Virginia Militia in the Revolutionary War

J. T. McAllister

HERITAGE BOOKS
2006

HERITAGE BOOKS
AN IMPRINT OF HERITAGE BOOKS, INC.

Books, CDs, and more—Worldwide

For our listing of thousands of titles see our website
at
www.HeritageBooks.com

A Facsimile Reprint
Published 2006 by
HERITAGE BOOKS, INC.
Publishing Division
65 East Main Street
Westminster, Maryland 21157-5026

Copyright © 1913 J. T. McAllister

— Publisher's Notice —
In reprints such as this, it is often not possible to remove blemishes from the original. We feel the contents of this book warrant its reissue despite these blemishes and hope you will agree and read it with pleasure.

International Standard Book Number: 978-1-55613-266-2

Table of Contents

INTRODUCTION.

Virginia's Share in the Military Movements of the Revolution.
Virginia Counties, Old and New.

PART I.

Summary of the Services of the Militia Arranged by Counties.

PART II.

Declarations of Virginia Militia Pensioners, §1 to §250.

PART III.

Militia Officers Appointed in Various Counties, §251 to §280.

PART IV.

Pensioners Residing in Virginia in 1835 who Received Pensions as Virginia Militiamen.

PART V.

Pensioners Residing Outside of Virginia in 1835 who Received Pensions as Virginia Militiamen.

GENERAL INDEX.

Acknowledgments

In the preparation of this book I have had the valuable assistance of Mr. Oren F. Morton, who, in addition to condensing the great mass of material into the shape in which it appears in sections from 1 to 251, prepared the articles which appear under the title "Virginia's Share in the Militia Movements of the Revolution," and "Virginia Counties, Old and New."

I wish also to acknowledge my indebtedness to Judge Lyman Chalkley, of Lexington, Kentucky, for procuring for me some of the declarations of record in that State, to Mr. W. G. Stanard, the Secretary of the Virginia Historical Society, and Dr. Henry R. McIlwaine, the Virginia State Librarian, for many courtesies shown me while engaged in the preparation of this book.

Introduction

This book does not profess to be a history of the Virginia Militia in the Revolution. No claim is made that it gives a complete list of the companies from any of the counties. Its purpose is to make available the material, some of which I have been gathering from time to time for a number of years. It is believed, however, that it is the first attempt to compile a considerable quantity of data on the subject. In a statement issued by the Secretary of War in 1832, he says that there are in his department no rolls of the State troops except those of Virginia, and no rolls of the militia except those of New Hampshire.

In regard to the Militia, very little is known and that little is extremely fragmentary.

In 1776 the available militia in Virginia is thought to have been about 45,000 men; probably it was never less than 40,000, of whom possibly one-fourth saw real service. Other states have counted their militia in the strength which they gave to the Revolutionary cause. For the lack of data Virginia has not received credit on this score. The reports of Secretary-of-War Knox fail to do justice to Virginia along this line. The figures given by him are mere estimates.

In 1776 a large number of Virginians were in the field against Dunmore. Some went to the relief of North Carolina and others were in the Cherokee Expedition in the West.

In 1778 Virginia had a number of militia in the operations in the West and for defense along the frontiers.

In 1779, Virginia was authorized to send militia to South Carolina.

In 1780, the militia were out in large numbers.

In 1781, 700 militia joined General Gates, some were at King's Mountain and others were serving around Norfolk. In the latter part of this year Dan'l Morgan had some of them serving in Green's Army. In 1781, practically all of the available militia of Virginia were summoned into service, taking part in the Battle of Guilford Court House, serving with Lafayette and at the Siege of Yorktown.

It is hoped that the material given in this book may throw some light on these services.

Most of the statements set out in this book were found by me in the counties where they were made. The word "county" is omitted in the statements where it will be easily understood. In some of the counties the declarations of the soldiers for pensions are spread in full upon the order book. In others they may be found filed with the papers of the term of court at which the application was made. Where not set out in full on the record book and not filed with the papers of the term, a very difficult proposition presents itself. I have frequently succeeded, however, in finding among the old musty files a package in which these declarations are wrapped up and have been preserved. Should all of these methods fail to disclose the statement, the only other method of procuring it is to obtain from the Bureau of Pensions at Washington, an abstract of the particular statements desired.

Frequently in the Clerk's Offices there will be found applications on which no pensions have been issued, due sometimes to a failure to supply proper proof, and at others because the service was not of sufficient length to bring the applicant within the terms of the pension law.

Under Chapters IV and V will be found the list of successful applicants for pensions whose pensions were granted solely on the ground of service as Virginia Militiamen. Many others who obtained pensions for service in the State Troops or in the regular service unquestionably served at times in the militia. There are several instances in the statements set out in this book where soldiers who held a high rank in the State troops or in the regular service later on served in the militia.

In Sections from 251 to 280 inclusive, I give the names of officers who were recommended or qualified in various counties in the State. While this does not necessarily mean that the person served, the probabilities are so strong as to make it almost a certainty.

I have followed various trails which were said to lead to muster rolls of Virginia Militiamen but found only the few which are set out in this book.

Virginia's Share in the Military Movements of the Revolution

In this article we present a bird's-eye view of those field movements of the Revolution, which immediately concern Virginia. It will interpret much of what is told in the pension declarations.

During the spring of 1775, Virginia committed herself to the cause of American Independence. In June, Lord Dunmore, the tory governor fled to a British war vessel, and from the safety of its deck he still made a pretense of asserting his authority. During the summer he gathered a few ships and with a force of British and tories he began to harry the shores of the Chesapeake. His style of warfare consisting in plundering plantation houses, maltreating women and children, stealing slaves, and burning seaports. In October he was repulsed from Hampton and in December was defeated near Norfolk. But on New Year's day, 1776, he cannoned and burned the last named town. General Andrew Lewis took command of the Virginia forces and drove Dunmore from his stronghold on Gwin's Island in the Chesapeake. The late governor sailed for England, and for three years the British had no foothold on Virginia soil. Yet their navy enabled them to dominate the sea, and the counties lying on navagable waters were thus kept in frequent alarm.

The first phase of the Revolution, as it relates to Virginia, was therefore the contest with Dunmore on the tidal waters. It was fought with militia, who came in part from the counties toward the Blue Ridge. The militia of the Tidewater continued to be called out here and there to repel the parties which landed from ships for the purpose of plunder.

The second phase consisted of trouble from the Indians on the western frontier. They had been stunned by their defeat at Point Pleasant, in 1774, but being urged on by British emissaries and white renegades, they at length began to harass the weak settlements in Kentucky, along the Holston, and toward the Ohio. To quell the Cherokees in the Southwest, a large force of militia was sent to the Holston early in the war. This army was in part made up of men from east of the Blue Ridge. But the militia of the Shenandoah

Valley were able to stand off the Indians who threatened them from the Northwest. The war parties of the red men scarcely ventured east of the Alleghany divide, yet the scattered settlements beyond were subjected to much distress. The wanton murder of Cornstalk, at Point Pleasant, was the immediate cause of the Indian raid into Greenbrier in 1778. The Indian depredations continued throughout the war, and garrisons had to be maintained in the frontier forts throughout the threatened area.

Being unmolested by any strong force, Virginia was free to raise and equip a number of regiments for the Continental service. Several of these took a distinguished part in the war in the Northern colonies. But for some time the militia were scarcely called upon except for the purposes already named.

The final phase of the Revolution in Virginia did not actively begin until the close of 1780, although in 1779, Clinton, the British commander-in-chief, had sent an expedition to ravage the coast. Unable to make head against Washington in the North, Clinton had carried the war into the South. Under Cornwallis, his armies overran South Carolina during the spring and summer of 1780, Georgia being already in their power. North Carolina was thus threatened from the South, and continued British success meant peril to Virginia from the same direction. To render the outlook all the worse, there were few disciplined Virginia troops who could be summoned to defend the State. The Virginia Continentals had been sent South as well as North. Gen'l Mathew's regiment had been captured at Germantown, Buford's had been massacred by Tarlton's troopers, and still other regiments had been included in the surrender of Charleston, to say nothing of still further losses. The drilled Continentals had proved themselves equal to the best British regulars, but although Virginia still had a somewhat numerous militia, they were untrained men and therefore at a great disadvantage when confronted by veterans.

In the fall of that year there was some apprehension that the Carolina tories under the energetic Ferguson, would push into Southwest Virginia. There was a considerable tory element in that region, and it was a further object to seize the lead mines in Wythe County. The militia were called out in their defense, but in October, Ferguson's army was annihilated at King's Mountain, men from Southwest Virginia contributing to this fortunate result.

In 1780, General Muhlenberg, the brilliant soldier who had quit the pulpit for the camp, was sent by Washington to take command in Virginia. Gathering some odds and ends of trained troops, and some militia, he drove the British General Leslie from Portsmouth. Next January, Benedict Arnold, the traitor, appeared with a larger force than was present to oppose him. He took Richmond and then fell back to Portsmouth, burning and plundering all along his line of march. At Portsmouth he was blockaded by the militia under Muhlenberg. General Lafeyette was now sent on by Washington with 1,200 regulars. To rescue Arnold, a still larger force of British was sent to Portsmouth, and Phillips, its commander, advanced and took Petersburg. Here he had an engagement with Steuben, who was in general command of the Americans, pending the arrival of Lafayette, whose approach prevented a second capture of Richmond. Phillips died of fever at Petersburg and Arnold resumed command of the British.

Meanwhile, Cornwallis had pushed the Southern army, under General Green, through North Carolina to the very border of Virginia. Notwithstanding the menace of the British army on the lower James, it was necessary to meet the new danger. Through great exertion, some 1,600 Virginia militia were collected to join Greene. Many of them were from the Valley counties. With their help he gave battle to Cornwallis, at Guilford, March 5th, and crippled him so badly that he made a tumultuous retreat to Wilmington. Greene advanced into South Carolina, and toward the end of May Cornwallis arrived at Petersburg and superseded Arnold.

The British army in Virginia was now about 8,000 strong. Lafayette with his much inferior force was pursued to the Rapidan, which he crossed at Ely's Ford. Cornwallis then moved toward the mountains. A raiding party under Colonel Simcoe destroyed the American magazines at the mouth of the Rivanna. Another expedition under Tarleton dispersed the State Legislature, at Charlottesville, but was deterred from pushing on to Staunton by the militia gathering to defend the mountain passes. Tarlton had been taught a lesson by his crushing defeat at the Cowpens, a few months earlier. Lafayette recrossed the Rapidan at Raccoon Ford. Cornwallis attempted to strike him on the flank, but was foiled by his adversary, who opened by night an old path since called the "Marquis Road," and took a strong position behind Meechums River to protect his stores. Cornwallis did not attempt to force conclusions, but under orders from Clinton retired toward the coast, followed by Lafayette, who on the Rapidan had been joined by Wayne with more troops from the army in the North.

Cornwallis had been ordered to take a position on the coast, so that he might be within supporting distance of Clinton at New York. This movement turned out to be his undoing. While executing it, two small engagements occurred near Williamsburg. The first known at the time as the battle of Hotwater, took place at Jenning's Ordinary, seven miles to the Northwest. Colonel Butler, a good officer under Lafayette, fell upon foragers under Simcoe, rescued the cattle they had taken, and handled the British roughly, but was forced to retire under the approach of Cornwallis to rescue his subordinate. The other fight, that of Green Spring, took place near Old Jamestown. The British were about to cross the James at this point, and Wayne, who was misled into thinking only a rear guard was on the north bank, made an impetuous charge against greatly superior numbers. He was repulsed with a loss of 118 men to the enemy's 80, but in alarm at the onslaught, Cornwallis did not deem it best to pursue and run into a possible ambuscade in return.

Cornwallis took post at Yorktown. In September, Washington arrived with a further re-enforcement and assumed general command. The gathering militia swelled the American army to a strength of 9,000 men, French under Rochambeau raising the total to 15,000. Being outnumbered two to one on land, and bottled up by the French fleet which commanded the bay, Cornwallis had to succumb to the inevitable. With his surender the war was practically at an end. During his almost unobstructed marches through the State, his armies wrought damage after the characteristic British fashion in the extent of about $10,000,000, the equivalent of probably three times that sum at the present day.

After the surrender of Burgoyne, in 1777, many of his men were sent to a military prison, at Winchester, others were quartered at Albemarle Barracks (now Charlottesville). The prisoners taken at the Cowpens were also sent to Winchester, as were likewise the soldiers in the army of Cornwallis. To guard all these prisoners of war many details of militia were called into service.

Virginia Counties, Old and New

Before the Old Dominion was torn into two states in 1861-3, the 149 counties of which it was then composed were grouped into two Districts; the Eastern and the Western, the line between them being the crest of the Blue Ridge. This division was thoroughly well known, and was recognized for administrative convenience and sundry other considerations. There has always been a marked difference in the origin, habits, and characteristics of the people of the two sections, and thus the Eastern District was the "Land of the Tuckahoe," while the Western was the "Land of the Cohee."

Of the present 69 counties of the former Eastern District, 58 were already in existence at the outbreak of the Revolution in 1775. During that time of strife, four new counties were formed; Fluvanna and Powhatan, in 1777, and Campbell and Patrick in 1781. Fluvanna was formed from Albemarle, Powhatan from Cumberland, Campbell from Bedford, and Patrick from Henry. Between 1784 and 1838 seven more counties were established; Appomattox, Franklin, Greenesville, Madison, Nelson, and Rappahannock. With one exception, all these newer counties lie against the Blue Ridge, and therefore in the more lately settled part of the old Eastern District.

The explanation given in the above paragraph will make clear why seven counties east of the Blue Ridge are never alluded to by name in the military movements of the Revolution. The names of officers and soldiers properly belonging to those areas must therefore be sought in the records of the older counties from which the newer ones were formed.

In the Western District the situation was vastly different. No portion had been settled for quite 50 years, and to a very great extent it was still an unoccupied wilderness. Because of these facts, there were, prior to 1776, only seven organized counties instead of the present 86. These seven were Augusta, Berkeley, Botetourt, Dunmore, Fincastle, Frederick and Hampshire. Berkeley then included Jefferson, Dunmore included most of Page, Frederick included Clarke and Warren, and Hampshire included Morgan, Mineral, Hardy, and Grant. The remaining and far greater part of the Western District was comprised in the enormous counties of Augusta,

Botetourt, and Fincastle, the jurisdiction of all of which was asserted as far as the Ohio river. Dunmore was soon renamed Shenandoah, and Fincastle disappeared because of its subdivision. During the war for Independence eight new counties arose in the Western District. Washington and Montgomery were formed in 1776 from a part of Fincastle. In the same year, Ohio, Monogalia, and Yohogania were formed out of the Northwest section of Augusta, the present county still retaining a frontage on the Ohio river. The other new counties, Rockingham, Rockbridge, and Greenbrier, were formed in 1778. Rockingham covered all the north of Augusta east of the Alleghany divide, and it then included nearly all of Pendleton and a portion of Page. Greenbrier, taken from Botetourt, reached to the Ohio river, while Rockbridge, formed from both Augusta and Botetourt, has always had substantially its present dimensions.

But Virginia, following the wording of her charter, claimed all the country to the west and northwest as far as the Mississippi, and the Great Lakes, and also that section of Pennsylvania lying west of the meridian, which constitutes the western line of Maryland. In the French and Indian and Revolutionary wars, these claims were maintained by force of arms. Thus Kentucky County, taken from Fincastle in 1776, afterwards became the State of Kentucky. Illinois County conquered from the British by George Rogers Clark and established in 1778, afterwards became the Territory Northwest of the Ohio, and out of it were carved the magnificent states of Ohio, Indiana, Illinois, Michigan, and Wisconsin. A boundary dispute with Pennsylvania was settled to the advantage of the latter state. By means of it, Virginia lost nearly all of Yohogania County, the fragment saved being annexed to Ohio County. She also lost a large part of Monongalia.

The few counties west of the Blue Ridge were not only large, but because of their great extent they possessed a considerable population. This was particularly true of Augusta and the counties southwest of it. It therefore explains the large number of officers and men who came from those counties as the boundaries then stood. Because of the additional circumstance that their inhabitants were nearly all white, they took a very conspicuous part in the Revolution. Probably no one county furnished so many soldiers as Augusta.

One other fact remains to be noticed. The Valley of Virginia had been settled such a length of time, that a majority of the men it sent into the Revolution were native to the soil. But this was not at all the case west of the Alleghany divide. The settlers west of the range were but a handful, and very few had been there so long as ten years. They were immigrants from the older counties of Virginia and from the neighboring states of Pennsylvania and Maryland.

Virginia Militia in the Revolutionary War---McAllister's Data

A summary placing by counties the service of the Virginia Militia as shown by the affidavits set out in this book

PART I.

NOTE:—*The references are to Sections.*

MEMORANDA:—In making up this summary no effort has been made to determine the correctness of the spelling of names or the accuracy of the revolutionary soldiers whose sworn statements are printed in a condensed form in this book.

ALBEMARLE

17—. Capt. James Garland's Company was in service at Albemarle Barracks, 9.
17—. Capt. ——— Hunton's Company was in service, 9.
17—. Capt. ——— Montgomery's Company was in service, 9.
17—. Lieut Henry Austin with some men were in service, 27.
17—. Capt. Miller's Company was in service below Richmond, 37.
17—. Capt. Mark Leak's Company was out in service, 99.
17—. Capt. Miller's Company was in service about Hampton, 35.
17—. Capt. John Scott's Company was out in service, 91.
17—. Capt. ——— Coursey's Company was out in service, 91.
17—. Capt. Mathew Leake's Company was in service at Cabin Point, 84.
17—. Capt. Nelson Thompson's Company was in service at Malvern Hill, 84.
1777. Capt, Landron Jones' Company served in the 1st Virginia, 99.
1777. Capt Jno. Harris' Company was out in service, 99.

1779. Lieut. Robert Jouett enrolled a number of men for service in the North, 64.
1779. Capt. Ambrose Madison's Company was in service at Albemarle Barracks, 91.
1780. Capt. Mark Leak's Company was in service at Cabin Point, 53.
1780. Capt. John Henderson's Company was in service at Cabin Point, 50.
1780. Capt. Wm. Grayson's Company was in service at Yorktown, 100.
1781. Capt. Benj. Harris' Company was in the regular service, 50.
1781. Capt. ——— Barrett's Company was in the Cavalry, 53.
1781. Capt. ——— Falkner's Company was out in service, 53.
1781. Capt. ——— Woodford's Company was in service near Richmond, 38.
1781. Capt. Nicholas Hammer's Company was in service at Albebemarle Barracks and joined Lafayette, 38.
1781. Capt. Mark Leak's Company joined Lafayette, 25, 100.
1781. Capt. John Harris' Company was in service at Half Way House, 25, 38.
1781. Capt. Dan'l White's Company joined Lafayette, 100.
1781. Capt. Benj. Harris' Company joined Lafayette, 100.
1781. Capt. John Burk's Company joined Lafayette, 100.
1781. Capt. ——— Lany's Company joined Lafayette, 100.
1781. Capt. Benjamin Harrison's Company was at the Seige of Yorktown, 9
1781. Capt. Benjamin Harris' Company was at Seige of York, 84.

For the list of Militia Officers who qualified in the County Court of Albemarle County, see Section 251.

AMELIA

1776. Capt. Rowland Ward's Company in service at Hampton, 159.
1776. Capt ——— Wilson's Company in service at Hampton, 159.
1777. Capt. Benj. Ward's Company in service about Petersburg, 81.
1777. Capt. Wm Craddock's Company in service at Cabin Point, 159.
1779. Capt John Knight's Company in service near Richmond and Norfolk, 193.

1779. Capt. Wm. Royall's Company in service in Richmond and Norfolk, 193.
1780. 300 Militia from this County in service near Chickamominy Swamp, 81.
1780. Capt. Watson's Company in service near Chickahominy Swamp, 81.
1780. Capt. Wm. Worsham's Company in service in the South as far as Charleston, 82.
1780. Capt. ——— Roberts Company, same, 82.
1780. Capt. ——— Fitzgerald's Company, same, 82.
1780. Capt. ——— Jones' Company, Same, 82.
1780. Capt. Wm. Worsham's Company in service near Richmond, 82.
1780. Capt. Wm. Worsham's Company in service near Petersburg, 82.
1780. Capt. John Ward's Company in service at Smithfield, 149.
1780. Capt. Wm. Craddock's Company at Battle of Camden, 159.
1780. Capt. ——— Price's Company at Battle of Camden, 159..
1781. Capt. ——— Company in service about Richmond, 149.
1781. Capt. Edward Booker's Company in service in Orange, 149.
1781. Capt. Edward Walker's Cavalry Company in service in Albemarle, 81.
1781. Capt. Peter Randolph's Company in service about Richmond, 81.
1781. Capt. John Knight's Company in service, 82.
1781. Capt. Wm. Worsham's Company in service, 82.
1781. Capt. Paulin Anderson's Company in "Wild Goose Chase," 193.
1781. Amelia men were gathering beeves for the army, 159.
1781. Capt. Lewis Ford's Company at the Siege of Yorktown, 193.

NOTE:—The Amelia Militia was discharged at Bird's Ordinary. Immediately after that Capt. Wm. Worsham, Capt. John Knight and 100 men were taken prisoners by Tarlton, 82.

NOTE:—In 1775, Capt. Markham's Company served in the First Virginia about Norfolk and was in the Battle of Great Bridge, 82.

MEMO.:—For the list of Militia Officers who qualified in the County Court of Amelia County, see Section 252.

AMHERST

1776. Capt. John Sale's Company served against Cherokee Indians, 18.
1778. Capt. John Trent's Company served against Indians on the Holston River, 189.
1779. The following Amherst Companies served this year at Albemarle Barracks, viz: Capt. John Sale's; Capt. David Woodrup's; Capt. Richard Ballinger's, 112, 17, 19, 39.
   Capt. Samuel Higginbotham's Company served below Richmond, 61.
1780. Capt. Ambrose Rucker's Company was out in service, 112.
1780. Capt. Younger Landrum's Company was in North Carolina, 10.
1780. Capt. John Morrison's Company served around Petersburg, 19.
1780. Capt. Richard Ballinger's Company was in service at Fort Powhatan, 61.
1780. Capt. James Barrett's Company and Capt. Tucker's Company at Yorktown, 100.
1781. The Companies of Capt. Younger Landrum, and Capt. James Franklin marched to North Carolina, got near to but not into the battle of Guilford. The men say they could have gotten there if they had been properly handled; Franklin resigned next day, 10, 17, 18, 19, 39, 40, 68.

   Col. Hugh Rose, the Colonel of the County, and Capt. Sam Higginbotham's Company and Capt. Caleb Higginbotham's Company were kept busy getting cattle to Williamsburg to feed the American forces, 39, 68.

   Some of militia were sent to guard the prisoners to the British ship below Jamestown, 17; and others were kept watching the tories in the county to keep them from disaffecting the negroes, 112.

   The Companies of Capt. John Stewart, Capt. John Loving, Capt. ——— Christian and Capt. Benjamin Higginbotham took part in the seige of York, 10, 19, 40, 134, 78.

No dates are given for the following services:

Capt. John Morrison's Company was raised to go to South Carolina, but was held in Virginia, 134.

Capt. Jacob's Company served at Albemarle Barracks, 31.
Capt. Richard Pamplin's Company served at same place, 106.
Capt. ——— Loving's Company served at same place, 134.
Capt. Richard Ballinger's Company served at Hood's Fort in Prince George County, 106.
Capt. John Christian's Company served below Richmond, 31.
Capt. John Phillips' Company served around Richmond, 31.
Capt. ——— Tucker's Company served at Williamsburg, 106.
Capt. ——— Dillard's Company served as guard at Court House, 106.
Capt. Stewart's Company was out in service, 106.

AUGUSTA

NOTES:—The service of militia in 1774 are included because the Battle of Point Pleasant in that year was really the initial battle of the Revolution.

Under the head of "Augusta" will be found services of many companies which later fell into the subdivisions of this large section of country then called Augusta.

There will also be found mention of some companies which may really belong to Rockingham, Greenbriar, Rockbridge, or Botetourt because of the dificulty in determining where they should be placed.

1774. Capt. Geo. Moffett's Company was six weeks at Clover Lick Fort 87.

1774. Capt. Geo. Moffett's Company built Fort Warwick, 117.

1774. Capt John Lewis' Company (raised at Warm Springs), was in the Battle of Point Pleasant, 60-73.

1774. Capt. Jno. Dickenson's Company in Battle of Point Pleasant, 79-115.

1774. Capt. Andrew Lockridge's Company at Battle of Point Pleasant, 74.

1774. Capt. Alexander McClenachen's Company at Battle of Point Pleasant, 136.

1774. Capt. Jno. Morrison's Company at the Battle of Point Pleasant, 136.

1774. Capt. Saml. Wilson's Company at Battle of Point Pleasant, 136.

1774. Capt. Geo. Mathews' Company at Battle of Point Pleasant, 136-117.

1774. Capt. Geo. Moffett's Company at Battle of Point Pleasant, 117.

Services for Which no Years are Given:

Capt. Thos. Smith's Company in service about Richmond, 130.
Capt. ——— McCoy's Company in service about Richmond, 86.
Capt. Geo. Poage's Company at Clover Lick Fort, 86.
Capt. ——— Buchannan's Company in service around Norfolk, 86.
Capt. ——— Company at Warwick Fort for three months, 73.

INDIAN SPIES IN SERVICE

1776 to 1779. John Bradshaw and others from Fort Cook, now in Monroe to Burnside's Fort, 12.
1776 or 1777. Adam Arbogast, 4.
1778. John Jones, William Morris, Leonard Morris, John Patterson, 115.
1779. Jacob Kennison from Fork Lick, on Elk River to Drenna's Fort and Little Levels, 48.
1782. Under Capt. Wm. Clendenning, 139.

1776. Capt. Jno Lyle's Company against Indians on Holston River, 98-136.
1776. Capt. Mathew Arbuckle raises a Company for service at Point Pleasant, 115.
1776. Capt. Jno. Lewis' Company at Warwick Fort and Clover Lick Fort, 33-76.
1776. Capt. Jno. Lewis raises a Company of regulars; goes into the Tenth Virginia; was in the battles of Brandywine and Germantown, 20.
1776. Capt. ——— Nall's Company against the Indians at Westfall Fort and Tygart's Valley, 119.
1777. Capt. McGuire raises a Company of regulars part of 16th Va.; was in the battles of Brandywine, Germantown, Guilford Court House and Hot Water, 186.
1777. Capt. ——— Smith raises a Company later commanded by Capt. Bell in regular service; was in battle of Monmouth, 13.

1777. Capt. Robt. Craven's Company against the Indians at Tygart's Valley, 34.
1777. Capt. ——— Buchannan's Company in service at Portsmouth, 162.
1777. Six men on duty at Wilson's Fort on Jackson's river, now Highland County, 33.
1777. Capt. Geo. Moffett's Company serving at Point Pleasant, 87-97-130.
1777. Some of the Militia under Capt. Mathew Arbuckle at Point Pleasant, 48.
1777. Capt. Mathew Arbuckle has Company on Elk River and later at Point Pleasant, 60.
1777. Capt. Jno McCoy's Company at West Fort, Louther's Fort, Nutter's Fort and Coontz' Fort, 4.
1777. Capt. Robt. M'Creary's Company at Warwick's Fort, 79.
1777. Capt. Samuel Vance's Company at Warwick's Fort and Clover Lick Fort, 33, 58, 76.
1777. Capt. Andrew Lockridges' Company at Vance's Fort (now Mountain Grove, Bath County), 58. 70.
1777. Capt. Wm. Pence's Company at Hacket's Fort, 139.
1777. Capt. Thos. Smith's Company at Point Pleasant, 98.
1777. Capt. Patrick Buchannan's Company capture tories near Peaked Mountain, now Rockingham County, Va., 133.
1778. Capt. ——— Company in service four months against the Indians on Jackson's River, 33.
1778. Capt. James Tate's Company in service at Lewisburg, now Greenbrier County, 133.
1778. Capt. Patrick Buchannon's Company in service at Lewisburg, 133.
1778. Capt. Francis Long's Company in service at Lewisburg, 133.
1778. Capt. Wm. Anderson's Company at Clover Lick Fort, 97.
1778. Capt. Wm. Craven's Company at Tygart's Valley, 139.
1778. Capt. Robt. Craven's Company at Fort McIntosh, 139.
1778. Capt. Saml. McCutcheon's Company at Fort McIntosh, 33.
Pack horses in service to Fort McIntosh, 117.
Teams sent from Staunton to take supplies of bacon from Orange and Culpepper to Washington's Army in the North, 124.

1778. Capt. Jno. McCoy's Company in service at Warm Springs, 4.
1778. Capt. Jno. McCoy's Company (Part of it), at Crab Bottom, 4.
1778. Capt. ——— Cooper's Company goes into regular service under Col. ——— Woodford, 87.
1778 or 1779. Capt Andrew Lockridge's Company for three months at Clover Lick Fort, 72.
1778 or 1779. Capt. Wm. Kincaid's Company at Fort Vance, Clover Lick Fort and West Fort, 92.
1778 or 1779. Capt. Jno. McCoy's Company at Richmond, 76.
1779. Capt. ——— McCreary's Company three months at Clover Lick Fort, 70.
1779. Capt. James Trimble's Company at Tygart's Valley and Fort Buchannon; 98, 111.
1779 or 1780. Capt Thos. Hickman's Company one month at Warwick's Fort, 72.
1780. Capt. Saml. McCutcheon's Company in service at Richmond, 22, 95, 107, 124.
1780. Capt. Jno Dickey's Company in service at Richmond, 22.
1780. Capt. Francis Long's Company, same, 22.
1780. Capt. Thos. Smith's Company, same, 22, 95.
1780. Capt. ——— Givens' Company, same, 22, 93, 124.
1780. Capt. John McCoy's Company at Richmond and Camp Holly, 33, 70.
1780. Capt. John McKittrick's Company at Fort Dinwiddie (near Warm Springs), and Fort Warwick, 111.
1780. Capt. Thos. Smith's Company with several other Militia companies guarded the General Assembly at Richmond, 97.
1780. Capt. James Tate's Company at the Battle of Cowpens, 63, 75, 118.
1781. Capt. Thos. Rankin's Company at Portsmouth, 136.
1781. Capt. Joseph Patterson's Company at Camp Carson, 22, 95.
1781. Capt. James Trimble's Company at Camp Carson, 22, 58.
1781. Capt. John Cunningham's Company at Camp Carson, 22, 58.
1781. Capt. Chas. Cameron's Company at Camp Carson, 20, 22, 58.
1781. Capt. Thos. Hickman's Company, 12, 22, 72.*
1781. Capt. Wm. Kinkead's Company at Portsmouth, 57, 74.
1781. Capt. ——— Stevenson at the Battle of Guilford Court House, 45.

---

*MEMO.:—For full account of this, see 22.

1781. Capt. James Tate's Company at the Battle of Guilford, Tate was killed and some of his men prisoners, 107.
1781. Capt. David Gwin's Company at Battle of Guilford, 76, 92.
1781. Capt. ——— Tate's Company joined main army Speedwell Iron Works, 133.
1781. Capt. ——— Smith's Company, same, 133.
1781. Capt. Thomas Smith's Company joined main army at Troublesome Iron Works, North Carolina, 97.
1781. Capt. John Smith's Company at the Battle of Guilford, 13.
1781. John Dickey's Company at Rock Fish Gap, takes charge of Prisoners captured at Cowpens, 98.
1781. Capt. ——— Company crosses Greenbrier River in pursuit of Indians, 4.
1781. Capt. James Bell has men in service impressing horses for the army, 97.
1781. Capt. David Gwinn's Company in service at Williamsburg, 33, 58.
1781. Capt. ——— Company in pursuit of Tarleton, 72.
1781. Capt. ——— Company at Charlottesville, 13.
1781. Capt. Peter Hull's Company at Battle of Jamestown, 72.
1781. Capt. John Brown's Company at Battle of Hot Water and Jamestown, 11, 79, 162.
1781. Capt. Chas. Cameron's Company at Battle of Jamestown, 20.
1781. Capt. Jno. Campbell's Company at the Battle of Jamestown, 22, 75.
1781. Capt. Chas. Haskins' Company at the Battle of Jamestown, 22.
1781. Capt. Jno. Dickey's Company at the Battle of Jamestown, 75. 95, 118, 163.
1781. Capt. Francis Long's Company at the Battles of Hot Water and Jamestown, 22, 198.
1781. Capt. Patrick Buchannon's Company at the Battle of Hot Water, 22, 111.
1781. Capt. John Givens' Company at the Battle of Jamestown, 87, 130, 134.
1781. Capt. Zachariah Johnson's Company at the Battle of Jamestown, 136.
1781. Capt. Wm. Bowyer and 108 mounted horsemen were at the Battles of New Kent Court House and Hot Water, 117.
1781. Capt. Samuel McCutcheon's Company in service for 20 days, 124.

1781. Capt. ———— Company at the Siege of York, 117.
1781. Capt. Francis Long's Company at the Siege of York, 22.
1781. Capt. Thos. Hicklin's Company at the Siege of York, 12, 70.
1781. Capt. ———— Trimble's Company at the Siege of York, 22.
1781. Capt. ———— Company at the Siege of York, 75.
1781. Capt. ———— Dickey's Company at the Siege of York, 22.
1781. Capt. ———— Buchannon's Company at the Siege of York, 22.
1781. James Bell's Company at Siege of York, 92.
1781. Capt. ———— Christian's Company at the Siege of York, 134.
1782. Capt. John McKittrick's Company in service at Tygart's Valley, 22, 118.
1782. Capt. Geo. Poage's Company three months at Warwick's Fort, 33.
1782. Capt. Geo. Poage's Company at Clover Lick Fort, 70.
1782. Lieut. John McCamie at Clover Lick Fort, 75.

MEMO.:—For the list of Militia Officers who qualified in the County Court of Augusta County, see Section 253.

BEDFORD

1776. Capt. Wm. Leftridge against Tories and Indians at Lead Mines, 47, 157.
1777. Capt. John Torbert's Company in service at Yorktown, 47.
1777. Capt. John Wilkerson's Company out in service, 157.
1777. Capt. Thomas Dooley's Company out in service, 157.
1778. Capt. Robt. Adams' Company guarding Lead Mines, 153.
1779. Capt Nathaniel Tate's Company joined Genl. Gates in North Carolina, 153.
1779. Capt. Charles Watkins' Company ordered to Jamestown, 153.
1779. Capt. ———— Company guarding at New London and Lynchburg prisoners taken at Cowpens, 47.
1780. Capt. Isaac Webb's Company conveying baggage wagons and live hogs from North Carolina to Mecklenburg, Va., 153.
1780. Capt. Alex. Cummins' Company in General Lawson's Brigade, 126.
1780. Capt Benj. Logan's Company guarding Kentucky frontiers, 153.

1780. Capt. John Renfro's Company against tories on New River, 157.

NOTE:—For a list of the Officers who qualified in the Militia in Bedford County, see Section 254.

BERKELEY

1777. Capt. Evens' Company was in the Battle of Brandywine, 122.
1778-'79. Capt. David Kennedy's Company was in service at Fort McIntosh, 59.
1780. Capt. ——— Sullivan's Company was in the Battle of Cowpens, and at Guilford Court House, 5.
1781. Capt. Edward Davis' Company served about Williamsburg, 59.
1781. Capt. John Hart Company was at the Siege of York, 59.
1781. Capt. ——— Coher's Company was at the Siege of York, 5.
1781. Capt. ——— Company guarded the prisoners taken at Yorktown, 148.

MEMO.:—For a list of the Officers who qualified in the Militia in Berkeley County, see Section 255.

BOTETOURT

NOTE:—It will be well to look under the services of the Augusta Militia as well as this head, as probably some services which should be under Botetourt are under Augusta.

1776. Capt. ——— Gilmer's Company served against the Indians on Holston River, 113.
1776 or 1777. Capt. ——— McKee's Company at Point Pleasant, 115.
1777. Capt. John Paxton's Company served at Point Pleasant, 112.
1778. Capt. James Tate's Company at Fort Savannah for one month, 133.
1778. Capt. P. Buchannon's Company at Fort Savannah for one month, 133.
1778. Capt. Francis Long's Company at Fort Savannah for one month, 133.
1778. Capt. Hugh Logan's Company to the relief of Donnally's Fort, 102.

1779. Capt. James Smith's Company served against the Indians in South West Virginia, 102.

1779. Capt James Barnett's Company served against Indians in South West Virginia, 102.

1779. Capt. Joseph Crockett's Company served at Williamsburg, 156.

1779. Capt. Wm. McClenahan's Company served against the tories in Montgomery, 156.

1779. Capt. James Barnett's Company served against the tories in Montgomery, 156.

1780. Capt. James Robinson's Company served in North Carolina, 114.*

1780. Capt. Alexander Handly's Company served in North Carolina, 114.*

1781. Capt. ——— May's Company served in North Carolina, was at the Battle of Reedy Fork, 133.

1781. Capt. John Cartmill's Company served in North Carolina, was at the Battle of Reedy Fork, 133.

1781. Capt. Mathew Wilson's Company was in North Carolina at the Battle of Reedy Fork, 133.

1781. Capt. ———Holston's Company was at the Battle of Reedy Fork, North Carolina, 133.

1781. Capt. ——— Bollar was at the Battle of Reedy Fork, N. C., 133.

1781. Capt. Wm. McClenahan's Company at the Battles of Alamance, Reedy Fork and Guilford, 156.

1781. Capt. ——— Hoyd's Company (?), at the Battle of Guilford Court House, 137.†

1781. Capt. Joseph Looney's Company was in service at Bottom's Bridge, 138.

1781. Capt. David May's Company at the Siege of York, 133.

1781. Capt. James Smith's Company at the Siege of York, 102.

No Date Given:

Capt. Mathew Arbuckle at Pittsburgh and Point Pleasant, 128.

Capt. ——— Company against tories at Lead Mines, 102.

For a list of the Officers qualified as Militia in Botetourt County, see Section 256.

---

*NOTE:—The 111 men in these Companies were reduced to 17.

†NOTE:—Section 137 contains a very full account of this Battlt.

BUCKINGHAM

177–. Capt. Wm. Dugrid's Company on guard at Albemarle Barracks, 26.
1781. Capt. Wm. Perkins' Company in Battle of Hot Water and Jamestown, 26.
1781. Capt. Silas Watkins' Company at Siege of Yorktown, 26.
1781. Capt. Wm. Giles' Company at the Siege of Yorktown, 26.

MEMO.:—A search of the records of Buckingham County failed to disclose any record of Militia Officers qualifying in it during the Revolution.

CAROLINE

The following companies were in service but the date is not given.
Capt. ——— Jameson, 85.
Capt. ——— Stevens, 85.
Capt. ——— Taylor, 85.
Capt. ——— Clark, 85.
Lieut. Littleberry Harrod, six months at Hobb's Hole, 190.
Capt. Wm Taliaferro's Company, 224.
Capt. ——— Company, 224.
Capt. Vivian Minor's Company at Williamsburg, 224.
1775. Capt. Phillip Buckner's Company in service, 219.
1776. Capt. Robt. Ware's Company in service at Williamsburg, 219.
1778. Capt. Elisha White's Company entered regular service for two years under Col. Chas. Porterfield, 190.
177–. Capt. John Marshall's Company was at Williamsburg, 211.
1779. Lieut. ——— Glenn had a Company in service at Malvern Hill, 211.
1779. Capt. Philip Johnson's Company at Williamsburg, 218.
1779. Capt. ——— Long's Company at Williamsburg, 85.
1780. Capt. James Johnson's Company at Battle of Camden, 35.
1781. Capt. Francis Cowherd's Company joined the First Virginia and was in the Battles of Guilford and Eutaw, 218.
1781. Capt. Ed. Bullock's Company was in service at Williamsburg, 35.
1781. Capt. Coleman Sutton's Company out in service, 158.
1781. Capt. Coleman Taylor's Company out in service, 158.
1781. Capt. Creed Haskin's Company in service at Yorktown, 211.

1781. Capt. Coleman Taylor's Company out in service, 158.
1781. Capt. ——— Coleman's Company in service at Yorktown, 219.

NOTE:—For a list of the Officers who qualified in the Militia in Caroline County, see Section 257.

CHARLOTTE

1776. Capt. Wm. Collier's Company joined Col. ——— Ruffins' Regiment at Petersburg and was in service near Gwynn's Island. Later it marched with regiment to Holston River against the Indians, 66.
1779. Capt. Wm. Morton's Company marched to North Carolina, joined Genl. Lincoln's Army, took part in attempt to storm British Fort at Stono Ferry, 66.
1780. Capt. Richard Gaine's Company was in service near Dismal Swamp, 184.
1781. Capt. Jesse Saunders' Company in service against Arnold, 184.
1781. Capt. Andrew Wallace's Company served in the Siege of Yorktown, 184.
1781. Capt. ——— Spencer's Company guarded the prisoners taken at Siege of Yorktown, 200.

MEMO.:—For a list of the Officers who qualified for the Militia in Charlotte County, see Section 258.

CHESTERFIELD

1776. Capt. Frank Goode's Company in service at Portsmouth, 2.
1777. Capt. Francis Smith's Company serving with First Virginia, 200.
1779. Capt Creed Haskins' Company serving at Hood's Fort in Surrey County, 199.
1780. Capt. ——— Booker's Company were in the South and at Gate's Defeat, 194.
1780. Capt. Archibald Walthal's Company in the South at Gate's Defeat, 194, 200.
1780. Capt. ——— Company at Gate's Defeat, 191.

NOTE:—These Companies were joined at Randolph Mills by the Militia from Caroline, Hanover and Henrico, who went with them to the South.

1780 or 1781. Capt Richard Crump's Company serving in Chesterfield, 15.

1780. Capt. ——— Company guarding the ferry at Westham and Tuckahoe, 200.

1781. Capt. Robt. Powt's Company joined Lafayette at Malvern Hill, 15*.

1781. Capt. Stephen Pankey's Company at the Battle of Guilford Court House, 191.

1781. Capt. David Patterson's Company served at Dinwiddie Court House, 194.

1781. Capt. Paul Patterson's Company served at Petersburg, 199.

1781. Capt. Paul Patterson's Company joined Lafayete, 199.

1781. Capt. David Patterson's Company was out for five weeks, 200.

1781. Capt. David Patterson's Company was at the Siege of York, 200.

Some of the Chesterfield Militia were in service around Petersburg, 82.

NOTE:—For a list of the Officers who qualified for the Militia in Chesterfield County, see Section 259.

CULPEPER COUNTY

1775. Capt. John Thorn's Company was out against Lord Dunmore, 148.

1776. Capt. ——— Bohannon's Company served three months near Norfolk, 148.

1777. Four companies including that of Capt. ——— Hill joined Washington above Philadelphia and were in the battle of Germantown.

1778. Capt. James Purvis' Company guarding prisoners at Albemarle Barracks, 249, 148.

1779. Capt. John Strother's Company guarding prisoners at Albemarle Barracks, 249.

1781. Capt. Ambrose Bohannon's Company joined Washington's Army at Malvern Hill and was with it to Yorktown, 94.

*QUERY:—It is uncertain whether the last two Companies mentioned belong in Cumberland or Chesterfield. Mention has been made above of Capt. Creed Haskins. He was probably the Cumberland Haskins of that same name who was appointed Captain in place of John Burton.

1781. Capt. Elijah Kirtley's Company joined Col. John Willis (of Hanover), and Genl. Morgan at Bird's Ordinary; was in Battles of Jamestown and Hot Water, 104.
1781. Capt. Saml. Ferguson's Company was in service about Richmond, 104.
1781. Capt. ——— Ferguson's Company joined Lafayette, 148.
1781. Capt. ——— Berkeley's Company was at the Siege of York, 148.
Capt. Henry Hill's Company met the British Prisoners taken at Burgoyne's surrender and guarded them to Albemarle Barracks, 94.
Capt. ——— Slaughter's Company joined Gen. Wayne's Army and served three months in Col. Barber's Regiment.

MEMO.:—No records are found in Culpeper showing the Militia Officers who qualified there during the Revolution.

CUMBERLAND

1776. Capt. Robt. Hughes' Company in service at Williamsburg, 54.
1779. Capt. Edward Munford's Company in service for three months, 15.
1779 or 1780. Capt. ——— Clarke's Company in service at Petersburg, 67.
1780. Capt. Richard Crump's Company in service at Hampton, 207.
1780 or 1781. Capt. Crad. Haskin's Company in service for three months, 6.
1780. Capt. Richard Crump's Company in service in Chesterfield, 15.
1781. Capt. Littleberry Mosby's Company in service at Petersburg, 207.
1781. Capt. Wm. Mayo's Company in service at Suffolk, 207.
1781. Capt. ——— Meredith's Company in service with Lafayette, 202.
1781. Capt. Wm. Meredith's Company in service in Chesterfield County, 6.
1781. Capt. Crad. Haskin's Company in service at Suffolk, 6.
1781. Capt. Robt. Powt in service with Lafayette, 15.

1781. Capt. ———— Company guarding old Cumberland Court House, 15.

1781. Capt. ———— Company guarding Seamen, 207.

NOTE:—For the list of Officers who qualified for Militia in Cumberland County, see Section 260.

DINWIDDIE

1779. Twelve Dinwiddie militiamen were serving under Col. John Banister in guarding the munitions of war at Petersburg, 144.

1780. A troop of cavalry from Dinwiddie County was in the Battle of Petersburg, 54.

17—. Capt. Fleming Bates' Company was in service, 144.

MEMO.:—No records were found in Dinwiddie County showing the Militia Officers who qualified there during the Revolution.

FAIRFAX

1777. Capt. ———— Moody's Company was in service in Pennsylvania, 77.

1777. Capt. Thos. Pollard's Company marched through Frederick and York and was at the battle of Germantown, 216.

1778. One of the Fairfax soldiers was on the ship which carried dispatches to France. An interesting account of this trip is found in §216.

1781. Capt. Thos. Pollard's Company was guarding Burwell's warehouse on York River, 216.

MEMO.:—No records were found in Fairfax County showing the Officers who qualified there during the Revolution.

FAUQUIER

Capt. Wm. Payne, whose statement will be found in §242, says that his Company was called out four or five times each year for three or four months; that the British were making havoc with the slaves and tobacco and burning in every direction, 242.

1777. Capt. Benj. Harris' Company in service, 239.
1780. Capt. John O'Bannon's Company served six months about Williamsburg, 240.
1780. Capt. John L. Chunn was in service about Williamsburg and Richmond, 241.
1780. Capt. James Winn's Company was in service in the South and in the Battle of Cowpens, 188, 238.
1780. Capt. Francis Triplett's Company was in the Battle of Cowpens.*
1781. Capt Benj. Harrison's Company was in service, 239.
1781. Capt. ―――― Company was at the Siege of Yorktown, 241.
1781. Capt Turner Morehead's Company was in service near Williamsburg, 244.
1781. Capt. James Winn's Company was at Siege of York, 244.

MEMO.:—For the Militia Officers who qualified in Fauquier during the Revolution, see Section 261.

FLUVANNA

1775. Capt. Thos. Holt was recruiting men in this County for several months, 27.
1777. Capt. Joseph Hayden's Company was in service about three months, 27.
17—. Capt. Saml. Richardson's Company was in service at Hampton, 51.
17—. Capt. Samuel Richardson's Company was in service at Williamsburg, 51.
1779. Capt. Samuel Richardson's Company was in service at Albemarle Barracks, 27.
1779. Capt. Joseph Hayden's Company was in service about Williamsburg, 27.
1780. Capt. Anthony Henderson's Company was in service at Albemarle Barracks, 51.
1780. Capt. Levi Thompson's Company was in service at Cabin Point, 32.
1781. Capt. Anthony Hayden's Company was in service at the time of Tarlton's Raid, 32.

*NOTE:—One of the Augusta County soldiers speaks of a Major Frank Triplett, of Fauquier, who was in this battle, see §75.

1781. At least one of the militiamen was engaged in making gun stocks for the army, 27.
1781. Capt. Richard Napper's Company was at the Siege of York, 51, 32.

MEMO.:—For the Militia Officers who qualified for the Revolution from Fluvanna County, see Section 262.

FREDERICK

1776. Capt. ——— Berry raised a company, served in the Eighth Va., 154.
177–. Capt. Charles Thurston's Company joined Lord Sterling's Command in New Jersey and was in the skirmishes at Piscatawney and Quibbletown, 142.
1777. Capt. ——— Helms' Company was in service three months, 142.
1778. Capt. ——— Gilkerson's Company guarding prisoners, 142.
1779. Capt. Geo. Ball's Company was in service for three months, 110.
1781. Capt. Joseph Gregory's Company was in service against the Indians, 129.
1781. Capt. Josiah Swearingen's Company was sent to Fort McIntosh, 138.
1781. Capt. Joseph Looney's Company was in service below Richmond, and also at the Siege of Yorktown, 138.
1781. Capt. ——— Bell's Company was at the Siege of Yorktown, 164.
1781. Some other companies were out at the Siege of York and guarded prisoners to Winchester, 110.

MEMO.:—For the Militia Officers who qualified in Frederick, see Section 263.

GOOCHLAND

1777. Capt. Thos. Harris' Company served two months about Williamsburg, 192.
1779. Capt. ——— Hatcher's Company was out in service, 147.
1779. Capt. Holman Rice's Company served two months in the Albemarle Barracks, 187.

1781. Capt. Geo. Williamson's Company was in the Battle of Guilford Court House, 192.
1781. Capt. ———— Company was at the Siege of York, 147.
1781. Capt. ———— Pier's Company guarded the prisoners taken at Yorktown, 147.

MEMO.:—For the Militia Officers who qualified during the Revolution in Goochland, see Section 264.

GREENBRIER

NOTE:—It is difficult to assign definitely under this head the services which were rendered by men who lived in Greenbrier territory. There will doubtless be found under the head of Augusta and Botetourt items which probably belong to Greenbrier.

1774. Capt. John Lewis' Company was in the Battle of Point Pleasant, 60.
1776. Capt. John Henderson's Company serving against the Indians at Cook's Fort, 44.
1777. Capt. Archibald Wood's Company was serving against the Indians on Bluestone, 44.
1777. Capt. Mathew Arbuckle had a company out against the Indians on the Head of Elk and later was at Point Pleasant, 60.
1776-1777. Read fully the statement of Wm. Pryor, 61, which is too full to be fairly abstracted here.
1780. Capt. Thomas Wright raises a Company to go against the Indians at Detroit. But it was marched to Lead Mines on Holston, and then to Logan's Station in Kentucky. It was also at McAfee's Station in Kentucky where Capt. James Armstrong was in command, 65.
1780-'81. Capt. A. Nickle raises a company to go to the Great Lakes, 60.
1781. The Militia of this company were in service at Laferty's Fort on Indian Creek, 34.

Capt. Mathew Arbuckle was one of the most noted soldiers of this County. After serving through the Indian Wars he was killed by a falling limb while riding beside Jackson River in the McClintic neighborhood, in what is now Bath County. His body was buried there near the place where he was killed. I have recently learned that his grave must be on the lower edge of the property now owned by the Hon. Geo. A. Revercomb on Jackson River.

MEMO.:—For the Militia Officers shown by the records to have qualified in Greenbrier in the Revolution, see Section 265.

HALIFAX

1777. Capt. ——— Moody's Company went to Pennsylvania, 56.
1779. Capt. ——— Witcher's Company joined Genl. Greene in South Carolina, 210.
1780. Capt. ——— Williams' Company was in service against the tories, 210.
1780. Capt. John Wynn's Company was in the battle of Guilford Court House, 210.
1781. Capt. James Turner's Company went South and was in the Siege of '96, 178.
1781. Capt. Henry Burnley's Company joined Genl. Lawson at Charlotte Court House and was in the Battle of Jamestown, 210.
1781. Capt. John Beckley's Company, same as above, 210.
1781. Capt. Wm. Clarke's Company, same as above, 210.
1781. Capt. John Falkner's Company was at Siege of York, 144.

HAMPSHIRE

1777. Capt. Moses Hutton's Company was in service at Fort Pitt and at Wheeling, 43.
1781. Capt. Geo. Ball's Company was in service, 43.
1782. Capt. ——— Company guarded the commissioners who ran the line between Virginia and Pennsylvania, 43.

HANOVER

177–. Capt. John Winston's Company was in service, 30.
1778. Capt. Thos. Nelson's Troops consisting of 100 cavalrymen were marched to Philadelphia, 143.

1780. Capt. Robt. Bolling's Company was in service near Norfolk, 143.
1780. Capt. John Price's Company was in service in the South at Gates' Defeat, 30.
1780. Capt. Thos. Doswell's Company was in service at Sandy Point, 30.
1781. Capt. Jno. Harris' Company was in service below Richmond, 38.
1781. Capt. Edward Bullock's Company joined Lafayette, 35.
1781. Capt. Nicholas Hammer's Company joined Lafayette on his "Wild Goose Chase," 38.
1781. Capt. Frank Coleman's Company was in service at Deep Spring near Williamsburg, 52.
1781. Capt. Robt. Bolling's Company was in service at Petersburg against Arnold and also in North Carolina, 143.
1781. Capt. John Thompson's Company was in service at Cabin Point and also at the Siege of York, 30, 35.

Some of the Militia from this County served at Albemarle Barracks, 38, 52.

HENRICO

For the Militia Officers who qualified for the Revolution in Henrico County, see Section 267.

HENRY

17—. Capt. Francis Shelton's Company in service against the tories on Dan River, 26.
1777. Capt. Peter Herston's Company went against the Indians on Holston River, 152, 157.
1781. Capt. Neely McGuire's Company in service on frontiers, 157.
1781. Capt. ——— Ruble's Company at the Siege of Yorktown, 152.

MEMO.:—For the Militia Officers who qualified in Henry County during the Revolution, see Section 268.

KING AND QUEEN

1776. Capt. Wm. Richard's Company was in service against Lord Dunmore, 36.

KING WILLIAM

Between 1776 and 1781 the companies under the following captains served:
Capt. Mordecai Abraham, 234.
Capt. Christopher Thompson, 234.
Capt. Mordecai Booth, 234.
Capt. Harry Quarles, 234.
1781. In this year the following Captains led their companies out and joined Lafayette:
Capt. ———— Drury, 234.
Capt. ———— Booth, 234.
Capt. ———— Abraham, 234.

LOUDOUN

1775. Capt. Simon Triplett's Company in service about Norfolk, 245.
17—. Capt Adam Wallace's Company of Regulars in service in South Carolina and at the Battle of Waxhaux, 168.
1777. Capt. John Thomas' Company in the Battle of Germantown, 28.
1777. Capt. Danl. Teagan's Company guarded the prisoners to Charlottesville, 245.
1781. Capt. Thomas Conner in service about New Kent Court House, 245.

MEMO.:—For the Militia Officers who qualified in Loudon County, during the Revolution, see Section 269.

LOUISA

1779. Capt. John Bias' Company in service, 131.
1780. Capt. ———— Company was in service under Col. Fontaine, 93.

1780. Capt. John Bias' Company joined the 2nd Va., went to North Carolina and was in Gates' Defeat, 131.
1781. Capt. Wm. Harris' Company was in service about Richmond, 93.
1781. Capt. Benjamin Harrison's Company was in service around Williamsburg, 93.
1781. Capt. ———— Harris' Company joined Lafayette in "Wild Goose Chase," 131.
1781. Capt. Jas. Watson, same, 131.
1781. Capt. ———— Phillips in the same, 176, 177.
1781. Capt. ———— White in the same, 176, 177.
1781. Capt. ———— Johnson in the same, 176, 177.
1781. Capt. Saml. Pettis' Company at the Siege of York, 131.

MEMO.:—For a list of the Militia Officers who qualified in Louisa County, during the Revolution, see Section 270.

LUNENBURG

1780. Capt. Wm. Hays' Company was out in service at the time of Arnold's Raid, 181.

MECKLENBURG

1779. Capt. Reuben Vaughan's Company joined Gen. Lincoln in South Carolina, and was in Battle of Stono, 169, 172.
1780. Capt. John Kendricks' Company was out in service, 172.
1781. Capt. John Brown's Company was called out three times, in one of which he was at the Battle of Guilford Court House, 172.
1781. Capt. Richard Whiten's Company was in the Battle of Jamestown, 169.

MONTGOMERY

NOTE.—It is very probable that some of these Companies may have gone out from Washington County instead of Montgomery. But I am listing them all under this head.

Services For Which No Date Can Be Fixed.

Capt. Danl. Trigg's Company in service against the Indians, 146.

Capt. ——— Company in service against the tories, 146.
Capt. Danl. Trigg's Company guarding Lead Mines, 146.
Capt. Isaac Taylor's Company serving with regulars, 146.
Capt. John Preston's Company in service against the Indians, 146.
Capt. John McCorkle's Company serving against the Cherokee Indians, 150.
Capt. ——— Company at Blackmore Station on Clynch River, 21.
Capt. ——— Company against Indians on Bluestone, 21.
Capt. ——— Paulin's Company in service in Kentucky, 185.
Capt. John Lucas' Company in service, 155.
Capt. Joseph Martin's Company against Indians, 21, 185.
1776. Capt. ——— Burns' Company against the tories, 145.
1776. Sergeant Aaron Scragg's Company on Bluestone, 145.
1776. Sergeant Mace Tacey's Company out under Col. Preston, 145.
1776. Capt. Abram. Trigg's Company against tories on Yadkin, 145.
1776. Capt. John Duncan's Company against Indians, 185.
1776. Capt. Henry Rolling's Company serving in Kentucky, 185.
1776. Capt. Joseph Floyd's Company against Indians on Greenbrier and New River, 146.
1778. Capt. Joshua Wilson's Company against Indians, 161.
1780. Capt. John Lucas' Company in service, 155.
1780. Capt. Arbam Trigg's Company against tories in North Carolina, 161.

For a list of the Militia Officers who qualified in the County Court of Montgomery County, see Section 271.

NOTTOWAY

1777. Capt. Gabriel Foulks was in service about Williamsburg, 174.
1779. Capt. Wm. Fitzgerald's Company went to North Carolina and was in Battle of Stono, 173, 174.
1780. Capt. ——— Gray's Company was out in service, 173.
1780. Capt. ——— Irby's Company was in service at Cabin Point, 173.
1781. Capt. ——— Overstreet's Company was at the Battle of Guilford Court House, 173.

MEMO.:—A search of the Records of Nottoway County fails to disclose a list of the Officers who qualified for the Militia in the Revolution.

ORANGE

For a list of the Militia Officers who qualified for the Revolution in Orange County, see Section 272.

PITTSYLVANIA

1776. Capt. John Dooley's Company was in service in Georgia, where Dooley was killed by an Indian, 42.
1777. Capt. John Donaldson's (or Donelson), Company was in service on the Holston River, 209.
1778. Capt. John Donaldson's Company was in service at Hatfields Fort and Lucas Fort on New River, 209, 214.
1780. Capt. Wm. Witcher's Company was in service in South Carolina, 214.

The companies of Capt. Isaac Clements, Capt. James Brewer, Capt. Azariah Martin, and Capt. ——— Paulin were in service in North Carolina, 151, 171, 209.

1781. Capt. James Turner's Company took part in the Siege of 96, 42.

Capt. Isaac Clement's Company was out in service, 56.

Capt. Joshua Martin's Company went into North Carolina, 141.

Capt. James Brewer's Company was in the Battle of Guilford, 212.

The Pittsylvania militia gathered at the Court House where six hundred prisoners taken at the battle of Cowpens, were delivered to them, 62.

Some of the militia served under Col. St. Geo. Tucker at Point of Forks, 217.

Capt. Chas. Wall's Company was in service at Cabin Point, 217.

The companies of Capt. Flemming Bates, Capt. Chas. Hutchings, Capt. Chas. Williams, and Capt. Wm. Dix, took part in the Siege of York, 42, 151, 174, 212, 213.

POWHATAN

Two companies, one under Capt. Edward Moseley, and the other under Capt. Thomas Harris went out from this County, but the year is not given, 248.

1777. Some of the militia were in service at Cumberland Old C. H., 54.

Capt. Robert Hughes' Company was in service three months at Hampton, 203.

1780. Capt. Littlebury Mosby's Cavalry Company was in service around Petersburg, 54, 197.

Capt. Richard Crump's Company was in service at Cabin Point, 202.

1781. Capt. Robert Hughes' Company joined Gen. Lawson at Hillsboro, N. C., and was in the battle of Guilford C. H., 196, 197, 198.

Capt. ——— Company was in service three months at Cabin Point, 196.

Capt. Hughes Woodson's Company was at the Siege of York, 196, 203.

Capt. Wade Mosby's Company and Capt. Horatio Turpin's Company served around Petersburg, 197.

Capt. ——— Porter's Company served at Burmuda Hundred, 198.

Some of the militia were guarding Monakin Ferry, 202.

Capt. George Williamson's Company was out in service, 203, 206.

MEMO.:—For the list of Militia Officers who qualified for the Revolution in Powhatan County, see Section 274.

PRINCE EDWARD

1775. Capt. Chas Allen's Company in service four months at Hampton, 24.

1776. Capt. Chas. Allen's Company at Hampton for four months, 16, 23.

1777. Capt. ——— Flournoy's Company was in service at Williamsburg, 24.

Capt. Luke B. Smith (a Professor in Hampden-Sidney College), led out a Company of Students, the Company served six weeks at Williamsburg, 197.

1778. Capt. Luke B. Smith's volunteer student company again in service for six weeks at Petersburg, 197.

Capt. ——— Ligon's Company and Capt. Chas. Allen's Company in service at Petersburg, 23, 24.

1779. Capt. Thos. Flournoy's Company guarded the magazine at Williamsburg, 7.

Capt. John Holcomb's Company served three weeks at Petersburg, 16.

1779-'80. Capt. Clark's Company was serving at Petersburg, 67.

1780. Capt. Chas. Allen's Company was serving at Petersburg, 7, 16, 29.

Capt. Phillip Holcomb's Cavalry company in service at Petersburg, occupying as barracks the Masonic Hall, 80.

Capt. Richard Holland's Company was guarding prisoners at Albemarle Barracks, 7.

1781. Capt. Andrew Baker's Company joined General Green near Dan River, was attached to Col. Otho H. Williams' regiment, 16, 54.

Capt Nathl. Cunningham's Company joined Gen. Green at Irvin's Ferry; was in the battle of Guilford C. H. Some of this Company conveyed prisoners to Halifax County; later went there for arms and wounded prisoners brought from Guilford, and conveyed these prisoners to British ship, at Jamestown, 23.

Capt. Ambrose Nelson's Company joined Gen. Green in North Carolina, but was not in battle of Guilford, 67.

Capt. Richard Allen's Company was stationed at Ratcliffe's old field in Col. Henry Skipwith's Regiment, 83.

Capt. Richard Holland's Company guarded prisoners from Pr. Edward C. H., to Albemarle Barracks, 16.

Military stores at Prince Edward C. H. (where Major Mazaret was in command), were being guarded, 2, 3, 195.

Capt. Flood's Company joined in the pursuit of Cornwallis, 24.

Capt. ——— Bird's Company was at the Siege of York, 67.

MEMO.:—For a list of the Militia Officers who qualified in Prince Edward County during the Revolution, see Section 275.

For the Muster Roll of Capt. John Morton's Company, see Section 275.

ROCKBRIDGE

1776. The Militia of this County were out against the Cherokee Indians, 125.
1776. Capt. Wm. McKee's Company went to Point Pleasant where it served for a long time at the Fort, 69.
1777. Capt. Chas. Campbell's Company was in service at Point Pleasant, 125.
1777. Capt. John Paxton's Company was in service at Point Pleasant, 112.
1778. Capt. David Gray's Company was in service against the Indians in Greenbrier County, 123, 105, 125.
1778 or 1779. Capt. Wm. Lyle's Company was in service on the frontier, 105.
1780. Capt. James Gilmore's Company was in service in North Carolina and in the Battle of Cowpens, 121.
1780. Capt. James Hall's Company, Capt. ——— Campbell's Company, Capt. David Gray's Company were in service around Richmond, 109, 137.
1781. Capt. James Buchannon's Company was in service near Williamsburg, 116.
1781. Capt. Andr. Moore's Company was in service around Norfolk, 105, 123.
1781. Capt. Saml. Wallace's Company was in service around Norfolk, 120.
1781. Capt. John Cunningham's Company was in service near Portsmouth.
    The Rockbridge troops under Col. John Boyer were camped near the Augusta Militia and Capt. John Cunningham was wounded, 12.
1781. At the time of Tarlton's Raid Capt. Wm. Moore's Company was in service, 120, 125.
1781. Capt. ——— Company was in the Battle of Hot Water, ———.
1781. Capt. James Buchannan's Company was in service in North Carolina, 182.
1781. Capt. Chas. Campbell's Company was out in service, 182.
1781. Capt. David Gray's Company was at the Siege of York, 105.
1781. Capt. Charles Campbell's Company was at the Siege of York, 115.
1781. Capt. Wm. Moore's Company was at the Siege of York, and guarded the prisoners to Winchester, 120.

MISCELLANEOUS

There were services in 1778 by Companies whose Captains' names are not given, see 105, 125; at the time of Tarleton's Raid, see 125—; at the siege of York, 125; and guarding troops at Albemarle Barracks.

MEMO.:—For a list of the Militia Officers who qualified in Rockbridge County during the Revolution, see Section 276.

ROCKINGHAM

NOTE:—As Rockingham County was not formed until 1778, and was taken from Augusta, reference should be had to the Augusta County list for some of the services of men in this County.

Services Under Which no Date Can Be Assigned

Capt. ——— Company at Fort Pitt, 5.
Capt. ——— Rush's Company under Col. Sampson Mathews, 119.
Capt. ——— Company at Warwick's Fort, 34.
1778. Capt. ——— Craven's Company against Indians in Tygart's Valley, 5.
1778. Lieut. John Rice's Company against Indians in Tygart's Valley, 34.
1778. Capt. Robt. Craven's Company at Koontz's Fort, 140.
1778. Capt. Wm. Kinkead's Company at Nutter's Fort, 34.
1778. Capt. Robt. Craven's Company against the Indians, 62, 140.
1780. Capt. Robt Craven's Company at the Battle of Cowpens, 62.
1780. Capt. Michael Cowger's Company at Great Bridge, 89.
1781. Capt. Geo. Houston's Company with Genl. McIntosh, 108.
1781. Capt. Geo. Houston's Company against tories on South Branch, 119.
1781. Capt. ——— Company in regular service, 119.
1781. Capt. ——— Company at Laverty's Fort, 34.
1781. Capt. Jeremiah Beazley's Company at Battles of Hot Water and Jamestown, 62.
1781. Capt. Geo. Houston's Company at Battle of Hot Water and Siege of York, 119.
1781. Capt. Michael Cowger's Company at the Siege of York, 140.

1781. Capt. Richard Rigger's Company at the Siege of York, 89.
1781. Capt. ——— Smith's Company at the Siege of York, 63.
1782. Capt. Wm. Smith's Company at Hinkle's Fort, 57.
1783. Lieut. Neel Cain's Company at Tygart's Valley and Clarksburg, 57.

MEMO.:—For list of the Militia Officers who qualified in Rockingham County, see Section 277.

SHENANDOAH

1777. Capt. John Hopkins' Company was in service at Point Pleasant, 127.
1778. Capt. Robt. Craven's Company was in service against the Indians in Tygart's Valley, 127.
17—. Capt. Jacob Rinker's Company was in service in South Carolina and guarded the prisoners taken at the Battle of Cowpens, 103.
1781. Capt. ——— Nevil's Company was in service at Fort McIntosh, 103.
1781. Capt. ——— Downey's Company was in service two months at Fort Frederick, 49.

MEMO.:—For a list of the Militia Officers who qualified from Shenandoah County during the Revolution, see Section 278.

SPOTTSYLVANIA

Without being able to give the date, the following companies are shown to have been in service:

Capt. William Mills' Company, 179.
Capt. James Cunningham's Company, 179.
Capt. ——— Tankersley's Company, 220.
Capt. ——— Holladay, 220.
Capt. Frank Coleman at Fredericksburg, 222.
Capt. Wm. Mills at Williamsburg, 223.
Capt. Francis Taliaferro at Hampton, 223.
Four companies probably about Williamsburg, 226.
Capt. McWilliams, 228.
Capt. John Scott, 228.

Capt. J. Craig, 235.
Capt. Thomas Bartlett, two months at Williamsburg, 276.
Capt Chas. Bibbing, 237.
Capt. Saml. Harris, 237.

The following companies were probably Regulars:
Capt. Alexander Parker's Company in 1779, 179.
Capt. Geo. Stubblefield's Company, 235.
Capt. Francis Taliaferro's Company, 235.
1775. Capt. Joseph Brock's Company served around Williamsburg, 236.
1776. Capt. Jos. Brock's Company served in New Jersey, 226.
1776. Capt. ——— Brock's Company served about Williamsburg, 223.
1779. Capt. John White's Company was in service, 220.
1780. Capt. Thomas Minor's Company served in North Carolina and was in the Battle of Camden, 229.
1780. Capt. ——— Coleman's Company guarded the Governor's palace at Williamsburg, 227.
1780. Capt. ——— Croucher's Company served around Petersburg, 222.
1781. Capt. John Carter's Company served around Fredericksburg and Hanover Court House, 236.
1781. Capt. Harry Stubblefield's Company served about Williamsburg, 235.
1781. Capt. Francis Coleman's Company served about Williamsburg, 235.
1781. Sergeant Benj. Robinson and eleven men guarded prisoners from the South to Staunton and Winchester, 219.
1781. Capt. Beverley Winslow's Company served about Williamsburg, 223.
1781. Capt. Geo. Craig's Company served about Williamsburg, 223.
1781. Capt. Thomas Towles' Company was in service, 225.
1781. Capt. Francis Coleman's Company in service about Fredericksburg, 225.
1781. Capt. Thomas Bartlett's Company joined Lafayette, 229.
1781. Capt. James Taylor's Company joined Lafayette, 229.
1781. Capt. Legg's Company served around Williamsburg, 231.
1781. Capt. Nicholas Payne's Company engaged in driving beeves

for use of the army at Yorktown, 236.
1781. Capt. Francis Coleman's Company at Siege of York and guarded prisoners to Winchester, 219, 228.
1781. Capt. ——— Tankersley's Company was in the fight at Osborne's and at the Siege of York, 222.
1781. Capt. Thos. Crouchers Company guarded the prisoners to Noland's Ferry on the Potomac, 231, 235.

MEMO.:—For a list of the Militia Officers who qualified for the Revolution from Spottsylvania County, see Section 279.

WASHINGTON

NOTE:—For the services of the Militia from this County, see the services listed under Montgomery County.

MEMO.:—For a list of the Militia Officers who qualified for the Revolution from Montgomery County, see Section 280.

Declaration of Virginia Militia Pensioners

PART II

Section No. 1

MASSIE, THOMAS.*—Nelson, Feb. 15, 1833. Born Aug. 22, 1748. In the Spring of 1775 he was chosen captain of a large company of volunteers to assist in protecting Williamsburg and the country between York and James rivers, against the depredations of Lord Dunmore and his myrmidons. Within the ensuing fall, he received a captain's commission to recruit a company of Regular soldiers to serve in the 6th Va. Reg. of the line on continental establishment. His Company, being recruited at the commencement of the following spring, he marched it to Williamsburg and united with the said 6th Regiment, then under command of Colonels Buckner and Elliott, and Major Hendricks. All the companies were nearly complete, some he believes, quite so, viz.: Capt. Samuel Cabell, Lieutenants Barrett and Taliaferro, and Ensign Jordan; Capt. Ruffin, two lieutenants and ensign; Capt. Johnson, two lieutenants and ensign; Capt. Hopkins, ditto; Capt. Garland, ditto; Capt. Cocke, ditto; Capt. Oliver Towles (a celebrated lawyer), and company officers; Capt. Gregory, ditto. He believes Capt. Worsham, or Dun and Avery. Also himself (Capt. Massie), Lieutenants Hockaday and Epperson, and Ensign Armistead. The companies were raised in different and distant parts of the State, and he had not even personal acquaintance with many of them, which,

---

*NOTE:—Except for the introductory lines, this declaration is given in full, the language of the original document being followed. It will be found of much interest. It throws important light on the treachery to the American cause of Gen. Charles Lee at the battle of Monmouth; a matter which was not fully cleared up by American historians for seventy or more years after it occurred.

together with the length of time, renders it difficult fci him to
remember every officer's name. After the Regiment was equipped
and armed, it marched out and camped in the vicinity of Williamsburg, where it entered into camp and military training; whence the
regiment was ordered to march to the North. Within the summer
following this was done under the command of Col. Buckner and
Major Hendricks (Lieut-Col. Elliott having withdrawn), Capt.
Ruffin died and he believes another officer, and several resigned or
withdrew. The regiment marched through Virginia by way of
Fredericksburg and the Northern Neck, through the upper part of
Maryland into Pennsylvania by way of Lancaster, leaving Philadelphia to the right; crossed the Delaware River above Trenton,
and passed through Jersey to Perth Amboy, where the regiment
was posted to defend that point and the country around until further
orders. Gen. Washington at that time having the greater part of
the main American army on Long and York Islands, soon after
the defeat of that army on those islands, he, with his said regiment,
was to march up the Sound by way of Newark. The storm and
capture of Fort Montgomery taking place, he met with Gen. Putnam
at Newark, and marched up the North River as high as Fort Lee.
The defeated army had crossed the Hudson, except a part th. had
marched on the east side of that river under command of Gen.
Chas. Lee. He, the said Thomas Massie, fell in the rear of those
retreating troops who had been appointed to cover their retreat and
marched the upper road by Springfield, Scotch Plains, etc., to New
Brunswick, on the Raritan River, where the troops to which he
was attached were attacked by the British Van. Having destroyed
a part of the bridge, the said American troops kept up a hot fire
with their artillery and small arms, with the British the whole day.
This checked the progress so much as to enable Gen. Washington
to cross the Delaware River with the retreating army, military
stores, etc. The troops to which he was attached (being unin-
cumbered), also had the good fortune to cross the Delaware without much loss. Gen. Washington having refreshed the troops and
received reinforcements recrossed the Delaware in the nig¹ t of
the 24th of December (he thinks), surprised and defeated a *lu* 'e
body of Hessians, posted at Trenton, captured about 900 of their
number, and crossed the river again with them. Several days subsequent, Gen. Washington, having received reinforcements, again cross-

ed the Delaware River with his army and took a post at Princeton. He, the said Massie, was for the two succeeding years generally employed on detached or particular service, consequently was seldom with the said Sixth Regiment or his company, which company was by this time much reduced. On the 1st day of January, 1777, he marched under the command of Gen. Scott (who headed a considerable body of troops), on or about the Princeton road and encamped in the evening on the Heights above Maiden-head. Soon after the van of an army under the command of Lord Cornwallis appeared, followed by the main body, said to amount to 12,000 men, and encamped in the place for the night. By dawn of the next day the enemy were in motion and filed off in columns to the American left, apparently to surround them. The Americans discharged two light field pieces of artillery at them, without return, and retreated down the road to a creek, which they crossed over a bridge and destroyed the same, and took possession of the ground on the Trenton side of the creek, then covered with large forest trees. Gen Hard at that time, being above with a large corps of Western Pennsylvania riflemen, the Americans kept the enemy at bay for several hours (he believes), before he could effect the passage of the creek with his large and heavy artillery. The Americans retreated up and slowly along the road to a summit of a hill, also covered with forest trees. Here Gen. Washington, accompanied by Gen. Green with reinforcements, came up. Here the Americans also skirmished (a considerable time), with the enemy before they retreated, and ultimately retreated to a long hill perhaps a mile to the west end of Trenton in view of the main American army. Here they formed and awaited the attack of the enemy. The day being now very far spent, the enemy appeared and approached the Americans in columns. As they were displaying we gave them a fire in single file from right to left, and retreated under a heavy fire of musketry and artillery, and formed under the protection of the main army in Trenton. A very heavy cannonade ensued directly between the two armies that lasted until after dark and has been called the cannonade of Trenton. Gen. Washington, having fortunately gained a grand point in eluding Cornwallis' intention of bringing him into a general action, made up large fires in front and left those who had been in the van during the day to keep them up. He immediately marched with his army, and taking the

Princeton road, reached that place early the next morning, defeated Col. Mahood, whom Lord Cornwallis had left there with troops to defend the place and its stores. Gen. Washington, having taken off these stores, etc., proceeded down the road by Kingston and Somerset Court House to Morristown, where he established posts on the Raritan in Jersey, viz., at Perth Amboy, Bonnontown and Brunswick. Gen Washington also established a line of posts opposite to them with a view of preventing the British garrisons from having intercourse with and marauding the country. He, the said Massie, was placed on this duty at Middle Post, Matuchen, under the command of Col. Hendricks, and served on it near five months. This duty was extremely severe by night as well as by day, constant patrolling, frequent skirmishes, some of them very bloody, nocturnal surprises, the cutting off of pickets, etc., always attended with loss of men and great fatigue. The British called in their posts about the first of June, and the American ports were evacuated about the middle of June. He, with the other officers, etc., who had been in this line of duty, joined the main army at Middlebrook. Sometime after, he and five other officers were sent to Virginia with instructions. He, on his return, joined the army under Gen. Washington at the White Marsh Hills. Shortly after, Gen Morgan returned with troops from the capture of Burgone's army. Our army then marched into winter quarters by way of the gulf to Valley Forge. He was soon detailed on duty under Gen. Morgan, who was to take post at Radnor, about half way between Valley Forge and the mouth of the Schuylkill River, with a view of cutting off the communication of the enemy from that part of the country which was effected. About this time (Feb., 1778), he was promoted to the rank of Major. In the Spring he commanded a large guard low in the lines not far above Philadelphia. Here he received Lord Cathcart, aide to Gen. Clinton, with a flag of truce and dispatches for Congress. Agreeably to orders, he, Cathcart, was not permitted to proceed further. The dispatches were read and delivered to Gen. Morgan. Immediately after, Gen. Clinton evacuated Philadelphia. He (Massie), marched under Gen. Morgan, through the city, proceeded up and crossed the river, and united with the main army. He, with Major Gibbs, was detailed to attend Gen. Morgan, who was appointed to command the light troops, etc., to interrupt and endeavor to retard the march of the British army through Jersey to Sandy Hook. The first attempt to retard their march was made at Allentown. This stopped them a day and some prisoners were taken. The second attempt was a complete surprise, from thick shrubbery in the pines, where 16 to 18 prisoners were brought off and a few killed with little loss to the Americans. Several other attempts were made to alarm and retard their march which succeeded so far as to enable Gen. Washington to march with his main army by Englishtown and obtain a position which gave him the power of bringing Gen. Clinton to a general engagement, in which it is believed he would have been entirely successful except for the flagrant disobedience of orders by Gen. Chas. Lee, who commanded the van of the American Army. On that, the 28th day of June, 1778 (an intense hot day), Gen. Washington ordered Gen. Lee to attack in full force. This, the said Massie, knows to be the fact, the orders having been communicated verbally by Gen. Washington through him (the said Massie), the evening before. On Gen. Lee's approach, the British army drew up in order for battle. Gen. Lee ordered a retreat which was done under a slow retreating fire for some time. Gen. Lee repeatedly sent orders to the officers commanding the several flanking corps not to advance and engage. This state of things continued until Gen. Washington came into the field himself, took the command, arrested Gen. Lee, and renewed the battle by bringing the troops into action. The battle at Monmouth Court House was a bloody and hard fought action. After the sunset the British army gave way, and it being too dark for pursuit, the American army lay on the field for the night, with a view to renew the battle the next day; but the British army in the night made a silent and rapid retreat, leaving their dead and wounded. Gen. Morgan, under whose command he, the said Massie, still acted was ordered to pursue the British early next morning, but they could not be overtaken except two or three hundred stragglers that were captured. Pursuit was continued to Middleton Heights immediately above Sandy Hook. After being there and thereabouts for several days, the troops marched up by Sposwood to Brunswick bridge on the Raritan River. Here we had a *feu de joie* in honor of the victory of Monmouth. From thence he marched to King's Ferry on the Hudson River and crossed to the White Plains in New York. Here he remained several weeks. From there, he, with several other officers, was ordered to Rhode Island to assist Gen. Sullivan at the siege of Newport, then in the possession of the British. A violent storm, however, with rain, etc., for several days having driven Count D'Estrey's fleet from the mouth of the harbor out to sea, rendered it impracticable for Gen. Sullivan to proceed with the siege; he consequently retired from the island, and the said Massie with the other officers detached as above stated returned and rejoined their respective regiments then encamped on the Hudson some distance above West Point, and on the opposite side.

Soon after this, the surprise and capture of Baylor's newly raised regiment of cavalry near Heroington, happened, when he with his regiment marched under the command of Gens. Woodford and Morgan with their troops to that neighborhood and took post on the strong heights of Paramus. By this time a large British force (said to amount to 6,000), under the command of Lord Cornwallis, had taken possession of the town of Hackensack, with a view of foraging the country, in which they did not succeed to much extent, owing to the vigilance of the American troops in attacking and repulsing their foraging parties. In a few weeks the British army returned to New York, and the said Massie with his regiment under the command of Col. Febiger was posted at Hackensack. Soon after this Col. Febiger was called off, and the said Massie was left in the sole command of the regiment. This was the second Virginia regiment on continental establishment. The officers were Captains Taylor, Parker, Calmen, Catlett, Stokes, Kennan, Gill, etc., as well as recollected at the distant date. He continued there until after the middle of December, when he with his command pursuant to orders marched into winter quarters at Boundbrook, on the north side of Raritan River (under the command of Gen. Lord Sterling, who commanded that division of the army), where he continued quietly for a considerable time. The British were confined to New York and its environs and employed in arranging and strengthening their posts of defense. Their embarcation of troops to our Southern States and other occurrence demonstrated the intention of moving the main seat of war there, with a view to attempt the subjugation of those states. Time progressing, it was known that Congress had determined to defend and save Charleston, if possible, and that the eight old Virginia regiments were doomed to that service. Those (8) regiments were then so much reduced in number that they were consolidated into (?) regiments (March, 1780). The officers whose commissions bore the highest rank, of course, took the command. The said Massie was of consequence a supernumerary officer, and, with Gen. Washington's permission, returned to Virginia, holding his commission (which he at this time has), ready and subject to duty with other supernumerary officers whenever called on or required.

He ranked as Major on the 20th of February, 1778, but did not take his commission from the war office (not having leisure to call for it), until the 20th of March, 1779. His commission as captain was literally worn and rubbed out in his pocket while on duty from the constant exposure to rain, hail and snow day and night. He acted alternately, under the command of Gens. Scott, Weedon, Sullivan, Morgan, Woodford, Gen. Lord Sterling, etc. He was afterwards under the command of Gen. Nelson as aidecamp in the winter of 1780 and 1781, when Arnold invaded Virginia and destroyed the public stores and houses at Richmond and arsenal and foundry, etc., at Westham, and was finally at the siege of Yorktown, and the surrender of that post with the British army, in October, 1781.

After the ratification of the treaty of peace, he received five thousand, three hundred and thirty-three and a third acres of land in the states of Ohio and Kentucky (the patents for which he now has), in consideration of his services as Major aforesaid. He likewise received some three per cent and six per cent certificates, not worth much at the time, afterwards sold, amount not recollected.

Section No. 2

ANDERSON, DAVID.—Prince Edward, Jan. 21, 1833. Enlisted May, 1777, serving as a private under Capt. Cadwallader Jones, in Col. George Baylor's Regiment till June, 1778, when he received a written discharge from Maj. Clough, of said regiment. Also volunteered as Minute Man, June, 1776, under Capt. Frank Goode, of Chesterfield County, and marched to Portsmouth, remaining there till about Dec. 20, same year, when he received a verbal discharge. In March, 1781, while living in Prince Edward County, was pressed into militia service as wagoner, by Henry Lipner commissary at

Prince Edward Court House, and made one trip, conveying stores to Halifax Old Town (Pittsylvania, C. H.). Then was guard at Prince Edward C. H. over military stores, and was collector of provisions for the army at Yorktown, serving with the exception of four or six weeks till the surrender of Cornwallis. Applicant was born in Cumberland (now Powhatan) County, Va., July 15, 1756. Discharged in 1787 because of hernia.

Section No. 3

ANDERSON, DAVID.—Prince Edward, Aug. 22, 1832. Born, 1756. Enlisted from Chesterfield in 1777, in the dragoons under Capt. Cadwallader Jones, serving under Col. George Baylor, First Lt. John Sleth (?), Second Lt. William Barrett. The term was for three years or during the war. Stationed at Fredericksburg till November, then went to Frederick, Md., and Lancaster and Reading, Pa. At Reading he had the smallpox. Crossed the Delaware to Princeton and Trenton, where he was discharged because of a rupture which still continues with him. Had served thirteen months. In 1776 he volunteered as a Minute Man under Capt. Frank Goode of Chesterfield, and was at Portsmouth during his term (according to recollection), of six months. He was then discharged. In March, 1781, was pressed into militia service as wagoner, by Harry Sepner, Commissary at Prince Edward C. H. Also acted as guard over military stores at that point, and as collector of provisions for the army at Yorktown. Was in service from a few days after the battle of Guilford until the surrender of Cornwallis, excepting a month or six weeks. Maj. Hazaret commanded at Prince Edward C. H.

Section No. 4

ARBOGAST, ADAM.—Pocahontas, Nov. 6, 1832. Born, 1760. Indian spy, 1776 or 1777. Drafted, and marched under Capt. John McCoy and Lt. Joseph Gwin to West's fort on West Fork of Monogahela, then down the river to Lowther's Fort, then lower yet to Nutter's Fort, where he remained much of the three months, and finally to Coontie's Fort, where troops were called in consequence of the Indians killing a write woman while she was spreading hemp in a field. Volunteered, 1778, as Indian spy under same Captain, and marched to Warm Springs, whence he, together with George Hull, John Gum, and Conrad Fleisher, were ordered to Crabbottom to guard that locality, and there remained the rest of his time. At another time he marched from his home (now Highland), across Greenbrier River to head of Seneca in pursuit of Indians. Date not given (1781?).

Section No. 5

ARGABRITE, JACOB.—Monroe, Oct. 15, 1832. Born in Lancaster County, Pa., Oct. 20, 1760. Came to Rockingham in boyhood. Volunteered for six months in May, 1778, under Capt. Craven for service against Indians. Was stationed at Westfall's and Hutton's forts in Tygart's Valley, except for a few days spent in reconnoitering. Volunteered at end of time for three more months. Then home two weeks, after which he was marched to Ft. Pitt and Tuscarora river, assisting at the latter place in building Ft. Laurence. The troops were commanded by Maj. Nall, Col. Crawford, and Gen. McIntosh, and sometimes by Col. Gibson. He knew Lt. Parks, who was killed by Indians between Ft. McIntosh and Ft. Lawrence, and saw him lying dead in the path. Col. Crawford therefore wanted to kill nine or ten Indians who had come for peace, but the other officers prevailed on him not to do so. Got home in February, 1779, without having been in any battle. In the fall of 1780, volunteered for 12 months in cavalry service under Capt. Sullivan, of Berkeley, and marched to South Carolina. Was in the battles of Cowpens and Guilford, and stationed a while at Salisbury. His time expired while command was at Bowling Green, Va., recruiting their horses. One Freeze was colonel (or major). Here he volunteered for an indefinite time in a rifle company under Capt. Coper, and was at the siege of Yorktown and one or two skirmishes. Was in the guard to convey away the prisoners. Taken sick at Williamsburg and discharged at Williamsburg, after having been in the service fourteen months after starting for North Carolina.

Section No. 6

BOATWRIGHT, JOHN.—Prince Edward, Aug. 22, 1832. Born in Amherst, 1764. Enlisted in winter of 1780-1, under Capt. Crad. Haskins, from Cumberland, and served three months, in Col. Posey's regiment, of Gen. Muhlenberg's command. In next tour was under Colonels Dolman and Parker, marching to Suffolk and Portsmouth, in which vicinity he was in several skirmishes, and then to Gen. Gregory's station, returning after a few days to Gen. Muhlenberg near Suffolk. Discharged after three months at Chuckatuck Mills. Also in 1781, served two months under Capt. William Meredith, of Gen. Steubin's command, campaigning in and about Chesterfield County.

Section No. 7

BRIGHTWELL, CHARLES.—Prince Edward, Sept. 13, 1832. Born about 1756, in King William. In 1779 served three months from Prince Edward under Capt. Thomas Flournoy, guarding the magazine at Williamsburg. The under officers were Lt. John Moore and Ensign John Allen. A Col. Hawes was in service at Williamsburg. Second term in 1780 of three months under Capt. Charles Allen. Marched to the Long Ordinary near Petersburg. Col. Randolph, Col. Meade, and Maj. John Holcomb were in the encampment. Third term, 18 days under (?) Capt. Richard Holland and Lt. Philip Mathews, guarding prisoners at Albemarle Barracks. Was drafted in each case.

Section No. 8

BOWLING, JAMES, SR.—Amherst, Aug. 20, 1832. Born 1752. Enlisted fall of 1775, under Capt. William Fontaine, serving in Second Virginia, under Col. Woodford, Lt. Col. Charles Scott, and Maj. Hardiman, John Marx being First Lt., Thomas Hughes, Second Lt., and one Robertson, Ensign. Served one year, campaigning about

Norfolk at the close of 1775. Was in the battle at Great Bridge about December 9th, where the enemy lost a brave officer, named Fordyce. The British were driven out of Norfolk to their ships, but their fleet cannonaded and burned the town. The American force remained some time at Norfolk, and on leaving it burned what was left. The return was by the same route, but the command remained some time in Suffolk because of sickness. Was discharged near Williamsburg. Served under Capt. Philip Thurmond as guard over the British prisoners in Albemarle Barracks; also as guard over paroled prisoners at Amherst C. H. Just before the capture of Cornwallis, he was on a tour under Col. Meriwether, the three services occupying about six months.

Section No. 9

BECK, JESSE.—Amherst, Aug. 21, 1832. Born in Albemarle, 1758. Prior to March, 1781, performed two terms of three months each in the Albemarle militia, guarding British prisoners. Was under Captain James Garland, who was killed by a sentinel at Albemarle Barracks. Was also under Capt. Hunton, or Capt. Montgomery. Col. Taylor, of Orange, was in charge. About March 1, 1781, under a draft of every fourteenth militiaman for 18 months, he became sergeant under Capt. Benjamin Harrison. The company made rendezvous in Hanover, where it was attached to the regiment under Col. Paddy and Maj. Finley. At Yorktown he saw the army of Cornwallis ground their arms. The regiment went into winter quarters at Old Cumberland C. H. In February, 1782, the corps was ordered into Southern Service and was in Georgia under Gen. Wayne, till November. Was discharged at Old Cumberland C. H.; in December, 1782, after nearly 21 months' service instead of eighteen. Remembers that when drafted each man was paid a bounty of $4,000, which by reason of depreciation was of little value. While in Georgia the army under Wayne watched Savannah, where the British were waiting transports to carry them home. Wayne's headquarters and his own encampment were at Mulberry Grove, the property of a tory, which, after confiscation, was purchased by Gen. Wayne.

Section No. 10

BLAIR, ALLEN.—Amherst, Oct. 15, 1832. Born, July 8, 1754, in Amherst. In 1780 was drafted three months under Capt. Younger Landrum and marched to join Gen. Gates in North Carolina, but before his time was out employed William Bowman, as substitute. In 1781 he again marched under Landrum, this time to join Gen. Greene. He was not in battle of Guilford, but so near that he saw dead and wounded men removed from the field. He saw Gen. Edward Stevens badly wounded in the thigh. Shortly after was again drafted, and under Capt. John Loving marched to Williamsburg, where he took sick of fever and was in hospital a considerable time. A little before the close investment of Yorktown, he was discharged from hospital and sent to the New Barracks. Soon the forces at this place were ordered to join the besieging army, but applicant was discharged, his time being nearly out and the surgeon deeming him too feeble for active service. Served six months in all.

Section No. 11

BROWN, JOHN.—Captain, 1781, of company raised on Cowpasture, in Bath. His lieutenant was Robert Thompson. Attached to regiment of Col. Samson Mathews, which served under Generals Wayne, Campbell, and Morgan. In battles at Hot Water and Jamestown, being captured in the latter. Died, 1830. Wife, Mary ———, Surviving children: 1 Margaret, married Joseph Wallace; 2 Rosanna, married Gerard Morgan; 3 Joseph; 4 John. Will mentions grandchildren: N. J. Brown Morgan, John Brown Wallace, Mary Ann Blackburn Brown.

Section No. 12

BRADSHAW, JOHN.—Pocahontas, Sept. 4, and May 7, 1833. Born, 1758. Went out in January, 1781, under Capt. Thomas Hicklin, Lt. Joseph Gwin, Ensign Thomas Wright in regiment of Col. Sampson Mathews. Was at Camp Carson near Portsmouth most of the winter. Discharged at Murdock's Mill, April 9, 1781. Was in one engagement within sight of Portsmouth, where Capt.

Cunningham, of Rockbridge, was wounded in the groin, and one private also wounded. Declarant was sergeant. Later, same year, was drafted for the Yorktown compaign, marching under Capt. Thomas Hicklin, and Col. Samuel Vance. After the surrender of Cornwallis he helped guard the prisoners to Winchester. Had served as Indian spy in the years 1776 to 1779 inclusive. Such services were not needed in the winter, as the Indians then kept in their quarters. The practice was for two men to leave Fort Cook, Monroe County, and be out three or four days each week, others taking their places on the return. They watched the gaps and low places in the mountains for thirty miles, to a point where they met the spies from Burnsides' fort. They were strictly forbidden to make a fire, no matter how inclement the weather. Died Jan. 6, 1835.

Section No. 13

BOYD, PATRICK.—Monroe, Sept. 17, 1832. Born 1759. Enlisted in Augusta in the regular service in Sept. ?, 1777, under Ensign Robert Kirk, the company being commanded by Capt. Smith and later by Capt. Bell. Col. Grayson commanded the regiment. Wintered at Valley Forge. Marched to Boundbrook, N. J. Was sick in camp at battle of Monmouth. After serving about 19 months and finding his health failing, he gave a man whose name he has forgotten, 100 pounds to take his place. At the same time was offered a lieutenant's commission if he would continue in service. Volunteered in 1781 under Capt. John Smith in Augusta, to go to North Carolina. Rendezvous at Waynesboro. Col. Moffet commanded the regiment. Marched by Lynchburg to Guilford, and was in the battle there over two hours. Reached home about one month later. Volunteered in September, 1781, under Col. Bowyer, to check the British from marching up country. When the regiment reached Charlottesville the town had been set on fire by the enemy. Marched to Gum Springs and to Richmond, where the enemy were seen leaving the city. Discharged about Oct. 1st, at Hickorynut Church, near Hot Water, after service of one month. Was in no battle while militiaman.

Section No. 14

COCKE, ANDERSON.—Prince Edward, Aug. 21, 1832. Born in Cumberland County, 1758. Living in Campbell. Declaration differs in no material respect from that of his comrade, William Wright.

Section No. 15

CARTER, POVALL.—Prince Edward, Sept. 14, 1832. Born, 1762, in Cumberland (since Powhatan). Enlisted under Capt. Edward Munford, December, 1779 (?), in the Light Infantry commanded by Col. Willis and Maj. Duval. Marched through Dinwiddie, Prince George, Surrey, etc. Had one skirmish near Bland's Ordinary. Discharged after three months. In spring of 1780 or 1781, served one term of four weeks, in Chesterfield, under Capt. Richard Crump and Col. Goode. In July, 1781, marched under Capt. Robert Powt to join Gen. Lafayette at Malvern Hill. Thence marched to Richmond and Pipington in pursuit of the British. Discharged after four weeks. Later served five weeks under Col. Moreby to guard prisoners at Old Cumberland, C. H. Was drafted for each term.

Section No. 16

CUNNINGHAM, JOHN.—Prince Edward, Aug. 21, 1832. Born, 1758. Enlisted May, 1776, in Militia company under Capt. Chas. Allen, Lt. Joseph Parks, and Ensign James Allen. Marched by Manchester, Williamsburg, and Yorktown to Hampton, where he was stationed under Col. Meredith and Maj. James. Discharged at Portsmouth after term of seven and one-half months. In May, 1779, volunteered under Capt. John Holcomb, serving about three weeks at Petersburg. In September, 1780, volunteered in Capt. Charles Allen's company of First Regiment, and after three months was given an honorable discharge. Was stationed at Petersburg under Col. E. Meade and Beverly Randolph. Early in 1781 volunteered under Capt. Andrew Baker, Lt. Joseph Parks, and Ensign Joseph Read, and joined Gen. Greene near the Dan river, where the company was attached to the regiment under Col. Otho H. Williams. Marched toward Hillsboro. In a skirmish at Whitsell's Mill about March 6, our troops gave back, Lt. Parks and private Ezekiel Parks being wounded. Company was discharged after one month. In May, 1781, volunteered under Capt. Richard Hilland, and served two or three weeks, being employed in conducting British prisoners from Prince Edward C. H. to Albemarle Barracks. Has always lived in Prince Edward.

Section No. 17

CASHWILL, HENRY.—Amherst, Sept. 17, 1832. Born in Amherst, 1757. In fall of 1779 served three months under Capt. John Sale, guarding prisoners at Albemarle Barracks, these being chiefly from Burgoyne's army. It February, 1781, marched under Capt. James Franklin, joining Greene's army the day after the battle of Guilford. During the battle his command was about 10 miles away and the cannon were heard. Thinks they might have taken part in the battle if they had used becoming alacrity. The company was then placed under Capt. Younger Landrum, of Col. John Holcomb's regiment and Gen. Lawson's brigade. In this tour he was Orderly Sergeant. Was discharged on Deep River after three months. In August, 1781, was again Orderly Sergeant under Col. Hugh Rose for three months, the service consisting of escorting a small body of British prisoners to a British vessel below Jamestown. Was drafted each time.

Section No. 18

CASH, BARTLETT.—Amherst, Oct. 15, 1832. Born in Amherst, 1757. In 1776 served three months under Capt. John Sale and Lt. James Franklin, of Col. Christian's brigade. The force he was in was to protect the frontier from the Cherokee Indians, then very troublesome. There was no battle. In 1781, under Capt. James Franklin. Joined Gen. Greene shortly after the battle of Guilford, serving then under Capt. Younger Landrum, Col. John Holcomb, and Gen. Lawson. Served in all six months, being drafted the second time.

Section No. 19

CASHWILL, WILLIAM.—Amherst, Sept. 17, 1832. Born in Amherst, 1762. Went out in militia February, 1779, under Capt. David Woodruf, and guarded prisoners at Albemarle Barracks three months. Volunteered, September, 1780, under Capt. John Morrison of a rifle company, and was stationed at Long Dairy, three miles out of Petersburg. There were present about 1,500 men under Gen. Steuben, and Gen. Lawson. February, 1781, he went out under Capt. James Franklin to join the army of Greene in North Carolina, but did not arrive in time for the battle of Guilford. They were near enough to hear the cannon and he thinks if the officers had pushed forward they might have been in time. Franklin resigned the day after the battle, and went home. The company was then put under Capt. Younger Landrum. Col. John Holcomb's regiment, Gen. Lawson's brigade. Was discharged at Deep River after three months' service. Total service, twelve months, three in each of four tours. Last tour began in September, 1781, under Capt. John Stewart. Was at siege of Yorktown and marched as guard to the prisoners to Winchester barracks, where he was discharged.

Section No. 20

CAMERON, CHARLES.—Bath, March 13, 1839. (Affidavit by Sarah, widow of said Cameron). Entered service December 3, 1776, as Lieutenant, under Capt. John Lewis in Tenth Virginia Continentals. Col. Adam Stephen commanding. Resigned, Jan. 3, 1778. Was in battles of Brandywine and Germantown. About January, 1781, drafted for three months. Captain of militia under Col. Samson Mathews. Subalterns being Lt. William Anderson and Ensign Robert Christian. Later, same year, served again as Captain of volunteer cavalry. Was in battle of Jamestown where he was adjutant of regiment, Samson Mathews being colonel and of Gen. Campbell's brigade. Last tour, two months. After Jamestown, became Captain in place of Capt. John Brown, taken prisoner. The lieutenant was Robert Thompson. 1782, appointed commissary for the district including Augusta, Rockingham and Rockbridge, serving as such from 12 to 18 months. Married Sarah Warwick (born

1772), May 3, 1792; died July 14, 1829, aged 76. December 3, 1776, elected First Lieutenant of First Company of Augusta, and reported, Feb. 1, 1777, that he had secured no recruits.

Section No. 21

CANTERBURY, JOHN.—Monroe, Jan. 19, 183–. Born in Prince William about 1761. Volunteered for one month in Montgomery to guard the frontier at Clinch River. Was at Blackmore Station on Clinch. Volunteered one month to guard the frontier on Bluestone river. Received no pay for either tour. Moved to Holston river, where he substituted three months for Samuel Douglas, and served at Logan's Station, Ky. Volunteered under Capt. Joseph Martin against the Indians. The troops marched across the French Broad to the Indian towns and were in several small skirmishes, but no regular engagement. They killed some Indians and took some prisoners, but the Indians evacuated their towns. Substituted for three months for a David Renfrow, and marched under Col. Campbell to the Santee river, where he joined Gen. Marion's army, then in camp. In one scouting party they took about 80 prisoners, brought them into camp, and sent them to Camden. Army remained in camp till Cornwallis surrendered. Declarant settled in Monroe, about 1784.

Section No. 22

CLARK, SAMUEL.—Monroe, Aug. 22, 1832. Born in Augusta, April 18, 1764. Entered as substitute for Thomas Means, in September, 1780, under Capt. Samuel McCutcheon, and Lt. John McCarney. Marched to Richmond along with the companies of Captains John Dickey, Francis Long, and Thomas Smith, and also one other company. The said five Augusta companies were stationed below Richmond, and after discharge marched back together. There was no engagement. Drafted three months in January, 1781, and marched under Capt. James Trimble to Fredericksburg, then to Sandy Point, where the James was crossed, then to within twenty miles of Portsmouth, where the British were in camp. The companies of

Captains John Cunningham, Charles Cameron, Joseph Patterson, and Thomas Hicklin were also in the march. Hicklin was cashiered for cowardice. The militia companies at this same point were commanded by Col. Sampson Mathews, Lt. Col. William Bowyer, and Maj. Alexander Robertson. Gen. Muhlenberg occasionally visited the station and seemed to be in command. The Rockbridge militia under Col. John Bowyer, were a few miles away. A captain or major named William Long was present for some time to drill the troops. Declarant with Cunningham's command was in a skirmish in which Cunningham was wounded. Discharged in April. Next month volunteered as substitute for John McCutcheon, a relative who was drafted three months and because of his family could not with safety leave home. His Captain was Patrick Buchanan, his Lieutenant, John Boyd. The companies of Captains John Campbell and Charles Haskins were in same troop. Field officers were Capt. Thomas Hughart, Lt. Col. John McCreery, Maj. Wilson. They marched into James City County, where the three companies joined Gen. Wayne. Soon after a foraging party of the enemy was seen about five miles from Williamsburg, and the companies of Buchanan and one each from Rockingham and Rockbridge were sent to drive them back. Maj. Willis, who was in command, was defeated, and the whole army marched to Jamestown, where it also was defeated. Declarant was wounded on the head by a British swordsman, and Col. Bowyer was taken prisoner. Declarant was taken to a hospital on Pamunkey river, and there remained till his discharge in August. Was then drafted three months under Capt. Francis Long. The companies of Captains Trimble, Dickey, and Buchanan also marched to Yorktown, where declarant remained till after the surrender. In April, 1782, volunteered three months against the Indians, and marched under Capt. John McKittrick to Tygart's Valley and to West Fork of Monogahala.

Section No. 23

DUPUY, JOHN.—Prince Edward, Aug. 13, 1832. Born Jan. 20, 1756. Enlisted June, 1776, as volunteer in State troops under Capt. Chas. Allen, Lt. Joseph Parks, Ensign James Allen, Col. Merriman being field officer and one Overton, Major or Adjutant.

Marched from Prince Edward C. H. through Richmond and Williamsburg to Hampton, where the army was stationed three or four months. Discharged at Portsmouth in January, 1777. In May or June of this year, under a draft on the young unmarried men of the State, requiring one year in the regular service, applicant hired a substitute named Estis, paying him $400. These troops marched north to join the army, and he knew nothing more of Estis. In 1778, during an alarm, and at which time applicant held a commission in his home company, he volunteered as a private under the above Charles Allen, and marched to Petersburg, the tour occupying a month or so. In January or February, 1781, he volunteered in his home County, Prince Edward, under Capt. John Bibb, himself being lieutenant. Bibb soon resigned and Nathaniel Cunningham was commissioned in his place. The company joined Gen. Greene at Irvin's Ferry, Halifax County, and was attached to Col. Cocke's regiment of Gen. Steuben's brigade. Was in the battle of Guilford. The second day afterward, applicant conveyed prisoners to Halifax C. H., Va., and delivered them to Nathaniel Hunt, stationed there to receive them. After this service, he returned home, according to order by Gen. Steuben, the tour lasting two or three months. Shortly after reaching home he was ordered to Halifax County to receive arms brought from Guilford battle field and convey them to Prince Edward C. H. In the same year, probably August, he was ordered to convey some wounded prisoners, sent from Guilford to Prince Edward C. H., and convey them to Gen. Lafayette, then at Ruffin's Ferry, King William County. From this point he took them on to Jamestown and delivered them to a British ship, the whole service occupying about one month. According to recollection his commission as lieutenant was by Patrick Henry. Henry Dawson, a witness to the declaration, served with applicant in 1776.

Section No. 24

DAWSON, HENRY.—Prince Edward, Sept. 7, 1832. Born in Amelia County, 1753. Volunteered from Prince Edward as minute man early in June, 1775. Company officers were Capt. Charles Allen, Lt. Joseph Parks, Ensign James Allen. The Colonel was one Merriman and one Overton was major or adjutant. Marched through Richmond and Williamsburg to Hampton, where the army lay three of four months. It then proceeded to Portsmouth, where applicant was discharged about Christmas. In 1777 he was drafted into the company of Capt. Flournoy and Lt. Moore, and after serving a while at Williamsburg a short while was discharged at Yorktown after a tour of three months. In 1778 was drafted into the militia company of Capt. Ligon and serving at Petersburg was there discharged after three months. In 1781 was drafted into Capt. Flood's Company and marched in pursuit of Cornwallis. This tour was also for three months. John Overstreet was major.

Section No. 25

DRUMHELLER, LEONARD.—Albemarle, Oct. 12, 1832. Born near Reading, Pa., about 1762. Came to Albemarle while small. Drafted in January, 1781, under Capt. John Harris, Lt. Thomas Jones, and Ensign William Jarman. Drew arms at Richmond. Stationed as fifer some time at Halifax House between Hampton and Yorktown. Discharged at Richmond in March. Drafted in May under Capt. Mark Leake. Joined the army under Gen. Lafayette near Richmond, marched to Raccoon Ford, where a junction was made with Gen. Wayne. Then through Orange and Louisa by the route still known as the "Marquis Road." The march was continued to Hampton, he being transferred to Capt. Miller's Company and frequently detailed for picket duty. Discharged at Malvern Hills in July. Again in minute service at Charlottesville, so continuing till after surrender of Cornwallis.

Section No. 26

DAVIDSON, GILES.—Amherst, Aug. 21, 1832. Born in Buckingham, 1762. Went out three months under Capt. William Dugrid at Albemarle Barracks, being substitute for Young Lee. He there enlisted under Capt. Garland Burnley for 12 months as guard to British prisoners. Later he volunteered under Capt. Francis Shelton, of Henry, who was raising a force to put down the tories, then causing alarm in the hollows of Dan River, on the North

Carolina line. Shelton's men visited persons known to be disaffected to the American cause and prevented injuries from tories. The headquarters was with a tory named McGowan, who lived in Henry. In 1781 he went out from Buckingham for three months under Capt. William Perkins, and was in the battles of Hot Water and Jamestown. He was at once called out again under Capt. Silas Watkins, who before Yorktown resigned and was succeeded by Capt. William Giles. Was present at Surrender of Cornwallis and helped to guard the prisoners to the Winchester Barracks, where he was discharged about Dec. 1, 1781.

Section No. 27

EAST, JAMES.—Rockbridge, Sept. 3, 1832. Born in Goochland, Aug., 1753. Entered service in Fluvanna in August, 1777, going out for three months under Capt. Joseph Hayden and Lt. Benjamin Anderson. Served under same officers in 1779 for three months at Williamsburg, Yorktown, and Hampton. On both tours Col. Samuel Cabell and Maj. George Thompson were field officers. Enrolled, January, 1781, and retained in County as maker of gunstocks, so continuing till the capture of Cornwallis, never understanding this service to be of private nature, and never being compensated therefor. Enlisted 1775 under Capt. Thomas Holt constantly employed with him in recruiting service for four months, then, because of the dissatisfaction of his parents, procuring James Burnley as a substitute. Also performed an irregular service of two months in 1779, guarding prisoners, especially Hessians, at Charlottesville. His Captain was Samuel Richardson, his lieutenant (probably), Thomas Thurman. Left Fluvanna, 1792.

Section No. 28

FIX, PHILIP.—Rockbridge, Nov. 6, 1832. Born near Reading, Pa., about 1754. Went out from Loudoun about September, 1777, as substitute for John Conrad. Company officers were, Capt. John Thomas, Lt. Samuel Potts, Ensign Thomas Wright. Marched from Leesburg through Frederick, Md., and York and Lancaster, Pa., to Chestnut Hill, making forced march to be in time for the battle of

Germantown, but was too late by a day or so. Later, his command surrounded the Rising Sun Tavern near Philadelphia, because of its being a harbor for the British. Discharged at York, Pa. Col. Clapham and Maj. West were regimental officers.

Section No. 29

GILLISPIE, GEORGE.—Prince Edward, Sept. 17, 1832. Born, 1752. In May, 1776, enlisted as minute man in the company of Capt. Charles Allen, Lt. Joseph Parks, and Ensign James Allen. It marched from his home County of Prince Edward to Hampton, by way of Richmond, Williamsburg, and Yorktown. At Hampton, Col. Meredith and Maj. James were in command. He was discharged at Portsmouth after service of seven and one-half months. In September, 1780, he volunteered under Capt. Charles Allen of the First Regiment, and marched to Petersburg, where other troops under Col. E. Meade and B. Randolph were stationed. His regiment then marched to near Portsmouth, where it was first under command of Gen. Robert Lawson and afterwards of Baron Steuben. After a tour of three months he was discharged thirty miles above Portsmouth. Applicant has no written discharge.

Section No. 30

GRUBBS, NATHAN.—Prince Edward, Aug. 21, 1832. Born in Hanover, 1757. First tour of nine months was in Virginia. Applicant was in no action. His Captain was John Winston, and he recollects his colonels as Elisha Meredith and Charles Dabney. The second tour, of six months, began in June, 1780. His Captain was John Price and his colonel was Holt Richardson. Was in Gate's defeat near Camden, S. C. At the end of his tour was honorably discharged. Served two subsequent tours in Virginia of three months each, one at Sandy Point under Capt. Thomas Doswell, and one at Cabin Point under Capt. John Thompson. He was also in the Siege of Yorktown, under Thompson. After the war lived in Louisa and Goochland, finally removing to Prince Edward.

Section No. 31

GILES, ISAIAH.—Prince Edward, Sept. 17, 1832. Born in Chesterfield, 1756. Performed a three months' tour under Capt. Jacobs, of Amherst, the time being spent in guarding prisoners at Albemarle Barracks. Col. Burnley and Maj. Meredith were in command. Second tour was under Capt. Richard Ballinger, this service being at Hood Fort in Prince George. His Company was the only one there. Third tour was under Capt. John Christian. He was at Richmond, Hobb's Hole, Bottom's Bridge, the Chickahominy, and other places. By recollection the tour was for three months and Gen. Lawson was in command. The fourth tour, of three mouths, was under Capt. John Phillips, and he served below Richmond. In the fifth tour, his father's wagon being impressed by Col. Gabriel Penn, of Amherst, he was assured by the said Penn that if he went with the wagon it would answer as a tour of duty. Length of his tour forgotten, but it included the Siege of Yorktown. All the tours were from Amherst.

Section No. 32

GRANT, ROBERT.—Amherst, Aug. 22, 1832. Born, 1761. Served three tours of two months each as drafted militiaman. About 1780 he marched from Fluvanna under Capt. Levi Thompson and Lt. Henry Martin to Cabin Point and put under Col. Holt Richardson. About a year later he went out under Capt. Anthony Haden, and Lt. Daniel Lightfoot, being again under Richardson, whose duty was to watch Hanover, Orange, and other counties. This was the time when Tarleton made his raid to Point of Fork and Charlottesville. The third time he went to the siege of Yorktown under Capt. Richard Napper, Lt. Zachariah King, and Ensign James Cole. His command was stationed on the Gloucester side of York River, under Col. Taylor and Maj. Campbell, to keep the enemy from escaping. The French fleet was lying off York River. He returned before the surrender. His companions were made no allowance for time spent in going into or returning from service. They were discharged *en masse* by their immediate company officers.

Section No. 33

GREEN, WILLIAM.—Bath, Sept. 11, 1832. Born, 1755. Drafted three months in September, 1776, as guard against Indians in Warwick's Fort, under Capt. John Lewis. In May, 1777, John Wilson applied to Col. John Dickenson for six men as a guard at his own fort on Jackson River. Declarant was drafted as one of these, serving three months. In September, 1777, drafted for three months under Capt. Samuel Vance at Clover Lick Fort. In 1778, drafted for four months against the Indians, serving on Jackson's River. Marched to Fort McIntosh on Ohio at Mouth of Big Beaver Creek, being under Capt. Samuel McCutcheon, of Gen. McIntosh's command. Was in no engagement. 1780, drafted for three months' tour under Capt. John McCoy. Marched to Richmond, remaining there eight or ten days, and was discharged after 24 days' service. 1781, drafted and served 34 days under Capt. David Gwin. Joined army at Hickory Neck Church near Williamsburg. In May, 1782, drafted for three months, serving under Capt. George Poage, at Warwick's Fort.

Section No. 34

GARTIN, NATHANIEL.—Monroe, Feb. 17, 1834. Born, 1759, in Orange. Moved to Rockingham, 1768. Entered service, 1777, as Indian spy in January and February. Capt. Robert Craven and Lt. Trout commanding the company. Marched to Tygart's Valley. Three months at Warwick's Fort. Indians had committed many depredations, and declarant was constantly examining the ways by which the Indians came into the settlements, so that he could give intelligence at the fort. No engagement. He and others pursued Indians, sometimes marching 40 or 50 miles a day and suffering extremely for want of provisions. A year later, the Indians still doing much injury in Tygart's Valley, he went out under Lt. John Rice, for three months. A year later still, marched 200 miles under Capt. William Kinkead to Nutter's Fort on West Fork of Mononga- hela, and served three months guarding farmers while at work in their fields. Settled in Monroe. In spring of 1781, having learned that the family of James Meeks on Indian creek, had been captured by Indians, he went to Laverty's fort on said creek as a volunteer, remaining three weeks reconnoitering between the mouths of the Bluestone and Indian Creek, and protecting the farmers while planting their corn.

Section No. 35

HILL, WILLIAM.—Prince Edward, Aug. 17, 1832. Born, July 22, 1758. Marched June 15, 1780, from Head Lynch's Tavern, Caroline County (under Capt. James Johnson, Lt. Pemberton, and Ensign Reuben Samuel), to Hillsboro, N. C., where a regiment was organized under Col. Holt Richardson, of King William County, Va., and Lt. Col. Glenn and Maj. Boyd and put into the brigade of Gen. Stevens. The army marched by Mast Ferry on the Pedee to near Camden, where there was a battle between Gen. Gates and Lord Cornwallis. After the retreat to Hillsboro and New Garden, applicant returned home in August. In February, 1781, he marched from Edmund Taylor's, Hanover County (under Capt. Edward Bullock), to Williamsburg, where a regiment was formed under Col. Mathews and Maj. Armistead. Then the command marched to Jamestown and Richmond, where it was joined by Gen. Lafayette and took part in his retreat. It was discharged the last of May. Three months later, he marched from John Morrill's Tavern, Hanover County, under Capt. John Thompson to Williamsburg, where a regiment under Col. Darke and Maj. Armistead was formed and put under Gen. Steuben. The troops were discharged at Yorktown, a few days before the surrender of Cornwallis. His services were in the Sixth Division of Carolina and the Fifth of Hanover. He removed to Prince Edward in 1781.

Section No. 36

HINES, WILLIAM, SR.—Prince Edward, Oct. 13, 1832. Born June 18, 1754 (in King and Queen?). Volunteered as minute man from King and Queen under Capt. William Richards and Lt. Hugh (?) Campbell, and marched to Gloucester about the time Dunmore and his troops lay near Gwin's Island. By permission of his commanding officer, he was on that island on a visit while the battle was going on, in which he took no part, nor was he in any engagement during that tour, which lasted about two months. He then hired his brother, John Hines, as a substitute for the rest of his term. Afterward, he went, in March, 1780, to Higgins' Station, Ky., three miles from Harrisburg, with a view of settling. In July, he volunteered for service against the Indians, only two old men being left at the station. His Captain was Hugh Megary (?). At the falls of the Ohio they joined Col. George Rogers Clark, and after a few days marched up the river in advance of him in pursuit of Indians. About the eighth day Col. Clark came on in boats, passed the company, and landed on the other shore. While in sight of Col. Clark the company was attacked by Indians, declarant being wounded by a ball which broke both bones in his right arm below the elbow. Next day he was sent with the other wounded to the falls of the Ohio, where he lay till December under the care of a surgeon before he was able to travel. He then returned to Higgins' Station. In this tour he was with Col. Clark only one night. During the winter he returned to King and Queen and was not fit for any more military service, since he could not straighten arm or fingers. Until his return he was out on the last tour five or six months. He went to see Col. Clarke after the latter returned from his expedition, and was told by him that he would have the necessary steps taken to have a pension allowed. A pension was granted, but he drew it only two or three times beginning with 1784 or 1785. He was some distance from Richmond, which fact was troublesome, and he was illiterate besides. For one month he was a substitute for William Sterling and served at Gloucester Town.

Section No. 37

HERRING, JAMES.—Albemarle, Oct. 19, 1832. Born in Albemarle about 1754. Four times in service; once under Lt. Henry Austin, of Gen. Nelson's command, for two months around Williamsburg. Second tour under Capt. Miller, of Col. Mathews' regiment. From an old field he saw the enemy's fleet seven miles distant in the river (James?). Discharged after two months at Brock's bridge. Third tour also two months and under Col. Mathews. Fourth term of one month at Charlottesville guarding a tory. Was drafted in each instance.

Section No. 38

HOGG, JOHN, Albemarle, Oct. 16, 1832. Born in Hanover, Sept. 15, 1763. About Jan. 6, 1781, he marched in the militia company of Capt. John Harris, Lt. Ralph Thomas, Lt. Thomas Jones, and Ensign William Jarman to Richmond, where they drew arms, and proceeded to the Halfway House, between Williamsburg and Yorktown. There they were stationed some time. Was discharged at Richmond, returning home about March 22. May 4, same year, marched under Capt. Nicholas Hammer and Ensign Charles Hudson to Albemarle Barracks, and then to the vicinity of Richmond to join Gen. Lafayette. After this the army made the "Wild Goose Chase," toward Fredericksburg and to the Raccoon Ford on the Rapidan, where Gen. Wayne joined the army. Then the march was through Orange and Louisa to Watson's Old Fields, where declarant was transferred to a company of light infantry under Capt. Woodford, Lt. Ruffin, and Ensign Bacon, of Muhlenberg's command. Near Richmond there was a skirmish with the enemy's light horse. The British were followed to Jamestown, where there was a smart skirmish from one o'clock till after sunset. He then marched with Muhlenberg's, Wagner's, and Campbell's brigades, to Goode's bridge on the Appomatox, where he was discharged July 24. A few days after his return home he was called out on duty at Charlottesville, until after surrender of Cornwallis. The minute men were compelled to be in place under penalty of serving six months. Applicant was drafted each time.

Section No. 39

HIGGINBOTHAM, BENJAMIN.—Amherst, Sept. 17, 1832. Born in Amherst, 1757. Called into the militia in 1779, under Capt. Richard Ballinger for three months, guarding prisons at Albemarle Barracks. Called again, 1781, under Capt. James Dillard, joining Gen. Greene in North Carolina, the day after the battle of Guilford, and serving three months. Later the same year served three months under Capt. Samuel Higgenbotham, driving cattle to Williamsburg for the main army. Was drafted each time.

Section No. 40

HARTLESS, WILLIAM.—Amherst, Sept. 17, 1832. Born in Caroline, 1754. Served in militia at Albemarle Barracks one month under Capt. Philip Thurmond in 1779. In 1781 went under Capt. James Dillard and joined Gen. Greene after the battle of Guilford. Later, same year, went out under Capt. Christian to Yorktown. After the surrender of Cornwallis he went to Winchester, conveying the prisoners. The last tours were each of three months and on all occasions he went out under draft.

Section No. 41

HIGGINBOTHAM, JAMES.—Amherst, Dec., 1832. Satisfactorily shown to the Court of Monthly Sessions that the said Higginbotham entered the Virginia service as Major of militia in 1776, serving around Williamsburg and continuing in duty as such till about 1778, when he was promoted to be Colonel (?), of the Ninth Regiment, Virginia Continentals. Continued to serve, principally as recruiting officer, till the close of the war. Shown also that said Higginbotham died intestate about March, 1813, aged above eighty years, leaving as heirs, Joseph C. Higginbotham, George W. Higginbotham, James Higginbotham, and Judith (Higginbotham) Dillard, but that letters of administration of his estate have never been granted.

Section No. 42

HARRISON, RICHARD.—Albemarle, Oct. 13, 1832. Born in Goochland, Sept. 10, 1757. Moved to Caswell County, N. C., 1775. March, 1776, volunteered against the tories who rose to protect their governor. His officers, Col. Saxton (?), Maj. William Moore, Capt. Adam Saunders. At Hillsboro troops were organized and then marched to Cross Creek, where there was news of the defeat of the tories by Col. Caswell, at Long Bridge. Discharged after five or six weeks. About December 1, 1776, marched from Pittsylvania County, Va., to Georgia under Capt. John Dooley and Lt. Boswell Smith. In Georgia, Capt. Thomas Dooley was killed by an Indian. Declarant was now in Continental service for 18 months, but then attached to no regiment. Next Captain was Boswell Smith. The troops in the two companies that marched to Georgia were promised a bounty of 200 acres, which he never received. All he did get was $8 in money. Discharged in Wilkes County, Ga., spring of 1778 and came home. Spring of 1781 was drafted from Pittsylvania, and marched to siege of Fort Ninety-Six, under Capt. James Turner. After Gen. Greene raised this siege he was in camp at the high hills of Santee, where his time expired, and he was sent back to Virginia in charge of prisoners. This service was for three months, eighteen days. In September, 1781, he went to the siege of Yorktown as substitute for his employer, John Lewis. Fleming Bates was captain. After surrender of Cornwallis he conveyed prisoners to Noland's Ferry on the Potomac. Was there discharged. Moved to Albemarle, 1784.

Section No. 43

HAWK, ISAAC.—Pocahontas, Sept. 5, 1832. Born, 1758. Entered service in Hampshire, March 10, 1777, under Capt. Moses Hutton, Lt. West Wade, Ensign Andrew Heath. Marched through "Yough (Youghigheny) Glades," to Fort Pitt, and thence to Wheeling by command of Gen. Hand. Was at Fort Wheeling six months. Jacob Ware and Jacob Crow were there killed by Indians, but not in any regular engagement. Aug. 10, 1781, was ensign under Capt. George Ball in Lt. Col. James Newell's regiment, of Hampshire County. Drafted for one month, Oct. 8, 1782, and marched from Big Capon, Hampshire County, to the Monogahela to guard the commissioners while running the line between Virginia and Pennsylvania. There was no engagement.

Section No. 44

HUTCHISON, WILLIAM.—Monroe, Oct. 17, 1835. Born in Augusta, 1757. In 1776 volunteered one year under Capt. John Henderson to guard the frontier. Began service in May at Cook's Fort. Marched across New River through the present County of Giles, then thinly peopled, and served as ranger, being on constant duty. The next spring volunteered under Capt. Archibald Wood to serve so long as the Indians might be troublesome. In the fall the company marched up Bluestone to the settlement near its head, to protect the people gathering their fodder. He was in places where probably few persons except Indians had ever been. Thus served four years (excepting one year that he and two others were detailed as spies by Capt. Woods), arduously and almost constantly ranging back and forth from Cook's fort to Wood's fort on Rich Creek. The country was wild and mountainous. Frequently he carried orders in the night time, when he could hear not far off the yell, the whistle, or the weary tread of the savage. If orders were to be sent express he was the man generally selected. Such service, however difficult or dangerous, he always performed, and as he believes to the full satisfaction of his captain and fellow-soldiers. During the year that himself, Philip Cavender, and Nicholas Woodfin were detailed as spies by Capt. Wood, he served at the imminent hazard of his life, lying out by night with no covering but his blanket and no shelter but the forest, the scream of the panther or the yell of the Indian reminded him of his duty to his country. After four years Capt. Gray, of Rockbridge took command of the company. In the spring of 1782, all signs of the savage disappearing from near the settlements, he left the service. When ordered by Capt. Gray to the head of Bluestone, after marching twenty miles, all but himself refused to go further. An old man named McGuire wished to go to the settlement, and one David Clay showing the way, we started and soon found we were pursued by some 10 or 12 Indians. Sometimes we were in mud to our knees, or in water to our necks. At dark the pursuers set up a tremendous yell, but we heard no more of them, and at length arrived where we were ordered, declarant having traveled 40 miles that day after nine in the morning.

Section No. 45

HAND, CHRISTOPHER.—Monroe, ——, 1833. Born in Ireland, 1758. Came to Virginia about 1773. Drafted in Augusta early in 1781, under Capt. Stevenson and Lt. Smith, of Col. George Moffett's regiment. Appointed orderly or first lieutenant. Company rendezvoused at Widow Tee's on Middle River, marched to Williamsburg, then to Norfolk, then with other militia to Gen. Greene's army at Guilford C. H. Was in the battle at that place, the Virginians forming the second line. The first line fled, but the Virginians stood their ground and fought hard till ordered to retreat by Gen. Stevens, their brave commander. A halt was made four or five miles from the battleground. The army retreated a little farther to Speedwell Iron Works, but returned to South Carolina. Discharged about Sept. 1, after serving eight months instead of the stipulated six. Was in no other engagement.

Section No. 46

JONES, THOMAS.—Made oath in Nelson that he enlisted December, 1776, under Capt. James Franklin, and soon made sergeant. Marched to Baltimore and then to Bound Brook, N. J. Affiant was often by the side of Franklin in the battle of Brandywine, and the latter's conduct was that of a brave officer. Shortly before the battle of Germantown Franklin left his company and was said to be sick. The company was in the battle, one man being killed and several (including declarant), wounded and removed to Reading. About one months later Franklin called at hospital and told him he was on his way home as his constitution would not stand the fatigues of the army. In 1780 at a militia muster in Amherst he heard Capt. Franklin asked why he was not at his post. The reply was that he returned home to enjoy his estate, the same as the inquirer.

THOMPSON, SMITH.—Made oath in Augusta that he was in the battle of Monmouth, June 28, 1778, and knew a James Franklin in Woodford's or Weedon's brigade, said Franklin being in the battle; that March 15, 1781, he saw the said Franklin, then a captain, in Gen. Greene's army at Guilford C. H., N. C.; that Franklin was attached to a regiment of Virginia Continentals; that he saw him the day after the battle in the tent of Col. John Greene.

FRANKLIN, JAMES.—Will made, March 11, 1813. Recorded in Amherst, August, 13, 1813. Gives his wife eleven negroes and his plantation on south side Rutledge Creek. Mentions Nancy C.,

Sarah W., and Betsy H. Franklin (daughters), and Jeremiah Franklin, bequeathing various property to the daughters, including a mill.

Section No. 47

JARVIS, FIELD.—Monroe, Jan. 21, 1833. Born in Westmoreland, April 25, 1756. Volunteered in 1776, serving three months at the lead mines in Wythe to keep the tories and Indians from taking them. His officers were Capt. William Leftridge and Lt. Stephen Saunders. When he went out he was living in Bedford. Volunteered there in September, 1777, for three months, under Capt. John Torbert and Lt. Arthur Mosely, and marched to Yorktown, where he served out his time. Moved to Monroe, 1781. Called out in 1779 by Col. James Calloway for guard duty at New London, Bedford County, the British prisoners taken at the Cowpens being confined there and at Lynchburg. In service ten days. Was in no battle.

Section No. 48

KINNISON, JACOB.—Pocahontas, Aug. 8, 1833. Born, 1757. Volunteered, 1777, under Capt. Mathew Arbuckle, then living in Little Levels of Greenbrier. Served the whole ten months at Point Pleasant, Arbuckle's subalterns being Lt. James Gilmer and Ensign John Williams. Only one company there. At end of ten months the Greenbrier men discharged by Gen. Hand, who came from Pittsburgh. A part of that company had enlisted for three years. Shortly before applicant was discharged, 700 men arrived at Point Pleasant under Colonels Dickenson and Skillern. April 15, 1779, re-entered service as Indian spy, and was expected to scour the country from Fork Lick on Elk River (including waters of Sleepy Creek, a branch of Greenbrier), to Drenna's Fort and Little Levels. Was almost continually in service, never being allowed at the fort more than two or three days at a time. Discharged October 15th.

Section No. 49

KELLER, CONRAD.—Monroe, Sept. 15, 1834. Enlisted for three years in Shenandoah, in 1776 or 1777. Served out said time as waiting man to Gen. Muhlenberg. Was drafted two months in 1781 or 1782, under Capt. Downey at Winchester. Served two months more at Fort Frederick on the Potomac.

Section No. 50

LEWIS, JESSE.—Albemarle, Oct. 13, 1832. Born in Albemarle, May 13, 1763. Drafted 1780, and served two months at Cabin Point under Capt. John Henderson, of Col. Holt Richardson's regiment, one Quarles being Major. In May, 1781, he substituted for William Eustis, who had been drafted for 18 months' service in the regular army, and marched under Capt. Benjamin Harris to rendezvoused at Old Chesterfield C. H., where Gen. Steuben was in command. Next march was to Point of Fork, a depot for military stores. On Tarleton's approach there was a retreat southwest to Staunton river and then to Hanover, to join the main army under Gen. Lafayette. Was at siege of Yorktown. After surrender of Cornwallis the command marched to winter quarters at Old Cumberland C. H., where declarant fell sick, procured a substitute, and received a written discharge from one Ferbecker (Febiger?). Was under command of Capt. Kirkpatrick and Lt. Thwait several months. His field officers most of the time he believes were Col. Gaskins and Maj. Polson.

Will dated Feb. 10, 1849. Codicil, March 20, 1849. Probated April 2, 1849. Mentions, 1, Polly Cravens; 2, Mary, daughter of Sophia Johnson; 3, Sarah T. L. Henkle; 4, James A. Henkle; 5, (daughters): Jane Barksdale, Elizabeth Maury, Sophia Johnson, Sarah F. Henkle; 6, (children of Sarah F. Henkle): Jesse L., Sarah Ann (Craven), Peter H., James A., Sarah T..L.; 7, Michael Johns, husband of Sophia.

Section No. 51

LOGAN, ALEXANDER.—Amherst, Aug. 22, 1832. Born Oct. —, 1761. Served four tours of two months each. In 1780 or 1781 was at Albemarle Barracks under Capt. Anthony Henderson, Col.

Taylor being in command, guarding prisoners. Next time, marched again from Fluvanna, under Capt. Samuel Richardson to the Halfway House between Yorktown and Hampton. Third tour also under Richardson and stationed at Williamsburg. Fourth tour under Capt. Richard Napper. Was at siege of Yorktown and stationed on Gloucester side of York River under (?) Col. Taylor, to keep enemy from escaping by land, the French fleet blockading the river. At one time had a certificate of pay which produced $2.50, being all the pay he had ever received. Was in no engagment, but pleased his officers.

Section No. 52

LANE, HENRY.—Amherst, Sept. 17, 1832. Born in Hanover, Nov. 26, 1745. In the spring of 1781 he lay in camp at Deep Spring near Williamsburg for four or five weeks, under Capt. Frank Coleman, George Stubblefield being Colonel of the Spottsylvania regiment and one Merriweather of his own. This tour was of three months. He paid for two others in beef, the law allowing such exemption. He next served a month at Albemarle Barracks.

Section No. 53

LIVELY, GODRILL.—Monroe, Aug. 19, 1833. Born about 1762. Drafted in Albemarle in September or October, 1780, under Capt. Mast Leake and marched to Cabin Point, where it was thought Arnold would land but did not. Discharged at Petersburg after one month. Drafted next May or June, serving one month about Richmond. Late in the fall of 1781 enlisted at Charlottesville for three years in the cavalry commanded by Col. (afterward Gen.), Armong (Armand?), being in Capt. Barrett's company, and served till the end of the war. The regiment was that winter at Charlottesville, then till the next fall at Staunton, and later at Winchester and at York, Pa. Discharged after 22 months in said regiment.

Section No. 54

MORGAN, WILLIAM.—Prince Edward, Sept. 17, 1832. Born, 1757. In summer of 1776 enlisted as private under Capt.

Robert Hughes and Lt. Edward Munford, marching from Cumberland County by way of Richmond and Williamsburg to Yorktown, where applicant was discharged after two months' service. In April, 1780, joined a troop of cavalry from Powhatan County, commanded by Capt. Littlebury Mosby and Lts. Horatio Turpin and Wade Mosby. The troop proceeded by way of Richmond, Williamsburg and Bottom's Bridge on Chickahominy to Petersburg, being joined meanwhile by a cavalry troop from Dinwiddie. At Petersburg applicant was in the battle in which Gen. Steuben was successful (?) over the British, who proceeded to Richmond and then down the James. At Richmond he was discharged after a tour of two months. Enlisted, 1777 or 1778, in Powhatan County, and at Old Cumberland C. H., served two months under Col. Mosby as Sergeant of the guard. 200 British soldiers were quartered there. February, 1781, joined a rifle company in Prince Edward, where applicant then resided. The company officers were, Capt. Andrew Baker, Lt. Joseph Parker, and Ensign Read. It joined Gen. Greene near the Dan river, and was attached to a regiment commanded (?) by Col. Call, of the Regular service. After one month returned to Prince Edward for provisions from the commissary, and then rejoined the army, which proceeded to Ramsay's Mill on Deep River. In North Carolina he marched under Gen. Robert Lawson to Halifax County, where he was discharged after a service of two months.

Section No. 55

MATHEWS, PHILIP.—Prince Edward, Aug. 20, 1832. Born, 1756. Enlisted in the spring of 1776, under Capt. Charles Allen, of Prince Edward, and marched by way of Manchester and Williamsburg to Hampton, where Col. Meredith and Maj. James took command. After two or three months he marched to Portsmouth and there remained until discharged, in December after a tour of seven months.

Section No. 56

MARTIN, JOSEPH.—Amherst, Sept. 17, 1832. Born in Fairfax, 1741. In Halifax, 1777, substituted for James Moseley under Capt. Moody and Lt. William Denical (?), and went into Pennsylvania on seven months' tour. Served near Head of Elk under Gen. Scott, of Washington's army. Still as minute man called out on five tours; once in erecting breastworks at Alexandria, once in guarding that town, two other times guarding Gen. Washington's home, the fifth time at Colchester. Does not remember length of tours. Went out from Pittsylvania, 1781, under Captains Isaac Clemens and Dicks and Lt. David Hunt. Reached home March 11th.

Section No. 57

McGLAUGHLIN, JOHN.—Bath, Sept. 11, 1832. Born about 1763. Went out Jan 1, 1781, under Capt. William Kinkead and Lt. Jacob Warwick, of Augusta (now Bath), serving in Col. Sampson Mathew's regiment. Was at Portsmouth three months, and on a Sunday morning was in a skirmish with the Britsh near that town. In 1782 or 1783, drafted for six months in Rockingham to serve against the Indians. Marched then under Capt. William Smith to Hinkle's Fort on the North Fork (Pendleton County). Was in no engagement. Next year went out under Lt. Neil Cain to Tygart's Valley and Clarksburg, the company being ordered out by Col Benjamin Harrison.

Section No. 58

McCAUSLAND, ANDREW.—Bath, Sept. 11, 1832. Born, July 14, 1757, in Chester County, Pa. Drafted three months, 1777, serving under Capt. Samuel Vance and Lt. John Cartmill; two weeks at Warwick's Fort, going then to Clover Lick Fort. In June, 1777 (or 1778), stationed one month under Capt. Andrew Lockridge at Vance's Fort on Back Creek. Drafted January, 1781, for three months, and marched under Capt. Thomas Hicklin, Lt. Joseph Gwin, and Ensign Thomas Wright to Camp Carson near the Dismal Swamp, so as to protect the road between that point and Portsmouth. Colonels Sampson Mathews and William Bowyer were in command. In June, same year, drafted 20 days to Williamsburg and Jamestown, serving under Capt. David Gwin, Lt. William McCreery, Ensign Alexander Wright.

Section No. 59

MORGAN, BENJAMIN.—Monroe, Nov. 19, 1832. Born at Philadelphia, Pa., 1761. Moved to Berkeley Co., Va., in boyhood. In 1778 (1779?), was drafted in the summer for three months under Capt. David Kennedy, of the packhorse service to Fort McIntosh, Col. Murray commanding at that post. Except for the last three weeks, helped to complete Fort Lawrence on Tuscarora River, seventy miles beyond Fort McIntosh. Discharged at the latter place. He saw Lt. Parks lying in a path after being killed by Indians. Volunteered about May 1, 1781, for three months under Capt. Edward Davis, marched by Fauquier C. H. and Fredericksburg to a point 40 miles below Williamsburg, where he joined his battalion, and then under Col. Darke and Gen. Lincoln toward North Carolina. Before getting that far the men were turned back to Yorktown and discharged. Was in no battle. Near Yorktown was pursued by a scouting party of British light horse, and in getting over a post and rail fence was cut in the shoulder. Drafted same year three months under Capt. John Hart and was at siege of Yorktown. Was of the guard for the portion of prisoners sent to Frederick, Md. Discharged about Christmas. Married Ann ———, 1784. Died Feb. 24, 1836.

Section No. 60

NICKLE, ISAAC.—Monroe, April 15, 1833. Born, 1752. In August or September, 1774, volunteered three months under Capt. John Lewis, and was in battle of Point Pleasant. Lt. John Henderson was in his company. Drafted from Greenbrier in August, 1777, to serve against Indians, under Capt. Mathew Arbuckle, and Col. Lewis. Served three weeks on Elk river and rest of three months at Point Pleasant. In 1780 (1781?), was drafted for three months under Capt. A. Nickle to go toward the Lakes, but owing to the condition of his family he hired Thomas Buchinal as substitute, giving him a mare worth $50. The troops were commanded by Col. Brown.

Section No. 61

PRYOR, WILLIAM.—Amherst, Oct. 15, 1832. Born in Albemarle (now Amherst), about 1752. Moved to the Great Kanawha in fall of 1773, and planted corn next spring, but was driven back to Amherst by Indians. Was at Point Pleasant, spring of 1775, and there saw Capt. Isaac Shelby, who had been left with the wounded after the battle the preceding October. Early in 1776 the Indians were so troublesome that he, with many others had to take shelter in the fort at Point Pleasant, and here substituted for James Frazer, in the command of Capt. Matthew Arbuckle, who was in charge of the fort. The subalterns were Lieutenants Andrew Wallace, James Thompson and Ensigns Samuel Wood and James McNutt. After serving out eight months for Frazer in the fall he enlisted under Arbuckle for two years. About this time Capt. William McKee, Lt. James Gilmer, and many privates came to Point Pleasant and were stationed under Arbuckle. Was often sent on detail with others up the Kanawha to a plantation to get corn, and was often a spy or on guard on the Ohio above the fort. In the fall of 1777, Colonels Skillern and Dickinson came on an expedition against the Shawnee towns. He met this force at the mouth of Elk. Among others of them were James Harrison and Micajah Goodwin. When they reached the fort, Lt. Gilmer went over the Kanawha to shoot turkeys and was there killed by unknown Indians. As soon as Gilmer's body was brought to the fort his men murdered Cornstalk, his son Ellinipsico, and another Indian, these Indians being held as hostages for the safety of the garrison and the settlers. While Skillern and Dickenson were at Point Pleasant, Gen. Hand, of the Continental army, came from Pittsburg and ordered a return, saying it was too late in the season to attack Chillicothe and other Indian towns. Hand ordered Arbuckle and McKee to shorten the pay and daily allowance of their men, saying they feasted too high. When this order was put into execution almost every man in the fort shouldered his gun and put on his knapsack, resolving to go home. But Col. McDowell told Hand of the impolicy of such measure and obtained permission to address the men, who on being promised their former pay and allowance, returned to duty. He himself took no part in the mutiny. Because of the murder of Cornstalk, the Shawnees, in the spring of 1778, mustered all their strength and besieged Point Pleasant several days. They killed Paddy Sherman and wounded Lt. Gilmer. Finding they could not take the fort they killed all the stock of the garrison and then started for the Greenbrier settlements. We knew of this from the Grenadier Squaw, said to be a sister of Cornstalk. She had taken shelter in the fort soon after its erection, and continued with us. When her own stock was killed she went out with spirits and became intoxicated, but overheard the Indians and told the officers of their plans. Capt. McKee then proposed that if any two men would go out and warn the Greenbrier people, he would so extend their furloughs as to be equivalent to a discharge, which itself he could not grant. John Inchminger and John Logan accepted and started, but returned the same evening. Philip Hammond and myself then agreed to go, but I gave way to my older brother, John, whom Hammond preferred and who was more experienced in Indian warfare. They were dressed in Indian style by the Granadier Squaw, and passed the Indians at some meadow about 12 miles from Donally's fort. They gave information and the settlers had been in the fort but a little while when the Indians attacked and a dreadful conflict ensued. Capt. Arbuckle was then in Greenbrier visiting his family. He and Capt. Lewis raised a company and forced their way into the fort. The Indians were driven off with much loss and Greenbrier was thus saved. During this expedition of the Indians, Gen. Clark stopped at Point Pleasant on his way to take Vincennes. In the autumn of 1778, there was a man in the fort named Morgan who had been a prisoner among the Indians many years. A squaw with him was said to be his wife. Morgan was in custody and ironed, and was to be taken to his father who had offered a large reward for his return. But finding himself lightly guarded, he and the squaw ran off and were never again heard of. Suspecting he would reach the Indian towns and tell that our time was nearly out, and that many of us would soon leave, the officers discharged many, including myself. In 1779 was drafted from Amherst for a three months' tour a little below Richmond. He served under Capt. Samuel Higgenbotham, of Col. Christian's regiment, and among his comrades were Zedekiah Shumaker, William Brown, and Samuel Allen. In 1780, he was out three months under Capt. Richard Ballinger, serving at Fort Powhatan, below Richmond, now (1832), Fort Jefferson. Among his comrades this tour were an elder brother, Nicholas Pryor, and Richard Tankersly.

Zedekiah Shumaker certified he served with declarant at Point Pleasant and below Richmond.

NOTE:—In a memorial of James Huston, who moved from the Cowpasture River to Kentucky, in 1783, and died there in 1818, aged 92, it is stated that he was out on a scout the day before the attack on Donally's Fort, and by means of his dog detected the approach of the Indians, and was thus enabled to warn the settlement. Houston's wife was Nancy McCreery, and he settled in Fayette County.

Section No. 62

PETERS, CHRISTIAN.—Monroe, Sept. 17, 1832. Born 1761. Drafted in Rockingham about June 1, 1779, to go to North Fork of South Branch of Potomac against the Indians, marching under Capt. Robert Craven. While stationed there the Captain received a commission to raise a company under a proclamation of the governor of South Carolina, offering 1,000 pounds of tobacco ($33.33) to each volunteer. Applicant accepted the position of corporal under said offer. With four others he returned with Capt. Craven to Rockingham, after being out about two months. The company was soon raised and started south about Sept. 1. At Hillsboro they lay two weeks waiting for other troops. They marched thence under Gen. Stevens to Cheraw Mills where they joined the army under Gen. Greene. A detachment was sent out to surprise some tories at the Black Swamp. The tories dispersed, but fourteen prisoners were taken. Part of the detachment was sent back with the prisoners, the other part marching to Georgetown, where twenty-eight prisoners and some supplies were taken. Another guard was sent off with the new prisoners, the rest of the force joining Gen. Morgan about 36 hours before the battle of the Cowpens. In the night the army moved about half a mile to the place chosen for a fight. Men were left to keep up the fires till daylight. The battle began about sunrise. Declarant was in the riflemen, on the right of the army, and in the third company from the right. They had the pleasure of taking 600 prisoners. Then the army moved back before Cornwallis' army to Salisbury, where declarant's company was detailed on the guard to convey the prisoners to Virginia.

By the time the army was fairly across the Yadkin, the advance of the British were on the other bank, but as the river was rising fast, they could not cross. The company's baggage wagon was lost, not being taken along. At Pittsylvania C. H. they delivered their prisoners to the militia of that county and were discharged in Rockingham in April. Declarant sold his bounty as part pay for a horse. In June, 1781, volunteered as sergeant under Capt. Jeremiah Beasley, and marched to Eastern Virginia, where command was attached to the regiment of Col. John Willis and Maj. Rucker, Gen. Campbell commanding the brigade. Declarant was in the battle of Hot Water, which lasted two hours and ten minutes, the Americans falling back to the shelter of Gen. Wayne's army. One man of the company was killed and fourteen wounded. In the battle of Jamestown, he was on the right, where there was little danger, but Gen. Wayne's regular troops suffered very much. Was out this time about four months, including a month, consumed in coming and going back. Total service, eleven months, in which he carried his own rifle, tomahawk, and butcher knife. Affidavit supported by John Dunn, a comrade.

Section No. 63

ROACH, JONATHAN.—Monroe, Sept. 17, 1832. Born in Rockingham, 1761. Enlisted in Orange, February, 1779, under Lt. John Goodalls for and during the time the British prisoners taken at Saratoga should be kept under guard. Served two years, three months, twenty-four days. Officers were Capt. Madison, Maj. John Roberts, Col. Taylor. Served at Winchester and Charlottesville. Discharged in May, 1781. In same year, substituted for James Craig, drafted from Rockingham for two months. Served under Capt. Smith, Maj. Long, Col. Samuel Lewis. Discharged eight miles from Yorktown eight days before surrender of Cornwallis Was in no battle. Moved to Monroe, 1785.

Section No. 64

ROBERTS, WILSON.—Albemarle, Oct. 12, 1832. Born in Albemarle, May 13, 1762. Volunteered for eighteen months under

Lt. Robert Jouett, and rendezvoused at Fredericksburg, April 25, 1779. The new recruits were there laid off into divisions and marched to Baltimore, his own under Capt. (?) Howard. They proceeded by water to the head of Elk, and the vessel running. aground, the command marched to the Blue Ball Tavern, thirteen miles from Philadelphia. Then they were ordered south, going by way of Fredericksburg to Petersburg, where the men were laid off into regiments. Declarant was in the Third Regiment, commanded by Col. Abraham Buford, of Gen. Scott's brigade. The regiment marched south the middle of March, 1780. About this time two field pieces were wanted at Charleston, S. C., and declarant's company volunteered to guard them. The regiment got within 25 miles of Charleston, which then, was under siege. There was then a retreat through Camden toward Salisbury. The day after leaving Camden they were overtaken at Hanging Rock, otherwise the Waxhaw Settlement, by the British Light Horse and infantry under Tarleton. This according to recollection was May 29th. Buford was defeated and it was the general opinion that out of about 500 men not more than 25 got entirely away without harm. Declarant made his way to Salisbury, where a remnant gathered and proceeded to Chesterfield C. H., Va. The regiment was again made up, still under command of Buford, and sent to Hillsboro, N. C., where declarant was discharged. About September, 1781, he was drafted for two months in the militia, and marched under Capt. Robert Sharp, to Richmond. Thinks his colonel was one Richardson. Soon after arrival at Yorktown, Cornwallis surrendered, and he was ordered back to Richmond to guard some prisoners or refugees. He was there discharged by Capt. Falkner, the tour being of two or three months.

Will made Aug. 20, 1836, probated July 3, 1837. Mentions, of children: Martha D. Kerby, John W. Roberts, William R. Roberts: of grandchildren: Sarah E. and John W. Kerby. Executors: J. W. and W. K. Roberts and Fayette F. Kerby. Possessed land, negroes, bank stock.

Section No. 65

ROBINSON, JOHN.—Monroe, Sept. 17, 1832. Born, 1749. Drafted in February, 1780, under Capt. Thomas Wright, of Greenbrier, for the alleged purpose of going against the Indians at Detroit, but was marched by Crytes (?) lead mines to the head of Holston, and thence to Logan Station, Ky., where it was decided that the troops were not to go to Detroit. Marched to McAfee's Station on Salt River, where Capt. James Armstrong was in command. The major under whom affiant served was Andrew Hamilton. Discharged here in August, 1780, his term of service calling for twelve months. Reached home the last of August in Company with twenty-eight others who had been in the same service. Among them were, James Alton, Swift Perry, and Edward Cornwell, all now dead; William Bushor, who moved to Kentucky, and James and John O'Hara and Thomas Alterberry, whom he knows nothing of. Was in no battle. In consequence of being from home he sustained a loss of $1,600 in the depreciation meanwhile of paper money held by him.

Section No. 66

SCOTT, WILLIAM.—Prince Edward, Sept. 17, 1832. Born in Ireland, Dec. 3, 1757. Enlisted 1775 or 1776 from Charlotte County for a term of one year in the militia. His company officers were Capt. Wm. Collier and Lt. Douglas Watson. Joined his regiment at Petersburg, commanded by Col. Ruffin and Maj. Glenn. The march was then by way of Williamsburg and Yorktown to Gwin's Island, where there was fighting several days with the British under Lord Dunmore. Several, he thinks seven, ships were destroyed after Dunmore was driven out. The' enemy then went up the river, the army watching his movements. News arriving that the Indians were troublesome on the frontier, the regiment, which was armed with rifles, marched to Holston river. A few days before its arrival there had been a battle between the vanguard and the Indians. The main body of the army went in pursuit, his regiment, then commanded by Col. Morgan being stationed at Holston (Long) Island, where it remained until the time of service expired. He had no written discharge because of the unpopularity of Morgan. The day before the discharge was to take place, the soldiers were told they would be mustered for the purpose. Next morning some men who wished to show their dislike to the Colonel broke his sword near the hilt and shaved the mane and tail of his horse.

Morgan rode off in a rage without issuing regular discharges, but saying he would do so at New London, Bedford County. He did not meet the men there nor did they get any written discharge. In February, 1778, applicant was drafted in Charlotte for a term, he believes, of two years. He hired John Scott as a substitute, gave him 100 pounds, and got a discharge for himself from Thomas Reed, the same stating the services was from Feb. 10, 1778, to March 16, 1778. The last tour was in 1779, when he was drafted about Feb. 1st into Capt. William Morton's Company, and marched south. At Salisbury, N. C., the command was joined by other Virginia troops and marched through Charlotte and Camden to the main army under Gen Lincoln. While there an attempt was made to storm a British fort at Stono Ferry, but the attack was repulsed. His discharge is dated July 13, 1779, and is signed by Maj. William Hubbard, of the Virginia Brigade. Applicant came to America in 1763, and moved to Prince Edward about 1782.

Section No. 67

SIMMONS, JEHU.—Prince Edward, Sept. 17, 1832. Born in Prince Edward, February, 1762. In 1779 or 1780, his father being drafted into the militia, he marched as a substitute under Capt. Clark, of Col. George Walker's regiment, both officers being of his County. They were ordered to Petersburg, where three other companies also assembled. In 1781 he volunteered for a second tour under Capt. Ambrose Nelson of Prince Edward and Ensign John Woodson and Benjamin Allen of Cumberland. The Command marched to join Gen. Greene at Guilford C. H., N. C. He was in Col. John Holcomb's regiment of Gen. Lawson's brigade. From recollection his major's name was Tucker. His regiment was not in the battle at Guilford, but a brother was wounded. Afterwards he marched with the army to Ramsay's Mill, where he was discharged. During the following summer he was drafted as a guard in the vicinity of Prince Edward C. H., Cornwallis being expected there. This tour he believes was of four weeks. Later in the summer he was drafted, and marched under Capt. Bird, of Prince Edward, to the siege of Yorktown. Maj. Charles Allen was the superior officer. At Yorktown he was under Col. Beverley Randolph, of Gen. Lawson's brigade. His command was detailed to convey the British prisoners to Winchester, and having been sick some time, he substituted a man in his place. The last tour was of four months by recollection, and he was sick some time afterwards. In every case he served full time and was honorably discharged.

Section No. 68

SMITH, PHILIP.—Amherst, Oct. 15, 1832. Born in Amherst, 1755. In 1781, marching under Capt. James Franklin, he joined Gen. Greene's army in North Carolina the day after the battle of Guilford. He was then put under Capt. Younger Landrum, Col. John Holcomb's regiment, Gen Lawson's brigade. In the following summer was in a tour under Capt. Caleb Higginbotham, driving cattle from Amherst to supply the army at Williamsburg. Served three and four months. Was drafted each time and was in no battle.

Section No. 69

SHUMAKER, ZEDEKIAH.—Amherst, Oct. 15, 1832. Born in Henrico about 1754. Went to the Great Kanawha and there resided till 1775, but returned because of Indians. In the autumn of 1776, enlisted two years under Lt. William Moore, of Rockbridge, some comrades being John Hogg, John Finney, Samuel Peters, and William Hicks, and marched to Point Pleasant. Other officers were Capt. William McKee, Lt. James Thompson, and Ensign James Gilmer. Capt. Matthew Arbuckle was in command at Point Pleasant, his subalterns being Lts. Andrew Wallace and Samuel Wood, and Ensign James McNutt.

Remainder of declaration is substantially the same as that of William Pryor. (Sec. 61). He adds that Inchminger and Logan declared they could not get by the Indians, that the Indians did not believe anyone would dare leave the fort, and that the reward offered by Morgan's father was $500. Also that Capt. Arbuckle's idea in sending off the men before their time was quite out was that otherwise the Indians might waylay them. He served a month or two guarding British prisoners at Albemarle Barracks, his Captain being Anthony Rucker.

Section No. 70

STEUART, EDWARD.—Bath, Sept. 12, 1832. Born, Feb. —, 1759 in Augusta (now Highland). About 1779 substituted for Joseph Beathe, in a three months' tour under Capt. McCreery, at Clover Lick Fort. Drafted about 1778, serving two months or over at Vance Fort under Capt. Andrew Lockridge. About 1780, drafted and served two months against the British. Marched under Capt. John McCoy to Richmond and Camp Holly. Drafted three months, 1781, serving at the siege of Yorktown, under Capt. Thomas Hicklin, Maj. John Wilson, and Col. Samuel Vance. Drafted three months, 1782, serving as ensign under Capt. George Poage, guarding the Augusta frontier at Clover Lick fort.

Section No. 71

STEUART, JOHN.—Bath, Sept. 12, 1832. Born Sept. 6, 1761, in Augusta (now Highland). Drafted, January, 1781, for three months. Marched down James. Crossed the river at Sandy Point and joined army next day. Then marched to Suffolk and Camp Carson, being stationed at the latter place during the winter. In March was marched to Portsmouth and back to Camp Carson, where he was discharged, April 10. Officers same as Edward Steuart's (Sec. 70). Again drafted three months and was at siege of Yorktown, where he was wounded on the hand by a sword cut.

Section No. 72

STEUART, JAMES.—Bath, Jan. 12, 1833. Born in Augusta (now Highland), Jan. 2, 1757. Drafted 1778, or 1779, for three months under Capt. Andrew Lockridge, at Clover Lick Fort. A year later went out one month under Capt. Thomas Hicklin to guard the frontier, and served at Warwick's Fort. Went out three months in 1781 against the British, the company officers being Capt. Thomas Hicklin, Lt. Joseph Gwin, Ensign Thomas Wright, and the regimental Colonels, Sampson Mathews and William Bowyer. They were stationed during the winter at Camp Carson near the Dismal Swamp, where he took a prisoner. He was often in scouting parties and in March they took some prisoners in a skirmish at Portsmouth. Discharged at Camp Carson. Drafted, June, 1781, on tour of 20 days, being in Capt. Peter Hull's Company of horse of Col. John McCreery's regiment. Was in the battle of Jamestown and then discharged. As substitute for James Carlile, served same year a month and ten days. Crossed and recrossed the James at Westham, in pursuit of Tarleton.

Section No. 73

SALISBURY, WILLIAM.—Pocahontas, Sept. 5, 1832. Born, 1742. Entered service at Warm Springs in May, 1774, under Capt. John Lewis, Lt. Samuel Vance, and Ensign Jacob Warwick, Col. Charles Lewis commanding the regiment. Was in battle at Point Pleasant. Drafted for three months at Warwick's Fort, 177–.

Section No. 74

SHARP, WILLIAM.—Pocahontas, Sept. 4, 1832. Born, 1740. Indian spy in 1773-'74. In service, summer of 1774 in company of Capt. Andrew Lockridge during the Point Pleasant campaign. William Mann and himself were sent by Gen. Andrew Lewis with a message to Gov. Dunmore, and did not rejoin the army till the morning after the battle at Point Pleasant. In September, 1764, had volunteered under Capt. Charles Lewis in an expedition against the Indians on the Muskingum. Returned next March. There was no engagement. The Indians gave up their captives. Lt. McClenahan was of the company. Colonels Field and McNeel were then members of it. Drafted, January, 1781, in Company of Capt. William Kincaid and Ensign James Trimble, of Col. Samson Mathew's regiment. Was in a skirmish with the British at Portsmouth. Discharged, April, 1781.

Section No. 75

SANS (SANDS?), SAMUEL.—Monroe, Aug. 22, 1832. Born, 1758. Substituted for William Dickey, who was drafted from Augusta late in 1780. Served under Capt. James Tate, whose major was Frank Triplett, of Fauquier. The regular officers were, Maj. Brooks, Col. Howard, and Gen. Morgan. Was in battle of Cowpens and was with Col. Washington when that officer captured 200 tories at Rugley's Mills. Discharged at Salisbury, after six months tour. Drafted three months in June, 1781, under Capt. John Campbell, Maj. Long, and Col. Charles Cameron. Was at battle of Jamestown, where he was commanded by Capt. John Dickey and Col. Hughart. Was also at Siege of Yorktown, and guarded prisoners to Winchester, where he was discharged. (Note: Declarant must have been called out twice in 1781). In 1782, substituted three months for Hugh Brown against the Indians, and marched under Lt. John McCamie (?), serving out his term at Clover Lick. Berryman Jones and Samuel Clark were comrades. The latter was wounded at Jamestown.

Section No. 76

SITLINGTON, ROBERT.—Bath, Sept. 26, 1832. Born 1749. In 1776, went out as substitute two months for Nathan Crawford, serving as ranger and spy at Warwick's Fort under Capt. John Lewis and Capt. Samuel Vance. Drafted 1777, for two months to serve against the Indians at Warwick, and Clover Lick Forts, under Capt. Samuel Vance and Lt. John Cartmill. Was in no engagement in either tour. Served four or six weeks against the British in 1778 or 1779 under Capt. John McCoy. Discharged at Richmond. Drafted for six weeks in 1781 and marched under Capt. David Gwin to Guilford. Was in the battle there, but received no wound.

Section No. 77

TAYLOR, JAMES.—Amherst, Sept. 17, 1832. Born in Fairfax, 1757. Went out as minute man from Fairfax in 1777, under

Capt. Moody and Lt. William Daniel. Served three months in Pennsylvania under Gen. Scott, of Washington's army. The corps to which he belonged being from Fairfax, it was placed in the center. He was afterwards out two tours at Alexandria, two in guarding Gen. Washington's estate, and one at Colchester.

Section No. 78

TURNER, WILLIAM.—Amherst, Aug. 21, 1832. Born in Albemarle, 1760. Served three months at Albemarle Barracks under Capt. Philip Thurmond. While there Capt. James Garland was killed by a sentinel on duty. Later was three months at Rocketts, below Richmond under Capt. John Christian. Still later, and again as orderly sergeant, he went out under Capt. Younger Landrum on the Guilford campaign. The company, which was attached to Gen. Lawson's brigade, was not in the battle. The next tour was at the Siege of Yorktown, and under Capt. Benjamin Higginbotham. He started as sergeant and on the way was commissioned ensign. However, a few days before the capitulation he, his captain, and others were discharged as supernumerary officers and ordered home.

Section No. 79

THOMPSON, ROBERT.—Bath, Jan. 8, 1833. Born about 1755. In 1774 volunteered against the Indians for three months. During battle at Point Pleasant was a guard at the Point. The battleground was half a mile above. Was under Capt. John Dickenson. In 1777, volunteered three months under Capt. Robert McCreery, serving at Warwick's Fort. Drafted, 1781, serving as lieutenant under Capt. John Brown. Was in battles of Hot Water and Jamestown, in Col. Samson Mathews' regiment.

Section No. 80

WALKER, WILLIAM T.—Prince Edward, Aug. 21, 1832. Born in Amelia, 1757. Drafted in summer of 1778. Marched under Capt. Edward Walker to Richmond, thence to Williamsburg, where the company remained several weeks, and finally to Hampton, where it was regularly discharged, the tour comprising about three months. At Hampton there was a report that the British were coming down Elk River. Because of the scarcity of lead, bullets were made from the lead in the church windows. In 1779, volunteered as private under Capt. E. Walker, of Amelia, and marched to Cabin Point, where the company was discharged, the tour covering two or three months. In 1780, volunteered in Capt. Philip Holcomb's Cavalry, of Prince Edward County, where applicant was now living. Marched to Petersburg and used Masonic Hall as barracks. This tour was also two or three months. Gen. Lawson was here in command.

Section No. 81

WOODSON, JOSEPH.—Prince Edward, Sept. 17, 1832. Born, 1751. Drafted from Amelia County, 1777, serving under Capt. Benjamin Ward two months. Stationed at Petersburg and there discharged. In the spring of 1780, the enemy lying off our coast and coming up our rivers, threatened Petersburg and Richmond, there was a call for 300 militia from Amelia. Applicant then served two months under Capt. Watson, of Col. William Giles' Regiment. The troops crossed the Appomattox below Petersburg and marched to the Chickahominy, where they were discharged. At the close of 1780, or early in 1781, applicant enlisted from Amelia in a company of cavalry under Capt. Edmund Walker, and marched by Cartersville, Point of Fork, and Albemarle C. H. to receive arms. The British were coming up the James and into the County. He was discharged in Amelia, never having been attached to any regular troops. In the spring of 1781, he enlisted in the State Legion to serve during the war. The Captain was Peter Randolph. The colonel was Everett Meade, and the majors were Diggs and Nicholas. The legion marched to Genito Bridge on the Appomattox, where it was stationed a short while, and then to Richmond to receive arms. Not being able to procure any it was stationed near Goode's bridge on the Appomattox, and did not join the troops about Jamestown and Yorktown. After the surrender of Cornwallis the troops to which applicant belonged were ordered to go home, after a service of about nine months, but to hold themselves in readiness for a future call, which however, never came.

Section No. 82

WORSHAM, WILLIAM.—Prince Edward, Aug. 20, 1832. Born, 1752. Enlisted for one year from Amelia County, in the First Virginia Regiment, in the summer of 1775. The company officers were Capt. Markham, First Lt. William Cunningham, Sec'd Lt. Joseph Scott, and Ensign Tarleton Woodson. The regimental officers were Col. Patrick Henry, and Major Francis Epps. Soon after his enlistment he marched to Winchester, then to Williamsburg, and afterwards to Norfolk. On the way to Norfolk the battle of Great Bridge took place between the advanced troops under Colonels Scott and Marshall, and the British, the latter retreating and after a few days of skirmishing embarking on their vessels. Norfolk was about this time burned, and the American troops remained to the end of his enlistment at Kemp's Landing. Afterwards, declarant was commissioned captain of militia, and with Captains Roberts, Fitzgerald, and Jones marched to aid the people of North and South Carolina, then much annoyed by the British and tories. At Halifax, N. C., they remained some time, and being joined by some of the militia of that State, were placed under the command of Col. Wylie Jones. They had marched near to Charleston about the time of Gate's defeat near Camden (Aug., 1780), when the militia returned, and his company was discharged in Amelia after a term of six months. In the fall of 1780, his company was again ordered out, and marched to Richmond and vicinity, being then under the command of Col. Abraham Greene and Maj. Philip Jones. After about two months the company was discharged. There was another call for the Amelia militia, and he marched with his company to Petersburg, where after two months of service under Col. Edmund Booker, he was discharged. Arnold and Philips appeared around Petersburg and Richmond, and the militia were called out frequently for short periods. In February, 1781, he again went out with his company for three months, and marched to the headquarters of Gen. Lafayette at Wilton near Richmond. Cornwallis came up from the South, and at Petersburg took general command of the British. It was the intention of Lafayette to attack them at different points at the same time. One division under Col. Barbour marched to Petersburg, while the other, under Lafayette in person, marched around to cross at Goose Island. Applicant was guide to

Lafayette, but Barbour arriving first atacked from Baker's Hill and the British retreated, going up the James to Point of Fork. Other troops coming in, the Amelia and Chesterfield militia were discharged at Bird's Ordinary, near Point of Fork. The day after his discharge, applicant with Capt. John Kinght, Lt. Archer Watshall and about 100 soldiers were taken prisoners on their way home by Tarleton. His commission was taken from him and he was detained as prisoner two months. After the battle of Jamestown, in July, he was discharged with the smallpox upon him. He was not again in service.

Section No. 83

WILTSHIRE, JOHN.—Prince Edward, Jan. 21, 1833. Born Feb. ·10. 1747. Enlisted for one year under Capt. Robert Watson and marched to Augusta, Ga., where the command was attached to Col. Joseph Habersham's regiment, of Georgia Continentals. Enlisted Sept. 1, 1776, and discharged next April because of sickness. Drafted May 13, 1781, and marched under Ensign Abner Watkins from Prince Edward to headquarters at Ratcliff's Old Field, where command was attached to Capt. Richard Allen's Company, of Col. Henry Skipwith's regiment and discharged at Malvern Hills, Aug. 11th.

Section No. 84

WOOD, SOLOMON.—Albemarle, Oct. 10, 1832. Born in Albemarle, Sept. 2, 1757. Served three tours as militiaman, First time went out under Capt. Matthew Leake and Lt. James Garland from Hart's store and marched to Cabin Point. Second time, under Capt. Nelson Thompson of Col. Reuben Lindsay's regiment, and was discharged at Malvern Hills. Third time under Capt. Benjamin Harris. Was at Siege of Yorktown, going thence as guard to the prisoners to Noland's Ferry on the Potomac where he was discharged. Drafted each time. Served nine months.

Will made May 15, 1832, probated Jan. 1, 1833. Wife, Mary.

Section No. 85

WILSON, RICHARD.—Amherst, Aug. 23, 1832. Born in Caroline, Dec. —, 1762. Drafted as Orderly Sergeant in 1779, and marched under Capt. Long to Williamsburg, where he was under Gen. Taliaferro guarding lower Virginia. Was in four other tours, of three months each, also as Orderly Sergeant. Remembers Gen. Lafayette, Gen. Muhlenberg, Col. McWilliams, Col. Mathews (at Jamestown), Col Johnston, Col. Innes at siege of Yorktown, Maj. Dabney (whom he joined at Culpeper), Maj. Duckleman. Maj. Boyce, Maj. Carey (at Yorktown), Captains Jamison and Stevens of the Port Royal Infantry, Captains Clark and Taylor, and subalterns: Tylor, Hampton, and Woolfolk. Was stationed at Port Royal, and during siege of Yorktown at Gloucester, and passed through at least thirteen counties.

Section No. 86

WANLESS, RALPH.—Pocahontas, Aug. 7, 1832. Born, 1757. Drafted from Calfpasture for three months under Capt. McCoy. In service half the time. Discharged at Richmond before reaching army. Was out two months as spy at Clover Lick under Capt. George Poage. Drafted nine months under Capt. Buchanan, serving part of said time at Norfolk.

Section No. 87

WOODELL, JAMES.—Pocahontas, Sept. 3, 1832. Born, 1752. Drafted from Augusta, 1774 (?), being stationed at Clover Lick six weeks under Capt. George Moffett. Drafted 1777, under same captain, and marched under Col. John Dickenson to Point Pleasant, where declarant was stationed a short while. Time, three months. Drafted, 1778, under Capt. Cooper, Col. Newell's Regiment, Gen. Woodford's Brigade. In service one year in Pennsylvania, New Jersey, and New York. Discharged at Middlebrook, N. J., February, 1779. Drafted, 1781, under Capt. John Given, of Col. William Bowyer's regiment, of Gen. Campbell's brigade, of Gen. Lafayette's army. Was in service three months and in battles of Hot Water and Jamestown. Was then First Lieutenant.

Section No. 88

WICKLEBACK, HENRY.—Monroe, Aug. 22, 1832. Born, 1755. Known in the army of the Revolution as Henry Squire. In December, 1778 (or 1779), entered service for nine months as a substitute at Ft. St. Lawrence. He was there under Capt. Uriah Springer, of Col. John Gibson's regiment, Gen. McIntosh being in general command. Marched to Ft. Pitt for a month, where he was under the command of Capt. W. Springer. Then returned to Ft. McIntosh for the rest of his time. Here again substituted for nine months, serving at Forts McIntosh, Pitt, and Wheeling. While at Ft. McIntosh was out with a scouting party of 15 to 20 men under Lt. Harris. Were attacked by some 40 Indians, but killed many of them. At Fort Pitt was sent out under Gibson and Crawford, when the advance guard was attacked by a large party of Indians, who were driven off and 10 of them killed. At time of entering army he lived in Greenbrier (now Monroe), and was employed by James Burnside to pack merchandise to Ft. St. Lawrence. It was on one of these trips that he substituted.

Section No. 89

WALKER, THOMAS.—Monroe, Sept. 17, 1832. Born Dec. —, 1764. Drafted in Rockingham four days after becoming sixteen, and marched under Capt. Michael Conger, joining Gen. Muhlenberg at Stone's Mills near Jamestown. A part of the regiment including himself marched to Great Bridge, remaining there a while and skirmishing. Marched then to Nottaway river, N. C., then back to Great Bridge, and then rejoined regiment, marching up and down the James till the three months were up. Drafted next July under Capt. Richard Riggen, marching to Richmond, then down the Pamunkey, crossing the same and joining Gen. Stevens. A part of the regiment including himself recrossed the Pamunkey, marched to the mouth of the Chickahominy, then to Williamsburg and Yorktown, where he was taken sick and discharged as unfit for duty three days before the surrender of Cornwallis.

Section No. 90

WISEMAN, JOSEPH.—Monroe, Aug. 22, 1832. Born in Pennsylvania, 1759. Drafted in the first militia from Bucks Co., Pa. Went out in August, 1776, under Capt. Thomas Berry, of Col. Mark Bird's regiment. Served in new Jersey and discharged at Paulus Hook in November. Moved to Rowan County, N. C., October, 1777. Volunteered in August or September, 1778, under Capt. Nickell and Lt. Chapman. Marched to Mecklenburg, C. H., where he was under the command of Col. Lock and Gen. Rutherford. Marched to the Ten Mile House near Charleston, then to the Two Sisters on Savannah river, where he joined Gen. Ashe immediately after his defeat, covering the retreat across the Savannah. Discharged at Salisbury, N. C., after nine months. July, 1779, substituted for three months, marched into Mecklenberg, where he was quickly discharged to go home and await further orders. No further call was made. Moved to Washington Co., Md., where under a call for every ninth militiaman, he was drafted for the war. He and eight neighbors, one of whom would have to be similarly drafted, hired a substitute for 45 pounds. Came to Monroe, 1794.

Section No. 91

YOUNG, JOHN.—Pocahontas, Aug. 8, 1832. Born, 1760. Entered service, 1779, under Capt. Ambrose Madison, Lt. Col. Francis Taylor, and Maj. John Roberts, being regimental officers. Garland Burnley was an officer in the regiment. Was in no engagement. Marched with British prisoners from Albemarle Barracks to Winchester, and was there discharged. Was in two previous tours under Capts. John Scott and Coursey. Was in no engagement.

Section No. 92

ARMSTRONG, WILLIAM.—Augusta, Oct. 26, 1832. Born on Little Calfpasture, December 12, 1759. In March, 1779 (1778?), was drafted for three months under Capt. William Kinkead and Ensign James Steele. Rendezvoused at Vance's Fort, marching thence to Clover Lick and to West Fork of Monongalia, where he was discharged in June. No other troops went out with the company. Drafted about March 1, 1781, and under Capt. Gwin, of Campbell's regiment, joined Greene's army in North Carolina. Their horses were then sent home. Was in the battle of Guilford. Discharged at Troublesome Iron Works, Rockingham County, N. C., one month after leaving home. In July drafted again under Capt. James Bell, Lt. John Wackub, and Ensign Alexander Crawford, of regiment under Col. Samuel Lewis and Maj. William Long. Was at Siege of Yorktown but no other engagement. Discharged two days before the surrender of Cornwallis.

Section No. 93

AILSTOCK, ABSALOM.—Rockbridge, —— —, 1832? Born in Louisa about 1763. Freeborn mulatto. Marched from Louisa about Dec. 1, 1780, it being rumored that the British were about to land on the coast, and was out four weeks. Regimental officers were Col. Fontaine and Maj. Winston. Discharged at Hanover C. H. About April 1, 1781, joined the Second Regiment under Capt. William Harris, the superior officers being Col. Richardson and Maj. Armistead. The British burned the tobacco warehouses in Manchester, the ruins of which applicant distinctly saw from Richmond side. Brigade stationed a while at Malvern Hills. The enemy were in the habit of coming this far up the James in boats, each with a gun at either end, their purpose being plunder. Two such boats and seventeen prisoners were taken by the regiment. Discharged in Spottsylvania in June. Called out next month under Capt. Benjamin Harrison and joined Nelson's brigade (called at Yorktown the Louisa Brigade), at Williamsburg, Col. Richardson being a field officer, but Maj. Martin taking the place of Maj. Armistead. After Washington arrived, the brigade marched on to Yorktown. During the siege, applicant was employed digging intrenchments for batteries and making sand baskets. After the French began the battle on Sunday morning, his regiment was put into the poplar redoubt for the purpose of charging into a gun battery.

Section No. 94

ALVERMAN, JOHN.—Botetourt, Sept. 7, 1832. Born in Culpeper, 1757. Volunteered under Capt. Henry Hill. Marched to meet, and to guard at Albemarle Barracks, the prisoners taken with Burgoyne. Col. James Taylor was in command at the barracks. Drafted under Capt. Slaughter, of Col. Barbour's regiment and joined Wayne, remaining three months. Drafted about May 1, 1781, under Capt. Ambrose Bohannan, joined Gen. Washington's army at Malvern Hill, marched thence to Yorktown. Taken sick, put in hospital at St. Peter's Church, New Kent County, and then discharged, Aug. 11, 1781.

Section No. 95

BELL, JOHN.—Augusta, Dec. 22, 1834. Born in Augusta, in Long Glade ,Sept. –, 1755. Late in September, 1780, went out as ensign for three months under Capt. Thomas Smith. Marched from rendezvous at Col. Esam's to just below Richmond, where he remained till discharged. No regular troops were there. Early in January, 1781, he substituted for his brother Francis, thinking the latter too young to bear the fatigue. Company officers were Capt. Joseph Patterson, Lt. Andrew Anderson, Ensign James Poage. From former rendezvous marched to Dismal Swamp, where he was discharged in April. In June called out as ensign for tour stated at twenty days, his captain being John Dickey, his lieutenant, Robert Campbell. Marched to Jamestown. Was in the battle there and in several little skirmishes. James Allen, Francis Gardner, and John Crawford were comrades at Jamestown; also Samuel Bell.

Section No. 96

BALSLEY, CHRISTIAN.—Augusta, Aug. 27, 1834. Amendatory declaration. Served at least twelve months in three tours.

Section No. 97

BELL, SAMUEL.—Augusta, July 28, 1834. Born, 1759. Drafted for three months in September, 1777, under Capt. George

Moffett, Lt. Joseph Patterson, Ensign Andrew Anderson. Col. John Dickenson and Maj. Samuel McDowell being line officers. Marched from rendezvous at mouth of Kerr's Creek by way of the Big Savannah (Lewisburg), and Walker's Meadows to Point Pleasant, where there was a fort garrisoned by a company of regulars under Capt. Arbuckle. It was understood that the troops were destined against Detroit, but in consequence of the late arrival of Gen. Hand from Pittsburgh, the expedition was abandoned, and in December applicant's command was ordered home, where he arrived Christmas eve. About May 1, 1780, applicant substituted for Benjamin Brown, a relative who could not leave home without great inconvenience. Marched under Ensign John Wilson to Clover Lick, where he joined his company under Capt. William Anderson and Lt. James Mitchell, and was discharged after three months. No other troops were at Clover Lick. In fall of 1780, applicant volunteered under Capt. Thomas Smith, Lt. (?), George Craig, Ensign John Bell. Marched to Richmond to guard the General Assembly. Several other militia companies were there. Discharged after two weeks. Then rejoined (not expecting to march far), Capt. Smith's company and marched into North Carolina, overtaking the main army at Troublesome Iron Works, the day after the battle of Guilford, and returning after a little above one month. The following May or June, Lt. Robert Kirk applied to Capt. James Bell (with whom applicant was serving) for men to help impress horses for the regular army. Applicant with a few others was so detailed, and served in Bath, etc.

Section No. 98

BELL, JOSEPH.—Augusta, Aug. —, 1832. Born in Augusta, Feb. —, 1755. Drafted in 1776. Rendezvoused at Lexington about July 15, and marched under Capt. John Lyle, of Col. Russell's regiment to the Great Island in Holston River, where the troops came under the command of Col. William Christian and proceeded against the Cherokees. Was stationed a while at a Cherokee town and returned after five months. Drafted next year. Marched from rendezvous at Staunton, about Sept. 22, 1777, under Capt. Thomas Smith, applicant being First Sergeant, and proceeded to Little Levels in Greenbrier, where the men were joined by other troops under Colonels John Dickenson, Samuel McDowell, and George Skillern. After being a while at Point Pleasant, the army was drawn up and Gen. Hand and Col. McDowell rode along the lines, announced the surrender of Burgoyne, and discharged the men. Got home middle of December. Went out again the middle of April, 1779, under Capt. James Trimble, of Col. Sampson Mathews' regiment, to serve against the Indians. Rendezvoused at Staunton April 16th, and marched to Tygart's Valley, returning in July. Ordered out again to rendezvous in Rockfish Gap, 1781, to guard the prisoners taken by Gen. Morgan at Cowpens. Last service was as ensign, rendezvous at Col. Esam's (Waynesboro), June 6, 1781. Marched under Capt. Francis Long, joining the troops of Col. Dandridge, of Gen. Lafayette's army. Was in action at Hot Water under Col. Willis; also in battle of Jamestown and at Yorktown during the siege. Was out four months. James Davis a comrade.

Section No. 99

BAILEY, JOHN.—Kanawha, (W. Va.), —— —, 1833. Drafted in Albemarle, 1777, under Capt. Landon Jones and Lt. James Wood, and attached to First Virginia under Gen. Nelson. Served six weeks, and a month later drafted under Capt. John Harris and Lt. Ralph Thomas. A third draft under Capt. Mark Leake and Lt. John Wharton. Total service, five months.

Section No. 100

BUSTER, CLAUDIUS.—Augusta, Sept. 25, 1832. Son of John Buster. Born in Albemarle, Nov. 24, 1763. Entered service in December, 1780, under Capt. William Grayson, Lt. William Gooch, Ensign Francis Montgomery, Orderly Sergeant Taulton (Tarlton) Woodson. Given arms at Richmond. Received into army at Yorktown by Gen. Nelson. Discharged next March. The companies of *Capt. James Barnett* and *Capt. Tucker* marched from Amherst at same time. The field officers were, Col. Dabney and Maj. Campbell. He served between Yorktown and Hampton. One night the British sailed up York River, landed at Halfway House, and destroyed some property. The Americans had left there the night before. Col. Mallory gave them battle, himself and several men being killed. In May, 1781, when it was rumored that the British were on their way to Richmond, there was a call for a great many men from Albemarle, and the following companies went into service: Capt. Daniel White's, Capt. Mark Leake's, Capt. Benjamin Harris', Capt. John Burke's, and Capt. Laney's. By a proclamation it was announced that if men who had served the winter before would now volunteer for six weeks, it should stand as a tour (of three months?). Applicant and many others so volunteered. His company officers were, Capt. Daniel White, Lt. Nathaniel Garland, Ensign Francis Montgomery, the whole force marching under Col. Reuben Linsday, and joining Gen. Lafayette on his retreat from Richmond. When Col. Linsday made return of his men he made no discrimination in favor of the volunteers, and all served three months. The army marched and countermarched until it fell back to Fauquier County. It then moved southwesterly to the Rapidan where it was joined by Wayne and Steuben. Col. Toles (Toler?), then took command of declarant's regiment. A Maj. McIlhany of the regular army, was also attached to the regiment. About this time the British cavalry got into Charlottesville, ran out the Assembly, and then retreated. Our army followed the British, but there was no fighting until the vicinity of Williamsburg was reached. There were then skirmishes at Hot Water and Hickorynut Church, and a considerable battle at Jamestown when the British went on board their ships. Applicant himself was in no battle. After the British took ship his company lay in camp at Malvern Hills until its discharge in August.

Section No. 101

CUNNINGHAM, JOHN.—Rockbridge, Sept. 3, 1832. Born, 1756. Marched under Capt. Bird in 1776, from Lancaster County, to Philadelphia, there transferred to Capt. Patton, and marched on to Amboy to join Gen. Robideau. Went out in 1777, also for two months, under Capt. White, marching to White Marsh, the British being in Philadelphia. Was under Gen. Irvine, who was Captured at Chestnut Hill. Was himself in several skirmishes. In 1781 served another two months guarding prisoners in Lancaster County, Capt. Patton again being his commander.

Section No. 102

CARTMILL, HENRY.—Botetourt, Sept. 7, 1832. Born in Chester County, Pa., 1754. Removed to Augusta, 1761. Feb. 26, 1779, commissioned ensign in Botetourt. Upon a requisition for troops to go against the Indians in the southwest of Virginia, he marched under Capt. James Smith to Nolachucky river, being joined on the way by Capt. James Barnett's Company from Roanoke. At Nolachucky about 400 men were found under command of Col. William Campbell. By a council of war it was determined not to pursue any farther. Returned after an absence of over three months, the distance to the Nolachucky being about 350 miles. Commissioned lieutenant April 14, 1781. Called into service and was at Yorktown during the whole siege, being under the command of Capt. James Smith. After the surrender he guarded prisoners for some distance beyond Williamsburg, when there being more force than was thought necessary he was permitted to return home. At the report that Donally's Fort in Greenbrier was attacked, he went as ensign under Capt. Hugh Logan to the relief of the settlers, but they were met by Capt. Hall, who told them the Indians had retired. At another time he ranged the mountains between Fincastle and Sweet Springs in search of Indians. Himself and many others assembled at the lead mines in Wythe to meet Col. Fergerson who was said to be advancing from the Carolinas with a large force of tories. After going as far as Stone House in Botetourt, they were stopped by Col. Skillern, commanding the Botetourt militia, until more men could be collected. News reaching them that the tories were dispersed, they returned home.

Section No. 103

CAMPER, JOHN.—Botetourt, Aug. 14, 1832. Born in Fauquier, 1749. Drafted in Shenandoah in 1781 (?). Rendezvoused at Steventown (New Market?). Marched under Capt. Nevill, and Col. Richard Campbell. Marched to Ft. McIntosh, then 74 miles farther to Yellow Creek. No encounter. Three months' service. Went out from Woodstock under Capt. Jacob Wrinker to Cheraw Hills, in South Carolina, where the troops went into winter quarters under Gen. Stevens. Was sent from there to guard the prisoners taken at Cowpens. Discharged at Albemarle Barracks after five months' service.

Section No. 104

COLVIN, BENJAMIN.—Boone County, Mo., June, 1832. Born in Culpeper, 1758. Entered service in April, 1778 (1781?), under Capt. Elijah Kirtley, of Culpepper, Col. John Willis, of Hanover, commanding the regiment. At first the expectation was to join Washington in the North, but news came the British were coming up the Potomac. Joined Gen. Morgan at Bird's Ordinary, Amelia County. At Bacon's Branch were joined by Gen. Muhlenberg. Moved toward Roanoke, where it was understood Tarleton was doing mischief, but he had left. Crossed James twenty miles above Richmond and about fifteen miles beyond met Gen. Wayne. A few days later a battle at Jamestown lasting two hours by the sun. At Hot Water there was a skirmish with a party of British who were robbing the country of cattle. They had a great many shut up in Gen. Lawson's field, but we got them all away. After Jamestown he was on scout duty and in some light skirmishes. Time was out Oct. 20, when the American army was at Bacon's Branch above Richmond. A day or two later, without going home he joined Capt. Samuel Ferguson's company just arrived from Culpeper and raised in affiant's neighborhood. Discharged in January, 1782, after service of nine months and ten days. Allowed $31.11 a year.

Section No. 105

DAVIDSON, JOHN.—Rockbridge, Aug. 8, 1832. Born in Rockbridge, Oct. 29, 1757. Was willing to go out in spring of 1778, being liable as unmarried man, but was induced by mother to hire substitute, who served twelve months. Drafted about June 1, 1778, serving in Greenbrier. Early in July, 1778 (1779?), served fifteen days under Capt. William Lyle driving packhorses loaded with flour and bacon to the troops on the frontier. Went out in January, 1781, under Capt. Andrew Moore, Lt. John McClung, Ensign James McDowell, the regiment being under Col. Bowyer. Rendezvous at Red House and marched to Portsmouth, where the regiment lay, except a month at Great Bridge. The Nansemond at Suffolk was crossed on a floating bridge. At Great Bridge were captured two twelve-pounder howitzers and about twelve prisoners. At Gum Bridge, near Dismal Swamp, there was a skirmish. Discharged about April 11th. Marched Aug. 7, 1781, under Capt. David Gay, who tried to induce him to be Orderly Sergeant. At Richmond the company formed with those of Augusta a battalion. Line officers were, Colonels Parker and Willis, and Gen. Muhlenberg. Proceeded to Ruffin's Ferry, thence to a point opposite Jamestown, 5,500 French being camped on north side. Their boats ferried the militia across. Then under Col. Samuel Lewis the companies marched to Yorktown, remaining there till Sept. 14, 1781.

Section No. 106

DAVIS, WILLIAM.—Alleghany, —— —, 1833. Born about 1756. Substituted in Amherst for John Tinsley, serving three months under Capt. Pamplin at Albemarle Barracks. Was again one month at same place under Capt. Ballinger, and as substitute for a young Tinsley. Next served three months for John McDaniel under Capt. Tucker, and was discharged at Williamsburg. Was detailed as a guard to take some British prisoners to Newport News. Next time was drafted three months, and served under Capt. Dillard as guard at Amherst C. H. Then volunteered under Capt. Stuart, serving eleven days. Colonels Taylor and Bland were in command at Albemarle Barracks.

Section No. 107

FULTON, ROBERT.—Augusta, Oct. 28, 1833. Born in Augusta, Nov. 18, 1760. Drafted, October, 1780, for three months, rendezvous at Waynesboro, and served at Richmond under Capt. Samuel McCutcheon, Lt. John McKenny, and Ensign David Gibson. Capt. Francis Long commanded until the arrival at Richmond. Drafted next February under Capt. James Tate, Lt. James Mitchell, and Ensign John Young, and was in battle of Guilford where Capt. Tate was killed and declarant taken prisoner. He was put into a prison ship in Cape Fear river and there confined till the middle of July. It was about Aug. 10th when he reached home, being unable to travel faster because of the feebleness produced by his confinement and treatment.

Section No. 108

GILLIAND, JAMES.—Bath, April 29, 1845. Declaration by Sheppard Gilliand, aged 59, son of Susannah Gilliand, widow of James. James came from Lancaster County, Pa., before the Revolution and settled in Rockingham, from which he went out on three tours of duty. One under Capt. George Houston, who gave him a discharge, Nov. 9, 1781. Was in a campaign under Gen. McIntosh. James died in 1810. Susanna in 1842, aged 92. Children: 1. John, born Nov. 11, 1768; 2. William, Oct. 7, 177–; 3. Jane, Jan. 3, 177–, married Jacob Lemon; 4. Samuel, April 28, 1775; 5. Henry, April 6, 1777; 6. Nancy, March 20, 1779, married Conrad Lemon; 7. Susanna, May 3, 1781, married John Shanklin; 8. James, Aug. 10, 1783; 9. Shepherd, Feb. 13, 1786; 10. Sarah, May 12, 1788, married Edward Wood; 11. Joseph, Dec. 23, 1790; 12. Elizabeth, March 6 (?), 1792, married John Carns; 13. Polly, June 20, 1796.

Section No. 109

HICKMAN, ADAM.—Rockbridge, Sept. 3, 1832. Born in Germany, 1762. Came to Rockbridge, 1768. Drafted about Oct. 1, 1780, under Capt. James (or William) Hall. Marched from rendezvous a mile below Lexington to Richmond and Petersburg. The company of Capt. Gray, also of Rockbridge, marched at same time. Tour was three months. Again drafted, May, 1781, marched to Sandy Point, where he crossed the James, then to Petersburg, where his recollection is that the Appomattox was crossed on a flatboat, the bridge having been burned by the enemy. After much further marching in this part of the State was discharged in August. William Miller, a comrade, certified that declarant was in the battle of Hot Water; that when the flat-boat on the Appomattox was upset by the horses in it, Hickman clung to a rope; and that he went by night to Williamsburg with a scouting party to surprise the British guard.

Section No. 110

HINKLE, HENRY.—Rockbridge, Aug. 5, 1833. Born in Pennsylvania, 1750. In 1779, went out from Frederick for three months under Capt. George Ball, served two other tours, the last extending till after the surrender of Cornwallis. Col. Darke commanded his regiment. Guarded prisoners to Winchester, and was discharged about two weeks later.

Section No. 111

HAMILTON, ALEXANDER.—Augusta, Aug. 29, 1833. Born in Augusta, Sept. —, 1759. Drafted for the protection of the frontier. Marched under Capt. James Trimble through Tygart's Valley to Fort Buchanan on West Fork of Monongahela. While there was in scouting parties but no battle. He thinks this service was in 1779. The discharge was in June, after at least two months service. Drafted for same purpose in spring of 1780, marching under Capt. John McKittrick from Jennings Gap, remaining a while at Fort Dinwiddie and serving the rest of the three months at Fort Warwick, from which he was sometimes out on scout duty. Third tour was from Waynesboro late in May, 1781. Marched under Capt. Patrick Buchanan of Col. Thomas Hughart's regiment to Richmond and below. Was in battle of Hot Water, June 26th, where his brother, James, was severely wounded. Was then detailed to attend his brother in a hospital in New Kent, the wound being considered dangerous. So remained till his time was out, when his brother, John, took his place as nurse. Col. (or Maj.?) Willis commanding their troops at Hot Water under Col. Butler, both being of the regular service.

Section No. 112

HARRISON, JAMES.—Rockbridge, Sept. 3, 1832. Born in Culpeper, Sept. 4, 1755. In fall of 1777, marched under Capt. John Paxton to Point Pleasant by way of Fort Donally. Gen. Hand soon arrived from Pittsburgh. Applicant witnessed the death of Cornstalk, his son Ellinipsico, and two other warriors, Red Hawk and Petalla. Returned shortly before Christmas. Gen. Hand disbanded the troops because of the lateness of the season and short supply of provisions. Applicant was drafted from Amherst in the Spring or summer of 1779 to serve under Capt. Shelton in guarding the British prisoners at Albemarle Barracks. Col. Taylor, of Orange, was in charge of them. The next term, also three months, he served there again, under Capt. Ambrose Rucker and Col. Taylor. This was the winter of 1780-'81. Next season, while Tarleton was above Richmond, he was called out by Col. Hugh Rose, of Amherst, to exchange British prisoners at Jamestown and deliver deserters from the American ranks (these being at New London, Bedford County), to American recruiting officers. Was thus engaged six months, and six months longer in patrolling his county twice a week to thwart any effort by the tories to disaffect the negroes.

Section No. 113

HIGHT, GEORGE.—Rockbridge, Dec. 3, 1832. Born in King and Queen, 1755. Removed while young to Amherst. In January, 1776, volunteered in Botetourt against the Cherokees, and marched under Capt. Gilmore to Crow's Ferry, now Pattonsburg, thence to Long Island on Holston, where he remained till about 3,000 men had assembled under Col. Christian. They marched for four weeks into the Indian country, destroyed five towns, and were discharged at Long Island. Enlisted in Rockbridge, Aug. 14, 1777, in Col. George Baylor's Light Dragoons to serve during the war.

In October, joined the regiment at Fredericksburg, remaining there five or six weeks, then marching to Reading, Pa., where he was inoculated for the smallpox. In February, 1778, the troop marched to the Raritan, and next month to Valley Forge. Here the Fourth Troop, to which he belonged, commanded by Capt. Cadwallader Jones, was employed by Gen. Morgan in preventing the people of the county from furnishing supplies to the enemy and in watching the movements of the latter. In the action at Monmouth, affiant was under the immediate command of Maj. Clough, of Lee's division. The regiment then proceeded to Hackensack, remaining there five or six weeks, then moving up the river. Sept. 23, it was surprised by Gen. Gray while asleep in barns. No quarter was given except to the Fourth Troop, all of whom were made prisoners, except affiant and John Walker, who escaped by getting in among the enemy. Col. Baylor was wounded and Maj. Clough was killed. Next day affiant joined the remnant of the regiment and wintered at Frederick, Md. In the spring they were joined by the Fourth Troop, now exchanged, and by some new recruits. Col. William Washington now took command, and they returned to New Jersey, again being employed in watching the enemy and preventing trading with him. Near the close of 1780, they marched south, arriving near Charleston, S. C., in March, 1780. Shortly after, learning that Tarleton was on his way from Savannah to Charleston, Washington whipped him, taking sixteen prisoners, including a colonel and a doctor. But later, Washington was surprised and defeated at Monk's Corner. The attack was so sudden that although the horses were saddled and bridled, there was not time to mount. Affiant was captured and after being dragged about with the army of Cornwallis some ten days, was put into a prison ship till after the surrender of Charleston. He was then placed in the barracks, there, but this being inconvenient to the British, he was again put on board a prison ship and confined till about August, when he was exchanged at Jamestown, Va. At Malvern Hills he found Capt. Cadwallader Jones, and was sent on to Maj. Call of Washington's regiment, who was recruiting in Orange, Albemarle, and Goochland. After the surrender of Cornwallis he was discharged in South Carolina, in the fall of 1782. Bartlett Fitzgerald, a comrade, certifies that in Grey's surprise Hight was cut down and left as dead.

Section No. 114

HEWITT, JOHN.—Botetourt, Sept. 5, 1833. Born Nov. 14, 1763, in Botetourt. Volunteered in Continental Line, Sept. 8, 1780, for six months, but order to march did not come till Oct. 27. Went out under Capt. James Robinson, Nov. 5, were joined by Capt. Alexander Handly's company, and marching under Maj. David Campbell joined Morgan two days after the battle of the Cowpens. There took the place of the Augusta and Rockbridge militia, who were about to be discharged. They acted bravely in the battle and guarded the prisoners to Virginia. Affiant's command was sent down the Catawba to act in concert with Gen. Davidson at McCowan's Ford, and by felling timber along the bank to prevent the enemy from crossing. A few hours after this preparation had been made a detachment of the enemy appeared on the opposite bank. As we were about to fire on them they retired. Before daylight next morning the British opened a heavy artillery fire on Gen. Davidson, who commanded lower down the river. After daylight they forced the passage and Davidson was killed. Meanwhile in a cold dark dash with heavy rain, the affiant's command got into the road on which Gen. Morgan was retreating and came up with it on the Yadkin, which was very much swollen by the rains. It was daybreak before the North Carolina militia got over, and took position a half mile up the river from the direct road to Salisbury. Next night they were attacked by a strong detachment of infantry supported by cavalry, and compelled to retreat. The army got over with the exception of a small part of the baggage. The last boat had put off when the British cavalry reached the river and fired on it with pistols, but without effect. In our skirmish, Capt. Hanley and John Allen were taken prisoners and a few men killed. The most of those who escaped had to cross the river in canoes. When the scattered troops assembled they marched to Guilford C. H., where they were permitted to rest a while, the enemy being detained by the flood in the Yadkin. Then they marched to Bruce's crossroad on the way where Col. ———— was cut to pieces by the British cavalry. The retreat continued till the Dan was crossed. After the Yadkin was crossed the army was commanded by Col. Williams. From the day after the battle of Cowpens they were employed night and day in throwing every possible difficulty in the enemy's path. The men were without tents and often without provisions. The fatigue, privation, and loss of sleep brought on sickness and death in that inclement season. When the two rifle companies crossed the Dan the 111 men were reduced to 17, and there were no officers but the major, who gave the remnant a verbal discharge, affiant being one of the 17. He volunteered Aug. 6, 1781, and marched to the siege of Yorktown under Maj. Patrick Locke, and after the surrender guarded prisoners to four miles beyond Winchester, where he was discharged the middle of November.

Section No. 115

JONES, JOHN.—Kanawha, (W. Va.), Jan. 15, 1833. Born Feb. 2, 1756. In 1773 he and two others settled on Great Kanawha, and next spring driven back to Muddy Creek by Indians. Built fort there under orders from Capt. Mathew Arbuckle. Was in the battle of Point Pleasant. In the middle of September, 1776, enlisted as regular soldier under Capt. Arbuckle. First Lt. Andrew Wallace, Second Lt. William Wood, Ensign John Gallagher. Served at Point Pleasant to close of 1777. The command was re-enforced by Botetourt men under Capt. McKee, Lieutenants William and John Moore, and Ensign James Gilmer. An attack by the Indians was repulsed and the savages then turned to Donally's Fort in Greenbrier. Two bold and daring soldiers, dressed in Indian costume, made their way thither and apprised the settlers of their danger in time to save them from extermination. Was employed as Indian scout in 1778-9 over a distance of 60 to 70 miles west of the inhabited section of country. William and Leonard Morris and John Patterson were scouts with him. Applicant mentions William Arbuckle, then at Ft. Mason.

Section No. 116

KELSO, JAMES.—Rockbridge, December 31, 1832. Born in Rockbridge, 1761. Drafted into militia service January 10, 1781, under Capt. James Buchanan, of Col. John Bowyer's regiment. Marched to Fredericksburg, Cabin Point, Smithfield, Portsmouth, and Williamsburg. Was in skirmishes near Portsmouth with British scouting parties. Volunteered when Tarleton made his raid on Charlottesville, marching to that place from Waynesboro, and serving one month. Drafted, September, 1781, under Capt. Charles Campbell, and was at Siege of Yorktown, after which was detailed to guard the prisoners to Winchester.

Section No. 117

KENNERLY, WILLIAM.—Augusta, July 22, 1833. Born in Culpeper, Feb. 4, 1752. Volunteered in Augusta, June, 1774, to serve against the Indians. Went out under Capt. George Mathews, William Robertson, being First Lieutenant and George Gibson, Second. Marched to Warwick's fort, where they joined Capt. George Moffett, whose men were building the fort. Declarant was left here in command of sixteen men, the rest of the company marching on to Point Pleasant, and returning after the battle. Discharged about Nov. 1st, after serving about four and one-half months. About June 1, 1778, was drafted into the Augusta militia. Owing to the domestic situation in his own and his father's family, his brother being also in service, declarant was asked by Col. Sampson Mathews to take charge of a brigade of pack horses to convey provisions to Fort McIntosh. He continued in this service till about the middle of November. In June, 1781, volunteered with 108 others as mounted infantry to go to lower Virginia. William Bowyer was captain and Samuel Bell and Charles Cameron were lieutenants. They joined Gen. Campbell at Richmond, and had a skirmish at New Kent C. H., and later at Hot Water. The troops marched and countermarched in the vicinity of Williamsburg. At the Siege of Yorktown, declarant was furloughed because of fever brought on by fatigue and exposure. Discharged late in October. Gen. Campbell served under Gen. Wayne.

Section No. 118

LEMON, JACOB.—Botetourt, June 7. 1832. Born about 1762. Enlisted in October, 1780, under Capt. John Tate, and joined the Southern army in South Carolina, serving in Col. Howard's

Maryland regiment. Was slightly wounded at Cowpens and discharged late in February, 1781, at Salisbury, N. C. Next May was drafted, and went out under Capt. John Dickey, marching to Williamsburg. Was in the action at Jamestown. Discharged at Camp Holly (Bottom's Bridge), sixteen miles below Richmond. Acted as sergeant in both tours. Drafted in 1782 under Col. John Moffett to guard the frontier at Tygart's Valley. Marched under Capt. John McKittrick and served full tour of duty.

Section No. 119

LEWIS, THOMAS.—Rockingham, Aug. 20, 1832. Born Jan. 26, 1760. Served in different tours under Captains Nall, Rush, and Houston, the last one a service of twenty days against the tories on the South Branch in 1781, doing at least ten days' guard duty on prisoners taken at Woodstock, from King's Mountain. Some of them were sick and one died on the road. Served under Capt. Houston at Yorktown in 1781, twenty days as lieutenant and adjutant. Drafted in 1781, for eighteen months in regular service Substitute hired without his knowledge. The tour under Nall, October, 1776, was against the Indians, who had done mischief that spring and summer, and was stationed at Westfall's fort and in Tygart's Valley. Second tour, under Rush, of Col. Sampson Mathew's command. Tour under Capt. George Houston was against Claypole's headquarters at Cape Capon. The establishment was entirely broken up. Was in battle of Hot Water.

Section No. 120

MOORE, WILLIAM.—Rockbridge, Aug. 7, 1832. Served three months and fifteen days, including going and returning, under Capt. Samuel Wallace, of Rockbridge, and Lt. Edmundson, being discharged about April 15, 1781, at Portsmouth. The company was in Col. John Bowyer's regiment of Gen. Muhlenberg's brigade. As captain of a volunteer company he later marched to Richmond soon after Tarleton's incursion to Charleston (?). Was gone about three weeks. Marched again about the middle of September, 1781, to Yorktown as captain of militia, being under Col. Samuel Lewis and Majors Long and McIlhany. From Yorktown, marched with the prisoners to Winchester, and was discharged there in December, returning to Rockbridge with not over twenty of the men he had taken out. Served also three other short tours.

Section No. 121

MILLER, WILLIAM.—Rockbridge, Sept. 3, 1832. Born in Pennsylvania, March 1, 1757. Drafted in Rockbridge. Marched October 9, 1780, under Capt. James Gilmore, Lt. John Carrothers, and Ensign John McCorkle. The last named was wounded in the wrist at Cowpens and died of lockjaw. At Hillsboro, N. C., the command joined Gen. Greene, was reviewed, and drew muskets. It then received orders to join Gen. Smallwood, then between Charlotte and Camden. At Salisbury, while on the march, applicant was taken from his company and ordered to the Catawba to guard Garrison's Ferry, being thus engaged for four weeks. When applicant was on his way to Smallwood, he heard that Morgan had gone to Charlotte and had sent the sick and disabled to the hospital. Capt. Gilmer advised applicant to go to hospital, but he preferred going on next day with the army. Was prevailed on to remain a short while with William Gilmer, a relative to the Captain and sick, and then to meet the army as soon as possible. But applicant was delayed and when he met his company it was returning from the Cowpens with prisoners. Served about seven months. Holds a certificate from Auditor of Public Accounts, showing he is entitled for his militia service to four pounds, eight shillings ($14.67). Came to Rockbridge about 1770.

Section No. 122

MASON, JOHN.—Rockbridge, Sept. 3, 1832. Born in Pennsylvania, 1740. Drafted fall of 1777, in Berkeley and marched under Capt. Evans, of Col. Campbell's regiment. Was in battle of Brandywine. Returned home next spring, being in service about six months, although the draft was for three. Later, marched from Augusta under Capt. Tate and was in battle of Guilford.

Section No. 123

McCLAIN, JOHN.—Rockbridge, Aug. 7, 1832. Served one tour of three months in Greenbrier under Capt. David Gray, of Rockbridge, in 1778. In 1781 served a tour of three months under Capt. Andrew Moore, Lt. John McClung, and Ensign James McDowell. Rendezvoused Jan. 10th at Red House, and served at Portsmouth and at Great Bridge near Norfolk under Col. Parker. Discharged April 11th. It took about fifteen days to get home. The certificate for said services was taken by the sheriff for tax. Born in north of Ireland, 1756.

Section No. 124

McCUTCHEON, WILLIAM.—Augusta, June 20, 1833. Born Nov. 27, 1758. Went into service in 1778, every tenth man among the militia who had not families being required to enter the regular service for one year. Took the oath June 3, and was ordered by Col. Sampson Mathews to drive a wagon from Staunton to Valley Forge. The wagon brigade to which he was attached was under Wagonmaster David Steele. They crossed the Blue Ridge by Rockfish Gap and took up a supply of bacon at Orange and Culpeper. Washington's army was met between Morristown, N. J., and the Hudson at King's Ferry. Soon after the battle of Monmouth they proceeded to White Plains. Declarant then presented to Gen. Greene a certificate from Col. Mathews, and asked to be returned to the ranks, his duties as wagoner being very tiresome. The request was refused. Discharged at Raritan River, June 1, 1779. Col. Thompson was wagonmaster general. Drafted, 1780, under Capt. Samuel McCutcheon, and Lt. John McCamie. Marched from Widow Tee's (Waynesboro), Sept. 1st, with the companies of Captains Smith, Long, Dickey and Given, and served three months at Richmond as guard, and were in no engagement. Long, the senior captain, acted as major. Declarant was Sergeant. Drafted in June, 1781, again under McCutchen, George Craig being lieutenant. The colonel was William Bowyer, the adjutant, Thomas Bell. Declarant served twenty days as Orderly Sergeant.

Section No. 125

McKEE, JAMES.—Rockbridge, Jan. 5, 1835. Born in Pennsylvania, March 14, 1752, died in Rockbridge, Aug. 14, 1832. Drafted from Rockbridge in Summer of 1776, for a tour of three months against the Cherokees, serving under Col. William Christian. Served a tour of three months in Greenbrier when the Shawnees attacked Donally's Fort. Third tour in fall of 1777, at Point Pleasant under Col. John Dickenson, Capt. Charles Campbell, and Lt. Samuel Davidson. Fourth tour as Ensign, Jan. 10, 1781, to April 25, 1781, and marched to Portsmouth. Was out two weeks the following June for two weeks when Tarleton plundered Charlottesville. Drafted three months in July and marched to headquarters at Westham near Richmond. Last draft of two months in October to march to Yorktown. Total service, seventeen months, twenty-nine days. Declaration by Nancy McKee, widow. Left a son, John T.

Section No. 126

MILAM, RUSH.—Kanawha, (W. Va.), Aug. 21, 1832. Born Oct. —, 1759. Entered Bedford County militia, 1780, under Capt. Alexander Cummins, Col. Meriweather's regiment, Gen. Lawson's brigade.

Section No. 127

O'ROARKE, DAVID,—Shenandoah, Oct. —, 1832. Born March 1, 1754. Volunteered three months in 1777, under Capt. John Hopkins, and Lt. Richard Regan, and served at Point Pleasant, when Colonels Dickenson and Skillern were there. Was not engaged with Indians. Went out again, May, 1778, in place of his brother, Philemon, who was drafted and had a family. Marched to Tygart's Valley under Capt. Robert Craven, Lt. Josiah Harrison, and Ensign Joseph Dictum. Served three months.

Section No. 128

PERSINGER, JACOB.—Alleghany, April 15, 1833. Born, 1749. Enlisted, 1774 (?), serving as corporal under Capt. Matthew Arbuckle, First Lt. Andrew Wallace, Second Lt. —— Wood, John Galloway, Third Lt., Ensign Samuel Walker, Maj. Nevis commanding the regiment. Left the service, October, 1778. Marched from Muddy Creek, Greenbrier, to Pittsburgh, and thence to Point Pleasant, where he was discharged. Was in no action. The assault on the fort at Point Pleasant took place during his absence.

Section No. 129

POWERS, WILLIAM.—Shenandoah (?), Oct. 1, 1833. Born in Frederick, 1765. Went out in 1781 with Capt. Joseph Gregory's company of Indian scouts. Stationed at Power's fort on Simpson Creek while spying the country. Went thence to Ohio river. Service, nine months. Volunteered as Indian scout, March, 1782, again serving under Gregory nine months. Went out again next march as spy. Was at mouth of Bingaman creek and where there had been an old Indian town. Discharged in December. During first tour Indians came into the neighborhood and killed John Tommis and six of his children and took one prisoner. Another time they killed John Owens. In second tour they killed James Owens and took Gilbert prisoner.

Section No. 130

ROBERTSON, JAMES.—Augusta, Aug. 28, 1833. Born in Augusta Nov. 16, 1751. Went out on a draft about Sept. 1, 1777, under Capt. George Moffett, marching to Point Pleasant and there remaining until discharged. The field officers were Gen. Hand, Col. Smithers, of Augusta, and Maj. Samuel McDowell, of Rockbridge. Was in no battle, but saw Cornstalk killed. Marched also to Richmond under Capt. Thomas Smith, but does not remember the year. Last tour, summer of 1781, immediately after Tarleton's raid to Charlottesville in an attempt to capture the legislature. Marched under Capt. John Given to near Jamestown, where he was in a skirmish. Capt. Given then went home and Capt. Charles Cameron was put in command. Discharged at Bottom's Bridge after a tour of three months, which was the common term of service.

Section No. 131

SHEPHERDSON, DAVID.—Rockbridge, Dec. 3, 1832. Born in Louisa, Aug. 3, 1763. Drafted in fall of 1779 for six months under Capt. John Bias, of Louisa. About June 19, 1780, having been transferred to Second Virginia Regiment, marched to Hillsborough, N. C., where he joined the Southern army under Col. Spencer and Gen. Stevens. His lieutenant was Thomas Shelton, his ensign, Anthony Winston. At Deep River himself and comrades nearly perished, having nothing but green crabapples to eat. 200 men were sent out to thrash some grain. Was in battle between Gates and Cornwallis, Aug. 16th. Affiant and his company retreated to Hillsborough and made rendezvous. Provisions soon became so scarce there that the captain advised the men to go home and get provisions and clothing, their clothing having been lost in the battle near Camden. So they went home, got suplies, and returned, but were advised to go home again, which they did and were honorably acquitted by a court martial. Was in active service three months. Drafted three months next spring under Capt. Harris. Marched to Williamsburg and back to Richmond, where he saw the British burning tobacco, etc., in Manchester. This expedition was called the "Wild Goose Chase." The company was relieved by another from Louisa. Later, was drafted three months under Capt. James Watson, who was succeeded by Capt. Samuel Pettis. Was attached to Gen. Weedon's brigade and stationed at Glouceester during the siege of Yorktown. Moved to Rockbridge, 1815.

Section No. 132

SIZER, JOHN.—Botetourt, Jan. 19, 1833. Born in Baltimore County, Md., 1759. Moved to Prince William, 1770, Rockingham, 1777. Volunteered, 1777, under Capt. (afterwards major) Ewell.

Volunteered for 18 months under Capt. Daniel Smith, marched to Fredericksburg, where he was under command of Capt. Adam Wallace. Enlisted for three years under Capt. Beverly and Col. Heath, and marched to Charleston, S. C., where he was transferred to Capt. Parker's Company, captured at the surrender of that city, and held as prisoner eighteen months. He was exchanged at Jamestown, Va., and at Richmond provided with money to get home. Col. Heath, Lt. Col. Wallace, and Maj. Stevenson were exchanged at same time. Col. Parker, who commanded a half-moon battery at Stono, was killed at the taking of Charleston within twenty steps of deponent. Volunteered in 1781 to drive a wagon loaded with flour from Rockingham to Yorktown, where he was detained during the siege to haul ammunition. After the surrender gave up the team he had impressed and went home. In service three years.

Section No. 133

TATE, JOHN.—Botetourt, Sept. 7, 1832. Born in Augusta, Aug. 6, 1761. In 1777, volunteered under Captains Patrick Buchanan and Thomas Smith, against a body of tories, who had assembled near Peaked Mountain. The leaders were put in jail and the followers dispersed. In May, 1778, information came of the Indian raid upon Donally's Fort, and the companies of Captains James Tate, P. Buchanan, and Francis Long were ordered to the rescue. Declarant marched under Tate. The companies remained at Fort Savannah (Lewisburg) about one month and were then discharged. Lord Cornwallis having tried hard to retake the prisoners captured at Cowpens, a requisition was made in January, 1781, on Botetourt, and Captains Mays, John Cartmill, Matthew Wilson, Holston, and Bollar were ordered into service. There was a heavy draft and applicant volunteered under Mays. Each man was ordered to provide himself with a horse and six days' provisions. The detachment marched under Maj. Thomas Rowland. After the Dan was crossed, the horses were sent back and the detachment soon joined the army under Gen. Greene, on the Haw. In a skirmish several of Mays' company were killed, applicant's detachment and the cavalry under Col. Lee being sent to bring on an action. A few days later Gen.

Campbell with the militia from Washington County came in. Next morning there was a battle on Reedy Fork, when Capt. Mays and all his men except applicant and thirteen others left the battlefield and went home. A day later, Captains Tate and Smith, from Augusta, joined the army at Speedwell Iron Works. They wanted applicant to join them, but he declined and went home after three months' service. About Aug. 1st, he volunteered under Capt. David Mays and marched from Boyd's Ferry near Pattonsburg and marched to Yorktown, being present during the whole siege. He was then sent with prisoners to Winchester, where he was discharged after three months' service. Discharge was signed by Lt. Wallace Estill. Henry Cartmill and John Hewitt were comrades at Yorktown.

Section No. 134

VINES, THOMAS.—Rockbridge, Nov. 6, 1832. Born in Amherst, 1756. Drafted to Albemarle Bararcks to guard Burgoyne's men. Marched under Capt. Loving and served four months. Colonels Burnley and Taylor commanded at the barracks at different times. Second tour under Capt. Josiah Martin to guard the prisoners taken in Carolina at Winchester, etc. Went out three months as substitute for John Campbell, of Augusta, marching under Capt. Given and Lt. William Robinson, Col. Robertson commanding the regiment. This was when Tarleton plundered Charlottesville. Joined Lafayette's army. Was in the battles of Hot Water and Jamestown. Was dismissed at the latter place, and when he reached home found orders to march again. Went back in July, under Capt. Christian, Lt. William Barnett, Ensign James Bell. Was at the Siege of Yorktown. Prior to this he volunteered under Capt. John Morrison, of Amherst, Lt. Thomas Yores, Ensign James Bell. The company was to go south, Capt. Morrison having served there. But as Arnold had come to Richmond, the command marched there remaining seven weeks. The enemy had gone after plundering, burning the rope walks, etc. Discharged at Petersburg after three months' service.

Section No. 135

VINEYARD, GEORGE.—Rockbridge, —— —, 18—. Adam Hickman certifies that he was reared in the same neighborhood with Vineyard and served with him in 1780, and knew him to be in a militia company at Richmond, 1781.

Section No. 136

WILSON, WILLIAM.—Augusta, Sept. 25, 1832. Born in Augusta, Nov. 7, 1745. Volunteered late in August, 1774, under Capt. Alexander McClenahan, Lt. William McCutchen, and Ensign Joseph Long, and marched to Point Pleasant together with the companies of Captains John Morrison, Samuel Wilson, George Mathews, and John Lewis. Captains McClenahan, Morrison, and Wilson were killed, the total loss being about 160. The army then advanced about eighty miles toward the Indian towns, returning to Point Pleasant, and waited there a week for provisions before resuming the return. In second tour volunteered in July, 1776, under Capt. John Lyle, Lt. William McCutcheon, and Ensign Joseph Long. From the rendezvous at Lexington the troops marched under Col. William Christian to the Holston river to protect the frontier against the Indians. There were only some light skirmishes. Disbanded in December. Drafted in 1781, serving under Capt. Thomas Rankin, Lt. Alexander Scott, and Ensign William Buchanan, his colonels being Sampson Mathews and William Bowyer. Rendezvous at Waynesboro, Jan. 11th, marching to Richmond, then Fredericksburg, then Portsmouth, where they joined Gen. Steuben's army. Was in two slight skirmishes. Disbanded at Portsmouth. Next volunteered in cavalry company under Capt. Zachariah Johnson, Lt. Charles Rankin, and Ensign Richard Madison. Marched about June 1st for Richmond, the British then retiring toward Williamsburg and the Americans pursuing. After the battle of Jamestown the troop returned, in August. His colonel was William Christian. Total service, about fifteen months.

Section No. 137

WILEY, ANDREW.—Rockbridge, —— —, 1832. Born in Rockbridge, July —, 1756. Drafted by Thomas Vance in 1777 to drive cattle to Point Pleasant. Went as far as mouth of Elk, where the company met a detachment from the fort to receive the cattle. Discharged after forty-two days. About March 1, 1778, entered the Continental service in the Virginia Line. Marched under Capt. Robert Sawyers to White Plains, N. Y., where the command joined Gen. Morgan, and applicant remained with him during the remainder of his term of twelve months, being discharged at Noland Ferry on the Potomac about May 10, 1779. Capt. Sawyer soon returned home and Capt. Andrew Wallace was killed in battle at Hanging Rock in the Carolinas. For this service he received about $6.00. In 1780-'81, he served as substitute under Capt. James Hall, and marched with two other companies under Captains Campbell and David Gray, and at Deep Run Church near Richmond joined Gen. Muhlenberg. Thence they marched down the north side of James above a battery near a British encampment opposite Norfolk, thence by Portsmouth, to Richmond, where he was discharged. Was in no skirmish. Again drafted three months about April 1, 1781, under Capt. Hoyd (Lloyd?), then of Botetourt, and joined Greene's army at Guilford. Was in the battle there, the Carolina militia forming the first line, the Virginia militia the second, and the Continentals the third. The Carolina men broke and ran at the outset. The riflemen to which applicant belonged were on the left, and when the Carolina men retreated, the British forces came down upon a ridge between the riflemen of the left wing and the command of Col. Campbell, who as applicant believes brought on the action. The enemy were swept off by the Virginia riflemen, but formed again and again, until finally they came down upon the ridge in columns, twelve and sixteen men deep, and were compelled (which party?) to ground their arms. Gen. Stevens was wounded and Capt. Tilford killed.

John Wiley certified that Andrew Wiley marched against the Whiskey boys (1794).

Section No. 138

WYSONG, FIATT.—Botetourt, Sept. 6, 1832. Born in York Co., Pa. Removed to Shepherdstown, (W. Va.) Drafted into militia service under Col. Morrison, remaining about five months. Company officers, Capt. Josiah Swearingen, Lt. Isaac Johns. Marched to Ft. McIntosh, thence under Gen. McIntosh to the Muskingum, where a fort was built. Discharged at Ft. McIntosh. While there saw Col. Richard Campbell, who was killed at Eutaw. In July, 1781, drafted and marched under Capt. Joseph Looney, Lt. Tosh, and Ensign William McClenahan to Battalion (Bottom's) Bridge below Richmond, and then to Yorktown, being present at the siege. Discharged in October.

NOTE:—There was a Capt. ——— Looney in Botetourt and this was probably a company from that County.

Section No. 139

WILTSHIRE, JOHN.—Prince Edward, Jan. 21, 1833. Born in Lancaster County, Pa., Aug. —, 1760. Came to Augusta in childhood. Entered militia service in September, 1775 (1777?), under Capt. William All and Lt. Jacob Pence, who raised a company to repel the Indians. The command marched by South Branch of Potomac to Hackett's Creek, which it garrisoned three months. Early in May, 1778, he went out under Capt. William (Robert?) Craven to succor Tygart's Valley, where several murders had taken place the preceding fall. The company marched across the Calfpasture and Bullpasture to the head of the Greenbrier, thence to the head of Tygart's Valley. Next September he went under Capt. Robert Cravens, of Col. Benjamin Harrison's regiment, to Ft. McIntosh. Just two years later, served again under Craven in Morgan's army in the South. In March, 1783, moved to Point Pleasant. Served as scout from 1782 to 1793 under Capt. William Clendennin and Col. George Clendennin. David Roberts was also a scout in 1789. In August, 1790, ——— fort was captured by Indians.

Section No. 140

ANSON, CHRISTOPHER.—Rockingham, Sept. 17, 1832. Born in Culpeper, 1759. Served first in 1778, under Capt. Robert Cravens at Koontz' Fort, Tygart's Valley. Next year served under Cravens as substitute for Peter Conrad. Served four years in all. In the south was under Col. Stubblefield, of Greene's army. At the Yorktown siege was orderly sergeant under Capt. Michael Cowger.

Section No. 141

ALLEE, DAVID.—Cooper County, Mo., May 6, 1833. Born in Pittsylvania, Va., April 25, 1762. Served in Henry, Spring of 1777 (1778?), under Capt. Peter Herston, Lt. William Ferguson. Joined seven other companies under Colonels Shelby and Christie, and on the French Broad the companies divided and went in different directions in pursuit of the Cherokees. They marched to the towns of Choto, Chilhowie, and Tuckaluckee. On the return they remained at Long Island on the Holston until Christie's treaty with the Cherokees was concluded. This service was six months. July, 1778, went out from Botetourt under Capt. Thomas Cummings, and Col. Charles Lynch. Had a fight with tories at the head of Little River in Botetourt, where they took Job Hale and William Terry, two tory captains. At Sinking Creek, in Montgomery, they disarmed a good many tories, and at Tom's Creek in Wythe, they disarmed others. Here they were discharged. Then volunteered under Capt. Joshua Martin, of Col. Abraham Penn's regiment, marched to the Dan River, and as the British were not in Virginia as reported, they were discharged, just after the battle of Guilford. Volunteered six months in the rangers under Capt. Arbuckle, who scouted the country from Daniel Rand's bottom on New River to Point Pleasant. Served another six months under Capt. Arbuckle and Col. Floyd, being stationed at Point Pleasant to watch the frontiers.

Section No. 142

ANDERSON, JACOB.—Montgomery, Sept. 3, 1832. Born July 3, 1758. Volunteered in Frederick under Capt. Charles Thurston and marched into New Jersey to join Lord Sterling. Was in skirmishes at Piscataway and Quibbletown, and discharged in April, 1777. Then drafted for three months under Capt. Helms, of Gen. Potter's brigade. Discharged at Chestnut Ridge near Philadelphia. In fall of 1778 enlisted under Capt. Gilkeson for one year to guard the prisoners at Frederick, Col. Smith being in command there. Joined a troop of horse in Baltimore, and marched to Philadelphia, where he was discharged. Drafted for eighteen months in 1781, and hired a substitute, but declarant had to give his obligation to Col. Darke to fill the place if it came to his term, but he did not go into service again.

Section No. 143

BOLLING, ROBERT.—From letter by same in 1835. Born 1762. Volunteered in spring of 1778, in Hanover, in a troop ot 100 cavalry under Capt. Thomas Nelson, of Yorktown, First Lt. George Nicholas, of Albemarle, Second Lt. Hugh Nelson, brother to Thomas. Troop raised for twelve months in pursuance of act of Congress. After being well disciplined, proceeded to Philadelphia, where command was told its services were not then necessary and was discharged Aug. 8th, with thanks of Congress in printed resolutions. Himself, early in 1780, as captain, raised a troop south of the James, Col. Bannister, of Dinwiddie, commanding the militia. Marched the troop into actual service under Col. Parker, of Gen. Muhlenberg's brigade, and held possession some time of Norfolk and Portsmouth. Early next spring resumed duty, new recruits having joined the troop, and remained in service till after the surrender of Cornwallis. In May a British force under Benedict Arnold captured Petersburg after a gallant resistance by the militia under Gen. Steuben. Was present in the action. Gen. Philips, who succeeded Arnold died at Petersburg a few days later in the home of writer's mother, Mrs. Mary M. Bolling. She with four single daughters were made prisoners. Cornwallis took command a few days later. Previous to the juncture of his force with Arnold's, writer went into North Carolina with a part of his troop to get information of the movements of Cornwallis. Two members, John Butts and Thomas Walker, were here captured. Writer was also in a skirmish seven miles below Petersburg.

Roster of Capt. Robert Bolling's Troop.

Bolling, Robert, *Captain*
Broadnax, William, *Second Lt.*

Scott, John, *First Lt.*
Briggs, John H., *Ensign.*

Privates

Atkinson, John
Atkinson, Roger
Avery, Edward
Bland, Richard
Bolling, Thomas T.
Bonner, Jeremiah
Barton, William
Butts, John
George, Frederick
Goodwin, Esau
Hodges, Robert
Howell, John
Hudson, Tuttle
Hudson, Irby
Kate, John
Kirkland, Benjamin

Lanier, Thomas
Morrison, John
Nicholas, John
North, John
Parkham, Nicholas
Randolph, Bret
Randolph, Henry
Scott, William
Shore, William
Smith, John
Starke, John
Stewart, Francis
Walker, Thomas
Walker, Robert
Walker, David
Watkins, John

Woodliff, Peter.

John Butts married Mary Anne, daughter of Daniel P. Claiborne and Mary A. (Maury) Claiborne.

Section No. 144

BOTT, FREDERICK.—Montgomery, Nov. 6, 1832. Born Oct. —, 1757. Volunteered in Dinwiddie, 1779, under Col. John Bannister to form one of a guard of twelve men and orderly sergeant to guard munitions of war at Petersburg. Was to serve eighteen months with privilege of hiring a substitute in case he did not retain his health. Fell sick after six months and hired substitute. Volunteered from Halifax under Capt. John Falkner and was at siege of Yorktown. Officers were, Capt. Fleming Bates, Col. Richardson, Gen. Samson (?).

Section No. 145

BELL, ROBERT.—Montgomery, Aug. 5, 1833. Born, 1759. Resident of County since 1762. Drafted 1776 (?), and served one month under Sergeant Aaron Scaggs on the Bluestone to guard Mares' (?) and McGuire's stations from the Indians, with whom there was frequent fighting. Three months later called out there again under Col. Preston and Sergeant Mace Tacy. Third tour was under Capt. Burnes against the tories at Buffalo Pond, Collin's mill, and the Wythe lead mine. Under Capt. Abraham Trigg marched into North Carolina and had a battle with the tories at Shallow Ford on the Yadkin. The wounded were left at Salem under physicians. Col. Preston and Maj. Joseph Cloyd were in command.

Section No. 146

CHARLTON, FRANCIS.—Montgomery, Feb. 4, 1833. Born Feb. 3, 1759. Went out in 1777 under Capt. Joseph Cloyd, Lt. Henry Patton, and Lt. Isaac Lorton, serving in April and July against the Indians on the Greenbrier and Giles frontiers. Second tour at same place under Capt. Daniel Trigg and Lt. McGee. Third tour, under Col. William Preston, was to disperse the tories in Montgomery who had turned out to meet the British advancing from the Carolinas. Col. Skillern was ordered from Botetourt for the same purpose. Fourth term under Capt. Daniel Trigg and Maj. Thomas Quirk was to guard the lead mines in Wythe from the British and tories. Volunteered from latter place under Capt. Isaac Taylor and went with the U. S. troops. Fifth term on Bluestone and in Abb's Valley, under Capt. John Preston. The order was because of the murder of the Moore family by the Indians. Total service, seven months.

Section No. 147

CLARK, MATTHEW.—Anderson, S. C., Oct. 5, 1832. Born in Goochland, Feb. 7, 1763. Before he was sixteen and therefore under age, he was permitted to join Capt. Hatcher's company, line officers being Col. Fleming and Maj. Morris. Was at siege of Yorktown, and then on detached service under Capt. Pier to convey away the prisoners. Before arriving at the military prison, he was left to take care of some who were sick.

Section No. 148

GRAVES, THOMAS.—Lincoln County, Mo., Sept. 17, 1832. Born in Culpeper, 1747. In 1775 went out under Capt. John Thorn and six other officers against Gov. Dunmore, who was trying to lock the wheels of government and stir up the Indians, and we drove him on board his vessels. We were governed by a body of wise men, like Patrick Henry and Edmund Pendleton, who found is in provisions and supported us upwards of six weeks, dismissing us with thanks. In 1776, the men were organized into divisions. Applicant was orderly sergeant under Capt. Bohannon, and marched to Norfolk and Long Bridge, being out three months. In 1777 ordered out when the British landed at Head of Elk and steered for Philadelphia. Went as orderly under Capt. Hill, Maj. William Roberts commanding the four Culpeper companies. We joined Washington above Philadelphia and were in the battle of Germantown. Soon after, we were put under regular officers, and sent down against the enemy's position at Philadelphia, where we felt some of the horrors of war. We marched and maneuvered day and night, sometimes in full view of the enemy's main army. Seldom an hour passed but we were shedding blood. We continued in perils of cold, hunger, and fatigue, our bed on the cold ground and our covering the canopy of the heavens. After six months we returned for winter quarters, without clothes and barefooted. In 1778, applicant was sergeant at the barracks guarding Burgoyne's troops until promoted by Maj. Roberts to be quartermaster *vice* James Straughton, also promoted. Was out four months. In 1781, called out in June, when the British took Richmond and made a raid to Charlottesville. Went as orderly under Capt. Ferguson. Joined the army under Lafayette and marched to Yorktown, where applicant was discharged. Two brothers were in the command, and one, Lewis Graves, being sick, substituted for him. After the surrender, applicant serving in a Berkeley company under Col. Hopkins (Clopham?) and Maj. Welch, helped to secure the prisoners. Was out about nine months. In the northern service was under Maj. William Roberts. Hired Lewis Prince as substitute eighteen months, paying him $250 and a good suit. Moved to Missouri, 1824. Died, March 14, 1834. Thomas N., the only son.

Section No. 149

HATTON, REUBEN.—Boone County, Mo., June 26, 1833. Born, 1762. Volunteered from Amelia, Oct. 1, 1780, under Capt. John (?) Ward, of Col. Mason's regiment and Gen. Lawson's brigade. Served as sergeant three months. Marched to Smithfield. Volunteered next February under Capt. Ford, and joined army at Westham above Richmond. Served three months as orderly sergeant around Richmond and Malvern Hills. From this point moved back, the enemy close upon us, but no battle. Gen. Wayne joined us at Culpepper, where declarant was discharged, in June. Then rejoined army in Orange under Capt. Edward Booker. Discharged in September and before he reached home heard that Cornwallis was taken. Married Joanne ——, Sept. 20, 1782. Died Aug. 16, 1841. Moved to Kentucky, 1794, and lodged in David Crevis' stillhouse until he could build.

Section No. 150

HOWE, DANIEL.—Montgomery, June 3, 1833. Born, 1758. Served seven tours of one month each, twice as lieutenant. Also one month in the Cherokee war under Capt. James McCorkle.

Section No. 151

HARRIS, JOHN.—Pittsylvania, 1832. Born, 1755. Marched from said County, June 11, 1780, under Capt. Isaac Clement and Benjamin Duncan to Hillsboro, N. C., joining the Third Virginia under Col. Glenn, of Stevens' brigade. At Massey's Ferry, Pedee river, declarant was left in a guard of 200 under Maj. Conoway to guard ferry and secure the boats, the main army moving on. After Gates' defeat many Virginia militia and others rendezvoused with the guard, and then all retired northward. Declarant discharged at Guilford C. H., in September at end of a three months' tour. Drafted next month and marched under Capt. James Brewer to Hillsboro. Transferred to Capt. Peter Mays, of Col. Stubblefield's regiment, and marched to Salisbury. Taken sick there. September, 1781, drafted under Capt. Charles Hutchings to march to siege of Yorktown, but being unable to travel was furloughed with orders to rejoin command as soon as possible. Was on the way to the front, when several of company were met telling of the surrender. Was out on other brief tours. Thomas Williams was a comrade at Massey's Ferry.

Section No. 152

JONES, DAVID.—Cooper County, Mo., May 6, 1833. Born in Pittsylvania, 1761. Enlisted from Henry, Spring of 1777, under Capt. Peter Herston and Lt. Ferguson. Marched to Long Island of Holston River, joined the army under Colonels Shelby and Christy. There a treaty was made. Service, three months. Next served under Capt. Ruble and Maj. Walker as Second Sergeant, and marched to Yorktown, where he joined Gen. Lawson's brigade. Discharged after surrender of Cornwallis. John Ross was a comrade.

Section No. 153

KING, WILLIAM.—Montgomery, Jan. 7, 1833. Born about 1755. Enlisted in Bedford, 1778, for two months as guard at the lead mines in Wythe under Capt. Robert Adams, Lt. M. Reynolds, and Col. Charles Lynch. Next spring his father, Avra King, being drafted by Capt. Charles Watkins, and Lt. Thomas Logwood, he went as substitute. They started for Jamestown, but were met by an express with the information that as the enemy had left their aid was not necessary. About fifteen days later, went as substitute for James Mays ,serving under Capt. Nathaniel Tate, Lt. Stephen Goggin, and Ensign Richard Edmondson, and marched to join Gen. Gates at Charlotte, N. C. Went into winter quarters at Cheraw Hills, S. C. During this march Gen. Greene assumed command and ordered Gates to Philadelphia under guard. Declarant marched under Capt. Isaac Webb, Lt. Charles Webb, and Ensign William Triplett to Mecklenberg, Va., as guard over baggage wagons and live hogs. Discharged at Bannister's Bridge. Following August, declarant volunteered under Col. Benjamin Logan to guard the Kentucky frontier, serving as minute man and scout. Logan joined Gen. Clarke at Bryant Station and marched to mouth of Licking River, where the regular troops were met. Marched to the Indian town at Standing Stone on the Great Miami, which with six others the declarant helped to burn. Army disbanded at mouth of Licking.

Section No. 154

LUCAS, BASIL.—Frederick, Va. ——, 1835. Listed in pension list as sergeant in Virginia militia. Born Aug. 12, 1757. Enlisted for four years in Maryland Line, Continental service, Capt. Resin Ball's Company of Col. Thomas Price's regiment. Died in Winchester, Sept. —, 1841, leaving a widow, Elizabeth.

Section No. 155

LUCAS, JOHN.—Montgomery, Aug. 8, 1832. Born July 15, 1749. Went out as captain about 1780 under Col. William Preston, and Lt. Col. Walter Crockett, and served at least six months. Was out twice afterwards under same officers. Resigned at end of war. Went into the Carolinas under Crockett to convey some British and tories from South Carolina to Moravian Town (Salem), N. C. Was engaged frequently in Montgomery, and under Preston surprised and captured some tories under Capt. McDonald. Was then detailed to guard them.

Section No. 156

LEWIS, ANDREW.—Montgomery, Nov. 7, 1832. Born Oct. —, 1758. Volunteered from Botetourt in February, 1779, under Capt. Joseph Crockett and Lt. Robert Sayers. Was stationed with other forces at Williamsburg till discharged in May. Gen. Andrew Lewis, his father, was commandant. No enemy appeared on land. Later in same year volunteered under Capt. William McClenahan and went into Montgomery against some tories who had organized for active service. The forces were under Col. William Preston and were engaged a month. Went again in same year against them as volunteer under Capt. James Barnett and Col. Hugh Crockett. Marched with other forces from Ft. Chiswell to Ramseur's Mill, N. C., where the British and tories had just been defeated, this fact determining the officers to return, the war lasting two months. Went out in February, 1781, under Capt. William McClenahan and Col. Hugh Crockett, and joined Greene's army in North Carolina. Declarant was in the engagement at Alamance and Reedy Fork. At Guilford was on outpost duty, under Colonels Williams and Howard. Total service one year. Was mounted on his own horse except in first tour. Never received a cent for his services, being then in affluence and only interested in sustaining his country.

Section No. 157

MURPHY, WILLIAM.—St. Francois County, Mo., May 7, 1833. Born March 12, 1759. Volunteered for three months, about Aug. 1, 1776, from Bedford under Capt. William Leftridge, Lt. Calloway, Ensign Joseph Bond. Guarded Chiswold lead mines till relieved by other troops. In April, 1777, was substitute three months for Lewis Dusee (?), who was drafted from Thomas Jones' Company in Henry. Served under Capt. Peter Herston, Lt. William Ferguson, Ensign Edward Tatum in Col. Christie's regiment. Marched 200 miles to Long Island in the Holston to stand guard during a treaty with the Cherokees. August, 1777, was substitute three months for Gwin Dudley, who was drafted into John Wilkerson's Company in Bedford. Served as Second Sergeant under Capt. Thomas Doley, Lt. Harry Talbott, and Ensign Calloway, and marched to Williamsburg. In 1778, substituted for William Cannon, drafted for five months into Robert Sevier's Company, Washington County, N. C. Joined Gen. Regulars in South Carolina about Dec. 1st, was appointed First Sergeant of a company organized, and served till March, 1779, under Capt. R. Sevier, Lt. Christopher Connaught, Ensign Charles Young, in Col. Peasley's battalion, Gen. Rutherford's regiment. In March, Sevier resigned and applicant became ensign. Detained till April 10th to await South Carolina recruits. Was in a battle on the Savannah and in some light skirmishes in Georgia. Volunteered in April, 1780, to serve three months against the Cherokees. Went as sergeant under Capt. Jno. Clark and Lt. John Bond, Gen. John Sevier being in general command. Marched to the headwaters of the Tennessee and killed a number of Indians, with the loss of Capt. Davis and Lt. Bond killed, and Jasper Terry wounded. Some horses were killed. In July, 1780, volunteered three months as private under Capt. John Renfro, Lt. Chatton Doggett, and Ensign Lewis Davis, in Col. Lincoln's so-called Light Horse of Bedford. Fought some tories on New River, taking their captain, William Terry, and getting his commission, which was from a British officer, and also a list of his men, all of whom we took and disarmed, excepting one, who got away. In June, 1781, a Thomas Runnels was killed by Indians, and Capt. Neely McGuire ordered our men in pursuit. Applicant volunteered and was one month in frontier service. In February, 1782, volunteered three months under Capt. John Clark, and Lt. John Murphy, of Washington County, N. C. (now Tenn.), Col. J. Brown commanding the regiment, and marched across Nolachucky and French Broad in pursuit of the Indians who had attacked Sherrill's Station on the frontier, losing one of their number in the attack. We overtook a band, supposed to number 60 to 100, and killed, as was said, thirteen of them. In August, 1782, drafted against the Indians again and hired George Doggett as substitute, but Gen. Sevier insisted that I go. Served under him in company of Capt. Thomas Wood and Lt. Vathan Breed, all the officers being of Greene Co. (Tenn.) We destroyed several Cherokee towns, killed a number of Indians, and took some prisoners. John Watts, a half-breed gave up a white woman named Jennie Ivey, who was taken from Roane's Creek a year before. Discharged in Greene

County (Tenn.) married Rachel ——, (born Nov. 15, 1764), Jan. 26, 1782. Husband died Nov. 2, 1833. John, oldest son, born in September, 1782. David Murphy, born, 1769, was half brother to William.

Section No. 158

LEWIS, THOMAS.—Vevay, Ind., Aug. 18, 1832. Born in Caroline, Dec. —, 1764. Went out in spring of 1781 under Capt. Coleman Sutton (Taylor?), of Col. Anthony Thornton's regiment. Again in June, 1781, under same captain and Col. Thomas Mathews. Again in September, 1781, same captain and Maj. Carey. Was drafted each time. Served in lower Virginia. At siege of Yorktown was second sergeant. After the surrender guarded prisoners to Winchester. Went to New York, 1798; to Indiana, 1818.

Section No. 159

MITCHELL, JOHN.—Montgomery, Sept. 3, 1832. Born about 1760. Drafted from Amelia in 1776 for no definite term. Served as fife major six weeks under Capt. Rowland Ward and Ensign Roberts. Only two companies were out on this service, the other being under Capt. Wilson. Marched to Hampton to prevent the British from landing, their fleet lying in the Chesapeake in full view. Drafted in fall of 1777, under Capt. William Craddock and Lt. Richard Craddock. The major in command was Dr. Cluman, a Frenchman. Marched to Cabin Point and Williamsburg. Was out six weeks. Served again in 1780 under Capt. William Craddock and Col. Richardson. Assembled at Hillsborough, N. C., and marched under Gen. Stevens, joining Gen. Gates the day before the battle of Camden. Next morning the action became general, and in the defeat, each man had to look out for himself. At Hillsborough remained about two weeks until the stragglers had pretty well come in. The forces to which applicant belonged were reduced to a regiment and placed under Col. Faulkner, Capt. Price commanding the company. They marched to New Garden to protect the Whigs from the tories, and finally applicant was discharged at Guilford C. H., after five months' service. Later, he was employed a month in Amelia collecting beeves for the army, this being in lieu of service in the ranks.

Section No. 160

RUTLEDGE, EDWARD.—Montgomery, Sept. 3, 1832. Born March 10, 1762. Volunteered in Augusta, January, 1781, and marched into North Carolina to receive the prisoners taken at Cowpens, and guarded them to the eastern border of Rockingham, where declarant's company was relieved by another, the service lasting three weeks. His captain was Francis Long. In April, volunteered for three months under Capt. F. Long, Col. Hughart, and Maj. Andrew Hamilton. Pursued Tarleton on his retreat from Charlottesville, and in vicinity of Richmond scouted to prevent depredations from raiding parties. Then marched to Jamestown, where a fight took place. At Burnt Ordinary was another skirmish. Near Williamsburg Hughart went home and Hamilton took command. Volunteered again under Long and was in Col. Vance's regiment at siege of Yorktown.

Section No. 161

RATLIFF, NATHAN.—Montgomery, July 1, 1833. Born, 1762. Entered service about June 1, 1778, serving one month against the Indians under Capt. Joshua Wilson and Lt. William Hungate. Went out again about July 1, 1780, under Capt. Abram Trigg, afterward a general. Marched to the Yadkin in North Carolina and defeated the tories in a skirmish. Eight months' service in all.

Section No. 162

THOMPSON, WILLIAM.—Boone County, Mo., July 2, 1833. Born in Augusta, 1749. Went out from said county in April, 1777, under Capt. Bohannan. Marched to Portsmouth, but the British had left after doing much damage in the vicinity, especially by fire. Drafted about April 1, 1781, under Capt. John Brown and Col. Bowyer, serving below Richmond. Was in the actions at Hot Water and Jamestown. In the latter his colonel was taken prisoner, but paroled after a few days. Discharged below Williamsburg, returning home in three or four days (?). In September his wagon was impressed with the team of a neighbor to haul forage and provisions to the army, and he went out with the wagon rather than trust it to another. The militia were discharged shortly after arriving at Richmond, but himself and wagon were impressed by Col. Sampson Mathews to make a trip from Petersburg to Taylor's Ferry on Roanoke. When near Petersburg on the return was again impressed to haul forage for the Light Horse. Reached his home in February. Allowed $23.33 per year.

Section No. 163

TEANEY, DANIEL.—Montgomery, Sept. 29, 1832. Born, April —, 1757. Drafted for two months in summer of 1776 from New Providence township, Philadelphia County, Pa. Constructed breastworks at Amboy, N. J., under Capt. John Edwards and Col. John Bull. Drafted again, 1777, for two months guarding the Delaware at Bristol, Pa., under Capt. Arnold Francis, Lt. Samuel Skein (Stein?), Col. Daniel Heister. Substituted same year two months for his brother, Henry Teaney, going out under Capt. William Davis and Col. John Bull, and marching to Head of Elk. Applicant was not in battle of Brandywine, having been sent off with baggage wagons the day before, and taking them twenty miles above Valley Forge. In 1779, settled in Augusta, and in October, 1780, was drafted under Capt. James Tate and Lt. John Blain and joined the Southern army beyond Salisbury, N. C. Was in battle of Cowpens and helped to bring back the prisoners. Was retained a month and six days beyond his three months' term, a battle having been expected with Tarleton. Drafted three months in summer of 1781, under Capt. John Dickey and Lt. John Campbell, and joined Gen. Muhlenberg. Was in battle at Jamestown and discharged at Bottom's Bridge.

Section No. 164

WYSOR, HENRY (Weizer).—Montgomery, Sept. 3, 1832. Born, 1754. Enlisted in February, 1776, under Capt. Berry in Frederick. Served in Eighth Virginia, Continental Line, commanded by Col. Muhlenberg and Col. Barsman. Joined it at Jamestown and marched by Halifax, N. C., to Charleston, and was there when Ft. Moultrie was attacked by the British fleet. Then marched to Savannah and Sunbury. At latter place was taken sick, remaining so three months, then was furloughed and went home. Three weeks later joined the army in New Jersey, and was attached to Morgan's Riflemen (serving therein under Captains Long and Knox, Lt. Craig, and Ensign Lovely (Lively?). Was at the capture of Burgoyne and the battle at Valley Forge (?), where my Major (Morris) was killed. Was also in other skirmishes. Discharged, February, 1778, at White House (White Marsh?), Pa. Drafted, 1781, under Capt. Bell, and was at the Siege of Yorktown. Furloughed about seven weeks later and not again called upon. Was sergeant while in service. Few of his company lived to return from the South. Gen. Morgan was a neighbor. Married in Frederick, about 1778.

Section No. 165

WOMACK, RICHARD.—Montgomery, Feb. 3, 1834. Born, 1753. Served under Captains Richard Allen, Cabell, and Benjamin Allen, Col. Shipwith, Lt. Col. Benjamin Allen, and Maj. Eppes. Volunteered in August, 1777, for several months, drafted in April, 1778, for six months, went out next November for six months. Fourth tour of six months, June, 1778. Fifth tour, spring of 1780. In all 28 months. Was in the battles of Long Island and Guilford, and in a skirmish. Served also under Captains Cox and Shelton. Lived in Pennsylvania when he enlisted.

Section No. 166

WANICOTT, RICHARD.—Montgomery, Oct. 2, 1832. Born in Pennsylvania, 1752. Served under Captains Daugat (Douthat?), Perkins, and Richard Allen, and Col. Henry Skippish, Lt. Col.

Benjamin Allen, and Maj. Eppes. Lieutenants were Cabell and Benjamin Allen. Volunteered in four tours: 1775(?), 1776(?), 1777(?), 1781, aggregating twenty-one months. Was in battles of Long Island and Guilford and a skirmish. Guarded prisoners at Old Cumberland C. H. Was also under Captains Evans, Cocke, and Shelton.

Section No. 167

BURNLEY, HENRY.—Columbia, Ga. Born, 1756. Removed to Georgia after the Revolution. Enlisted from Bedford, Va., March, 1776, in Fifth Virginia, Continental Line, under Capt. Harry Terrell, First Lt. John Goggins, Second Lt. Thomas M. Reynolds, Ensign Robert Watkins, Col. Josiah Parker commanding. Volunteered under Col. Daniel Morgan and went with him, Col. Butler and Maj. Morris to Saratoga, in 1777. Was also in the battles of Germantown and Guilford. In the latter he was a volunteer under Capt. William Jones. Discharged at Valley Forge.

Section No. 168

BALLARD, JOHN.—Augusta, June 26, 1820. Born about 1760. Enlisted in Loudoun, in Continental Line, under Capt. Adam Wallace, of Col. Buford's regiment. In camp at Petersburg the following winter. Marched with Buford into South Carolina and taken prisoner at Waxhaw, where he was badly wounded. He received three cuts on the head, a stab in the side with a bayonet, and one finger was nearly slashed off. At Petersburg he suffered severely from exposure and because of his wounds he cannot dress or undress himself without assistance.

Section No. 169

CUNNINGHAM, ANSEL.—Jackson, Ga., Nov. 6, 1832. Born in Mecklenburg, Va., July 27, 1763. Substituted in 1779 for John Stephens, serving six months under Capt. Reuben Vaughan. Joined Gen. Lincoln in South Carolina. Was in the battle of Stono.

In a scouting party the day before took two small vessels in Stono river. Drafted under Capt. Richard Whitton, marched to Jamestown, was in a skirmish on the James, and retreated to Coles' Ferry. Soon after, joined Lafayette's army below Richmond, was in the battle at Jamestown, and was discharged at Yorktown. Died about 1840.

Section No. 170

FLOWERS, ABSALOM.—Sussex, May 2, 1833. Born, 1758. Enlisted Jan. 1, 1781, under Capt. John Powell, Lt. Edward Powell, and Ensign Rochelle, in Col. Meriweather's militia. Rendezvoused at Ball's Ordinary, Sussex, and served mostly about Cabin Point until discharged in April. Called out in April, 1781, serving under same officers, except Capt. John Massenburg (Massingbird?), who was wounded in the hip in a fight at Petersburg. Four other comrades were also wounded. The call was to relieve some militia at Petersburg, but next morning they were attacked and compelled to retreat. Lt. Powell marched the command to the Chesterfield coal mine, where they remained about ten days. The enemy moving toward Richmond to burn that city, the troop marched there and joined a strong force under Lafayette. Arnold then made a sudden retreat to Petersburg and the American army lay at Richmond some time. Discharged after eight weeks. Called out next October under Capt. Nathaniel Newson, who resigned at Surry C. H., and was succeeded by Lt. Thomas Newson. Served at siege of Yorktown.

Section No. 171

HOPKINS, JAMES.—Pittsylvania, Sept. 17, 1832. Born Feb. 22, 1765. Substituted for James Hopkins, Sr., spring of 1780, and marched under Capt. Azariah Martin, Lt. William Holt, Ensign Leroy to Hillsboro, N. C. There transferred to Fourth Virginia militia under Col. Lucas, of Gen. Stevens' brigade, and after having some drill were sent on to join the army under Gates. From Rugeley's mill marched at 10 p. m., Aug. 15th to surprise the enemy, who however, marched at the same hour. The armies met in the night, there was a sharp skirmish between the advanced guards, a line was formed, and the men stood under arms till daybreak, when there was a shameful defeat. No rendezvous had been designated and the men lost all their baggage, including all clothing but what they had on. Under these circumstances a considerable part of the company went home, but a court of inquiry ordered them back to serve eight months under regular officers. Under Capt. Paulin we marched back to Hillsboro, and there transferred to Capt. Graves, of Culpeper, assigned to take command of men from a few other counties, who had committed the same offense. Under Gen. Greene the army went into winter quarters on the Cheraw Hills, S. C. In February there was a general order releasing the married men belonging to the eight months company, and Capt. Graves returned with the discharged men. Capt. Webb and Lt. Webb took command of those still in the army. Shortly after this, Gen. Morgan defeated Tarleton at Cowpens and had to make a rapid retreat with his prisoners. Gen. Greene marched to cover Morgan's movement, leaving the small eight months company to guard the camp and the mills that were supplying flour and meal. At length Capt. Webb received orders to follow with about ten wagons loaded with flour and meal and a drove of 400 hogs. We were in the rear of both armies, and had to change our course because of Cornwallis' march. In Mecklenburg we delivered the supplies to a commissary, having safely brought them through a region infested with British and tories. Our time being nearly up, we were permitted to petition Gen. Greene that he discharge us, we being worn out with fatigue and nearly naked. He did so.

Section No. 172

KIDD, JAMES H.—Gwinnett, Ga., Aug. 13, 1833. Born, 1765. Drafted in Virginia into Capt. Reuben Vaughan's company, January, 1779. Joined Gen. Lincoln at Bacon's Bridge near Charleston, S. C. Was in battle at Stono. Discharged in Virginia in July. Was under 15 when he went out, but from his desire to enter the army he reported himself old enough to go on the militia roll. Served two months in 1780 under Capt. John Kendrick,.

and three in 1781, under Capt. John Brown. Was at battle of Guilford. From Ramsey's Mill was sent to Albemarle with prisoners and discharged there. After this the company were required to present their discharges in order to draw some salt, and applicant never saw his again. Born in Mecklenburg.

Section No. 173

NANCE, JAMES.—Pittsylvania, Sept. 17, 1832. Born in Nottoway, Feb. 2, 1762. Drafted Feb. 9, 1779, under Capt. William Fitzgerald, Lt. Charles Irby, Ensign Bowling Hall, joined Col. David Mason at Halifax, N. C., and Gen. Lincoln at Stono, S. C. Was in the battle at Stono, June 20, from beginning to end. Discharged at Camden, S. C., in August, having acted as fifer. In 1780 was out under Capt. Gray and Col. White. In fall of same year was drafted under Capt. Irby and marched by Cabin Point to Nansemond. Was to go into the cavalry under Charles Irby on condition that he could get a horse, and if he could not, his absence in search of one was to count as furlough. Not finding one in his home neighborhood, and Elisha Gunn being called out to join Gen. Greene, he and Gunn changed tours. Marched under Capt. Overstreet to Troublesome Creek, N. C., and was in the battle at Guilford. Was discharged at Ramsey's Mill, Chatham County. Moved to Wake County, N. C., 1801.

Section No. 174

NANCE, WILLIAM M.—Pittsylvania, Sept. 17, 1832. Born Jan. 18, 1760, in Nottoway. Substituted for William Mitchell in 1777, entering service under Capt. Gabriel Folks, Lt. John Knight, and Ensign William Brookin. At Williamsburg Joined Col. Vivian Brookin's regiment. Served under Gen. Nelson and discharged at Hampton. Drafted February, 1779, serving in same company with James Nance (§173). Was orderly sergeant during this six months tour. In 1781, drafted from Pittsylvania and served at siege of Yorktown, under Capt. Charles Williams, and Lt. Dix (Hunt?).

Section No. 175

PITTMAN, JAMES.—Madison County, Ga., Oct. 2, 1832. Born in Amelia, March 4, 1756. Enlisted from Columbus County, Ga., in 1776, served two months under Capt. German in Col. Marbury's regiment, and four as lieutenant, guarding the Georgia frontier. Went into Florida to take St. Augustine, but the expedition failed. Was in a fight with the British. Served again six months on the frontier, and another tour under Col. Few, during which there was a fight with the enemy between Savannah and Augusta, and Few retreated. Served four months under Capt. Sinkfield and Col. Williamson, while the tories were troublesome in South Carolina. After the surrender of Charleston he thought South Carolina and Georgia entirely in the hands of the enemy, and went as refugee into Virginia, where he served two weeks guarding the prisoners taken at Cowpens. Returned to Georgia after peace. Died Dec. 25, 1850. Children: 1. John G; 2. Noah W; 3. Timothy; 4. Teresa (married Wilson Strickland); 5. Martha (married Abner Wells); 6. America (married Benjamin W. Cash); 7. Sarah (married Samson Lay); 8. Lucinda (married Henry Harris); 9. Pleasant O.; 10. Martin H.; 11 Sir James; 12. Nancy (married Silas Smith); 13. Elizabeth. 9, 10, 11, 12, 13 died prior to 1850, leaving children, except, (?) Elizabeth.

Section No. 176

PERKINS, SAMUEL.—Madison County, Ky., Aug. 13, 1832. Born about 1761. Went out from Louisa in 1781 under Capt. Philips. Served under General Demarcus* and Wayne. Also other tours under Captains White and Johnson. Married Susanna Pass in Louisa, 1798. Died Sept. 27, 1839, leaving seven children.

Section No. 177

PERKINS, ANTHONY.—Madison County Ky. Born about 1757. Brother to Samuel Perkins. Enlisted under Capt. Philips, of Gen. Wayne's army. Marched from Louisa in pursuit of the British but never came to an engagement. Served other tours under Captains White and Johnson. Total service fourteen months.

---

*Lafayette. Some of the soldiers knew him only as DeMarquis or Demarcus.

Section No. 178

PERKINS, JOHN.—Franklin, Tenn. Born in Halifax, May 11, 1765. Enlisted as Thomas Carson, April, 1781, as substitute for Alexander Moore, under Capt. James Turner. Was at the siege of Ninety-six and discharged in Mecklenburg, N. C. Moved in 1782 to Caswell County, N. C., and was there drafted for eighteen months under Capt. Elijah Moore and Capt. Rhodes. Discharged at Ten Mile House near Charleston. He used the name Thomas Carson because while he was an infant his mother, Mrs Mary Perkins, married Thomas Carson, a widower, one of whose children was John. After his stepfather died in 1783, his mother told him his real name and he used it thence forward. Married Frances ———. Died in Hardin County, Tenn., June 16, 1840.

Section No. 179

DAVIS, THOMAS.—Woodford County, Ky., Aug. 18, 1818. Born in Spottsylvania, 1761. Enlisted April 25, 1779, for eighteen months. Served under Capt. Alexander Parker in Col. Richard Parker's regiment. Substituted for his brother, Benjamin Davis, under Capt. William Mills and James Cunningham. Discharged at Williamsburg. Drafted the day after his return home and was at siege of Yorktown: Total service 18 (22?) months, for which applicant received $60.

A supporting affidavit adds these particulars: Jesse Davis, of Prince William, was private, Jan. 1, 1777, to Jan. 6, 1778; Lieutenant thence forward to October, 1778, when he became captain. Died, February, 1782. His brother, Pressley Davis, was killed in battle of Long Island, 1776. John, another brother, died in hospital of smallpox.

Capt. Davis married Nancy Melton, of Prince William, about 1775. Children: 1. William M., of Frankfort, Ky; 2. Nancy (married ——— Reynolds), Frankfort.

Section No. 180

HULL, PETER.—Captain, 1779, and as such commanded a troop of cavalry in Yorktown campaign. Married Barbara Keith.

Children: Henry, Peter, Susanna, Barbara, Adam, Jacob, Elizabeth. Muster roll of his company Second Battalion, Augusta militia, 1779. Taken from the list written by Lt. Seybert, and given in Morton's History of Highland County (Va.).

Peter Hull, *Captain*
Nicholas Seybert, *First Lt.*

Henry Fisher, *Second Lt.*
Jacob Hoover, *Ensign.*

Privates

Arbogast, Adam
Arbogast, David
Arbogast, John
Arbogast, Michael
Bennett, Jacob
Bennett, John
Bennett, William
Blizzard, Thomas
Bodkin, Hugh
Bowman, John
Burner, Abraham
Conrad, Ulrich, Jr.
Crummett, Frederick
Duffield, Abraham*
Eckard, Abraham
Eckard, Philip
Ellsworth, Jacob
Eye, Christopher
Fleisher, Conrad
Graham, Francis
Gum, Isaac
Gum, Jacob
Gum, William
Hammer, Balsor
Harper, Nicholas
Hoff, James
Hogg, John*
Hoover, Michael
Hoffman, George

Lantz, Conrad
Lantz, Joseph
McQuain, Alexander
Mullenax, John
Mullenax, James*
Null, Henry
Peninger, John
Pickle, Christian
Puffenberger, George
Rexrode, George
Sheets, George
Simmons, George
Simmons, John
Simmons, Leonard
Simmons, Mark
Simmons, Michael
Simmons, Peter
Smith, Mark
Smith, Sebastian
Snider, John
Stone, Sebastian
Stout, George
Summers, Paul
Summerfield, Thomas
Wagoner, Adam
Wamsley, John
Wamsley, William
Wamsley, James*
Whiteman, Henry

*Under 18 years of age.

Hull, Adam
Ingram, Uriah
Jordan, Andrew

Wilfong, Jacob
Wimer, Philip
Yeager, John

Section No. 181

MOORE, DAVID.—Cole County, Ky., Nov. 13, 1832. Born in Amelia, Nov. 20, 1763. Enlisted in Lunenburg, fall of 1780, as substitute for his father, Robert. Served under Capt. William Hays, Lt. Hays, Ensign Gill. Marched to rendezvous at Jamestown, then to Portsmouth, which Lord Dunmore (?) had garrisoned. There was a skirmish between scouting parties. Col. Daniel Morgan (?) with his riflemen attacked a fort, causing a loss to the enemy of 18 to 20 men, as stated by a deserter. Dunsmore abandoned the fort during the night. Later, marched under Colonels Morgan and Dowbman (?) through Dismal Swamp to Elizabeth, a small place destroyed by the British. Returned home next spring soon afer battle of Guilford. A week or so later substituted for John Mathews, of Brunswick, under Capt. House. Marched to Point of Fork, finding an engagement going on. Then retreated about two days before the British. When his three months expired, permission to return home was refused. Next night the orderly sergeant went off with muster rolls together with several men, and the following day there was no one to call the roll and permission to go home was given. Went to Missouri, 1819. Allowed $30, a year, March 4, 1831.

NOTE:—Arnold, not Dunmore, had a British force at Portsmouth about the time applicant first enlisted. Morgan was at that time camping in the Carolinas, not in Virginia.

Section No. 182

POTTERF, CASPER.—Preble County, O., March 23, 1833. Born in Lancaster County, Pa., Dec. 19, 1759. Moved to Virginia about 1778; to Ohio, about 1800. Drafted, winter of 1777-8, in Frederick, Md., under Capt. John Bannerd. Enlisted again, January, 1781, under Capt. James Buchanan, of Rockbridge. Discharged in

April at Gregory's Camp, N. C. Enlisted next August under Capt. Charles Campbell, of same county. Discharged at Winchester Barracks. Total service, nine months.

Section No. 183

BUCK, JOHN.—Greenup County, Ky., October —, 1820. Born Dec. 20, 1752. Drafted from Culpeper, July 4, 1776, for 18 months, under Capt. Kilpatrick and Col. Chambers Begger. Served out his time.

Section No. 184

MOORE, GEORGE.—Boone County, Mo., Feb. 6, 1833. Born 1761. Enlisted in Charlotte, Dec. 25, 1780, under Capt. Richard Givens for three months. One month later reached headquarters of Gen. Muhlenberg near Dismal Swamp. The traitor, Arnold, with 1,600 British was fortifying himself in Portsmouth. Affiant volunteered in a company of 50 under Capt. Jesse Saunders, Lt. David Caldwell, and Ensign Carter, of Col. Dick's and Maj. Thomas' regiments. Two companies of infantry were in two miles in front of the main army toward Arnold's line. We often skirmished, killed some of the enemy and taking some prisoners. Capt. Armand, a Frenchman who commanded a company of light horse, charged on the enemy's guard and took them all, without a gun being fired on either side. The enemy at one time came out of their works and fired on us, but on our advance they retired. Our only damage was one man wounded in the thigh. We marched against a fort on the Blackwater held by the British, who fired on us with cannon, but for want of artillery we made no attack. After dark they sent a boat down the river for reinforcements. We took the boat with an officer, eight men, and some clothing. We also took some horses around the fort. Arnold evacuated Portsmouth in March. We were discharged in April.. Middle of next August called out under Capt. Andrew Wallace and marched for Yorktown to join Washington's army. When within two miles we laid out our camp and went to digging trenches. Affiant and three others of company were employed in artillery service. We began firing Oct. 9th, and after a few days moved our guns nearer. Generals Lafeyette, Wayne, and Lincoln I saw frequently with the men in the entrenchments. Gen Knox, the commander of the artillery, was one day at one of the batteries looking through his spyglass, when a cannon ball struck the top of the post by which he was standing. A splinter struck his ear and made it bleed freely. After the surrender, Sergeant Elijah Clark, Samuel Marshall, John Paulet and affiant had orders to take some Carolina tories from Williamsburg to Richmond, where we drew provisions to last us home. Moved to Missouri, 1810.

Section No. 185

KINCAID, JAMES.—Lafayette County, Mo., Nov. 5, 1833. Entered service while living at Castlewood on Clinch, 25 miles from Abingdon. The settlers in Powell's Valley had been driven out by Indians, and many of them hid their "plunder," not being able to bring it to a place of safety. Capt. John Duncan and company were ordered out to guard the people so that they might bring their goods into the settlements. Applicant was one year with him. Capt. Joseph Martin was at this time stationed at Rye Cave on Clinch to guard the frontier. The brothers, John and James, Bunnil (?) were scouts under him. We met these spies and went with them to Martin's Station in said valley, but all had fled. One refugee, Capt. (Robert?) Davis met us. He had lived at Owen's Station, ten miles below Martin's. Duncan sent five men to go with him to Owen's to collect his "plunder." On the way back Indians in ambush fired on them, killing Bowman and wouning James Bunnill and —— Johnson. Bunnill, Davis, and another man got in that night. Next day Duncan went down with all his force, including affiant, save a few left to guard the wounded. Davis took us to where an Indian stood that he shot at. We found a good deal of blood and followed the trail, but after a while it seemed that the party scattered. We buried Bowman and returned to Owen's. Bunnill grew very sick and we took him to Rye Cave. All were dismissed in about a month. The above took place 1776 (?) in summer time. Next went to Kentucky under Col. John Bowman, of Bedford, Henry Rolling (?) being captain, and made for ——— Station. Near Abingdon one William Bush told our captain he would raise a lieutenant's quoto (24 men), if he could command it under Rollins. He secured the men, affiant and brother Joseph enlisting by consent of father. Overtook Bowman at ford of Cumberland River and joined company of Capt. Paulin (?). Arrived at Boonesboro about August, 1777. The only other stations in Kentucky were Logan's and Harrod's. Stayed 16 to 20 days to let the people get in their corn, which they could not do the year before, because of the Indians. Col. Calloway, who lived with his family in the fort, expected to return with Bowman, but failed to catch up. When he came back to the fort reported a man killed on the trail we had come by, and that the Indians had massacred seven or eight families around Castlewood. Affiant and brother and several others became uneasy about the home folks, and the colonel granted a discharge. On the way back we met the Clinch scouts, who confirmed the report and said the families not killed had fled. We had been gone about 50 days. Next expedition was to Illinois under Col. John Montgomery. About 130 men and recruits were sent to Clarke and Montgomery, and it was understood by us that the army would go to Detroit. Affiant and brother, Joseph, enlisted. At Long Island in Holston we were met by Col. Evan Shelby and 40 militia, and went by canoes to Chicamauga, where in a skirmish we killed a few, took some prisoners, stayed two months, and collected a good deal of Indian plunder. Shelby returned and Montgomery went to join Clarke.

Section No. 186

BELL, SAMUEL.—Augusta, April 28, 1823. Certificate by Joseph and Sarah Bell. Entered Sixteenth Regiment, Virginia Continentals, as ensign, March 8, 1777. Served under Captains McGuire and Thomas Bell and Col. William Grayson. Was in the battles at Brandywine, Germantown, Guilford, and Hot Water. In last fight was wounded in eight or nine places and captured. Parolled by the enemy and continued to the end of the war as a supernumerary officer. Died in Staunton, 1788, leaving as legatees, Joseph, Sarah, Thomas, and John Bell.

Section No. 187

ROUNTREE, WILLIAM.—Henrico, Sept. 3, 1832. Born in Goochland, Jan. 3, 1763. Went out in March, 1779, with Capt. Holman Rice, Lt. Edward Herndon, of the regiment of guards under Col. Francis Taylor and Morgan Roberts. Served at Albemarle Barracks two months.

Section No. 188

MURPHY, JOHN.—Fauquier, Aug. 31, 1832. Born at Dublin, Ireland, Jan. 1, 1733. Went out Sept. 4, 1780, under Capt. James Winn. Was a comrade with Thomas Obannon. (See his declaration).

Section No. 189

BURFOOT, TANDY.—Powhatan, Aug. 15, 1832. Born in Goochland, 1761. Drafted from Amherst about 1778 and marched under Capt. John Trent against the Indians on Holston. Took fever after eight weeks and was furloughed. Drafted from Amherst and served about Richmond under Capt. Nicholas Cabell. Total service, six months.

Section No. 190

COLLINS, JOHN.—Powhatan, Aug. 15, 1832. Enlisted in Carolina about 1778 under Capt. Elisha White and Col. Charles Porterfield, serving two years in state defense. Discharged at Richmond. Guarded prisoners at Winchester, was six months at Hobb's Hole on Rappahannock under Lt. Littlebury Harrod, and three months on a vessel at Warwick in care of prisoners. Born about 1758.

Section No. 191

HALL, JAMES.—Powhatan, Sept. 19, 1832. Born in Chesterfield, 1761. Was at Gates' defeat. Next spring (1781) returned to North Carolina under Capt. Stephen Pankey. Being in Class

Two, of the militia, was not called out so early as some others. Was also in battle at Guilford. Served about two years, both as volunteer and drafted man. Memory defective.

Section No. 192

HATCHER, SETH.—Powhatan, Nov. 21, 1832. Born in Goochland, Jan. 13, 1760. Went out in September, 1777, under Capt. Thomas Harris, and served two months at Williamsburg and Yorktown. Next tour under Capt. George Williamson. At Hood's Landing they fired in the night on a landing party of the enemy, and afterwards marched to Suffolk. Under Williamson he crossed the Roanoke at Taylor's Ferry and was wounded at Guilford. Eight months' service.

Section No. 193

HUTCHINSON, JAMES.—Powhatan, Sept. 19, 1832. Born in Amelia, 1762. Went out first in 1779 under Capt. John Knight as substitute for Mackness Goode, of Amelia, and served three months about Richmond and Norfolk. Second tour was in same year and locality, and under Capt. William Royall, Lt. John Royall, and En. William Robertson. The third began in April, 1781, when he joined the army at Malvern Hills, and was in the retreat to Rapidan. This time he was under Capt. Paulin Anderson, Lt. William Crowder, and En. William Wood. Fourth tour began Aug. 1, 1781, and was at Yorktown under Capt. Lewis Ford. Total service, one year.

Section No. 194

JACKSON, HENRY.—Powhatan, Sept. 19, 1832. Born in Chesterfield in 1761. About 1780, the Chesterfield militia were called South. At least two companies started under Captain Booker and Archibald Walthall. Affiant was with latter. After waiting at Randolph's Mill for the Caroline, Hanover, and Henrico militia to come up. Col. Faulkner led the regiment across the Roanoke at Taylor's Ferry and on to Hillsboro, where Gen. Stevens was in command until Gen. Gates arrived. In the battle at Camden he was wounded in the leg by a bullet. There was a rally at Hillsboro. He reached home in December. In February, 1781, he went out under Capt. David Patterson, but after lying at Dinwiddie C. H. three weeks they were discharged by Capt. (?) Col. (?) Robert Goode, though told to be ready at call. After the battle of Guilford he was again called out and served in Virginia. Total service, nine months.

Section No. 195

MAXEY, JOHN, SR.—Powhatan, March 21, 1833. Born in Prince Edward in June, 1764. First tour was early in 1781, guarding stores at Prince Edward C. H. The only officer there was Serg't Alexander McClardy. Next substituted for Benjamin Hart, the company with another from Buckingham marching under Maj. John Overstreet, of Prince Edward, to Malvern Hill, crossing the James at Carter's Ferry. Under Col. Towles the command was constantly in motion. A week or two after his discharge he substituted for his brother, Shadrach Maxey (married), and marched to Yorktown under Capt. Nathaniel Cunningham. After the surrender he guarded prisoners to Winchester.

Section No. 196

MOSBY, HEZEKIAH.—Powhatan, Oct. 18, 1832. Born in Powhatan, Jan. 12, 1760. First called out in 1781, under Capt. Robert Hughes. Crossed Roanoke at Boyd's Ferry and joined Gen. Lawson at Hillsboro. Was in battle of Guilford and discharged at Ramsay's Mill. Second tour began almost immediately after. Half of the three months spent at Cabin Point, the other half was in marching up and down the James. The last tour was under Capt. Hughes Woodson, at siege of Yorktown, after which he guarded prisoners as far as Williamsburg. Nine months' service.

Section No. 197

MOSBY, WADE.—Powhatan, Sept. 19, 1832. Born in Powhatan in 1761. About 1777 affiant joined a number of his fellow students at Hampden-Sidney Academy (later a college), in forming a volunteer company. Luke B. Smith, a professor, was captain. Subalterns were, Lt. Samuel Venable and En. Samuel Hackley. Served six weeks at Williamsburg. Was then sixteen years old. A year later the company again went out for six weeks under the same officers, serving at Petersburg. Affiant then quit college, and in fall of 1779 or spring of 1780, was Second Lieutenant under his brother, Capt. Littlebury Mosby (later a General). At Petersburg they joined the cavalry under Col. Banister, of Gen. Lawson's command. The call was because hostile vessels came near on the James. After the defeat of Gates there was a heavy call, and affiant went out under his brother-in-law, Capt. Robert Hughes, serving as adjutant of the regiment. At Moore's Ordinary in Prince Edward, Capt. Cameron, of Buckingham took ill, and affiant was appointed in his place. Was in battle of Guilford under Col. B. Randolph. Col. Carrington, quarter-master-general, laid off the battleground. A fifth tour quickly followed, because Gov. Jefferson wrote Littlebury Mosby to raise all the cavalry he could and go to the aid of Lafayette. L. Mosby called on his subalterns, affiant raising a company and Horatio Turpin another, L. Mosby leading the battalion as major. It lay at Petersburg until the British, under Gen. Phillips arrived, and then the cavalry covered the retreat, taking up the bridge over the Appomattox after the army had crossed. Affiant was then much on vidette service under Col. Call, his own father, militia commandant of county, keeping him to watch Cornwallis while the latter was about Richmond, which was four or five weeks. Married Susanna ———, April 13, 1785. Died June 1, 1834. Widow made application, Oct. 1, 1838.

Section No. 198

MOSELEY, ARTHUR.—Powhatan, Aug. 15, 1832. Born about 1762 in Powhatan. Drafted in 1780. Went into North Carolina under Capt. Robert Hughes, crossing Roanoke at Peyton's Ferry.

Was in battle at Guilford. Later, served at Bermuda Hundred, etc., under Capt. Porter, and was at Westham, when Gen. Wayne's army was set over the James. All the boats were taken up to Jude's Ferry, seventeen miles above Richmond, and all the boats at Micham Ferry were brought down, and were guarded the whole summer. Served almost continuously till end of war.

Section No. 199

ROSS, WILLIAM.—Powhatan, Aug. 15, 1832. Born in Chesterfield May 10, 1763. Drafted April 15, 1779, in Chesterfield under Capt. Creede Haskins and En. Archer. Served at Hood's Fort in Surry under Capt. Richard Hill, of the Artillery. Went out again in February, 1781, under Capt. Paul Patterson and Col. Robert Goode, and started for the Carolinas, but at Dinwiddie C. H. the command was countermarched to Petersburg. Third tour began a week or so after second ended and under same officers. Joined in the retreat from Petersburg, crossed the James at Tuckahoe, and marched to Richmond to join Lafayette's army. With several others was taken prisoner in Chesterfield by British cavalry and kept till September. Was in a skirmish at Sudbury in Chesterfield. Discharged at Portsmouth.

Section No. 200

SHORT, ARCHIBALD.—Powhatan, Aug. 15, 1832. Born in Chesterfield, in December, 1758. Took oath in 1776. About 1777 enlisted as regular for three years under Capt. Francis Smith, a recruiting officer of the First Regiment. After a few weeks procured a substitute. About June, 1780, substituted for Samuel Short, of Chesterfield, under Capt. Archibald Walthall. Waited at Randolph's Mill till the militia from Caroline, Hanover, and Henrico came up. Col. Faulkner led the regiment to Hillsboro, where it lay till the Virginia and North Carolina militia assembled. After Gen. Gates arrived, the army proceeded to near Camden, where it was defeated, but rallied at Salisbury. Affiant was in hospital there about a month and discharged for ill health, not reaching home for about two months more. A third tour was to guard the ferries at Westham and Tuckahoe. A fourth tour of about five weeks was under Capt. David Patterson. Was discharged before the battle of Guilford under same captain he served at siege of Yorktown, and then guarded prisoners, under Capt. Spencer, of Charlotte. Total service, about two years.

Section No. 201

SLEDD, JOHN.—Powhatan, Sept. 19, 1832. Born in Hanover, 1760. Enlisted in 1779, under Capt. Benjamin Timberlake, of the garrison regiment. Served two years and three months guarding prisoners. Discharged at Winchester, May, 1781, by Col. Taylor. Was not outside of State.

Section No. 202

STOVALL, LITTLEBERRY.—Powhatan, Oct. 18, 1832. Born, 1765. First tour in 1780, when fifteen years old. Substituted for his father, who was drafted, and marched under Capt. Richard Crump, to Cabin Point. After his discharge was put at once on muster list. Later in same year was drafted to join Gen. Gates, but was discharged as too feeble. Next year he served under Col. Goode in Chesterfield. Another tour was as volunteer for his relative, William Hobson, of Cumberland, who was drafted. Under Capt. Meredith he joined Lafayette at Richmond and was discharged at Raccoon Ford. The last tour began a few days later, when he guarded Manokin Town Ferry till surrender of Cornwallis. Total service, about eight months.

Section No. 203

TONEY (TORREY?), JOHN.—Powhatan, Aug. 15, 1832. Born in Powhatan (then Cumberland) about 1755. First tour, three months, about 1777, under Capt. Robert Hughes, serving about Hampton in the fall. Second tour in Chesterfield, under Capt. Wm. Mays and Col. Goode. Third tour under Mays and Hubbard, serving at Richmond, Petersburg, and Suffolk, and being in a skirmish at Hood's Landing on the James. Fourth and fifth tours in 1781, under Capt. Geo. Williamson. Last tour at Yorktown, under Capt. Hughes Woodson, who had been a regular officer. Total service about fifteen months.

Section No. 204

TUCKER, THOMAS.—Powhatan, March 21, 1833. Born in Powhatan, 1755. First tour early in 1781 when he marched to Guilford C. H., under Capt. Robert Hughes and Col. B. Randolph. Discharged at Ramsey's Mill. Second tour, soon afterward, was under Col. Holcombe at Cabin Point and Smithfield.

Section No. 205

WATKINS, EDWARD.—Powhatan, Aug. 15, 1832. Born in Powhatan, 1747. After 1778, in almost constant service under Capt. Williamson. Taken prisoner in battle at Guilford, but escaped after three days. There served under Maj. Tucker and Colonels Randolph and Holcomb. Was called out for Yorktown, but got a substitute.

Section No. 206

WATKINS, EDWARD, SR.—Powhatan, Feb. 20, 1833. Took oath Sept. 20, 1777. Himself and Edmund Wooldridge furnished William Edwards as a substitute for two years. First three tours were as drafted man under Capt. George Williamson, at Williamsburg, and Cabin Point. At the latter place Gen. Lawson was in command, and there was a skirmish. In third tour crossed Roanoke at Peyton's Ferry. Was taken prisoner at Guilford, but escaped after three days. His papers were then taken from him. Williamson resigned after reaching Guilford and was succeeded by Hubbard. Affiant was called on far the Yorktown campaign, but furnished Daniel Langsden as substitute.

Section No. 207

McLAURINE, WILLIAM.—Cumberland, June 5, 1832. Volunteered May, 1780, under Capt. Richard Crump, Lt. Vincent Markham, and En. James Smith, the latter being a Baptist preacher. Col. Robert Goode commanded the regiment, which served around Hampton. The second tour was under Capt. William Mayo, and began in January, 1781, the command marching to Suffolk. On one occasion the company being surprised in the night, the captain tried to make the men fight, but they ran, although being in larger number they could have taken the opposing force. The command was always on the move and did much night duty, once taking five or six British loaded with jewelry and other plunder. Third tour began next March, and was in the cavalry under Capt. Littlebury Mosby. The service was in detachments. Affiant witnessed the fight at Petersburg. The American army retired to the Midlothian Coalpits, twelve miles away. Affiant went home for a fresh horse, and rejoined the army at Malvern, where he was always on scout duty by night. At one time he could hear conversation on a British vessel. This service was for three months and the company was complimented by Jefferson in a letter to Capt. (afterward Gen.) Mosby. The last tour was in guarding prisoners, mostly seamen.

Section No. 208

BRADLEY, DANIEL.—Pittsylvania, Aug. 22, 1832. Enlisted from Cumberland, July 1, 1780, in First Virginia for eighteen months. Was under Capt. White and enlisted by En. Belew. Was in the battles of Guilford and Eutaw, the siege of Ninety-Six, and at the capturing of Scotch Lake a blockhouse at Camden, and the forts at Friday's, Thompson's, and Augusta. Was in camp on High Hills of Santee. Capt. Morgan was wounded at Eutaw.

Section No. 209

CHANEY, ABRAHAM.—Pittsylvania, Aug. 22, 1832. Born in 1760. Volunteered under Capt. John Donaldson, Jr., Lt. Moses Hutchings, and En. Joseph Williams, and marched to Holston River.

Capt. Donaldson with affiant and fourteen other men ranged after the Cherokees for two weeks. Second tour (1778) was to Hatfield Fort on New River, and under Capt. Donaldson and Lt. John Gwinn. In winter of 1780-'81 was drafted under Capt. Clements and marched to Hillsboro, where he was ill ten weeks and hired his brother, John Chaney, as substitute. Total service, one year.

Section No. 210

FERGUSON, ROBERT.—Pittsylvania, Aug. 22, 1832. Born in Halifax in 1761. In 1779 substituted for Bezaliel Wier, and served under Capt. Witcher, marching to join Gen. Lincoln in South Carolina. Next spring as a volunteer under Capt. William and and Col. John Cleveland, affiant served against the tories, and also drove cattle for Joseph Terry to Wilkes C. H., N. C. Next December he went out as substitute for William Bennett, serving under Capt. John Winn. On this tour he was in the battle at Guilford and was discharged at Ramsey's Mill. In April, 1781, was drafted under Capt. Henry Burnett, serving later under Captains John Beckley and William Clark. Joined Gen. Lawson at Charlotte C. H., was several weeks at Malvern Hill and was in the battle of Jamestown. Just after his return home in August he enlisted as wagoner with William McGraw and served one year. Total service, thirty months.

Section No. 211

ANDERSON, JACOB.—Pittsylvania, Aug. 22, 1832. Born in Caroline in 1760. First tour was under Capt. John Marshall and at Williamsburg. Second, in 1779, around Malvern Hill, was under Col. Richard Allen, Lt. Glenn, and En. John Daniel, of Col. Henry Skipwith's regiment. The third was under Capt. Creed Haskins, in the Yorktown campaign. Total service, seven months. Drafted in each instance.

Section No. 212

SMITH, JOHN.—Pittsylvania County, Sept. 17, 1832. Born, 1744. Drafted under Capt. James Brewer and afterward William Dix. Was in battle of Guilford and discharged at Haw River, March 30, 1781. Under Dix served in Yorktown campaign, and discharged at Noland's Ferry on Potomac, by Capt. Charles Williams, while guarding prisoners to Winchester.

Section No. 213.

JEFFRIES, WILLIAM.—Pittsylvania, Sept. 17, 1832. Born in Richmond County, 1758. Enlisted in Virginia Line at same time with Samuel Colston, and under Capt. Jeffries. Was inoculated for smallpox. At Valley Forge joined the Fifteenth Regiment and served two years. In 1780 volunteered under Capt. Joshua Stone and was discharged at High Rock, N. C. About Aug. 1, 1781, was drafted under Capt. William Dix, Lt. David Hunt, and En. Clement McDaniel, and served under Col. Meriwether in siege of Yorktown. Discharged at Noland's Ferry, while guarding prisoners to Winchester.

Section No. 214

WRAY, DAVID.—Pittsylvania, Sept. 17, 1832. Born in Brunswick, 1751. Volunteered in April or May, 1778, against the Indians on New River, serving under Capt. John Donaldson. Was at Lucas Fort, etc. In 1780 volunteered under Capt. William Witcher to join Gen. Lincoln in South Carolina, and served five months. Was sick at the time of the battle of Stono. Guarded to Virginia the prisoners taken at Cowpens, then was ordered back to North Carolina and at Guilford guarded wagon train. Served about ten months, and was in no battle.

Section No. 215

DIXON, WILLIAM.—Pittsylvania, Aug. 22, 1832. Born, 1762. Enlisted for three years in the fall of 1780, under one

Wheatley, a recruiting officer for the Continental cavalry regiment of Col. Litterell, who was killed at Lindley's Mill. Other officers were Col. Read, Maj. Douglas, Capt. Richeson, Capt. Trowton. The command was often out to suppress tories. Just before battle of Guilford, affiant was detached to guard ammunition to Hillsboro.

Section No. 216

DOVE, WILLIAM.—Pittsylvania, Aug. 22, 1832. Born in Charles County, Md., Nov. 27, 1758, and moved to Fairfax in boyhood. On arrival of express saying the British had landed at Head of Elk in August, 1777, he volunteered under Capt. Thomas Pollard and Col. Rumley, and marched by way of Frederick and York to join Washington's army. While ill with smallpox at Lancaster he heard the cannon at Germantown. Discharged in November. Next September was a marine on the "General Washington" to carry dispatches to France. The officers were Capt. Francis Speake, and Lt. Samuel Walker. The Captain and Lieutenant of the Marines were William Sanford and William Pearson. The surgeon was William Ramsey. The voyage of eighteen days was said to have been the fastest known. On leaving Brest, ninety vessels were convoyed out by French warships. Near Cape Henry the "General Washington" took a British privateer and brought her to Alexandria. In March, 1780, affiant sailed again on same ship, which convoyed some merchantmen out of the Chesapeake. On the way to Amsterdam a large British merchantman was taken. Affiant and seven other men were detailed as crew for same, and brought the ship and four prisoners to Philadelphia, but never received a cent of prize money. In July, 1781, volunteered as corporal under Capt. Thomas Pollard, whose company was attached at Malvern Hill to the regiment under Col. Meriwether and Maj. Hardy. Its duty was guarding Burwell's warehouse on York River.

Section No. 217

SMITH, JOSEPH.—Pittsylvania, Sept. 17, 1832. Substituted in January, 1781, for Harmon Miller. Served under Capt. Charles Wall, Lt. Bates, En. Daniel Wilson. Was at Cabin Point six weeks, then joined Gen. Muhlenberg at Portsmouth. In a second tour substituted for his father, James Smith, in April. Served at Point of Fork, under Col. St. George Tucker. Discharged at Malvern Hill, July 28, 1781. Born in Maryland in 1763 and came to Halifax before the war.

Section No. 218

PETTIS, JOHN.—Spottsylvania, Aug. 7, 1832. Drafted in Caroline about 1779, under Capt. Philip Johnson and served at Williamsburg. Later was with Samuel Coleman in First Virginia, Continental Line, and was under Capt. Francis Cowherd and Col. Samuel Hawes. Was in the battles at Guilford and Eutaw, and was discharged at Salisbury about January, 1782. Total service, about eighteen months. Died July 1, 1833.

Section No. 219

SORRELL, JOHN.—Spottsylvania, Aug. 7, 1832. Born in Caroline about 1760. Volunteered, 1775, under Capt. Philip Buckner. Second tour, under Capt. Robert Ware, began in April, 1776, service being around Williamsburg. Third tour began May 1, 1781, under a draft in Spottsylvania. Was sent with eleven other men under Sergt. Benjamin Robinson to guard prisoners from the South to Staunton and Winchester. At Fredericksburg, was employed to roll back to the warehouses some tobacco that had been concealed. Drafted for Yorktown campaign under Capt. Coleman and was ill some time. Two redoubts were stormed Sunday evening and next morning he asked Dr. Tankard to allow him to report for duty. The captain and others having gone home sick he gave the papers to Reuben Plunkett, orderly sergeant, and reported fit for duty. Witnessed the British prisoners stack their arms and marched back further orders. Volunteered in first and second tours. Confined to house and lot for eleven years.

Section No. 220

STEARS, RICHARD.—Spottsylvania, Aug. 7, 1832. Born, Sept. —, 1762. Drafted in June, 1779, and served under Captains John White, Tankersley, and Holladay. Was at the surrender of Cornwallis.

Section No. 221

STEARS, JOHN.—Spottsylvania, Aug. 7, 1832. Born in 1755. Enlisted in Seventh Regiment, Virginia Line, under Capt. Oliver Towles, and Lt. Benj. Alsop. Served at Fredericksburg and Williamsburg. Was discharged for ill health in August, 1776. Died, Jan. 18, 1837.

Section No. 222

TURNLEY, FRANCIS.—Spottsylvania, Aug. 7, 1832. Born, 1762. In first tour, drafted under Capt. Croucher, October, 1780, and discharged at Petersburg. In second, drafted under Capt. Frank Coleman and served at Fredericksburg. In third, under Capt. Tankersley, he was in the fight at Osbornes and at the surrender of Cornwallis. Total service, ten months. Died Dec. 18, 1836.

Section No. 223

CHEW, HARRY.—Spottsylvania, Aug. 7, 1832. Born Sept. 23, 1758. First tour of duty was at the first of the Revolution under Capt. Brock, John Brock being a comrade. The second was under Capt. Beverley Winslow, whose company with that of Capt. John Craig was under Maj. George Thornton, and later, Col. Sampson Mathews. This tour was also to Williamsburg, which Gen. Scott abandoned at Arnold's approach. Col. Mathews retreated to Richmond and was there joined by Col. Samuel Temple, of Caroline. After Arnold's retreat, the command was ordered forward to Williamsburg, but was dismissed at Dincastle's Tavern, twelve miles west of that town, by Col. Innes, who succeeded Mathews. Third tour was under Winston, quartermaster of regiment under Mathews.

Fourth tour, under Capt. William Mills, was to Williamsburg to join Mathews. Last tour was as ensign under Capt. Francis Taliaferro, First Lt. Henry Bartlett, Second Lt. John Wigglesworth, and Thomas Towles, quartermaster. From rendezvous at Fredericksburg to Hampton the minute men were under Maj. Andrew Buchanan. Affiant was always a volunteer. (Note.—The tours were given as remembered and not in order of time.)

Section No. 224

TRIBBLE, GEORGE.—Spottsylvania, Sept. 3, 1832. Enlisted for nine months as minute man in Virginia Line, serving under Capt. Vivian Minor, of Caroline, and Col. Richard Johnson. Joined Maj. Andrew Buchanan at Williamsburg. Was out in six other tours under Capt. William Taliaferro and others. Joined Lafayette's army in Culpeper and was at siege of Yorktown. In one fight at Gloucester. Born in Caroline in 1757.

Section No. 225

VASS, PHILIP V.—Spottsylvania, March 3, 1833. Born in County, Feb. 17, 1763. Served three tours in 1781, under Captains Thomas Towles and Francis Coleman. In the last was substitute for Harry Chew. Served in the defense of Fredericksburg, in Lafayette's retreat, and in siege of Yorktown.

Section No. 226

STANARD, LARKIN.—Spottsylvania, Aug. 6, 1833. Born in County, May —, 1760. Cadet in U. S. service under Col. Mordecai Buckner, Lt. Col. Thomas Aylett, and Maj. James Hendricks. Later was private under Captains Joseph Brock, Thomas Bartlett, ——— Winslow, and ——— Craig. Under Richard Young was purchasing commissary. Enlisted Jan. 1, 1776, and served in New Jersey. Being oldest cadet was entitled to preference in case of vacancy, but Col. Buckner appointed his nephew, a junior cadet. Therefore affiant and several others went home at the close of the year, having ranked and messed as an officer. Was subsequently a volunteer private in four tours, campaigning about Williamsburg. Total service, twenty-three months.

Section No. 227

MOORE, ALEXANDER.—Spottsylvania, June 3, 1833. Born in County in 1760. Drafted about 1780, under Capt. Coleman and guarded Governor's palace at Williamsburg. Then enlisted under Serg't Major Thomas Hood and guarded Gen. Greene's baggage wagons. Ordered back from North Carolina with same wagons. Last tour was in Yorktown campaign. Total service, about thirteen months.

Section No. 228

FALCONER, SAMUEL.—Spottsylvania, Feb. 4, 1833. Born in Orange about 1757. Volunteered once, drafted twice. Served under Captains McWilliams, John Scott, and Francis Coleman. Last tour was at siege of Yorktown and in guarding prisoners to Winchester.

Section No. 229

ALSOP, BENJAMIN.—Spottsylvania, Nov. 6, 1832. Born in County, March 17, 1758. Marched about June 1, 1780, to Hillsboro, N. C., and made quartermaster there. Was under Capt. Thomas Minor, Lt. John Holladay, Second Lt. Lewis Holladay, En. Robert Durrett; regimental officers being Col. George Stubblefield, Lt. Col. Joseph Spencer, Maj. William Moseley. Was in battle at Camden, after which the army partially rallied at Hillsboro. In May, 1781, was nominated Lieutenant under Capt. Thomas Bartlett, and was transferred to the company of Capt. James Taylor. Joined Lafayette's army at Raccoon Ford, the regimental officers being Col. James Meriwether, and Majors Hardiman and McWilliams. Total service, nine months.

Section No. 230

SMITH, PHILIP.—Spottsylvania, Oct. 1, 1832. First tour from King and Queen in Seventh Division of Militia under Capt. Munstall Banks. The six other short tours were also in the Yorktown peninsula and under Captains Christopher Howard, William Courtney, John Lines, and John Haskins. Was drafted in every instance. Born in King and Queen in 1757. Moved to Spottsylvania in 1799.

Section No. 231

CASON, EDWARD.—Spottsylvania, Oct. 1, 1832. Born in County, 1752, died March 13, 1834. Was six months in Continental Line from Hanover, serving in Seventh Division under Capt. Price and Col. Holt Richardson. Was at battle of Camden. Next year was drafted from Spottsylvania and marched to Williamsburg under Capt. Legg and Col. Thomas Meriwether. Third tour was in guarding prisoners from Yorktown to Noland's Ferry, serving under Captain Croucher and Lt. Branham.

Section No. 232

CASON, WILLIAM.—Spottsylvania, Oct. 1, 1832. Served, 1776-'9, in Second Regiment, State Line, serving under Capt. Quarles, Lt. Benj. Edmundson, and Col. Thomas Minor. Was at Monmouth and Stony Point.

Section No. 233

POWELL, PTOLEMY.—Born, 1767. Just before the surrender of Cornwallis was accepted as substitute for a brother in the army at Gloucester, while the brother was home two weeks on furlough. Served under Maj. Campbell in same company with Enoch Breeden.

(NOTE:—This information is given by Breeden.)

Section No. 234

BREEDEN, ENOCH.—Spottsylvania, Oct. 1, 1832. Born in Maryland, Jan. —, 1759. Came to Charles City County, 1766. His father went into the army and never came back. Himself and mother then went to King William, where two brothers lived. Served several short tours from the summer of 1776, till October, 1781. being under Col. Hickman and Captains Mordecai Abraham, Christopher Thompson, Mordecai Booth, and Harry Quarles. Both volunteered and was drafted. Substituted for his married brothers, Moody and Caleb. King William County was very liable to depredation by British ships. The last service began in January, 1781, when he was under Captains Drury, Booth, and Abraham, of Col. Charles Dabney's First Regiment. Joined Gen. Stevens at Four Mile Creek in Henrico, retreated into Culpeper, crossing the Rappahannock at Ely's Ford and recrossing at Raccoon Ford. Then marching by Pogue's Mill, the army took the Marquis road to Mechunk Creek in Albemarle. In the advance to Richmond Steuben joined Lafayette. Affiant was then some time in camp at Sim's Neck, on Pamunky, and joined Gen. Weedon at White House Ferry. At siege of Yorktown was stationed at Ware Church near Gloucester. The three King William Companies discharged a few days before the surrender.

Section No. 235

PENDLETON, PHILIP.—Spottsylvania, Oct. 1, 1832. Born in County, April 6, 1758. Served twelve months in Continental Line as minute man. Capt. George Stubblefield going into the regular army, he was then under Capt. Francis Taliaferro. Next volunteered under Capt. J. Craig, and served fifty days, also at Williamsburg. The last tour was under Captains Harry Stubblefield and Francis Coleman, they being under Majors McWilliams and Hardyman. After surrender of Cornwallis, went with prisoners as far as Nolan's Ferry, serving under Capt. Thomas Croucher.

Section No. 236

PIERCE, JOHN.—Spottsylvania Sept. 3, 1832. Volunteered in August, 1775, under Capt. (later Col.) Joseph Brock. Guarded the public buildings at Williamsburg under Gen. Charles Scott. Discharged two years later. Second tour of two months also at Williamsburg and under Capt. Thomas Bartlett and Col. Thomas Nelson. Third tour began Jan. 10, 1781, when he served under Capt. John Carter as orderly at Fredericksburg and Hanover C. H. The fourth was next fall and under Capt. Nicholas Payne, he collected beeves and drove them to Williamsburg.

Section No. 237

JONES, THOMAS.—Spottsylvania, Sept. 3, 1832. Born, 1757. Enlisted for twelve months, serving under Captains Charles Bibbing (?) and Samuel Harris. The company was not to be attached to a regiment, but to be ready for any call. After discharge was ordered for duty and hired George Hampton as substitute.

Section No. 238

OBANNON, THOMAS.—Fauquier, Aug. 31, 1832. Born in 1757. Drafted Sept 4, 1780, under Capt. James Winn and marched into the Carolinas to join Smallwood and Morgan. Was at the taking of Rugely, but not in the battle of Cowpens because detailed to collect the sick and take them to Salisbury, N. C., after which he was ordered to take them on to Virginia. Was quartermaster sergeant.

Section No. 239

MOFFETT, JESSE.—Fauquier, Aug. 31, 1832. Born 1759. Served under Capt. Benjamin Harrison during fall of 1777, and a second tour of three months beginning in July, 1781.

Section No. 240

PAYNE, AUGUSTINE.—Fauquier, Aug. 31, 1832. Born, 1762. Tour of six months beginning in November, 1780, and under Capt. John Obannon at Williamsburg. Called out next fall, but excused because of injured foot.

Section No. 241

MONROE, GEORGE.—Fauquier, Aug. 31, 1832. First tour of six months began in November, 1780. Service was at Williamsburg and Richmond under Capt. John L. Chunn. Second of three months; was at siege of Yorktown and guarding prisoners to Winchester. Born in County, 1762.

Section No. 242

PAYNE, WILLIAM.—Fauquier, Aug. 31, 1832. Lived at Falmouth in 1776, and was captain of militia. Was often called out, usually four or five times each year, for an aggregate of three or four months annually. The enemy were making havoc in the slaves and tobacco, keeping the whole country in alarm, and burning in every direction, so that desperate exertions had to be made against them. His service was usually at various points on the Potomac and Rappahannock, the last tour being at the siege of Yorktown. In 1780, moved to Westmoreland and was made captain there.

Section No. 243

WITHERS, SPENCER.—Fauquier, Aug. 30, 1832. Born, 1756. Went out from Warrenton, summer of 1780, under Capt. Francis Triplett, to Hillsboro, N. C. Served in Morgan's brigade against the tories. Tarleton pursued Morgan forty miles to the Cowpens. Affiant was then sick. Next June was in Col. Edmund's regiment and stationed at Ruffin's Ferry, on the Pamunky. Was in the retreat to Raccoon Ford, where Gen. Wayne joined the army. Was at siege of Yorktown. Guarded prisoners to Winchester. Discharged at Ashby's Gap about Christmas.

Section No. 244

MURRAY, REUBEN.—Fauquier, Aug. 29, 1832. Born, 1762. First tour in spring of 1781, under Capt. Turner Morehead, and Colonels Armistead, Churchill and Dabney. Was at Williamsburg till the British advanced. Second tour at siege of Yorktown under

Captains James Winn and Linn Sharp and Col. Elias Edmonds. Was made sergeant. Guarded prisoners to Winchester and there discharged.

Section No. 245

ETHALL, ANTHONY.—Fauquier, Aug. 29, 1832. Born in Loudoun, Feb. —, 1757. Went out in September, 1775, serving six months under Capt. Simon Triplett. Witnessed the burning of Norfolk. Did guard duty at the old lighthouse near Hampton, which burned before he left the vicinity. Col. William Grayson and Maj. Lever Powell were regimental officers. From June till Christmas, same year, excepting about 10 days in harvest time, affiant was in same company guarding battery and breastworks. Drafted early in 1777, to guard Hessian prisoners on their way to Charlottesville. Company commander was Capt. Daniel Teagans. In summer of 1781, was drafted under Capt. Thomas Connor and Col. Meriwether and campaigned around New Kent C. H.

Section No. 246

WELCH, SYLVESTER, SR.—Fauquier, July 23, 1832. Born 1762. Enlisted in Northumberland, 1777, under Samuel Denny, in First Virginia Artillery, serving three years. Regimental officers, Col. Charles Harrison, Lt. Col. Edward Carrington, Maj. Christopher Holman. Company commander, Capt. Jonathan Dandridge. Was at Valley Forge and Monmouth.

Section No. 247

OWEN, ELISHA.—Powhatan, Aug. 6, 1838. Served about twelve months in 1780-'81. Married Elizabeth ———, in 1779. Died, 1832. Declaration by widow.

Section No. 248

AMMONETT, CHARLES.—Powhatan, Nov. 12, 1832. Born in Powhatan, Oct. 13, 1758. Served four tours under Captains

Thomas Harris and Edward Moseley. Was in a skirmish below Petersburg, where several of the enemy were killed. Guarded boats at Judes Ferry. Both volunteered and was drafted.

Section No. 249

STEWART, JOHN.—Spottsylvania, Aug. 7, 1832. Born, 1761. Enlisted in 1778, from Culpeper under Capt. James Purvis, Col. Francis Taylor, and Maj. John Roberts, and served till June, 1781, guarding prisoners. Later was drafted under Capt. Nicholas Payne and Col. Meriwether, served at Yorktown, and guarded prisoners to Winchester, about Dec. 1st. Declaration by widow.

Section No. 250

WILSON, ABRAHAM.—Spottsylvania, Aug. 7, 1832. Born in Spottsylvania, 1759. Drafted from Culpeper in February, 1779, under Capt. Joseph Strother, serving at Albemarle Barracks and on the seaboard. A second tour, under Capt. Frank Coleman, was at Yorktown. Service, eighteen months.

Officers of the Virginia Militia in the Revolution

PART III.

The lists here given for the counties of Albemarle, Amelia, Bedford, Berkley, Botetourt, Caroline, Chesterfield, Cumberland, Fauquier, Fluvanna, Frederick, Goochland, Greenbrier, Henrico, Loudoun, Louisa, Orange, Powhatan, Rockbridge, and Spottsylvania, were compiled directly from the County Order Book, excepting Albemarle (in part), and Spottsylvania. The records of Fluvanna and Greenbrier were found somewhat deficient, and those of Henrico were very much wanting. Nothing was found in Buckingham, Culpeper, Dinwiddie, Fairfax, Hampshire, Nottoway, Prince George, Prince William, or Stafford.

These lists give the date of nomination or commission, and wherever possible, the captains under whom the lieutenants and ensigns served. It is evident that the record was not always complete. In some instances an officer was undoubtedly sworn in, although only the date of recommendation can be found on the Order Book.

Where a name, as of "John Smith," appears twice, it is because it is not clear that in each instance the same person is designated. And as a higher rank usually means that the officer has previously served in one or more lower grades, only the highest rank found is given in the lists.

Where a date is given without any explanatory mark, it means that the person is known to have held the indicated rank in the year mentioned.

The special abbreviations used are the following:
Co. Lt.—County Lieutenant.
Cp.—Captain.
Lt.—Lieutenant (when there is nothing to show whether first or second.)

F. L.—First Lieutenant.
S. L.—Second Lieutenant.
En.—Ensign.
S.—Sworn into office.
A.—Appointed by county court.
R.—Recommended by county court.
N.—Nominated by county court.
    The three last expressions were all in use, but seem as a rule, to have the same force.

Com'd—Date of Commission by governor; bearer subsequently sworn in.

P'ner—Prisoner of war in hands of the enemy.

Res.—Resigned.

Section 251—Albemarle
A—(From Wood's History of Albemarle.)

Allen, David, Cp.
Ball, Erasmus
Chiles, Micajah
Davis, Isaac
————, John Lowery
Durrett, Richard
Flait, William
Foulk, Matthew
Frazier, Falzy
Garland, Edward
Gilliam, George, Lt.
Gilmer, George, Lt.
Harper, Richard
Harris, Richard
Henderson, John
Henderson, John
Henderson, Bennett
Henderson, William
Johnson, William
Lewis, Charles, Cp.
Lewis, Charles L.
Lewis, William, T, Sergt.

Lewis, Isham
Lewis, William
Lewis, Micajah
Lindsay, Reuben
Marks, John, Lt.
Marks, Hastings
Martin, John, Sergt.
Martin, Thomas, Jr., Corp.
Martin, Hudson
Martin, Thomas, Cp.
Mills, Frederick William, Cp.
Mills, Bernard
Mitchell, Thomas
Quarles, James, Cp.
Strachan, Thomas.
Thompson, Nelson
Walker, Thomas
Wood, William, Sergt.
Wood, William
Wood, Isaac
Wood, John
Wood, John

(NOTE:—The dates of commission for the above are May 2, and July 11, 1775.)

B—(*From Papers of George Gilmer.*)

Barksdale, Samuel
Bowen, Micajah
Boyd, William
Burke, Henry, Cp.
Burke, John, Cp.
Butler, Cp.
Carr
Carr, Makins
Collins, John
Dowell, Major
Dunn, James
Garland, Nathaniel, Lt.
Gentry, George
Gentry, James
Going, Sherod
Gooch, William, Lt.
Grayson, William, Cp.
Hall, Nathan
Hall, John
Hardin, George
Harris, Benjamin, Cp.
Harris Robert, Cp.
Harris, William
Hawkins, Reuben, Cp.
Hill, Richard
Huckstep, Charles
Hudson, John, Cp.
Johnston, Richard
Jordan, William

Keblinger, Adam
Leake, Mark, Cp.
Lewis, Nichols, Cp.
Lindsay, Reuben, Col.
Martin, John, Cp.
Maupin, Cornelius
Maupin, Daniel
Maupin, William
McCardle, Samuel
Meriwether, James
Meriwether, Thomas
Munday, Jonathan
Peper, John, Lt.
Leamond, Ephriam
Southerlin, Kenneth
Snow, Richard
Spradling, John
Spinner, Richard
Strange, David
Taylor, John
Thacker, Nathaniel
Thomas, Absolam
Thomas, John
Thompson, Leonard, Lt.
Thompson, Roger
Thompson, George, Lt.
Wheeler, Micajah
White, Daniel, Cp.
Wood, John

Woodson, Tarleton, Sergt.

C—(*From Order-Book of* 1783.)

Brisco, William, Cp.—S. May 8, 1783—vice James Wood.
Henderson, John, Lt.—1783.
James, Thomas, Cp.—S. May 8, 1783—vice John Henderson.
Moore, James, En.—S. May 8, 1783—under T. Jones.

Mosley, Daniel, En.—R. Nov. 13, 1783.
Nicholas, William, Col.—1783.
Reid, John, En.—R. May 8, 1783—under Brisco.
Thomas, Ralph, Cp.—R. Nov. 13, 1783—vice Benj. Harris.
Thomas, Joseph, Lt.—R. Nov. 13, 1783, under R. Thomas.
Wingfield, Charles, Lt.—R. May 8, 1783—under Jones.
Wood, James, Cp.—1783.
Woodson, William, Lt.—R. May 8, 1783—under Brisco.

Section 252—AMELIA

Anderson, Paulin, Cp., 1777.
Anderson, Henry, F. L., S. April 23, 1778—of Nottoway County.
Anderson, Francis, Jr., F. L, January 22, 1778—under Jones

Bagley, George, F. L., S. May 25, 1780.
Bass, William, En., S. April 23, 1778.
Beadle, John, S. L., N. June 22, 1780.
Bolling, Robert, Lt. (?), S. June 22, 1780.
Booker, Edmund, Lt. Col., S. May 25, 1780.
Booker, George, S. L., R. August 28, 1777—under E. Booker.
Booth, John, S. L., October, 26, 1780.
Bowling, Robert, Cp. S. October, 26, 1780—vice W. Jones.
Bridgforth, Thomas, S. L., S. June 22, 1780.
Brooking, Robert E., Cp., S. Sept. 20, 1777.
Brown, Thomas, En.? June 22, 1780.

Chaffin, Joshua, F. L., S. Oct. 26, 1780—under L. Ford.
Chappell, John, En., S. Oct. 26, 1780.
Cobbs, John C., S. L., R. June 22, 1780—under W. Craddock.
Cocke, Chastain, Cp., S. Sept. 20, 1777—of 19th Co.
Craddock, Henry, S. L., S. April 23, 1778.
Craddock, Richard, S. L., S. Jan. 22, 1778.
Craddock, Richard, ?, S. June 22, 1780.
Craddock, William Crass, Cp., S. June 22, 1778—vice Ward.
Craddock, Charles, En., S. June 26, 1776—(probably same as William C.)

Crowley, William, ?, S. June 22, 1780.
Dennis, John, Cp., S. April 23, 1778—vice Munford.
Durham, Joshua, F. L., R. Nov. 23, 1780—under R. Bowling.

Edward, Robert, En., S. Oct. 24, 1776.
Elliot, John, S. L., R. Sept. 20, 1777—under R. Graves.

Finney, William, Cp., S. Oct. 20, 1777.
Finney, John, En., S. Oct. 20, 1777.
Fitzgerald, Francis, F. L., S. May 25, 1780.
Ford, Lewis, Cp., S. March 25, 1779.
Ford, William, Cp., S. March 25, 1779—vice Brooks.
Fowlkes, Gabriel, Cp., S. April 22, 1779.
Fowlkes, Gabriel, Lt. Col., S. April 23, 1778.

Gibbs, William, S. L., S. March 25, 1779.
Giles, ———, Col., S. April 23, 1778.
Goode, Mack, En., R. October 26, 1880.
Gray, John, F. L., S. August 28, 1777—under T. Short.
Green, Abraham, Cp., S. June 22, 1780.
Green, Samuel, S. L., R. April 23, 1778.
Greenhill, William, Cp., S. Sept. 20, 1777.
Grigg, James, En., S. May 25, 1780.

Hall, Bowler, F. L., S. June 22, 1780.
Harrison, William, S. L., R. April 23, 1778—under Capt. Walker.
Holloway, William, En., R. Nov. 23, 1780.
Howson, John, En., S. Aug. 28, 1777—under W. Watson.
Hudson, Robert, Cp., R. Oct 26, 1780.

Irby, Charles, S. L., S. Aug 28, 1777—under N. Winn.

Jenkins, James, Col. S., July 27, 1780—2d Battalion.
Jennings, Joseph, Cp., S. Sept. 20, 1777.
Jeter, Presly, En., S. May 25, 1780.
Johnson, Arthur, En., S. Sept. 20, 1777—under P. Jones.
Jones, Richard, F. L., S. Oct. 26, 1780.
Jones, Batt, Lt. S. June 22, 1780.
Jones, Daniel, Cp., S. April 22, 1779.
Jones, Thomas, En., S. Sept. 20, 1777—under R. Ward.
Jones, William, Cp., S. Sept. 20, 1777.
Jones, Philip, Cp., R., June 22, 1780.
Jordan, Thomas, En., R. Nov. 27, 1777—under R. Winn.

Knight, John, ?, S. June 22, 1780.

Lewis, Griffin, S. L., S. Oct. 20, 1777.
Locke, Richard, En., S. Sept. 20, 1777.

Manere, John, S. L., S. Jan. 22, 1778—under W. Jones.
Marshall, Abraham, F. L., S. May 25, 1780.
Marshall, John, En., R. April 23, 1778.
Marshall, Alexander, S. L., R. Aug. 28, 1777—under B. Ward.
McNabb, Alexander, S. L., S. Aug. 28, 1777.
Mitchell, Thomas, En., R. Jan. 22, 1778—under R. Jones.
Mitchell, Thomas, —?—S. June 22, 1780.
Mitchell, Evans, En., S. Sept. 20, 1777—under A. Green.
Munford, Edward, Cp., May 25, 1780—of 20th Company.

Newman, Rice, En., R. Aug. 28, 1777—under A. Green.
Noble, Joseph, En., R. June 22, 1780.

Oglisby, Richard, Cp., S. May 25, 1780.
Osborne, Abner, ?, S. June 22, 1780.
Osborne, William, Jr., Cp., S. May 25, 1780.
Overton, Thomas Perkins, S. L., S. Oct. 26, 1780.

Randolph, Peter, F. L., S. Oct. 20, 1777.
Roberts, Jacob, En., S. May 25, 1780.
Roberts, Pleasant, Cp., S. June 22, 1780—vice P. Jones.
Roberts, Alexander, F. L., S. May 25, 1780.
Robertson, William, S. L., R. May 25, 1780—under R. Ogilsby.
Royall, John, F. L., S. June 22, 1780.
Royall, Littlebury, F. L., S. June 22, 1780.
Royall, William, F. L., S. Sept. 20, 1777.
Royall, John, S. L., S. Sept. 20, 1777.
Royall, John, F. L., S. ?, June 22, 1780.

Sherwin, Samuel, Col., A. April 23, 1778.
Short, Thomas, Lt. Col., S. May 25, 1780.

Tabb, Edward, Cp., R. April 23, 1778—under J. Jenkins.
Tabb, John, Col., R. Aug. 28, 1777.
Towers, John, Jr., En., S. May 25, 1780.
Tucker, Daniel, En., S. Aug. 28, 1777.

Vaughan, James, F. L., N. Oct, 26, 1780.
Vaughan, Robert, F. L., R. June 22, 1780—under E. Booker.
Vaughan, Robert, Cp., S. Sept. 20, 1777.
Walker, ———, Cp., 1777.
Walthall, John, F. L., S. April 22, 1779—under Capt. Finney.
Ward, Rowland, Jr., Cp., S. May 25, 1780—vice D. Jones.
Ward, Rowland, Sr., Maj., S. April 23, 1778.
Ward, John, En., R. Sept. 20, 1777.
Ward, Benjamin, Capt., 1777.
Watkins, Samuel, S. L., R. Nov. 23, 1780.
Watson, Luke, S. L., S. Oct. 20, 1777.
Watson, William, Cp., 1777.
Wells, William, En., S. Oct 20, 1777.
Wells, Thomas T., S. L., S. Sept. 20, 1777.
Williams, Philip, F. L., S. Sept. 20, 1777.
Winn, Richard, Cp., 1777.
Wilson, Charles, F. L., R. April 23, 1778.
Wilson, ———, Lt. Col., A. April 23, 1778.
Willson, Thomas Branch, Maj., S. Oct. 20, 1777—probably same as above.
Wood, William, Jr., S. L., S. Jan. 22, 1778—under P. Anderson.
Worsham, William, En., S. March 25, 1779.

Section 253—Augusta

NOTE:—See also Rockingham for Robert Craven, Robert Davis, Reuben Harrison, John Hopkins, Abraham Lincoln, William Nall, John Skidmore, and Daniel Smith.

Allen, William, Lt., S. April 17, 1782—under J. Campbell.
Anderson, William, Lt., R. April 17, 1782—under J. McKittrick.
Anderson, William, Cp., 1777.
Anderson, Robert, En, R. April 17, 1782—under J. McKittrick.
Anderson, Andrew, Cp., R. Aug. 18, 1781—vice Joseph Bell.
Anderson, George, S. L., R. May 18, 1779—under T. Rankin.
Anderson, George, En., S. Feb 20, 1781.
Baskins, Charles, Cp., R. Feb. 20, 1782—vice Zachary Johnson.
Baskins, James, F. L., S. Oct. 20, 1780.

Bell, Joseph, En., S. Aug. 15, 1780—under J. Dickey.
Bell, James, Cp. S. Aug. 15, 1780.
Bell, Joseph, Cp., S. Aug. 15, 1780—vice David Bell, res. Aug. 15, 1781.
Bell, David, Cp., 1777—died 1780.
Black, Samuel, S. L., S. Oct. 20, 1778—under R. McCreery.
Blair, Joseph, En., R. Feb. 17, 1778—under J. Cunningham.
Bogart, Cornelius, En., R. Sept. 19, 1780—under B. Wilson.
Boggs, Thomas, Cp. R. Aug. 19, 1778—vice M. Humble.
Bowyer, William, Lt. Col., S. Feb. 16, 1779—2d Batallion.
Boyd, John, En., R. May 20, 1777.
Bratton, George, Lt. S. May 22, 1782.
Bratton, James, Cp. R. Aug. 21, 1781—vice W. Kinkead.
Brown, John, Cp., S. May 15, 1781—vice J. Cartmill.
Brownlee, Alexander, En., R. May 19, 1778—refused to serve.
Buchanan, David, Lt., R. Aug. 18, 1781—under P. Buchanan.
Buchanan, William, En., S. Dec. 20, 1780—under S. McCutchen.
Buchanan, Patrick, Cp., 1777.

Calbraith, William, En., S. Mar. 22, 1782.
Cameron, Charles, Col., S. Feb. 20, 1782.
Campbell, John, Cp., S. April 17, 1782—vice J. Patterson.
Campbell, Charles Cp., 1777.
Campbell, Robert, F. L., S. March 17, 1778.
Carpenter, Michael, F. L., S. Aug. 19, 1778—under W. Lowther.
Cartmill, John, Cp., S. Nov. 21, 1780—vice R. McCreery.
Christian, Robert, Jr., S. L., S. Aug. 15, 1780—under F. Long.
Clark, Robert, Lt., S. Aug. 19, 1777.
Clemons, Casper, F. L., R. May 18, 1779—under T. Rankin.
Coger, Michael, Cp., S. Nov. 23, 1777—vice W. Naile.
Colbraith, William, En., S. March 22, 1782.
Connerly, Arthur, En., S. April 17, 1782.
Coulter, Michael, Lt., S. Feb. 20, 1781—2d Battalion.
Craven, Robert, Cp., 1777.
Crawford, Alexander, En., S. Nov. 11, 1780—under J. Cartmill.
Crawford, James, S. L., R. Aug. 19, 1777.
Crouch, Joseph, Cp., S. March 16, 1779.
Cunningham, John, Cp., S. Aug. 19, 1777.

Davis, Robert, Cp., 1777.

Day, Joseph, En., R. Aug 21, 1781—under G. Poage.
Dickey, John, Cp., S. Aug. 15, 1780—vice W. Henderson.
Ewing, James, En., R. 1777.
Finley, William, Cp., S. Aug. 15, 1780—vice R. Thompson.
Fleisher, Henry, En., S. June 20, 1781.
Fleisher, Henry, S. L., Oct. 22, 1778—under J. McCoy.
Frazier, James, S. L., S. Oct. 20, 1778.
Frazier, James, Cp., 1777.

Garner, John, S. L., R. Aug. 19, 1778.
Gibson, David, En., S. May 18, 1779—under J. Patterson.
Gibson, James, S. L., S. Oct. 20, 1778.
Gilmer, John, Cp., 1777.
Given (Gwin?), David, Cp., S. June 20, 1781—vice Oliver.
Given, John, Cp., S. Feb. 17, 1778—vice Laird.
Graham, James, En., S. Oct. 20, 1778.
Graham, Christopher, Lt., S. May 11, 1777.
Gray, David, Cp., 1777.
Gwin, Joseph, F. L., R. Aug. 21, 1781—under T. Hicklin.
Gwin, David, S. L., S. Feb. 16, 1777—became Cp.

Hamilton, Patrick, En., R. March 16, 1779.
Hamilton, Charles, Cp., S. June 18, 1782—vice D. Gwin.
Hamilton, Andrew, Jr., En., S. Sept. 15, 1778—under W. Kinkead.
Hamilton, John, Cp., R., Aug. 20, 1777—(Tygart's Valley).
Harper, Nicholas, F. L. (?), 1778.
Harris, Robert, S. L., S. Sept. 17, 1777—under S. McCutchen.
Harrison, Reuben, Cp., 1777.
Hempenstall, Abraham, En., S. April 20, 1778.
Henderson, William, Cp., 1777..went to Kentucky about 1780.
Hewitt, Thomas, Cp., 1777.
Hicklin, Thomas, Cp., S. March 17, 1778.
Hogshead, James, Jr., En., R. Aug. 19, 1778—under J. Trimble.
Hopkins, John, Cp., 1777.
Hughart, Thomas, Col., S. Sept. 19, 1780—2d Battalion.
Hull, Peter, Cp., S. June 20, 1781—vice J. McCoy.
Humphreys, Jonathan, Lt., S. Nov. 21, 1780.

Johnson, James, Lt., S. March 22, 1782—under C. Baskins.
Johnson, Zachary, Cp., S. Aug. 20, 1777—res. Feb. 20, 1782.

Kenny, Robert, Cp., S. Oct. 21, 1778—vice A. Robertson.
Kinkead, William, Cp., S. Sept. 15, 1778—vice A. Lockridge—res. Aug. 21, 1781.

Lincoln, Abraham, Cp., 1777.
Lockridge, Andrew, Maj., S. Sept. 15, 1779.
Logan, William, En., A. March 19, 1782—under S. McCutchen.
Long, Joseph, Lt., S. Nov. 22, 1780—under F. Long.
Long, Francis, Cp., 1777.
Lowderson (Robertson?), William, Cp., R. Aug. 19, 1777—(West Fork).
Lowther, William, Cp., R. Sept. 17, 1777—(West Fork).
Lyle, John, Cp., 1777.

Madison, Richard, S. L., R. May 19, 1778.
Mathews, Richard, En. R., Oct. 21, 1778—under J. Trimble.
Mathews, Sampson, Lt. Col., S. May 19, 1778.
Maxwell, Alexander, F. L., S. March 16, 1779.
McClenahan, William, En., R. Dec. 16, 1777—under A. Robertson.
McCoy, John, Cp., 1777.
McCreery, John, Lt. Col., S. Aug. 15, 1780.
McCreery, William, Lt., S. June 20, 1781—under C. Cameron.
McCreery, Robert, Cp., 1777.
McCune, John, F. L., S. Oct. 21, 1778—under R. Kenny.
McCutchen, Samuel, Cp., S. Sept. 17, 1777—under S. McCutchen.
McKenny, John, F. L., S. Sept. 17, 1777.
McKittrick, John, Cp., S. April 17, 1782—vice J. Trimble.
McKittrick, John, En., R. Aug. 21, 1781—vice Gardner.
McMahon, John, S. L., S. June, 16, 1778—under W. Anderson.
Meteer, Thomas, En., R. Aug. 19, 1778.
Mitchell, James, S. L., R. May, 19, 1778.
Moffett, George, Col., S. June 16, 1778.
Moore, Andrew, Cp., 1777.

Nall, William, Cp., 1777.

Oliver, John, Cp., R. Nov. 21, 1780—vice S. Vance.

Patterson, Joseph, Cp., S. May 18, 1779—vice W. Anderson.
Peebles, John, Cp., 1777.
Pence, George, Cp., 1777.

Perry, Joshua, En., S. May 22, 1782.
Poage, James, Lt., S. Mar. 20, 1782.
Poage, John, Jr., En., S. Mar. 20. 1782.
Poage, George, Cp., S. June 20, 1781—vice Oliver—2d Battalion.
Pringle, Samuel, Cp., 1777.

Rankin, James, En., R. May 18, 1779.
Rankin, Thomas, Cp., S. May 18, 1779—vice R. Kenny.
Reader, Anthony, Cp., R. Aug. 19, 1777—vice Adam Reader.
Reader, Adam, Cp., 1777.
Robertson, William, Cp., S. March 16, 1779.
Robertson, Alexander, S. L., R. Aug. 19, 1778—under R. Kenny.
Robertson, Alexander, Maj., S. Oct. 21, 1778.
Rucker, Samuel, Lt., S. May 15, 1781—under J. Oliver.

Scott, Alexander, S. L., R. Dec. 16, 1777—under A. Robertson, res. 1781.
Seybert, Nicholas, F. L., S. March 16, 1778—under J. McCoy.
Shaw, Robert, S. L., R. Aug. 19, 1777—under T. Smith.
Shirley, Valentine, En., R. Aug. 19, 1777.
Simpson, Alexander, Cp., S. Nov. 18, 1778.
Skidmore, John, Cp., 1777.
Smith, Daniel, Cp., 1777.
Smith, Thomas, Cp., 1777.
Smith, John, En., S. Sept. 17, 1777—under R. McCutchen.
Steel, James, En., S. Oct. 20, 1778—under R. Thompson.
Stephenson, John, Cp., 1777.
Stewart, Ralph, Cp., 1777.
Stewart, Alexander, Cp., 1777.

Tate, William, Cp., S. Aug. 21, 1781.
Tate, James, Cp., 1777—killed at Guilford.
Teter, Paul, Cp., 1777.
Thomas, James, En., S. Aug. 19, 1778.
Thompson, Robt., Lt., S. Nov. 21, 1781.
Thompson, Robert, Cp., 1777.
Thompson, Alexander, Col., R. May 19, 1778—refused to serve.
Trimble, James, Cp., S. Sept. 15, 1778—vice G. Moffett.

Vance, Samuel, Col., R. Aug. 21, 1781.

Waddell, Joseph, Lt., S. Aug. 15, 1780—under W. Henderson.
Warwick, Jacob, F. L., S. March 16, 1779—under S. Vance.
Warwick, Jacob, Cp., R. March 20, 1777.
Wauchub, John, S. L., S. Sept. 19, 1780.
Westfall, Jacob, Jr., F. L., R. Sept. 19, 1780—under B. Wilson.
White, John, Lt., S. April 20, 1779.
Wier, Samuel, En., R. May 20, 1777.
Wilson, John, Maj., S. March 20, 1781—2d Battalion.
Wilson, David, En., S. Aug. 15, 1780—vice Brownlee.
Wilson, Benjamin, Cp., S. March 17, 1778—(Tygart's Valley).
Wilson, Matthew, Cp., S. Nov. 23, 1777.

Young, Patrick, En., S. May 15, 1781—under C. Cameron.
Young, James, S. L., R. Oct. 21, 1778—under J. Young.
Young, John, Cp., 1777—res. Nov. 18, 1778.

Section 254—BEDFORD

Adams, Robert, Cp., R. Feb. 24, 1778.
Adams, James, S. L., R. Feb. 24, 1778.
Adams, James, Cp., R. May 29, 1781.
Alexander, Robert, Cp., S. June 27, 1779.
Anderson, Jacob, S. L., R. June 29, 1779.
Anthony, Joseph, S. L., A. Oct. 26, 1778.
Arthur, Benjamin, Cp., R. Sept. 29, 1781.

Beard, David, Cp., S. Sept. 23, 1780.
Beard, Samuel, Cp., S. Sept. 23, 1780.
Brown, Shildrake, En., S. Aug. 28, 1780.
Bryan William, En., S. Dec. 28, 1778.
Bullock, Josias, Cp., S. April 24, 1781.
Bullock, James, Cp., S. Feb. 28, 1780.
Burnley, Harry, En., S. May 28, 1781.
Burnley, Henry, F. L.,R. April 24, 1781.
Burns, James, S. L., R. Aug. 28, 1780.
Butler, Alexander, F. L., S. Aug. 28, 1780.
Butterworth, Benjamin, Lt., R. Sept. 24, 1781.

Callaway, James, Jr., Cp., R. Oct. 22, 1781.
Callaway, John, Maj., R. Sept. 24, 1781.

Callaway, Charles, Cp., S. April 24, 1781.
Callaway, James, Co. Lt., S. Dec. 28, 1778.
Callaway, Chesley Dudley, F. L., S. Sept. 28, 1778—removed from County, 1779.
Callaway, William, Lt. Col., S. March 23, 1778.
Campbell, John, En., R. May 23, 1780.
Charter, Thomas, Cp., R. May 28, 1781.
Cheetwood, Jace, En., S. May 24, 1779.
Chiles, John, Cp., S. Nov. 24, 1778—res. Sept. 24, 1781.
Clark, Micajah, En., R. Sept. 24, 1781.
Clark, Robert, Cp., S. Sept. 28, 1778.
Clayton, En., S. March 27, 1780.
Clayton, John, Cp., S. April 24, 1781.
Cobb, Charles, Cp., R. Feb. 28, 1780.
Cobb, Robert, F. L., R. Nov. 22, 1779.
Cobb, Edward, S. L., R. Nov. 22, 1779.

Doggett, Chatton, Cp., S. Feb. 28, 1780.
Davis, Joseph, S. L., R. Nov. 23, 1778—under T. Arthur.
Davis, Samuel, F. L., R. Nov. 23, 1778—under T. Arthur.
Davis, Henry, F. L., R. Feb. 24, 1778.
Demoss, Thomas, F. L., S. May 24, 1779.
Divers, John, F. L., R. May 28, 1781.
Dooley, George, F. L., R. May 24, 1779.

Early, Jacobus, F. L., R. May 28, 1781.
Early, Jacob, Cp., R. Feb. 24, 1778.
Early, Jeremiah, Col., S. Dec. 28, 1778.
Eidson, Henry, En., R. Sept. 24, 1781.
Ewing, William, F. L., S. Sept. 23, 1780.

Farley, Francis, En., S. Sept. 23, 1780.
French, Daniel, En., S. June 26, 1780.
Franklin, Edmund, En., R. Feb. 24, 1778.
Franklin, Owen, En., R. Feb. 24, 1778.
Fuqua, Moses, S. L., S. Feb. 28, 1780.

Gilbert, Samuel, F. L., R. May 28, 1781.
Gilbert, John W., Cp., S. Nov. 22, 1779.
Gilbert, Daniel, S. L., S. Nov. 22, 1779.
Gilbert, Preston, Lt., res. Sept. 24, 1781.

Gilliam, Zachariah, En., S. Sept. 28, 1778.
Gilliam, Zachariah, S. L., R. Nov. 22, 1779.
Green, James, S. L., S. July 25, 1780.
Green, Moses, F. L., S. Feb. 28, 1780.
Greer, James, F. L., R. Sept. 24, 1781— (Green?).
Griffith, Benjamin, En., R. Nov. 23, 1778.
Gwatkins, Charles, Cp., R. Sept. 24, 1781.

Haile, Richard, En,. R. April 26, 1779.
Haynes, Parmenas, Cp., R. Sept. 24, 1781.
Hayth, Thomas, F. L., S. April 24, 1781—(Heath?).
Helm, John, S. L., S. March 27, 1780.
Helm, Thomas, F. L., S. Feb. 22, 1779.
Henderson, William Gent, En., R. May 28, 1781.
Hudnall, William, F. L., S. May 25, 1778.
Hunter, John, Jr., En., S. Nov. 22, 1779.

Innes, Harry, En., Oct. 22, 1781.
Irvine, Andrew, F. L., S. May 28, 1781.
Irvine, John, S. L., S. March 27, 1780.
Irvine, Robert, F. L., S. June 29, 1779.

James, William, F. L., R. Oct 25, 1779.
Jeter, Henry, F. L., R. May 28, 1781.
Johnson, Thomas, En., S. Dec. 28, 1778.
Jones, Thomas, En., R. April 24, 1781
Jones, William, F. L., S. Feb. 28, 1780.
Jordan, William, Cp., S. April 24, 1781.

Leftwich, Augustine, F. L., S. May 28, 1781.
Leftwich, William, Lt. Col., S. Feb. 28, 1780.
Leftwich, Uriah, En., S. May 24, 1779.
Logwood, Thomas, Cp., R. Sept. 24, 1781.
Lumpkin, Thomas, En., R. April 24, 1781.
Lynch, Anselm, F. L., R. Sept. 24, 1781.
Lynch, Charles, Esq., Col., R. Feb. 24, 1778.

Martin, David, S. L., S. March 22, 1779.
McIroy, Hugh, F. L., S. March 27, 1780—(McElroy?).
McReynolds, Thomas, Cp., S. Nov. 12, 1779.
Milam, William, S. L., R. Sept. 24, 1781.

Miller, Simon, Jr., En., R. July 26, 1779.
Mitchell, Daniel, En., S. May 24, 1779.
Moon, Jacob, Jr., En., R. June 29, 1779.
Moore, Jacob, S. L., S. Aug. 28, 1780.
Moseley, Arthur, S. L., R. June 29, 1779.
Murray, Thomas, Lt., R. Oct. 22, 1781.

Namee, Cornelius, S. L., R. July 26, 1779.
Nance, Thomas, En., S. May 24, 1779.

Otley, John, Cp., R. Mar. 23, 1778—(Ottey?)

Parrow, Daniel, En., S. Aug. 28, 1780.
Pate, Matthew, F. L., R. Feb. 28, 1780.
Pate, Anthony, Cp., R. Feb. 24, 1778.
Pate, Thomas, En., S. Nov. 23, 1778.
Patrick, John F., gent., En., S. Feb. 28, 1780.
Phelps, John, F. L., R. Feb. 24, 1778.
Poindexter, Joseph, Cp., S. Sept. 28, 1778.
Price, Bowen, Cp., R. May 28, 1781.
Price, Brown, F. L., S. June 29, 1779.

Quarles, John, Col., res. Dec. 28, 1778.

Rentfree, Isaac, F. L., S. Nov. 23, 1778.
Rentfree, William, Cp., S. May 25, 1778.
Rentfro, Isaac, En., R. May 28, 1781.
Rentfro, Mark, En., S. Feb. 28, 1780.
Rice, Benjamin, F. L., R. April 24, 1781.
Richeson, Jonathan, Cp. R. Feb. 24, 1778.
Russell, James, S. L., R. Feb. 28, 1780.

Slaughter, John. En., R. Feb. 26, 1781.
Smith, Jonathan, S. L., R. April 26, 1779.
Steel, Alexander, F. L., S. Nov. 22, 1779.
Stith, Joseph, En., S. Aug. 28, 1780.

Talbott, Haile, Cp., S. Aug. 28, 1780.
Tate, Jesse, F. L., S. May 25, 1778.
Tate, Edmund, S. L., R. May 26, 1778.
Taylor, Skelton, F. L., S. Aug. 28, 1780.
Terrill, Harry, Maj., S. Feb. 28, 1780.

Terrill, Peter, Cp., S. Feb. 28, 1780.
Terry, William, Cp., S. May 28, 1781.
Thornhill, William, En., R. May 24, 1779—under Capt. Ottey.
Trigg, William, Lt. Col., S. Dec. 28, 1778.
Trigg, John, Cp., R. Feb. 24, 1778.
Turnbull, George, F. L., S. Aug. 28, 1780.

Vardiman, William, F. L., S. May 24, 1779.

Walden, Richard, En., S. Aug. 29, 1780.
Ward, John, Jr., En., R. Sept. 24, 1781.
Ward, John, gent., Maj., S. March 22, 1779—res. Sept. 24, 1781.
Watkins, Robert, Cp., S. May 25, 1778.
Watts, Thomas, Cp., R. Feb. 24, 1778.
Wood, Peter, F. L., R. April 26, 1779.
Wooten, Hinman, En., S. Nov. 24, 1778.
Wright, David, Cp., R. May 24, 1779.

Section 255—Berkeley

Baldwin, John, Cp., 1780.
Bameslee, F. L., R. May 15, 1781—under E. Lucas.
Buckles, Robert, Jr., S. L., S. May 15, 1781—under W. Lucas.
Buchannon, Alexander, En., May 15, 1781—under Porterfield.

Clarke, George, Cp., 1781.
Collitt, Isaac, Lt., R. May 15, 1781.
Cook, Giles, Jr., Lt., R. May 15, 1781—under R. Ransom.
Crane, James, En., A. Nov. 19. 1776.

Downe, John, En., R. May 15, 1781—under J. McCormick.
Druggett, James, En., R. Nov. 21, 1780—under C. Morrow.
Dundane, James, Cp., 1780.

Fink, Jacob, En., R. Sept. 18, 1781—under A. Noble.

Hart, John, Cp., R. April 17, 1781.
Hunter, David, Jr., Lt., R. April 17, 1781—under J. Hart.

Jones, John, En., R. May 15, 1781—under J. Richardson.

Lucas, William, Cp., R. May 15, 1781—vice E. Lucas .
Lucas, Edward, Cp., res. March 20, 1781.

McCormick, John, Cp., S. May 15, 1781.
Metcalf, Allen, En., R. May 15, 1781—under J. Swearingen.
Miller, Zachariah, En., R. April 17, 1781.
Morrow, Charles, Cp., 1780.

Noble, Anthony, Cp., 1781.

Pendleton, Philip, gent., Col., A. April 15, 1777—vice V. Swearingen.
Porterfield.

Ransom, Richard, Cp., R. May 15, 1781—vice E. Worthington.
Richeson, James, Cp., R. May 15, 1781.

Sanders.
Shirley, David, En., R. May 15, 1781—under G. Clark.
Snider, Jacob, Lt., R. Sept. 18, 1781.
Snider, Jacob, Jr., Cp., S. May 15, 1781.
Snider, Nathaniel, Lt., R. Aug. 15, 1780.
Stephens, Robert, Cp.—res. Dec. 17, 1776.
Sturgis, William, En., R. May 15, 1781—under R. Ransom.
Swearingen, Josiah, Cp., 1781.
Swearingen, Van, gent., Co. Lt., A. Feb. 15, 1777.

Thornberry, Thomas, Lt., R. May 15, 1781—under J. Swearingen.

Veal (?), David, En., R. Sept. 18, 1781—under A. Noble.

Washington, Samuel, Co. Lt., res. Feb. 15, 1777—brother to Gen. Washington.
Willis, Robert Carter, gent., Lt. Col., A. Feb. 15, 1777—vice P. Pendleton.
Worthington, Ephriam, Cp., 1781.

Section 256—Botetourt

Allen, Hugh ("Big Mouth"), S. L., R. May 10, 1781—under Pryor.
Anderson, John, Cp., 1777.
Armstrong, Andrew, F. L., R. April 12, 1781—under J. Neely, Jr.
Armstrong, John, Cp., 1778.

Baird, John, Cp., A. July 12, 1781—vice Hanley.
Barnett, Cp., 1781.
Bollar, John, Cp., S. April 8, 1779.
Brown, ———, Cp., 1777.

Cartmill, Thomas, Cp., S. May 11, 1780.
Cartmill, Henry, Lt., R. April 13, 1780—under J. Cartmill.
Cartmill, John, Cp., R. April 13, 1780—in Logan's old company.
Collin, Moses, En., S. May 13, 1777.
Cook, ———, Cp., 1777.
Crockett, Hugh, Maj., S. March 10, 1778.

Donally, Andrew, Maj., R. March 10, 1778.
Dean, ———, Cp., 1778.

Earn, ———, Cp., 1781.
Eavons, ———, Cp., 1781.
Eddins, David, En., R. April 12, 1781—under J. Martin.
Estill, Wallace, F. L., R. April 12, 1781—under J. Galloway.

Fleming, James, En., R. April 12, 1781—under Hanley.
Frazier, George, F. L., A. July 12, 1781—under J. Baird.

Galloway, John, Cp., R. April 12, 1781.
Gillis, Thomas, En., A. April 13, 1781—under J. Wood.
Gilmore, ———, Cp., 1777.
Ginn (?), ———, Cp., 1778.
Givens, ———, Cp., 1777.
Gordon, William, S. L., R. April 12, 1781—under Eavons.

Hall, James, Cp., 1777.
Hamilton, William, Cp., 1777.
Hamilton, Andrew, Cp., 1777.
Hampkins, Uriah, En., R. May 10, 1781—under Pryor.
Hanly, ———, Cp., 1781.
Harley, ———, Cp., 1778.
Henderson, James, Lt. Col., R. March 10, 1778.
Holstin, ———, Cp., 1781.
Holster, ———, Cp., 1780.
Hull, Peter, Cp., 1780.
Hutcheson, James, S. L., A. April 13, 1781—under Smith.

Lewis, John, En., R. April 12, 1781—under J. Lewis.
Lewis, John, Cp., R. April 12, 1781—of New Company.
Lewis, Andrew, F. L., R. April 12, 1781—under J. Lewis.
Lewis, Samuel, Col., R. March 10, 1778.
Lockhart, Patrick, Maj., A. July 12, 1781.
Logan, John (?), Cp., 1778.
Loony, ———, Cp., 1781.

Martin, Josiah, Cp., 1781.
May, David, Cp., 1781.
McArnold, William, S. L., R. April 13, 1780.
McClenahan, William, Lt. Col., A. July 12, 1781—vice T. Rowland.
McFarran, Samuel, En., A. April 13, 1781—under Smith.
McFarran, Rowland, Cp., 1777.
McGeorge, Thomas, En., R. April 12, 1781—under Eavons.
McMurtry, ———, Cp., 1778.
McNeely, William, S. L., R. April 12, 1781—under J. Barnett.
McRoberts, John, S. L., A. Jan. 12, 1781—under P. Lockhart.
Mills, ———, Cp., 1781.

Neely, ———, Cp., 1781.
Neely, Robert, S. L., R. April 12, 1781—under J. Neely.
Neely, James, Jr., Cp., R. April 12, 1781—vice W. McClenahan.
Neely, William, En., S. April 15, 1778.

Pauling, ———, Cp., 1778.
Paxton, John, Cp., 1777.
Paxton, William, Cp., 1777.
Peck, Adam, En., A. Jan. 12, 1781—under P. Lockhart.
Poage, George, Col., S. Sept. 3, 1778.
Pryor, ———, Cp., 1780.

Reaburn, Joseph, S. L., A. July 12, 1781—under H. Watterson.
Reaburn, James, En., R. April 12, 1781—under Barnett.
Robinson, Isaac, S. L., A. July 12, 1781—under Pawlings.
Robinson, ———, Cp., 1778.
Robinson, John, Cp., before 1777.
Robinson, Hercules, Cp., 1777.
Robinson, William, Lt. Col., res. April 12, 1781.
Rowland, Thomas, Lt. Col., R. April 12, 1781.
Rutledge, John, F. L., A. July 12, 1781—under H. Watterson.
Rutledge, George, Cp., A. July 12, 1781—vice J. Woods.

Scott, William, En., A. Sept. 13, 1781—under J. Baird.
Semley, Alexander, En., R. April 13, 1780.
Skillern, George, Co. Lt., R. July 13, 1780.
Smith, James, Cp., 1778.
Smith, Henry, Cp., 1778.
Stewart, John, Co. Lt., R. March 10, 1778.

Tosh, James, En., R. April 12, 1781—under J. Neely.

Vimands, Elijah, En., A. July 12, 1781—under Smith.

Section 257—Caroline

Alcock, Thomas, Lt., S. Dec. 1777.

Baynham, Gregory, F. L., S. March, 1778—under R. Graham.
Beazley, Thomas, En., R. May, 1781.
Boutwell, John, Lt., S. May, 1778.
Brame, John, En., R. Feb., 1778—set aside by court.
Broaddus, Thomas, F. L., Nov., 1779—under Fletcher.
Buckner, Richard, Maj., S. Feb., 1778.
Buckner, Philip, Cp., S. Dec., 1777.
Buckner, William, Cp., S. Nov., 1777.

Coleman, Daniel, F. L., R. May, 1779—under G. Madison.
Coleman, Julius, S. L., R. May, 1779—under G. Madison.
Coleman, Samuel, Cp., S. Jan. 1779—vice P. Johnson.
Collins, William, Lt., S. June 12, 1779.
Connor, William, S. L., R. May, 1779.
Connor, Francis, En., S. Nov., 1777.

Daniel, James, En., R. Nov., 1779—under Fletcher.
Dejarnet, Joseph, F. L., R. May, 1781—under J. Sutton.
Downer, John, Lt., S. Nov., 1777.
Durritt, William, Cp., S. June 12, 1778—vice W. Marshall.
Durritt, Richard, F. L., S. June 12, 1778.

Ellis, Thomas, En., S. March, 1779—under R. Graham.

Faulkner, Johnson, F. L., R. Nov., 1777.
Fitzhugh, John, Lt., S. Dec., 1777.
Fletcher, ———, Cp., 1779.

Graham, Duncan, Jr., S. L., S. March, 1779—under R. Graham.
Graham, William, Lt., S. Dec., 1777.
Graham, Robert, Cp., S. March, 1778.
Gravatt, John, En., R. Jan., 1779—under S. Coleman.
Gray, William F., F. L., R. May, 1781—under Jameson.
Guy, Thomas, F., S. L., R. May, 1781—under J. Sutton.
Guy, George, Cp., S. Nov., 1777.

Hall, John, En., R. Jan., 1779—under P. Stern.
Hawes, Thomas, En., R. May, 1779.
Higgen, Joel, En., R. May, 1779.
Hord, Thomas, F. L., S. Aug., 1778—under W. Streshly.
Hord, James, F. L., Aug., 1778.
Hord, John, Lt., S. May, 1778.

Jameson, David, En., S. Dec., 1777.
Jeter, Ambrose, En., R. May, 1778.
Johnson, Philip, Maj., S. Jan., 1779—vice J. Minor.
Jones, Thomas, F. L., R. Nov., 1778—under E. Jones.
Jones, John, Cp., res. Nov., 1777.

Kay, James, En., S. Jan., 1778.

Long, William, F. L., R. Jan., 1779.
Long, John, Cp., S. Feb., 1778.
Lowry, Thomas, Col., S. June 12, 1778.

Madison, George, Cp., R. May, 1779—vice J. Marshall.
Marshall, John, Cp., S. Dec., 1777.
Mitchell, William, En., R. Nov., 1779.

New, Anthony, Cp., S. Dec., 1777.
Norment, Samuel, En., S. Dec., 1777.
Norment, John, Lt., S. Dec., 1777.

Quarles, Roger, Cp., res. May, 1779.

Rawlins, Samuel, En., R. Feb., 1778.
Rennolds, James, S. L., R. Nov., 1779.
Richeson, Joseph, Cp., S. Jan., 1779—res. May, 1781.
Roy, Mungo, En., R. Nov., 1777.

Sale, Samuel, S. L., R. Nov., 1779.
Samuel, William, En., R. May, 1779.
Samuel, Reuben, Lt., S. Jan., 1778.
Streshly, William, Cp., 1779.
Sterns, Peyton, Cp., 1778.
Sutton, James, Cp., R. May, 1781.
Temple, Samuel, Cp., S. Nov., 1777.
Terrell, George, En., S. Dec., 1777.
Thilman, John, Cp., res. Nov., 1777.
Thompson, John, Lt., S. Dec., 1777.
Thornton, Anthony, Jr., Lt. Col., S. Nov., 1777.
Thornton, George, Lt., S. Dec., 1777.
Timberlake, Lewis, S. L., S. Dec., 1777—under P. Johnson.
Tompkins, Francis, Cp., R. May, 1779—vice W. Durrett.
Tompkins, Robert, Cp., R. May, 1779.
Turner, Daniel, Lt., S. Feb., 1778.
Twiner, Daniel, S. L., R. Nov., 1777.
Tyler, Richard, S. L., R. Oct., 1779—under F. Tompkins.
Tyler, John, Lt., S. Dec., 1777.
Tyler, George, S. L., R. May, 1779—under R. Tompkins.
Upshur, Jeremiah, F. L., R. Nov., 1779—under Streshly.
Upshur, James, gent., Lt. Col., S. March, 1778.
White, Ambrose, En., R. Nov., 1778.
White, Chilion, Lt., S. Dec., 1777.
Winn, Benjamin, F. L., S. July, 1779.
Woolfolk, John, Lt., S. Jan., 1779.
Woolfolk, Charles, Lt., S. May, 1778.
Wyatt, Richard, En., S. Feb., 1778.

Section 258—Charlotte

Bacon, ———, Cp., 1777.
Brown, Langston, Lt., S. Dec., 1777.
Friend, ———, Cp., 1777.
Goode, ———, Cp., 1777.
Harvey, ————, Cp., 1777.

Hubbard, Cp., 1777.
Hubbard, William, Maj., S. June, 1780—(same as preceding).
Jameson, William, gent., Cp., S. November, 1779.
Morton, Jacob, Cp., S. July, 1779.
Morton, Josiah, Lt. Col., S. June, 1780.
Morton, Joseph, S. L., S. Nov., 1777.
Morton, William, Cp., 1777.
Read, Edmund, Lt., S. Nov., 1777.
Read, Jonathan, Lt., S. Nov., 1779.
Thornton, Francis, S. L., S. March, 1780.
Watkins, Joel, Col., S. August, 1780.
Watson, William, En., S. November, 1777.

Section 259—Chesterfield

Archer, Field, En., A. March 2, 1781.
Archer, Henry, S. L., S. Oct. 3, 1777—res. March 2, 1781.
Archer, John, F. L., S. Oct. 3, 1777—under A. Walthall.
Armistead, Robert, S. L., R. Oct. 3, 1777—under R. Booker.
Barker, John, Cp., A. June 6, 1777.
Barker, Richard, Cp., A. June 6, 1777—vice T. Bolling.
Bass, Joseph, En., A. April 6, 1781—under B. Branch.
Bass, Joseph, Lt. Col., S. Jan. 4, 1777.
Bass, Archibald, Cp., A. May 5, 1780.
Black, William, Cp., R. Jan. 3, 1777.
Bolling, Thomas, Maj., S. Jan. 4, 1777.
Booker, Richard, Cp., S. Aug. 1, 1777.
Botte, John, Co. Lt., S. Jan. 4, 1777.
Bough, ———, Cp., 1777.
Bragg, William, F. L., A. Mar. 6, 1778.
Branch, Edward, F. L., A. April 6, 1781.
Branch, Benjamin, gent., Cp., res. May 5, 1780.
Branch, James, En., R. Oct. 3, 1777.
Brooking, Robert, En., A. Aug. 6, 1779.
Cheatham, Matthew, S. L., A. April 6, 1781.
Cheatham, Samuel, S. L., S. Dec. 5, 1777.
Cheatham, Henry, Cp., S. Aug. 1, 1777.

Clark, Sallyson, En., R. Oct. 3, 1777.
Cogbill, George, F. L., A. Nov. 3, 1780.
Cogbill, ———, Cp., res. Nov. 3, 1780.
Covington, Thomas, S. L., A. March 6, 1778.
Covington, Richard, En., R. Nov. 7, 1777.
Covington, Thomas, F. L., S. Dec. 5, 1777—under R. Booker.
Dance, Ezekiel, S. L., A. April 6, 1781—under B. Ward.
Elam, Bartilot, En., A. March 2, 1781—under H. Cheatham
Elam, Samuel, S. L., A. Nov. 7, 1777.
Elam, Richard, S. L., S. Nov. 7, 1777.
Elam, Branch, En., S. Nov. 7, 1777—res. March 2, 1781.
Ellyson, Onan, En., S. Oct. 3, 1777.
Farmer, John, Jr., F. L., S. Oct. 3, 1777—under H. Cheatham.
Farrar, John, S. L., R. Oct. 3, 1777—under T. Wooldridge.
Fowler, Luke, S. L., S. Aug. 4, 1780—under R. Wooldridge.
Fowler, John, S. L., S. Oct. 3, 1777—under R. Goode.
Gibbs, William, En., R. Oct. 3, 1777.
Goode, Thomas, F. L., A. May 5, 1780.
Goode, Francis, gent., Cp., R. Oct. 3, 1777—res. Dec. 5, 1777.
Graves, King, Cp., A. Nov. 3, 1780—vice Cogbill.
Harris, ———, Cp., 1777.
Haskins, Robert, Col., S. Aug. 1, 1777.
Hill, William, En., S. July 7, 1780—under G. Markham.
Hill, John, F. L., S. Oct. 3, 1777—under R. Booker.
Hylton, John, En., R. Oct. 3, 1777—under B. Moseley.
Logwood, Archibald, F. L., S. Oct. 3, 1777—under T. Wooldridge.
Markham, George, Cp., S. Dec. 5, 1777.
Moodie, James, F. L., S. Dec. 5, 1777—under F. Goode.
Moseley, William, En., S. Nov. 7, 1777.
Moseley, Blackman, F. L., S. Oct. 3, 1777—under Bough.
Newberry, Joseph, S. L., S. Oct. 3, 1777—under B. Moseley.
Osborne, Edward, En., R. Sept. 6, 1776.
Pankey, Stephen, F. L., Oct. 3, 1777—under G. Markham.
Patterson, David, F. L., S. Oct. 3, 1777—under R. Goode.
Polard, Thomas, S. L., A. March 2, 1781—under Bough.
Randolph, William, Cp., S. Dec. 5, 1777—res, Aug. 6, 1779.
Robertson, John, F. L., A. Aug. 6, 1779—under R. Haskins.
Robertson, George, Lt. Col., A. June 4, 1779.
Rowlett, John, En., R. Dec. 5, 1777.

Rowlett, William, En., A. April 6, 1781.
Royall, John, F. L., A. Aug. 6, 1779—under J. Archer.
Scott, Walter, S. L., S. Oct. 3, 1777.
Taylor, Joseph, En., S. Dec. 5, 1777.
Walthall, William, En., A. Nov. 3, 1780.
Walthall, Archibald, Cp., S. Oct. 3, 1777—vice G. Robertson.
Ward, Benjamin, Cp., A. Aug. 6, 1779—vice W. Randolph.
Wells, Isham, Lt., S. July 7, 1780—under B. Ward.
Wells, Joseph, En., A. March 6, 1778.
Winfrey, Henry, S. L., A. Nov. 3, 1780.
Wooldridge, Robert, En., S. Aug. 4, 1780.
Wooldridge, Thomas, Cp., S. Oct. 3, 1777—vice Harris.

Section 260—Cumberland

Allen, Richard, Cp., 1777.
Allen, Samuel, En., S. Aug. 25, 1777.
Allen, Archer, Cp., 1777.
Allen, Benjamin, S. L., S. Aug. 25, 1777—under R. Allen.
Anderson, William, S. L., S. Aug. 25, 1777—under Scott.
Anderson, Robert, Cp., S. March 26, 1781.
Baine (?), John, En., S. Aug. 25, 1777.
Ballon (?), Charles, Cp., S. Sept. 28, 1778—vice W. Hobson.
Ballon, William, S. L., S. May 22, 1780.
Booker, Richard, F. L., S. July 28, 1777.
Burton, John, S. L., S. Aug. 25, 1777.
Burton, John, En., S. March 26, 1781.
Carrington, Joseph, gent., Cp., S. July 28, 1777.
Carrington, George, Jr., gent., Maj., S. July 28, 1777—res. Feb. 26, 1781.
Clarke, William, F. L., R. Sept. 28, 1778.
Daniel, William, F. L., S. April 23, 1781—under A Allen.
Gilliam, James, En., S. April 23, 1781.
Glen, James, S. L., S. Aug. 24, 1778—under M. Woodson.
Guttery, Bernard, F. L., S. Aug. 24, 1778—under M. Woodson.
Guttery Alexander, Cp., S. April 23, 1781.
Harrison, Benjamin, En., S. April 23, 1781.
Haskins, Creede, Cp., S. Aug. 25, 177—vice J. Burton.

Hatcher, John, F. L., R. March 27, 1780.
Hatcher, John, En., S. March 27, 1780.
Hobson, Benjamin, S. L., S. April 26, 1779.
Hobson, William, gent., Cp., S. July 28, 1777—res. Sept. 28, 1778.
Hobson, John, En., S. May 22, 1780.
Hudgens, William, F. L., S. Aug. 25, 1777.
Keeling, George, F. L., S. March 26, 1781—under Wilson.
Meredith, William, En., S. Aug. 24, 1778—under M. Woodson.
Noel, John, En., R. Aug. 25, 1777—under R. Allen.
Parker, Charles, En., R. May 26, 1781.
Randolph, Beverley, Col., S. July 28, 1777.
Richardson, Martin, S. L., S. March 26, 1781.
Scott, ———, Cp., 1777.
Skipwith, Henry, Lt. Col., S. July 28, 1777.
Taylor, Samuel, S. L., S. Aug. 26, 1777.
Thompson, Bartlet, F. L., R. May 26, 1781—under Haskins.
Townes, William, S. L., S. April 23, 1781.
Turpin, William, En., S. Aug. 26, 1777.
Williams, Samuel, En., com'd, Feb. 26, 1781.
Wilson, ———, Cp., 1777.
Woodson, Miller, Cp., 1777.

Section 261—Fauquier

Ash, Francis, S. L., S. April 26, 1779.
Ashby, Lewis, En., R. March 24, 1778.
Atwell, Francis, gent., Cp., S. Sept. 28, 1778.
Ball, William, S. L., R. Nov. 27, 1780.
Ball, William, Cp., S. Aug. 25, 1777—vice J. Webb.
Ball, John, En., R. March 22, 1779—under F. Atwell.
Ball, Benjamin, F. L., R. March 22, 1779.
Baker, John, F. L., R. Oct. 25, 1779—under Kincheloe.
Barnett, Ambrose, En., S. March 27, 1780.
Bayles, William, Cp., R. July 23, 1781.
Ball, John., Cp., R. Oct. 25, 1779.
Ball, Charles, Cp., res. Nov. 24, 1777.
Blackwell, Samuel, gent., Lt. Col., R. Aug. 27, 1781.
Blackwell, James, F. L., S. June 28, 1779—under T. Weaver.

Blackwell, William, Cp., S. July 26, 1779.
Blackwell, John, gent., Lt. Col., S. Sept. 28, 1778—1st Battalion.
Boggers, Jeremiah, En., R. Sept. 25, 1780.
Bradford, John, En., S. July 23, 1781.
Bradford, Alexander, F. L., R. March 22, 1779.
Bronaugh, Samuel, En., R. May 22, 1780.
Bronaugh, Thomas, gent., Cp., S. May 25, 1778.
Buckner, Aylett, Maj., S. May 25, 1778.
Chilton, Charles, gent., Cp., S. April 27, 1778.
Chunn, John Thomas, Maj., R. Aug. 27, 1781.
Churchill, Armistead, gent., Col., S. May 25, 1778—2d Battalion.
Combes, John, En., S. May 25, 1778.
Conway, Thomas, Jr., Cp., R. May 22, 1780.
Craven, John, En., R. Nov. 27, 1780.
Deering, John, Lt., R. Aug. 27, 1781.
Digges, Edward, gent., Maj., R. Nov. 24, 1777—2d Battalion.
Donaldson, William, En., S. June 22, 1778.
Edmonds, William, gent., Co. Lt., R. Aug. 27, 1781.
Edwards, Thomas, S. L., R. March 22, 1779—under F. Atwell.
Eustace, William, Jr., F. L., R. July 23, 1781.
Fletcher, John, Lt., S. May 22, 1780.
Flowers, Daniel, Cp., 1780.
Foley, James, Jr., Cp., R. Oct. 25, 1779.
French, John, S. L., S. Aug. 24, 1778.
Fuller, Rodham, En., S. Sept. 28, 1778—under W. Blackwell.
Fuller, Joshua, Lt., S. Aug. 25, 1777.
Garrington, John, F. L., Sept. 26, 1780.
George, ———, Cp., 1777.
Grigsby, William, Cp., R. March 24, 1778.
Harris, Thomas, F. L., S. May 25, 1778.
Harrison, Bevor, F. L., R. March 24, 1778—under W. Grigsby.
Hathaway, John, Cp., S. March 27, 1780.
Hathaway, James, F. L., S. April 27, 1779.
Heale, William, S. L., S. March 27, 1780.
Helm, Thomas, Cp., S. May 28, 1781.
Hogan, John, S. L., R. Oct. 23, 1780.
Hunt, William, S. L., Oct. 25, 1779.
James, John, En., R. July 23, 1781.
James, Thomas, S. L., R. March 22, 1779.

James, Joseph, Cp., S. Sept. 28, 1778.
Jennings, Baylor, En., S. May 22, 1780.
Jennings, Augustine, F. L., S. March 27, 1780.
Jennings, William, Cp., S. June 22, 1778.
Jennings, Berryman, En., S. May 25, 1778—under T. Bronaugh.
Kemper, Peter, Jr., En., S. March 27, 1780.
Keith, Alexander, Cp., R. Aug. 27, 1781.
Keith, Thomas, S. L., R. March 24, 1778—under T. Morehead.
Kenton, William, Lt., S. May 25, 1778.
Kincheloe.
Layton, Robert, F. L., S. May 25, 1778.
Martin, John, S. L., S. July 26, 1779—under T. Weaver.
Mauzy John, S. L., R. May 22, 1780.
Metcalf, John, En., R. Aug. 27, 1781.
Moffett, John, gent., Maj., R. March 24, 1778—2d Battalion.
Morehead, Turner, Cp., S. May 25, 1778.
Nash, William, S. L., R. March 24, 1778—under W. Grigsby.
Neale, Matthew, En., R. March 22, 1779—under F. Triplett.
Nelson, Thomas, En., S. March 27, 1780.
Nelson, Joseph, En., S. May 22, 1780.
Norris, William, F. L., R. March 24, 1778—under F. Atwell.
Obanon, Samuel, S. L., R. Sept. 25, 1780.
Payne, Francis, En., S. Feb. 22, 1779.
Pearle, Samuel, S. L., R. Nov. 27, 1780.
Peyton, Henry, F. L., R. Oct. 25, 1779.
Pitckett, Martin, gent., Col., R. Aug. 27, 1781—2d Battalion.
Pope, William, Cp., S. May 25, 1778.
Prince, Hubbard, S. L., R. March 24, 1778.
Ransdell, Wharton, En., S. Sept. 28, 1778.
Ransdell, William, En., S. May 25, 1778—under T. Morehead.
Rixie, Richard, Cp., R. May 22, 1780.
Rogers, George, S. L., S. June 28, 1779.
Seaton, William, En., R. March 24, 1778—under F. Triplett.
Settle, William, Cp., 1777.
Sharpe, Sinsfield, Cp., R. July 23, 1781.
Smith, Joseph, Lt., R. Aug. 27, 1781.
Smith, Rolly, F. L., S. March 26, 1781.
Smith, William, En., R. March 22, 1779.
Smith, Augustine, En., S. July 26, 1779.

Smith, Thomas, Lt., S. June 22, 1778.
Shumate, Daniel, S. L., S. Nov. 23, 1778—res. July 23, 1781.
Sutherfer (?), Richard, En., R. Oct. 23, 1780.
Taylor, Joseph, F. L., S. July 26, 1779—under F. Atwell.
Timberlake, Epapproditus, S. L., R. Sept. 26, 1780.
Toley, James, Cp., R. Aug. 27, 1781—(Foley?).
Triplett, Francis, Cp., S. Sept. 28, 1778—vice Bell.
Warren, William, En., R. Sept. 2, 1778.
Weaver, Tilman, Cp., R. March 24, 1778.
Webb, John, Cp., 1777—died about March, 1777.
Wheatley, Joseph, Cp., S. May 22, 1780.
Wickliffe, William, En., R. Sept. 2, 1778.
Williams, Charles, Cp., S. Aug. 25, 1777.
Winn, Minor, Lt., S. March 27, 1780.
Withers, James of Jas., Cp., R. Aug. 27, 1781.
Withers, James of Thos., S. L., R. March 24, 1778.
Withers, William of Jno., S. L., R. Nov. 24, 1777.

Section 262—Fluvanna

Adams, James, Jr., S. L., R. Sept. 4, 1777.
Anderson, Benjamin, F. L., S. Sept. 4, 1777.
Beckley, John, F. L., S. Sept. 4, 1777.
Duncan, George, Cp., S. Sept. 4, 1777.
Haden, Anthony, En., com'd, Sept .4, 1777—res. April 2, 1779.
Haden, Anthony, gent., Cp., R. April 2, 1779—vice J. Napier.
Haden, Joseph, Cp., S. Sept. 4, 1777.
Haden, John Mozeley, F. L., S. Sept. 4, 1777.
Haden, John M., En., S. April 2, 1779—under L. Thompson.
Haden, William, gent., En., S. April 2, 1779—under J. Napier.
Hall, Richard, F. L., R. April 2, 1779—under D. Tilman.
Hancock, Benj., En., R. April 2, 1779—under A. Haden.
Haslip, Henry, S. L., S. Sept. 4, 1777.
Henry, William, gent., Lt., S. Sept. 4, 1777.
Johnson, William, En., S. Sept. 4, 1777.
Lee, Benjamin, En., S. Sept. 4, 1777.
Martin, Benjamin, En., S. Sept. 4, 1777—(Benj. Moss?).
Martin, Henry, F. L., A. Sept. 4, 1777—under L. Thompson.

Martin, John, S. L., S. Sept. 4, 1777.
Martin, William, S. L., R. Sept. 4, 1777.
Mays (Mayo?), Joseph, S. L., N. May 6, 1779—under D. Tilman and in place of T. Tinsdale.
Moore, Jesse, S. L., R. Sept. 4, 1777—refused to qualify.
Moss, Alexander, F. L., S. Sept. 4, 1777.
Napier, John, gent., Cp., S. Sept. 4, 1777—res. April 4, 1779.
Napier, Richard, Cp., S. Sept. 4, 1777.
Napier, Thomas, gent., Col., S. Sept. 4, 1777.
Omohundro, Richard, En., S. June 4, 1778—under R. Napier.
Thompson, George, gent., Maj., S. Sept. 4, 1777.
Thompson, Leonard, gent., Cp., S. Nov. 6, 1777.
Thompson, Roger, gent., Lt. Col., S. Nov. 6, 1777.
Thurmond, Thomas, Cp., S. Sept. 4, 1777.
Tilman, Daniel, F. L., S. Sept. 4, 1777.
Tilman, Daniel, Cp., S. Dec. 3, 1778—vice G. Duncan.
Tinsdale, Thomas, S. L., com'd Sept. 4, 1777—under G. Duncan.
Williamson, John, S. L., S. Sept. 4, 1777.
Woody, William, S. L., R. April 2, 1779.
Wynne, Thomas, En., S. Sept. 4, 1777.

NOTE:—No record later than April 2, 1779.

Section 263—Frederick

Abernathy, William, Lt., S. June 3, 1777.
Bobb, Peter, Cp., S. Nov. 6, 1776.
Baldwin, Thomas, Cp., S. Nov. 6, 1776.
Barnett, George, En., S. March 7, 1780.
Barrow, John, En., S. May 2, 1780.
Bell, George, gent., Lt., S. Aug. 5, 1777.
Bell, George, Cp., R. Aug. 4, 1779.
Berry, Francis, Cp., R. Aug. 4, 1779.
Branson, Amos, En., R. Aug. 4, 1779.
Brinker, Henry, En., S. May 2, 1780.
Brown, James, Lt. R. Aug. 4, 1779.
Burk, James, En., R. Aug. 4, 1779.
Bush, Vance, Lt., R. Aug. 4, 1779.
Byerly, Robert, En., R. Aug. 4, 1779.

Cockley, Jacob, Cp., R. Aug. 4, 1779.
Calmes, Marquis, Lt. Col., R. Feb. 4, 1777—res. Aug. 4, 1779.
Calvert, Samuel, gent., Lt., S. Oct. 5, 1779.
Camp, John, Lt., R. Aug. 4, 1779.
Carter, Joseph, Cp., R. Aug. 4, 1779.
Catlett, John, Lt., R. Aug. 4, 1779.
Catlett, John, Cp., S. Oct. 7, 1777.
Catlett, Henry, Lt., R. Aug. 4, 1779.
Cochran, James, En., R. Aug. 4, 1779.
Combs, Benjamin, Lt., R. Aug. 4, 1779.
Crim, Jacob, Lt., R. Aug. 4, 1779.
Daniel, Hugh, En., R. Aug. 4, 1779.
Denny, Samuel, En., R. Aug. 4, 1779.
Denny, Robert, Lt., S. March 7, 1780.
Dobbins, Edward, En., S. May 2, 1780.
Dorsey, Joshua, Lt., 1777.
Eastin, Johnston, En., S. May 2, 1780.
Elkins, Benjamin, Lt., R. Aug. 4, 1779.
Evans, William, Lt., R. Aug. 4, 1779.
Frost, William, Cp., R. Aug. 4, 1779.
Gilham, Peter, Lt., R. Aug. 4, 1779.
Gilkerson, Samuel, Cp., R. Aug. 4, 1779.
Hampton, Thomas, En., R. Aug. 4, 1779.
Hancher, William, En., R. Aug. 4, 1779.
Harrell, John, En., R. Aug. 4, 1779.
Heaton, James, Lt., R. Aug. 4, 1779.
Helphingston, Philip, Lt., R. Aug. 4, 1779.
Hill, John, Lt., R. Aug. 4, 1779.
Hisewanger, John, Maj., S. Sept. 7, 1779—vice R. White.
Hiskill, Peter, En., R. Aug. 4, 1779.
Hiskill, Adam, Cp., R. Aug. 4, 1779.
Horseley, Richard, En., S. May 2, 1780.
Kemp, John, En., S. May 2, 1780.
Kindrick, Christly, Lt., R. Aug. 4, 1779.
Kendrick, Abraham, Cp., R. Aug. 4, 1779.
Kennedy, David, Col., S. April 1, 1777—vice J. Smith.
Larrich, John, Cp., R. Aug. 4, 1779.
Laurence, James, Lt., R. Aug. 4, 1779.
Lindsay, Abraham, Lt., R. Aug. 4, 1779.

McCormick, Francis, Lt., R. Aug. 4, 1779.
Merser, Aaron, Cp., R. Aug. 4, 1779.
Myers, Jacob, Cp., R. Aug. 4, 1779.
O'Brien, John, En., S. Nov. 6, 1776.
Pyles, Joshua, Lt., R. Aug. 4, 1779.
Redman, Jeremiah, Cp., R. Aug. 4, 1779.
Rice, John, Cp., S. March 8, 1780.
Rinherbo, Casper, Cp., R. Feb. 4, 1777—vice R. White.
Simerall, James, Lt., R. Aug. 4, 1779.
Smith, Samuel, Lt., R. Aug. 4, 1779.
Smith, John, gent., Co. Lt., res. Feb. 4, 1777.
Stribling, William, Lt., R. Aug. 4, 1779.
Taylor, Richard, En., R. Aug. 4, 1779.
Taylor, William, Cp., R. Aug. 4, 1779.
Vance, William, En., R. Aug. 4, 1779.
White, Robert, Lt. Col., R. Aug. 4, 1779—vice M. Calmes.
Wilson, Hugh, En., S. Aug. 7, 1781.
Wolfe, Henry, En., R. Oct. 7, 1777.
Wolfe, John, En., R. Oct. 7, 1777.
Wood, James, gent., Co. Lt., res. Feb. 4, 1777, to become colonel in Continental Line.

Section 264—Goochland

Allen, Richard, S. L., S. Feb. 15, 1781.
Allen, James, F. L., A. April 21, 1778.
Bennett, James, En., S. March 27, 1779.
Bibb, Richard, Maj., S. May 17, 1778.
Blackwell, John, S. L., S. Aug. 17, 1778.
Bradshaw, Robert, En., S. Feb. 15, 1781.
Britt, John, En., S. Feb. 15, 1781.
Britt, Obadiah, En., S. May 18, 1778.
Cole, William, S. L., S. May 17, 1780—under S. Richardson.
Cox, Edward, En., S. Dec. 15, 1777.
Curd, John, Jr., Maj., S. May 17, 1780.
Curd, Edmund, Cp., A. April 21, 1778—vice W. George.
Duke, Edward, Cp., 1780.
Ellis, Stephen, S. L., A. July 21, 1777—under E. Leak.

George, James, Jr., S. L., S. Feb. 16, 1778.
George, William, Cp., 1777.
Guerrant, John, Maj., A. Aug. 20, 1781.
Guerrant, John, Jr., En., S. Feb. 15, 1781.
Hancock, Major, En., S. May 17, 1780.
Hanley, Hezekiah, En., A. July 21, 1777.
Harding, Thomas, En., S. Feb. 15, 1781.
Harris, Nathaniel, En., A. July 21, 1777.
Hatcher, Thomas, Cp., S. May 17, 1780.
Henley, Hezekiah, En., A. July 21, 1777.
Herndon, John, S. L., S. May 17, 1780.
Holman, Tandy, Cp., R. Nov. 19, 1781.
Hopkins, John, gent., Col., S. May 17, 1780—res. Aug. 20, 1781.
Johnson, Peter, F. L., S. Feb. 16, 1778.
Johnson, Walter, Lt., A. July 21, 1777—under J. Ware.
Lacy, Matthew, En., S. May 17, 1780.
Lacy, Elliott, En., S. May 17, 1779.
Leak, Josiah, Cp., 1777.
Leak, Elisha, Cp., 1777.
Lewis, Nicholas, En., S. May 17, 1780—under E. Duke.
Lewis, Joseph, S. L., S. May 17, 1780—under E. Duke.
Lewis, Robert, gent., Col., S. Nov. 15, 1779.
Massie, Thomas, En., A. April 21, 1778.
Massie, Nathaniel, Cp., 1777.
McCaul, William, En., S. Dec. 15, 1777.
Miller, Thomas, F. L., S. Feb. 15, 1781.
Miller, William, Cp., A. Sept. 15, 1777—in 10th Division—res. Nov. 19, 1781.
Morris, Nathaniel G., Co. Lt., A. Aug. 20, 1781.
Overstreet, James, F. L., A. April 21, 1778.
Parrish, Sherwood, S. L., S. May 17, 1780.
Parrish, Tolley, gent., Col., S. May 17, 1780.
Payne, George, Lt. Col., A. Aug. 20, 1781.
Payne, Josias, Jr., S. L., S. May 17, 1779.
Peers, Anderson, Lt., S. Dec. 15, 1777—under E. Leak.
Perkins, Francis, En., S. May 17, 1779.
Perkins, John, S. L., S. Feb. 16, 1778.
Pledge, Francis, En., S. May 17, 1779.
Price, Charles, F. L., A. April 21, 1778—vice S. Williams.

Price, Meredith, Lt., S. June 16, 1777.
Paine, Nathaniel, S. L., S. Feb. 15, 1781.
Redford, Edward, F. L., S. Feb. 15, 1781.
Redford, Milner, F. L., S. May 17, 1780—under E. Smith.
Richardson, Samuel, Cp., S. May 18, 1778—vice J. Ware.
Robards, Lewis, En., S. May 17, 1779.
Royster, Thomas, S. L., A. Sept. 15, 1777.
Rutherford, David, F. L., S. May 17, 1780—under H. Parrish.
Sampson, Stephen, Cp., 1777.
Smith, Edward, Cp., S. May 17, 1780.
Smith, Obadiah, S. L., A. April 21, 1778.
Towles, Stockley, Cp., A. Sept. 15, 1777—in 9th Division.
Wade, Dabney, F. L., S. May 17, 1780—under E. Smith.
Ware, James, S. L., S. Dec. 15, 1777.
Ware, John, Cp., 1777.
Webber, Philip, F. L., S. May 17, 1779.
Williams, Soloman, Lt., S. July 21, 1777.
Woodson, John, gent., Co. Lt., S. Sept. 27, 1779—res. Aug. 20, 1781.
Woodson, Isham, S. L., R. March 15, 1779.
Woodson, Josiah, En., S. Dec. 15, 1777.
Woodson, John Stephen, S. L., A. July 21, 1777—under S. Sampson.

Section 265—Greenbrier (W. Va.)

(NOTE:—The commissions indicated below were dated 1780 and 1781, the first Order Book appearing to have been lost.)

Anderson, John, Cp.
Clendenning, George, Cp.
Clendenning, William, Lt.
Davidson, George, Lt.
Davis, William, En.
Donally, Andrew, Col.
Glass, Samuel, Cp.
Graham, Cp.
Gregory, ———, Cp.
Hamilton, Samuel, Cp.
Hamilton, William, Cp.

Henderson, John, Cp.
Johnson, James, Cp.
Kelly, Alexander, Cp.
McCoy, ———, Cp.
Miller, Hugh, Cp.
Richard, Elijah, Cp.
Renick, William, Cp.
Shelton, Thomas, Cp.
Thompson, ———, Cp.
Ward, William, Cp.
Williams, Samuel, En.
Wood, Archibald, Cp.
Wright, ———, Cp.

Section 267—Henrico

NOTE:—The Revolutionary records prior to near the date given below were burned by the British.

RECOMMENDATIONS OF OCT. 1, 1781.

Adams, Richard, F. L.
Giles, William, En.
Hollman, Nathaniel, F. L.
Hondle, Hezekiah, En.
Johnson, Benjamin, S. L.
Price, John, Cp.
Turpin, John, Cp.
Turpin, Sugly, S. L.

Section 268—Henry

Adams, William, S. L., A. March, 1780—under H. Critz.
Barksdale, John, F. L., A. April, 1781—under B. Martin.
Barton, David, S. L., A. June, 1780—under O. Rubell.
Barton, Joshua, F. L., S. June, 1780.
Bedford, Thomas, F. L., S. June, 1780—under B. Martin.
Carlan, Daniel, Cp., S. April 20, 1778.
Choice, Tully, Cp., A. Aug., 1780—vice F. Reeves.

Choice, William, S. L., A. Aug., 1780—under T. Choice.
Conway, John, En., A. Aug., 1780—under P. Hairston.
Cowden, James, Cp., S. June, 1780.
Critz, Haman, Jr., Cp., 1780.
Davis, John, S. L., com'd, March, 1779—under T. Smith.
Dillard, John, Cp., A. July, 1780—vice J. Shelton.
Fontaine, John, Esq., Cp., S. June, 1780—vice J. Salmon.
Haile, Thomas, Cp., S. June, 1780—vice P. Vardaman.
Hairston, George, Cp., S. June, 1780—vice G. Waller.
Hairston, John, Cp., res. June, 1780.
Hairston, George, Cp., S. June, 1780—vice G. Waller.
Hairston, Peter, Cp., A. July, 1780.
Halbert, William, S. L., A. March, 1780—under E. Shelton.
Harris, Peter, En., com'd March, 1779—under T. Henderson—vice J. Wells.
Henderson, T., Cp., 1779.
Hill, Swinfield, Cp., A. March, 1779—vice E. Short.
Hill, Thomas, En., com'd, June, 1781—under T. Haile.
Hughes, Archilaus, Esq., Co. Lt., A. March, 1780—res. July, 1780.
Jones, Joseph, F. L., com'd June, 1871—under T. Haile.
Jones, Thomas, F. L., A. July, 1780—under J. Rentfro.
Lyne, Edmund, Lt. Col., res. April 20, 1778.
Lyne, Henry, Esq., Cp., res. June, 1780.
Lyon, James, Esq., Lt. Col., A. March, 1780.
Lyon, Stephen, F. L., A. March, 1779—under E. Shelton.
Martin, Brice, Cp., 1780.
Menifee, William, En., A. July, 1780—under T. Haile.
Miller, John, En., A. March, 1780—under H. Critz.
Murphy, John, En., A. March, 1779—under T. Haile.
Nance, Reuben, En., A. October, 1779—under J. Wells.
Owen, Christopher, En., A. April, 1781—under B. Martin.
Penn, Abraham, Col., R, March, 1780.
Petect, James, Cp., S. June, 1780—vice J. Hariston.
Prunty, Thomas, En., A. August, 1780—under T. Choice.
Redd, John, S. L., A. April, 1780—under B. Martin.
Reeves, Frederick, Cp., res. August, 1780.
Rentfro, William, S. L., com'd June, 1781—under Petect.
Rentfro, John, Cp., A. July, 1780.
Rentfro, Joshua, S. L., A. July, 1780—under J. Rentfro.

Reynolds, George, F. L., A. August, 1780—under P. Hairston.
Rogers, David, En., A. March, 1779—under E. Shelton.
Ross, Daniel, S. L., A. June, 1780—under O. Rubell.
Rubell, Owen, Cp., S. June, 1780.
Ryan, William, F. L., A. August, 1780—under T. Choice.
Salmon, John, Esq., Cp., res. June, 1780.
Shelton, James, Cp., res. July, 1780.
Shelton, Eliphaz, Cp., A. March, 1779—vice J. Lyon.
Short, Edward, Cp., 1779.
Small, Matthew, Co. Lt., R. July, 1780.
Small, Matthew, S. L., S. April 20, 1778—under T. Henderson.
Smith, Gideon, En., A. June, 1780—under O. Rubell.
Smith, Thomas, F. L., A. March, 1780—under H. Critz.
Smith, Thomas, Cp., com'd March, 1779.
Spencer, James, En., A. July, 1780—under J. Dillard.
Standifor, Luke, S. L., com'd June, 1781—under T. Haile.
Standifor, William, En., A. July, 1780—under J. Rentfro.
Taylor, George, F. L., A. July, 1780—under J. Dillard.
Taylor, William, S. L., A. July, 1780—under J. Dillard.
Thomas, Austin, En., res. September, 1780.
Tunstall, William, Esq., Co. Lt., res. March, 1780.
Turner, John, F. L., S. June, 1780.
Vardaman, Peter, Cp., 1780.
Waller, George, Esq., Maj., A. June, 1780—vice J. Lyon.
Wells, John, Cp., A. October, 1779—res. August, 1780.
Wells, Matthew, S. L., A. October, 1779—under J. Wells.

Section 269—Loudoun

Adams, Francis, En., S. March 12, 1781.
Alexander, John, gent., Lt. Col. S. April 9, 1781.
Ball, Farling, Cp., S. May 13, 1777—vice G. Shaffer.
Beaver, ———, Cp., 1777.
Benham, John, En., S. June. 12, 1780.
Binns, John, gent., F. L., S. March 13, 1781.
Binns, Charles, Jr., S. L., S. March 13, 1781.
Boggess, Henry, En., S. Oct. 11, 1779.
Boggs, Vincent, En., R. Sept. 9, 1777.

Bullskin, ———, Cp., 1777.
Butler, Joseph, Cp., S. Oct. 13, 1782.
Cleveland, James, Cp., S. Jan. 11, 1780.
Coleman, James, gent., Maj., S. March 10, 1777.
Cox, Samuel, Cp., 1777.
Davis, ———, Cp., 1777.
Debell, William, Lt., S. May 12, 1781.
Dehaven, Abraham, F. L., S. June 11, 1781.
Douglas, Hugh, gent., Cp., S. May 12, 1781.
Douglas, William, gent., Cp., S. Aug. 11, 1777.
Elgin, Gustavus, Cp., S. Oct. 13, 1782.
Elgin, Francis, Jr., En., S. Aug. 9, 1779.
Elliott, William, En., S. April 12, 1779.
Eskridge, Charles, Lt. Col., S. April 13, 1779.
Feagan, Daniel, Cp., S. May 11, 1778.
George, William, Cp., S. March 11, 1782.
Greenup, ———, Cp., 1777.
Hancock, Simon, Cp., R. Sept. 9, 1777—vice W. Smith.
Hixon, Timothy, gent., Cp., S. Oct. 13, 1782.
Humphrey, ———, Cp., 1777.
Irey, Philip, Cp., R. March 9, 1778—refused to qualify.
Jones, ———, Cp., 1777.
Katon, Jacob, En., S. June 14, 1779.
Kennon, Thomas, gent., Cp., S. May 12, 1781.
Kilgore, George, F. L., S. Aug. 9, 1779.
King, Smith, gent, Lt., S. May 12, 1781.
Lewis, Thomas, gent., Cp., S. Aug. 11, 1777—vice W. Smith.
Lewis, Joseph, Cp., 1777.
Lewis, John, gent., Cp., S. May 13, 1777.
Linton, John, gent., Cp., S. April 10, 1781.
Luckett, John, Cp., S. June 8, 1778.
Marks, Elisha, Cp., R. March 9, 1778—vice P. Irey.
McGeach, John, Cp., S. March 13, 1781.
McMaken, Alexander, gent., Maj., S. April 9, 1781.
McMichen, ———, Cp., 1777.
Miles, Josias, En., R. May 13, 1777—under T. Respess.
Minor, John, Cp., 1777.
Moffett, Josiah, gent., Cp., S. March 13, 1781.
Moss, John, gent., Cp., R. Jan. 13, 1777.

Nolard, Samuel, gent., Cp., S. May 12, 1781.
Nolard, Philip, Cp., S. May 13, 1777.
Ousley, ———, Cp., 1777.
Owley, William, F. L., R. Sept. 9, 1777.
Payne, Henry, F. L., S. June 14, 1779.
Pierce, Thomas, Cp., S. March 12, 1781.
Reed Jacob, Maj., R. June 11, 1781—held up to await a decision as to procedure between Reed and A. Maken.
Respess, Thomas, Cp., S. March 10, 1777.
Saunders, Gunnell, Lt., R. Jan. 13, 1777.
Saunders, John, En., R. Jan. 13, 1777.
Shaffer, ———, Cp., 1777.
Shores, Thomas, Cp., S. March 12, 1781.
Sinclair, John, Lt., R. May 13, 1777—under T. Respess.
Slater , ———, Cp., 1777.
Smith, Nathan, Cp., 1777.
Spurr, ———, Cp., 1777.
Stanhope, William, Cp., S. Aug. 11, 1778.
Stover, Cp., 1777.
Summers, George, gent., Cp., R. May 13, 1777.
Tarflinger, Henry, gent., Lt., res. Oct. 13, 1782.
Taylor, John, gent., F. L., S. Feb. 11, 1782.
Taylor, ———, Cp., 1777.
Thomas, Enoch, gent., Cp., S. Oct. 13, 1782.
Thomas, Moses, Cp., res. Aug. 11, 1777.
Triplett, Simon, Esq., Col. S. Oct. 8, 1781.
Vandevender, Isaac, En., S. Sept. 15, 1778—under J. Lewis.
Vanover, ———, Cp., 1777.
Vincell, Adam, Cp., S. Oct. 13, 1777.
West, George, Maj., S. May 11, 1778.
Whaley, James, Jr., S. L., S. Aug. 9, 1779.
White, ———, Cp., 1777.
Wildman, Joseph, Lt., S. Aug. 9, 1779.
Wycoff, ———, Cp., 1777.

Additional Recommendations

Adams, Nathan, Lt., May, 1778.
Asbury, George, En., Aug. 1778.
Barkley, Scarlet, Lt., May, 1778.

Benham, Peter, En., May, 1778.
Botts, Joshua, Lt., May, 1778.
Butcher, Samuel, Lt., May, 1778.
Carnan, William, En., March, 1778.
Cleveland, James, Cp., Nov. 8, 1779.
Cox, Samuel, Maj., May, 1778.
Debell, John, Lt., July 12, 1779.
Dodd, John, En., March, 1778.
Farnsworth, Henry, Lt., May, 1778.
Grant, Isaac, En., May, 1778.
Henry, John, Cp., May, 1778.
Hutchison, William, En., July 12, 1779.
King, Thomas, S. L., March, 1778.
Lewis, Daniel, S. L., March, 1778.
Marks, Thomas, Lt., Aug., 1778.
Mason, George, Lt., May, 1778.
McClain, Robert, Cp., May, 1778.
McClellan, William, Cp., May, 1778.
Millam, Thomas, En., Nov. 8, 1779.
Robinson, William, Lt., Aug., 1778.
Russell, Francis, Lt., May, 1778.
Russell, John, Lt., May, 1778.
Russell, Robert, En., Aug. 1780.
Shore, Richard, En., May, 1778.
Shrieve, John, En., A. 1779.
Smith, Nathan, S. L., June, 1780.
Taylor, George, Lt., May, 1778.
Thatcher, John, En., May, 1778.
Thomas, Thomas, S. L., Aug. 1780.
Walter, John, Lt., May, 1778.
White, Joel, En., June, 1780.
Williams, John, Lt., May, 1778.
Williams, Thomas, En., Feb. 14, 1780.

Section 270—Louisa

Anderson, Turner, Lt., S. April 9, 1781.
Anderson, David, Cp., 1777.
Anderson, Richard, Col., 1777.

Bagby, William, En., S. July 10, 1780.
Bagby, ———, Cp., 1777.
Bias, John, Cp., S. June 8, 1778—died, 1781.
Bigger, David, F. L., S. Jan. 11, 1779.
Bradburn, Butler, S. L., S. March 12, 1781.
Brown, John ,En., R. June 12, 1780.
Clark, William, En., S. Oct. 12, 1779—under Mosby.
Cole, Samuel, Lt., S. Oct. 12, 1779.
Cosby, John, gent., S. L., S. Oct. 9, 1780.
Crutchfield, John, F. L., R. 1782.
Dabney, Samuel, En., S. June 9, 1777.
Fontaine, Aaron, En., R. April 13, 1779.
Fox, John, Cp., 1776.
Garland, Nathaniel, Cp., 1777.
Garrett, Harvey (Henry?), Cp., S. March 12, 1781.
Glenn, Beverley, En., S. Aug. 11, 1777—under R. Phillips.
Green, Forrest, En., R. April 10, 1779.
Harris, William, F. L., S. March 12, 1781.
Harris, Frederick, F. L., R. April 10, 1779.
Henson, Samuel, S. L., R. April 14, 1778—under S. Richardson.
Hughes, William, Cp., S. Jan. 11, 1779.
Hughes, Joshua, En., S. April 13, 1779.
Jackson, William, S. L., S. Aug. 11, 1777.
Johnson, Richard, S. L., S. March 12, 1781.
Johnson, George, Lt., S. June 12, 1780.
Johnson, Henry Ashton, S. L., R. April 10, 1779—under J. Watson.
Johnson, Christopher, En., S. Oct. 13, 1777.
Johnson, Thomas, gent., Cp., A. Sept. 9, 1776.
Lumsden, George, Cp., S. April 13, 1779.
Meriwether, William, En., R. Oct. 12, 1781.
Meriwether, David Wood, F. L., S. June 14, 1779.
Michie, George, S. L., R. Dec. 10, 1781.
Michie, Robert, S. L., R. June 12, 1780.
Michie, James, S. L., S. Sept. 8, 1777—under S. Richardson.
Minor, Garrett, Cp., 1777.
Moorman, James, En., S. March 12, 1781.
Mosby, ———, Cp., 1777.
Nelson, John, gent., Maj., S. June 8, 1778.
Overton, Walter, S. L., S. June 13, 1779.

Paulet, Richard, Cp., S. Dec. 10, 1781—vice J. Bias.
Petis, Samuel, En., R. Aug. 13, 1781.
Phillips, Richard, Cp., 1777.
Poindexter, John, Cp., 1777.
Price, Hezekiah, F. L., R. April 14, 1778.
Ragland, Samuel, Cp., 1777.
Richardson, Samuel, Cp., S. June 9, 1777.
Roberts, James, S. L., S. Sept. 8, 1777—under Mosby.
Ross, John, En., S. Sept. 8, 1777.
Sanders, John, Cp., S. Oct. 12, 1778—vice D. Anderson.
Seay, John, Lt., S. June 8, 1778.
Shelton, Thomas, F. L., R. Oct. 12, 1781.
Shelton, Samuel, En., R. April 14, 1778.
Shelton, Peter, En., S. Aug. 11, 1777—under J. Fox.
Smith, William, Lt., S. Nov. 11, 1776.
Street, Joseph, S. L., R. April 14, 1778.
Terrill, Thomas, S. L., R. Oct. 12, 1781.
Thompson, Joseph, En., R. April 10, 1779.
Thompson, William, S. L., S. Sept. 8, 1777.
Thompson, ———, Cp., 1777.
Timberlake, John, S. L., R. April 14, 1778.
Truman, Obadiah, En., S. March 12, 1781.
Waddy, Samuel, En., R. June 12 ,1780.
Walden, Lewis, En., S. Sept. 8, 1777.
Wasley, Robert, S. L., S. Jan. 11, 1779.
Watson, James, Cp., S. Jan. 11, 1779.
White, John, Cp., R. Sept. 9, 1776.
White, William, Cp., A. Aug. 11, 1777.
White, William, Co. Lt., S. June 8, 1778.
Wilson.
Winston, James, gent., F. L., S. March 12, 1781.
Winston, Anthony, S. L., R. June 12, 1780.
Yancy, St. Charles, Cp., R. Oct. 12, 1781—vice W. Hughes.

Section 271a—Monongalia

Pay roll of Capt. William Haymond's Company, of Monongalia County Militia on duty at Pickett's Fort, near Morgantown from the 15th of April until the 12th of June, 1777.

William Haymond, Capt.
Morgan Morgan, Lieut.
James Johnston, Ensign
Zarah Ozban, Sergt.
Amos Ashcraft
John Doherty
Edmond Chaney
Jereh. Chaney
David Morgan
Thos. Haymond
Willm. Pettyjohn
Amos Pettyjohn
Robt. Campbell
John Ice

Frederick Ice
Henry Hank
Peter Popens
Levy Carter
John Carter
Fredk. Huklebery
Jarvis Brumagen
Jeremiah Simson
Valentine Kennett
Evan Morgan
Ruben Boner
James Morgan, Sr.
John Lemaster
James Morgan, Jr.

NOTE:—For above list I am indebted to Mr. Henry Haymond, of Clarksburg, W. Va., who has in his possession the original pay roll.

Section 271—Montgomery

Adams, John, F. L., R. Nov. 6, 1781—under Montgomery.
Alcorn, John, S. L., R. Nov. 6, 1781—under Montgomery.

NOTE:—Robert Alcorn was in S. C. in 1782.

Bailey, Benjamin, F. L., S. May 13, 1778—under W. Bobbet.
Bobbet, William, Cp., R. March 4, 1778—over part of Trigg's Company.
Bright, Albertus, En., A. April 5, 1781—under Trigg.
Brown, Peter, En., R. Sept. 7, 1779—under H. Patton.
Bryson, John, S. L., R. June 2, 1779—under J. Henderson.
Buchanan, William, Cp., 1777—absent in Kentucky service, September, '77.
Buchanan, Robert, Cp., 1777.
Burk, ———, Cp., 1777.
Burns, James, Cp., R. Sept. 7, 1779—vice J. Cloyd.
Calhoun, William, En., A. April 5, 1781—under Buchanan.
Campbell, Charles, En., S. April 6, 1779—under Buchanan.
Campbell, William, S. L., R. Jan. 6, 1778—under R. Buchanan.
Campbell, Samuel, Lt., S. May 6, 1777—com'd Oct. 21, 1775.

Cavanaugh, William, Lt., A. April 5, 1781—under G. Pearis.
Cavanaugh, Charles, En., A. April 5, 1781—under G. Pearis.
Chapman, John, S. L., R. Nov. 6, 1781.
Cline, Nicholas, En., S. March 4, 1778—sold land to Mitchael Cline, 1785.
Cloyd, Joseph, En., S. Sept. 8, 1779—died, 1833.
Cloyd, ———, Cp., 1777.
Cock, James, F. L., R. Sept. 8, 1779.
Cox, ———, Cp., 1777.
Crawford, James, F. L., R. June 2, 1779.
Crawford, John, Lt., S. March 3, 1778.
Crockett, Walter, Lt. Col., S. Oct. 5, 1779.
Crockett, John, F. L., R. Sept. 3, 1777—under J. Montgomery.
Crockett, Andrew, S. L., R. Sept. 3, 1777—under Drapier.
Dack (Doak?), Joseph, S. L., R. Nov. 6, 1781—under W. Ward.
Davis, William, S. L., R. Sept. 7, 1779—under J. Burns.
Davis, Robert, F. L., S. Jan. 6, 1779—under R. Buchanan.
Dean, William, S. L., R. Nov. 6, 1781—under W. Glavis.
Doak, Samuel, En., R. Sept. 8, 1779.
Doak, William, Cp., 1779—res. Nov. 6, 1781.
Downing, James, F. L., S. May 5, 1778.
Drapier, ———, Cp., 1777.
Edwards, Frederick, Cp., com'd Aug. 16, 1780.
Estis, Richard, F. L., S. Sept. 8, 1779—under H. Gardiner.
Evans, Jesse, Lt., S. March 4, 1778.
Ewing, Samuel, Cp., A. April 5, 1781—vice Pierre.
Ferguson, Samuel, En., A. April 5, 1781—under J. Moore.
Finley, James, Cp., R. Nov. 6, 1781—vice J. Stephens.
Foster, Thomas, F. L., R. June 2, 1779—under Pierce.
Francis, Henry, Cp., S. March 3, 1778.
Gardiner, Henson, Cp., S. Sept. 8, 1779—for part of Cloyd's Company, on Walker Creek.
Glavis, William, F. L., R. Nov. 6, 1781—under J. Newell.
Hatfield, Andrew, Cp., R. Nov. 6, 1781—vice J. Lucas.
Hays, John, Cp., R. Nov. 6, 1781—head north fork of Holston.
Henderson, John, Cp., R. March 4, 1778—for part of Cox's Company—died, 1813—wife, Mary. Children: 1 Joseph, 2 John, 3 Jonas, 4 Robert, 5 Samuel, 6 Thomas, 7 William, 8 Sarah

(married Mitchell), 9 Polly (married Bean); had much property.
How, Daniel, S. L., R. Sept. 7, 1779—under H. Patton; sold land to James Hoge, 1783.
Inglis, David, En., R. Sept. 1, 1778.
Inglis, William, Col., S. Jan. 4, 1777.
Johnson, Benjamin, F. L., S. June 2, 1779.
Justice, Moses, S. L., R. Nov. 6, 1781—under J. Hays.
Kettering, Laurence, En., R. Jan. 6, 1778—under R. Buchanan.
Kincannon, Francis, S. L., R. June 2, 1779—under W. Love.
Love, Robert, F. L., R. Nov. 6, 1781—under J. Finley.
Love, William, S. L., R. Nov. 6, 1781—under J. Finley.
Love, William, Cp., S. June 2, 1779.
Lovel, William, F. L., R. Nov. 6, 1781—vice J. Hays.
Lovel, Markel, En., R. Nov. 6, 1781—under J. Hays.
Lucas, John, Cp., A. Mar. 3, 1778—vice T. Burk.
Mageehe (McGee), Samuel, S. L., R. March 4, 1778—under Trigg.
Maguire, William, En., R. March 3, 1779—under J. Moore.
Maxwell, James, Cp., 1779.
McCorkle, James, Cp., 1777.
McDonald, Magnus, En., R. Sept. 3, 1777—under J. Montgomery.
McFarlane, John, En., A. April 5, 1781—vice N. Cline.
McMullen, William, F. L., R. Sept. 7, 1779—under J. Burns.
Moffett, Robert, F. L., S. May 13, 1778.
Montgomery, Joseph, Cp., A. Nov. 6, 1781—vice A. Trigg.
Montgomery, Michael, Cp., 1778.
Montgomery, James, Cp., S. Sept. 3, 1777—vice W. Buchanan.
Moore, James, Cp., S. May 13, 1778—on Bluestone river.
Mure (Muir), Alexander, F. L., R. Sept 7, 1779—under H. Patton.
Mure, Richard, En., S. March 3, 1778—under Pearce (or Pierce).
Neely, Alexander, S. L., R. June 2, 1779—under Pearce.
Newell, James, Cp., A. April 5, 1781—vice H. Francis (Frazier?).
Owens, Richardson, Cp., R. June 2, 1779.
Osborn, ———, Cp., 1777.
Parks, William, En., R. Nov. 6, 1781—under Montgomery.
Patton, Henry, Cp., R. Sept. 7, 1779—vice J. Cloyd; bought land of Henry Gardner, 1780.

(NOTE:—Robert, William, Thomas and James Montgomery were grand jurors in Fincastle County, 1774, the first being foreman).

Pearce,* ———, Cp., 1777—abroad in 1781.
Peary (Pearis), George, F. L., R. March 3, 1779—under J. Moore.
Preston,† William, Co. Lt., S. Jan. 4, 1777.
Robertson, James, gent., Lt. Col., S. April 2, 1777.
Saunders, Stephen, Cp., A. Nov. 6, 1781—vice J. Pearce.
Sayers, Robert, En., R. Nov. 6, 1781—under J. Newell.
Sayers, Thompson, En., S. Jan. 6, 1778—under Drapier.
Scurry, Eli, S. L., R. Sept. 8, 1779.
Shaw, Joseph, En., R. Nov. 6, 1781—under J. Finley.
Smith, Jarvis, En., R. June 2, 1779—under W. Love.
Snide, Christian, F. L., R. Nov. 6, 1781—under A. Hatfield.
Stephens, ———, Cp., 1777.
Swift, Flour, Cp., R. Sept. 8, 1779.
Taylor, ———, Cp., 1777.
Thompson, Henry, F. L., S. Jan. 6, 1778—under Cloyd.
Trigg, Abram, Cp., A. April 5, 1781—com'd, May, 1780.
Trigg, Daniel, Cp., R. April 2, 1777.
Vancel, Edmund, En., R. March 4, 1778—under D. Trigg, died, 1815.
Wall, Adam, En., S. Sept. 8, 1779.
Ward, William, Cp., R. Nov. 6, 1781—vice W. Doak.
Ward, John, F. L., R. Nov. 6, 1781—under W. Ward.
Ward, Alexander, En., R. Nov. 6, 1781—under W. Ward.
White, James, En., A. April 5, 1781—under W. Love.
Wood, ———, Cp., 1777.

Section 272—Orange

Barbour, Thomas, Esq., Maj., S. July 23, 1778.
Biddle, Lewis, F. L., S. May 25, 1780—under E. Shackleford.
Brookman, Samuel, Lt., R. Feb. 27, 1777.

---

*(NOTE:—Perhaps Richard, who died in 1822, leaving widow, Peggy, and children: Samuel, Thomas, Jonathan, Richard, William, Sarah (Garlich), Phœbe (Thompson), Abagail).

†(NOTE:—William Preston, of Jefferson County, Ky., died in 1821, and will was recorded in Botetourt. Married Caroline Hancock. Children: Henrietta, Maria, Caroline, Josephine, Hancock, William C., Susanna. He had a brother, Francis. He provided that $6,000 be expended on the education of his two sons.)

Bruce, ———, Cp., 1777.
Buckner, William, Cp., A. May 28, 1778.
Burnley, Zachariah, J., Co. Lt., S. July 23, 1778.
Burton, May, F. L., S. May 27, 1779.
Cave, Belfield, S. L., S. May 27, 1779.
Chambers, Thomas, F. L., A. May 25, 1780—under R. Graves.
Coleman, James, En., S. May 25, 1780—under Z. Herndon.
Connor, Timothy, F. L., A. May 25, 1780—under R. C. Webb.
Conway, Catlett, Cp., res. May 25, 1780.
Craig, Toliver, Cp., S. July 24, 1777.
Daniel, Robert, Cp., S. May 25, 1780—vice C. Conway.
Daniel, Vivian, Cp., res. May 23, 1776.
Graves, Richard, Cp., S. Aug. 27, 1778—vice C. Bruce.
Hansford, Benoni, F. L., S. Aug. 27, 1778.
Hawkins, James, Cp., S. March 25, 1779.
Head, Benjamin, Cp., R. May 28, 1778.
Head, James, En., S. Sept. 25, 1777.
Herndon, John, En., A. May 25, 1780.
Herndon, Zachariah, Cp., S. May 25, 1778.
Hubblefield, George (Stubblefield?), F. L., S. Nov. 27, 1777—under Bruce.
Ingram, William, En., A. May 25, 1780—under J. Hawkins.
Jameson, James, S. L., A. May 25, 1780—under G. Waugh.
Jameson, William, En., S. April 1, 1779.
Johnson, Robert, F. L., A. April 1, 1779.
Johnson, ———, Cp., 1777.
Kenton, Ambrose, En., A. Sept. 25, 1777.
Lindsay, Caleb, F. L., S. Oct 23, 1777—under R. Thomas.
Madison, James, gent., Co. Lt., res. May 28, 1778.
Mallory, Uriel, Cp., 1777.
Martin, Robert, En., S. Aug. 27, 1778—under W. Buckner.
Miller, Lewis, S. L., S. May 25, 1780—under Z. Herndon.
Miller, Robert, Cp., S. May 27, 1779—vice B. Head.
Mills, Nathaniel, Cp., R. Feb. 27, 1777.
Moore, Reuben, F. L., A. May 25, 1780—under G. Waugh.
Moore, Francis, Jr., Cp., 1777.
Moore, William, Maj., res. May 28, 1778.
Newman, Alexander, En., S. May 25, 1780.
Pannill, John, S. L., S. Nov. 23, 1780—under R. Graves.

Price, Richard Moore, Lt., S. May 27, 1779.
Porter, Abraham, Lt., N. March 25, 1779.
Porter, Charles, Jr., Lt., S. April 1, 1779.
Proctor, John, S. L., S. May 28, 1778.
Robinson, John, En., S. May 25, 1780—under R. C. Webb.
Rowland, Thomas, S. L., A. May 25, 1780.
Saunders, James, S. L., S. May 25, 1780—under R. C. Webb.
Scott, John, Jr., F. L., S. May 25, 1780—under Z. Herndon.
Scott, James, En., A. April 1, 1779—under Z. Herndon.
Scott, John, gent., Cp., res. May 28, 1778.
Shackleford, Edmund, Cp., S. May 25, 1780—vice C. Conway.
Shackelford, Zachary, S. L., S. Oct. 23, 1777.
Singleton, Manoah, S. L., S. Aug. 28, 1777.
Sisson, Caleb, En., S. April 1, 1779.
Smith, William, S. L., S. Nov. 27, 1779—under C. Conway.
Smith, George, Cp., res. May 28, 1778.
Taliaferro, George, Lt. Col., A. Map 28, 1778.
Thomas, Robert, Cp., S. Oct. 23, 1777—vice N. Mills.
Thomas, Rowland, S. L., A. May 25, 1780.
Waugh, George, Cp., S. May 25, 1780.
Webb, Richard C., Cp., A. May 25, 1780—vice Craig.
White, Richard, En., S. May 27, 1779.
White, Jeremiah, Cp., res. May 28, 1778.
Willis, Moses, S. L., A. May 25, 1780—under J. Hawkins.
Wright, William, F. L., S. May 25, 1780.
Young, William, S. L., S. Aug. 27, 1778—under W. Buckner.

Section 274—Powhatan

Clemons, William, En., A. June 20, 1781—under E. Munford.
Cox. Edward, S. L., S. July 16, 1778—under R. Crump.
Cox, Edward, F. L., A. June 20, 1781—under E. Vaughan.
Crump, Richard, gent., Cp., S. Oct. 16, 1777—vice Wm. Gay.
Crump, Richard, Maj., R. June 20, 1781—vice Thos. Harris, prisoner of war.
Drake, James, S. L., R. Aug. 21, 1777—under R. Crump.
Eggleston, John, S. L., A. June 20, 1781—under W. Mays.
Fleming, William, gent., Co. Lt., S. Aug. 21, 1777.

Gay, William, Cp., res. Aug. 21, 1777.
Harris, John, Esq., Lt. Col., S. Aug. 21, 1777.
Harris, John, gent., Co. Lt., R. June 20, 1781—vice L. Mosby.
Harris, John, Jr., gent., En., S. July 20, 1780—under I. Porter.
Harris, Thomas, gent., Cp., S. Aug. 21, 1777.
Harris, Thomas, Maj., R. May 18, 1780.
Harris, Francis, E., En., A. May 21, 1778—under E. Munford.
Haskins, Edward, Esq., Maj., S. Aug. 21, 1777.
Haskins, Edward, gent., Lt. Col., S. July 20, 1780.
Haskins, Edward, gent., Col., R. June 20, 1781.
Haskins, Thomas, Esq., Cp., S. Aug. 21, 1777.
Hubbard, Thomas, F. L., S. May 18, 1780—vice Thos. Stegar.
Hughes, Robert, Cp., S. Oct. 16, 1777.
Hughes, David, En., S. May 18, 1780.
Hughes, David, F. L., R. June 20, 1781—under W. Mosby.
Lescur, Marshall, S. L., S. May 18, 1780.
Ligon, John, En., A. June 20, 1781.
Lockett, Gideon, En., N. Nov. 19, 1778—under G. Williamson.
Logwood, Edmund, S. L., R. Aug. 21, 1777—under R. Hughes.
Markham, Vincent, gent., F. L., S. June 18, 1778—under E. Munford.
Markham, Vincent, gent. Cp., A, June 20, 1781.
May, Joseph, S. L., R. Aug. 21, 1777.
Mays, William, gent. Cp., S. Aug. 21, 1777.
Mays, William, Lt., R. June 20, 1781—vice E. Haskins.
Merriott, Triplett, En., R. Aug. 21, 1777—under T. Harris.
Merriott, Tapley, En., A. Dec. 21, 1780—under E. Munford.
Merriott, Tapley, S. L., R. June 20, 1781—under E. Munford.
Mosby, Lyttleberry, Esq., Col. S. July 17, 1777.
Mosby, Littleberry, Gent., Co. Lt., R. May 18, 1780—vice Wm. Fleming.
Mosby, Littleberry, Gent., Co. Lt., res. June 20, 1781.
Mosby, Poindexter, Esq., Cp., S. Aug. 21, 1777—res. May 21, 1778.
Mosby, John, S. L., R. Aug. 21, 1777—under T. Haskins.
Mosby, Benjamin, S. L., S. May 21, 1778—under E. Munford.
Mosby, Benjamin, F. L., A. June 20, 1781—under E. Munford.
Mosby, Wade, Cp., A. June 20, 1781—vice R. Hughes, p'ner of war.
Moseley, John, Lt. S. March 19, 1778.
Moseley, John, F. L., S. Dec. 17, 1778—vice G. Williamson.
Moseley, Thomas, En., S. Feb. 18, 1779—under G. Williamson.

Munford, Edward, Cp., S. May 21, 1778—vice P. Mosby.
Pleasants, Samuel, S. L., A. June 20, 1781—under E. Vaughan.
Poor, William, F. L., S. Dec. 18, 1777—under R. Hughes.
Porter, Isaac, Cp., S. May 18, 1780.
Povall, John, S. L., S. Nov. 19, 1778.
Radford, George, En., S. May 18, 1780—vice R. Smith.
Saunders, Samuel, Hyde, En., R. Aug. 21, 1777—under R. Crump.
Smith, George, S. L., S. May 21, 1778.
Smith, George, F. L., R. May 18, 1780—under I. Porter.
Smith, Robert, En., R. Aug. 21, 1777—res. May 18, 1780.
Smith, William, F. L., A. June 20, 1781—under V. Markham.
Stegar, Thomas, F. L., S. Oct. 16, 1777—under W. Mays, res. May 18, 1780.
Stegar, Hans, S. L., S. May 18, 1780.
Stovall, George, En., R. Aug. 21, 1777.
Stratton, John, En., A. June 20, 1781—under W. Mosby.
Swann, John, F. L., R. Aug. 21, 1777—under R. Hughes.
Thompson, Josiah, F. L., R. Aug. 21, 1777—under P. Mosby.
Tucker, James, S. L., A. June 20, 1781—under W. Mosby.
Vaughan, Edmund, F. L., S. May 18, 1780.
Vaughan, Edmund, Cp., A. June 20, 1781—vice R. Crump.
Williamson, George, F. L., S. May 21, 1778.
Williamson, George, Cp., S. Nov. 19, 1778—vice T. Haskins.

Section 275—Prince Edward

The list herein given is from a list contributed by Alfred J. Morrison, in the Virginia Magazine of History, April, 1913, and taken by him from the records. The following officers were appointed and commissioned in May, June and July, 1777.

Captains:
    Josiah Chambers
    John Bibb
    David Walker
    Andrew Baker

Lieutenants:
    Charles Allen
    Jacob Woodson
    John Dabney
    Sharpe Spencer

Ensigns:
>Benjamin Allen
>James Carter
>Richard Holland
>William Rice

Second Lieutenants:
>Robert Goode
>William Wooton
>Henry Young

It appeared from an order made in July, 1777, that the following were then Captains of Militia Companies:
>———Clarke
>——— Owen
>———Ligon
>——— Bigger
>Thomas Flournoy
>——— Chambers
>William Bibb

In 1778 the following Captains were appointed:
>John Bibb
>George Carrington

In 1778 the following Lieutenants were appointed:
>John Dupuy
>Thomas Lawson

In 1778 the following Ensigns were appointed:
>———Bigger, Jr.
>Yancy Bailey

In 1779 the following Captains were appointed:
>Williamson Bird (in place of Chas. Venable, resigned)
>Richard Holland
>Sharpe Spencer
>Thomas Moore

And reference is made to the following persons as being, or having been Captains of companies:
>Geo. Booker
>Saml. Venable
>Henry Walker, Dec'd
>David Walker, Dec'd

In 1779 the following Lieutenants were appointed:

Nicholas Davis
Robert Venable
Geo. Booker
Jesse Watson
William McGehee
Ambrose Nelson
John Langhorn

In 1779 the following Ensigns were appointed:

James Parks
Drury Watson
Thomas Watkins

In 1779 Thomas Haskins was recommended as Colonel of the Militia of the county and George Walker as Lieutenant Colonel.

In 1780 the following were recommended or appointed as Captains:

Thomas Lawton
Dick Holland
Jacob Woodson

In 1780 the following were recommended or appointed as Lieutenants:

Jesse Watson
Drury Watson
William Price, Jr.
Joseph Parks
James Clark
James Wright

As Ensigns:

Stephen Pettus
John Bell
William Booker

In 1781:

John Nash recommended as County Lieutenant
Geo. Walker as Colonel
Thomas Flournoy as Lieut. Colonel
John Clark as Major

In 1781 the following were appointed as Captains:
Stephen Neal
James Clark
Ambrose Nelson (in place of John Bibb)

In 1781 the following were appointed as Lieutenants:
Nathaniel Allen
John Richards
Geo. Pulliam
George Foster
William Wooten
John Clarke, Jr.
James Parks
John Bell

In 1781 the following were appointed as Ensigns:
Philip Mathew
Robert Walton
Peyton Glenn
William Galespie

Muster Roll of Capt. John Morton's Company, of Prince Edward militia, June 28, 1781.

OFFICERS

Captain John Morton*
First Lt. John Holcomb
Second Lt. Obadiah Woodson
En. Edward Wood
Sergeant James Morton
Sergeant Samuel Anderson
Sergeant Charles Stogg
Sergeant Charles Anderson
Corporal Robert Lawton
Corporal Thomas Hastie
Corporal William Wright
Corporal William Chambers

PRIVATES

Anderson, Parsons
Ascul, William
Baldwin, Thomas
Bigger, William
Bird William
Boas, Michael
Brown, Isham
Byrk, Thomas
Casey, William
Chaffin, Isham
Chaffin, Christopher
Cocke, Anderson

*NOTE:—Capt Morton had eight sons in the service.

Boas, Meshack
Cunningham, Nathaniel
Cunningham, John
Daniel, George
Davidson, Edward
Davidson, William
Davidson, David
Davis, Charles
Durham, Nathaniel
Edmunds, Jacob
Fore, Francis
Foster, Joshua
Fraser, John
Fraser, Thomas
Fugue, William
Garratt, Alexander
Gillispie, William
Hales, Peter
Hampton, Nathan
Holman, Alexander
Hord, William
Howerton, James
Jennings, Isham
Jennings, James
Johnson, William
King, Thomas
Lee, John
Lee, Archibald
Leigh, Charles
Martin, Samuel
McGehee, William
Morton, Thomas
Newcomb, Julius
Parker, Glover
Peak, Aaron
Pierce, Thomas
Pillon, Jasper
Rain, Nathaniel
Robertson, David
Rutledge, Dudley
Sharp, Moses
Smith, Robert P.
Smith, John
Smith, Alexander
Spaulding, John
Sutherland, Philemon
Southerland, William
Taylor, George
Thompson, John
Tuggle, Benjamin
Tuggle, Thomas
Walker, Thomas
Walker, William, 1
Walker, William, 2
Watkins, Abner
Webster, John
Whitlock, Josiah
Wilburn, Thomas
Woodson, Anderson
Woodson, John
Wright, Archibald

Section 276—Rockbridge

Alexander, Joseph, F. L., S. Nov. 3, 1778.
Brown, John, gent., Co. Lt., S. April 7, 1778.
Buchanan, James, Cp., S. Aug. 3, 1779—vice S. Steel.
Campbell, Charles, gent., Cp., S. May 5, 1778.

Carruthers, John, F. L., S. Aug. 4, 1778.
Cloyd, David, Cp., R. March 8, 1780.
Cunningham, James, S. L., S. Nov. 3, 1778.
Davis, James, S. L., S. July 7, 1778.
Davison, Samuel, S. L., S. July 7, 1778.
Elliott, James, Cp., S. Nov. 3, 1778
Evans, Andrew, En., S. July 7, 1778.
Gay, John, gent., En., S. May 4, 1779.
Gilmore, John, gent., Cp., S. May 5, 1778.
Gilmore, John, gent., Lt. Col., S. April 7, 1778.
Gilmore, James, Jr., Cp., S. May 5, 1778.
Gray, David, gent., Cp., S. May 5, 1779.
Hall, James, Cp., S. May 5, 1778.
Harrison, Thomas, Cp., S. July 4, 1780.
Hay, James, En., S. May 4, 1779.
Hodge, James, Lt., S. Nov. 3, 1778.
Huston, James, En., R. Nov. 2, 1779.
Lyle, James, En., R. July 4, 1780—under S. Wallace.
Lyle, John, Cp., S. May 5, 1778.
Maxwell, Audley, En., R. March 8, 1780.
McCampbell, James, En., R. Nov. 7, 1780.
McClung, John, Lt., S. Nov. 7, 1780—under S. Wallace.
McClung, William, Jr., En., R. Nov. 2, 1779.
McDowell, Samuel, gent., Col., S. April 7, 1778.
McKee, Robert, F. L., S. Dec. 2, 1778.
McKenny, John, Lt., R. Nov. 7, 1780.
McMath, William, Lt., S. Sept. 5, 1780.
Moore, Andrew, Cp., S. May 6, 1778.
Patterson, Samuel, F. L., S. Sept. 1, 1778.
Paxton, John, Cp., S. May 5, 1778.
Paxton, William, Cp., S. May 5, 1778.
Poage, Robert, S. L., S. July 7, 1778.
Steel, Samuel, Cp., S. May 5, 1778—res. May 5, 1779.
Steel, Thomas, S. L., R. Nov. 2, 1779.
Stuart, Alexander, Maj., S. April 8, 1778.
Taylor, William, Lt., R. March 8, 1780.
Tedford, Alexander, Cp., S. Nov. 7, 1780.
Tedford, John, En., S. May 4, 1779.
Walker, Alexander, S. L., S. July 7, 1778.

Wallace, John, En., S. Sept. 5, 1780.
Wallace, Samuel, Cp., S. May 5, 1778.
Weir, George, Lt., S. April 7, 1779.
Wiley, Alexander, En., S. Sept. 5, 1780—under T. Harrison.
Wallace, David, En., S. May 11, 1780.
Wallace, Samuel, Cp., 1777.
Walter, William, S. L., R. April 12, 1781—under J. Lewis.
Watman, Henry, Cp., 1871—under J. Wood.
Watterson, Henry, Cp., A. July 12, 1781—vice G. Rutledge.
Wilson, ———, Cp., 1780.
Wood, James, Cp., A. July 13, 1781—vice W. Robinson.
Wright, James, Cp., 1778.

Section 277—Rockingham

Baker, Michael, Cp., R. May 29, 1781—vice J. Fitzwater.
Baker, Nicholas, Cp., S. Sept. 24, 1781.
Baxter, George, Cp., S. March 22, 1779.
Beazley, Jeremiah, Cp., S. March 27, 1780.
Bird, Andrew, Cp., S. May 24, 1779.
Bogg (Hogg?), Thomas, Cp., S. May 25, 1778.
Bryant, Peter, Lt., S. Aug. 27, 1781.
Cain, Cornelius, F. L., R. Oct. 25, 1780.
Carn, Nicholas, Lt., S. May 25, 1779.
Chrisman, George, Cp., S. March 26, 1781.
Coger, Michael, Cp., S. June 22, 1779.
Conrad, Stephen, Cp., S. Aug. 27, 1781—vice J. Beazley.
Craven, Robert, Cp., S. March 23, 1779.
Davidson, Josiah, Cp., 1780.
Davis, Robert, Cp., S. March 23, 1779—res. Nov. 24, 1781.
Dictum, John, S. L., R. Nov. 23, 1779—under J. Harman.
Dictum, Joseph, F. L., R. Oct. 23, 1780.
Eberman, William, Lt., R. Sept. 24, 1781—vice R. Minnis.
Erwin, Benjamin, En., R. Oct. 25, 1780—under T. Bogg.
Evans, Evan, Lt., S. Nov. 23, 1778.
Fitzwater, John, Cp., S. March 28, 1780.
Fitzwater, Thomas, S. L., R. March 28, 1780—under J. Fitzwater.
Frazier, James, Cp., S. June 22, 1779.

Gordon, Thomas, S. L., S. March 22, 1779.
Hamilton, Gawen, Maj., R. May 29, 1781—was also Lt. Col.
Hardman, John, F. L., S. March 22, 1779.
Harman.
Harrison, Benjamin, Lt. Col., S. May 25, 1778.
Harrison, Josiah, Cp., S. March 27, 1780.
Harrison, Josiah, En., R. March 26, 1781—under R. Morris.
Harrison, Robert, En., S. Sept. 24, 1781—under J. Harrison.
Harrison, Reuben, Cp., S. May 25, 1778.
Harvie, John, S. L., S. April 24, 1780.
Herring, William, Cp., R. Nov. 23, 1780.
Hevener, Jacob, En., S. March 27, 1780.
Hewitt, Thomas, Cp., S. May 25, 1778.
Hinkle, Isaac, Cp., S. Sept. 24, 1781—vice A. Thompson.
Hopkins, John, Cp., S. June 22, 1779.
Huston, George, Cp., S. March 28, 1780.
Huston, John, S. L., S. Nov. 28, 1780—under G. Huston.
Johnson, Andrew, Cp., S. March 22, 1779.
Keister, Frederick, Lt., S. Sept. 28, 1778.
Kyger, Christian, Lt., S. Aug. 27, 1781.
Lewis, Thomas, gent., En., S. Aug. 27, 1781.
Lincoln, Abraham, Cp., 1779.
Lincoln, Jacob, Lt., S. March 26, 1781.
Lingul, Paul, En., S. Nov. 23, 1778.
Minnis, Robert, Lt., res. Sept. 24, 1781.
Morris, Reuben, Cp., S. March 26, 1781.
Morris, William, S. L., S. Nov. 23, 1778.
Moyer, Philip, Lt., S. April 24, 1780.
Nelson, Daniel, En., R. Nov. 23, 1779—under G. Huston.
Nolle (Nall?), William, Lt. Col., S. March 27, 1781.
Painter, Christopher, En., S. May 25, 1779.
Patton, Benjamin, Cp., R. Nov. 24, 1781.
Pence, James, Cp., 1779.
Pirkey, John, Lt., S. Aug. 27, 1781.
Rader, Anthony, Cp., S. May 25, 1778.
Reagon, Richard, F. L., S. April 27, 1779—under D. Smith.
Rice, John, S. L., S. May 25, 1778.
Robinson, John, S. L., R. Aug. 27, 1781.
Ruddle, George, Cp., S. March 22, 1779.

Ruddle, John, Lt., S. Sept. 24, 1781.
Rush, John, Cp., S. March 22, 1779.
Rutherford, Joseph, S. L., S. March 27, 1780—under R. Reagan.
Rutherford, Elliot, En., S. March 27, 1780—under R. Reagan.
Shanklin, Andrew, F. L., R. Nov. 23, 1779—under G. Huston.
Skidmore, John, Maj., R. April 28, 1778.
Smith, Abraham, Co. Lt., S. May 25, 1778—res. Nov. 24, 1781.
Smith, Daniel, Col., S. May 25, 1778.
Smith, Daniel, Cp., S. May 25, 1778.
Smith, Joseph, F. L., S. May 25, 1778.
Smith, Joseph, S. L., S. April 27, 1779.
Smith, Reynolds (Benjamin?), En., S. March 27, 1781.
Smith, Robert, F. L., S. March 27, 1780—under R. Reagan.
Smith, William, En., S. May 25, 1778.
Smith, Benjamin, En., R. Aug. 27, 1781.
Stratton, Seraiah, Cp., R. Oct. 25, 1780.
Thompson, Andrew, Cp., res. Sept. 24, 1781.

Section 278—Shenandoah

Crookshank, John, Cp., S. July 27, 1780.
Galladay, David, En., S. Sept. 1, 1780.
Lambert, Jacob, En., S. Aug. 26, 1779.
Leath, John, Lt., S. June 29, 1780.
Nitherson (?), John, Maj., S. June 29, 1780.
Plumley, Matthew, Lt., S. Sept. 1, 1780.
Price, Evan, Lt., S. Aug. 26, 1779.
Reaner, Ulrich, Cp., S. July 27, 1780.
Riggins, William (?), Cp., S. June 29, 1780.
Riggins, Charles, En., S. June 29, 1780.
Sehorn, John, Cp., S. July 27, 1780.
Snapp, Philip, En., S. Aug. 26, 1779.
Syler, William, En., S. Nov. 25, 1779.
Windle, Philip, Lt., S. Aug. 26, 1779.

Section 279—Spottsylvania

Bartlett, Thomas, Cp., 1781.
Bartlett, Harry, gent., S. L., S. Sept. 18, 1777.

Brock, Joseph, Jr., En., S. June 15, 1780.
Carter, John, gent., Cp., S. Sept. 18, 1777.
Chew, John, gent., S. L., S. Sept. 18, 1777.
Chew, John, Jr., gent., S. L., S. Sept. 18, 1777.
Clayton, Thomas, gent., En., S. Sept. 18, 1777.
Coleman, Francis, Cp., R. July 19, 1781—vice W. Mills.
Collins, Bartlett, F. L., S. Nov. 17, 1780.
Dudley, Peter, En., S. Nov. 17, 1780.
Durrett, Robert, S. L., S. Sept. 21, 1780—under T. Minor.
Hardin, John, En., S. Feb. 19, 1779.
Holladay, James, En., S. Dec. 21, 1780—under Stubblefield.
Johnson, Benjamin, gent,, S. L., S. Feb. 19, 1779.
Legg, John, gent., Cp., S. May 17, 1781—vice W. McWilliams.
Lewis, John Z., En., S. Nov. 16, 1780.
Mason, John, Lt., S. Oct. 19, 1780—under T. Towles.
McCalley, John, Cp., S. Nov. 17, 1780—died about 1782.
McWilliams, William, Lt. Col., S. Aug. 16, 1781.
Meals, John, gent., Cp., S. Feb. 19, 1779—vice G. Thornton.
Miller, Thomas, gent., F. L., S. Sept. 18, 1777.
Mills, William, gent., Cp., S. Sept. 17, 1777—res. July 19, 1781.
Minor, Thomas, Cp., 1782.
Owens, James, S. L., S. Nov. 17, 1780.
Page, Mann, Esq., Lt. Col., S. July 19, 1781.
Sharpe, Thomas, Lt., S. Oct. 19, 1780—under White.
Smith, Robert, gent., F. L., S. Sept. 18, 1777.
Stubblefield, ———, Cp., 1780.
Tankersley, John, Cp., R. July 19, 1781—vice T. Bartlett.
Taylor, James, gent., Cp., S. Sept. 21, 1780.
Thornton, George, gent., Maj., S. Nov. 16, 1780.
Towles, Thomas, gent., Maj., S. Aug. 16, 1781.
Tutt, James, gent., Cp., S. April 2, 1776.
Washington, Charles, Lt. Col., S. Oct. 19, 1780.
White, ———, Cp., 1780.
Wiglesworth, James, S. L., S. Dec. 21, 1780—under Stubblefield.
Winslow, Beverley., Co. Lt., S. July 19, 1781.
Wright, William, En., S. Sept. 21, 1780.
Yates, Robert, gent., S. L., S. Sept. 18, 1777.

Section 280—Washington

Adams, Cp. Geo.
Allison, Lt. Chas.
Anderson, Cp. John.
Anderson, Lt. John.
Barnett, En. Alex.
Beattie, Lt. David.
Berry, Lt. John.
Black, Lt. Joseph.
Blackburn, Lt. Wm.
Bowen, En. Arthur.
Bowen, En. Rees.
Bowen, Cp. Wm.
Buchanan, Capt. Robt., Sr.
Campbell, Lt. Col. Arthur.
Campbell, Lt. Charles.
Campbell, Cp. John.
Campbell, Cp. John.
Campbell, Lt. Col. William.
Casey, En. Wm.
Christian, Cp. Gilbert.
Colvill, Cp. Andr.
Coulter, Lt. John.
Crabtree, En. James.
Craig, Cp. Robt.
Davis, En. John.
Davis, En. Robt.
Dickenson, En. Henry.
Duncan, Cp. John.
Dysart, Cp. James.
Edminston, Majr. Wm.
Edmiston, Cp. Wm.
Elliott, En. James.
Frazier, Lt. John.
Freeland, En. Geo.
Fulkerson, Lt. James.
Hays, Lt. Saml.
Kinkead, Cp. John.
Kincannon, Lt. Andr.
Lewis, Cp. Aaron.
Litton, En. Solomon.
Looney, Ensign John.
Lowny, Ensign John.
McClelland, Ensign Abraham.
Maxwell, Lt. Geo.
Maxwell, Lt. James.
Martin, Cp. Joseph.
Mastin, Cp. Thomas.
Montgomery, Cp. James.
Neal, En. Wm.
Price, Lt. Thos.
Ramsey, En. Josiah.
Robertson, Cp. James.
Rosebrough, En. Wm.
Shaw, En. James.
Shelby, Col. Evan.
Shelby, Cp. James.
Shelby, Cp. John, Sr.
Smith, Maj. Daniel.
Snoddy, Lt. John.
Topp, Lt. Roger.
Ward, Lt. David.
Whitten, En. Thomas.
Wilson, Ensign John.
Wylie, Lt. Alex.

Pensioners Residing in Virginia in 1835 who Received Pensions as Virginia Militiamen

PART IV.

(Embracing those residing in what is now W. Va.)

NOTE:—This list is arranged alphabetically, but is so arranged as to give, in alphabetical order, the counties in which the pensioners lived. Owing to this arrangement the exact alphabetical arrangement of the names was not possible.

NOTE:—The figures indicate age of person named.

NOTE:—The initials I. S. stand for Indian Spy.

Adams, Henry, Bedford Co., 73.
Andrew, Thos., Bedford Co., 72.
Arthur, Wm., Bedford Co., 72.
Alverson, Jno, Botetourt Co., 76.
Agee, Jacob, Buckingham Co., 77.
Anderson Jas., Cabell Co., W. Va.
  (Alias Asha Crockett).
Arrington, Adler, Campbell Co., 73.
Anderson, Nathan, Chesterfield Co., 70.
Andrews, Isham, Chesterfield Co.
Armstrong, Jno., Essex Co., 72.
Abshire, Abraham, Franklin Co., 70.
Adams, Elisha, Franklin Co., 71.
Akers, John, Franklin Co., 76.
Abbott, Wm., Halifax Co., 78.
Ashcroft, Jno., Harrison Co., 97.
Armstead, Wm., Mathews Co., 76.
Andrews, Vorney, Mecklenburg Co., 80.

Arnot, Henry, Monroe Co., W. Va., 73.
Argubute, Jacob, Monroe Co., W. Va., 74.
Ayers, Sergt. Elisha, Patrick Co., 74.
Anderson, Jacob, Pittsylvania Co., 72.
Arboghart, Adam (Arbogast), Pocahontas Co., W. Va., 74.
Ammonet, Charles, Powhatan Co., 76. (Died April 14, 1833).
Alley, Abraham, Prince George Co., 71.
Allstock, Absalom (Ailstock), Rockbridge Co., 74.
Ammon, Christopher, Sergt., Rockingham Co., 75.
Augubright, Geo., Rockingham Co., 75.
Alsop, Lt. Benj., Spottsylvania Co., 76.
Alcock, Lt. Thomas, Stafford Co.

Bull, Curtis, Accomack Co., 72.
Bull, Danl., Accomack Co., 75.
Bowden, Micajah, Albemarle Co., 81.
Bell, Corp. Christopher, Amherst Co., 80.
Blair, Allen, Amherst Co., 80.
Bonner, Wm., Bath Co., 74.
Bailey, Philip, Bedford Co., 86.
Barton, Corp. Elisha, Bedford Co., 76.
Blankenship, Abraham, Bedford Co., 74.
Bond, Sergt Wright, Bedford Co., 74.
Brown, Henry, Bedford Co., 74.
Brown, Thos., Bedford Co., 86.
Banks, Jacob, Buckingham Co., 77.
Branch, Olive, Buckingham Co., 74.
Bloss, Valentine, Cabell Co., W. Va., 77.
Brooks, Jas., Campbell Co., 74.
Brooks, Nelson, Campbell Co., 75.
Browne, Henry, Campbell Co., 74.
Beadles, Edmund, Caroline Co., —.
Bass, Edward, Jr., Chesterfield Co., 80.
Bass, Jno., Chesterfield Co., 73.
Bernard, Benj., Chesterfield Co., 77.
Barton, Richard, Chesterfield Co., 82.
Blankenship, Josiah, Chesterfield Co., 76. (Died March 26, 1833).
Bradley, Sergt. Austin, Culpeper Co., 87. (Died Dec. 15, 1832).
Brown, Danl., Sergt., Culpeper Co., 85. (Died July 14, 1833).

Brown, Jno, Culpeper Co., 74.
Brown, Wm., Culpeper Co., 76.
Bass, Jno, Dinwiddie Co., 74.
Bolling, Capt. Ro., Dinwiddie Co., 75.
Ball, Stephen, Essex Co., 72.
Beazley, Ephriam, Essex Co., 72.
Beale, Richd. E., Fauquier Co., 74.
Blackwell, David, Fauquier Co., 84.
Brizendine, Wm., Sr., Franklin Co., 91.
Barr, Jas., Frederick Co., 81.
Beatty, Henry, Frederick Co., 94.
Blakeman, Ensign Geo., Frederick Co., —.
Buckner, Sergt. Philip B., Frederick Co., 83.
Bishop, Hy., Floyd Co., 77.
Brooks, Thos., Goochland Co., 90.
Bailey, Thos., Halifax Co., 73.
Bates, Ensign Jas., Halifax Co., 74.
Bunton, Wm., Halifax Co., 70.
Berry, Wm., Hampshire Co., W. Va., 90.
Brinkley, Lt. Henry, Hampshire Co., 73.
Bills, Jno E., Hardy Co., W. Va., 71.
Bolener, Adam, Hardy Co., 67.
Bailey, Jos., Harrison Co., W. Va., —.
Bell, Rich'd, I. S., Harrison Co., W. Va., —. (Va. Cont. Line.)
Brake, Jno., I. S., Harrison Co., W. Va., —.
Burns, Michael, Henry Co., 83.
Bailey, Isham, Kanawha Co., W. Va., 79.
Bailey, Wm., Kanawha Co., W. Va., 80.
Beadless, Joel., King William Co., 73.
Butler, Jno., King William Co., 70.
Bibb, Thos., Lewis Co., W. Va., 80.
Bonnett, Peter, I. S., Lewis Co., W. Va., 70.
Brown, Isacher, Loudoun Co., 73.
Butler, Jacob, Loudoun Co., 76. (Died June 9, 1833.)
Badger, Thomas, Louisa Co., 73.
Bullock, David, Louisa Co., 73. (Died Feb. 16, 1833.)
Bragg, Wm., Luenburg Co., 73.
Brandon, Thos., Mecklenburg Co., 88.

Butler, Jos., Mecklenburg Co., 76.
Bertrug, Peter, Monongalia Co., W. Va., 84.
Boon, John, Monroe Co., W. Va., 79.
Bell, Sr., Robt., Montgomery Co., 75.
Byrd, Wm., Nansemond Co., 71.
Breeding, John, New Kent Co., 76.
Boaz, Sergt. James, Patrick Co., 85.
Boman, John, Patrick Co., 75.
Boyd, James, Patrick Co., 71.
Blechhynden, Charles, Pendleton Co., W. Va., 76.
Blizzard, Burton, Pendleton Co., W. Va., 77.
Borer, Charles, Pendleton Co., W. Va., 74.
Blankenship, Jno, Pittsylvania Co., 74. (Died Oct. 28, 1832.)
Bradshaw, John, I. S., Pocahontas Co., W. Va., 75.
Bass, Sr., Wm., Powhatan Co., 71.
Boatwright, John, Prince Edward Co., 71.
Brightwell, Charles, Prince Edward Co., 78.
Bell, John, Prince William Co., 71.
Brown, Thos., Preston Co., W. Va., 74.
Bartleys, James, Rockingham Co., 74.
Berry, Benj., Rockingham Co., 76.
Bryan, Wm., Rockingham Co., 72.
Beal, Shadrach (of Ben), Southampton Co., 71.
Beall, John, Southampton Co., 76.
Bullock, Sergt. James, Spottsylvania Co., 73.
Bishop, Wm., Surrey Co., 37.
Booth, Beverley, Surrey Co., 82.
Buckhart, Henry, Smythe Co., 73.
Bowling, Jarrett, Tazewell Co., 72.
Brickey, Wm., Westmoreland Co., 78.
Brookover, John, Wood Co., W. Va., 74.
Blackard, Will-you-be, Wythe Co., 76.
Biggs, Jno., Bedford Co., 69.

Chase, Robt., Accomack Co., 73.
Carr, Mickens, Albemarle Co., 72.
Collins, Jno., Albemarle Co., 86.
Campbell, Jno., Amherst Co., 83.

Campbell, Anthony, Bedford Co., 74.
City, Jacob, Bedford Co., 73.
Cartmill, Lieut. Hy., Botetourt Co., 80.
Congleton, Moses, Brooke Co., W. Va., 70.
Criswell, Richd., Brooke Co., W. Va., 86.
Cummins, Ro., Brooke Co., W. Va., 82.
Clairborne, Leonard, Buckingham Co., 73.
Campbell, Wm., Campbell Co., 85.
Candler, Wm., Campbell Co., 82.
Carson, Wm., Campbell Co., 85.
Cobbs, Jno., Campbell Co., 75.
Corneyle, Jacob, Campbell Co., 83.
Clark, Jas., Chesterfield Co., 84.
Condrey, Jno., Chesterfield Co., 74.
Cox, Bartlett, Cumberland Co., 82.
Cole, Francis, Dinwiddie Co., 83.
Cogghill, Thos., Essex Co., 71.
Croxton, Carter, Essex Co., 72.
Cooper, Barnabas, Fayette Co., W. Va., 74. (Died Jan. 6, 1833.)
Cooper, Eiles, Franklin Co., 86.
Cooper, Sterling, Franklin Co., 74.
Campbell, Jno., Frederick Co., 74.
Crutchfield, Stapleton, Goochland Co., 75. (Died June 29, 1833.)
Chandoin, Lewis, Goochland Co., 80.
Comer, Jno., Grayson Co., 81.
Childrey, Wm., Halifax Co., 74.
Crump, Henry, Hampshire Co., W. Va., 77.
Chrisholme, Ensign Walter, Hanover Co., 102.
Carn, Jno., Harrison Co., W. Va., 92.
Coplin, Benj., Harrison Co., W. Va., 84.
Crimm, Harman, Harrison Co., 84.
Cunningham, Walter, Harrison Co., W. Va., 85.
Christian, Ro., Kanawha Co., W. Va., 70.
Carlton, Benoni, King George Co., 71.
Carlton, Humphrey, King George Co., 81.
Cain, Sergt. Jno., Lewis Co., W. Va., 76.
Cartington, Jno., Lewis Co., W. Va., 70.
Coteral, Thos., Lewis Co., W. Va., 72.

Cox, Philip, Lewis Co., W. Va., 71.
Cuthright, Jno., Lewis Co., W. Va., 80.
Coombs, Jno., Loudoun Co., 80.
Copeland, Jas., Loudoun Co., 75.
Cooksey, Chas., Lunenburg Co., 72.
Canedy, Leroy, Madison Co., 77.
Clutterbuck, Jas., Madison Co., 74.
Callis, Geo., Mathews Co., 74.
Christian, Jno., Mathews Co., 73.
Clibourn, Wm., Mecklenburg Co., 68.
Cunningham, James, Mecklenburg Co., 70.
Chalflin, Solomon, Monongalia Co., W. Va., 82.
Clayton, Elisha, Monongalia Co., W. Va., 77.
Chambers, Sergt. Robt., Monroe Co., W. Va., 80.
Charlton, Francis, Montgomery Co., 75.
Clarke, Samuel, Monroe Co., W. Va., 70.
Canafax, Wm., Monroe Co., W. Va., 75.
Campbell, Henry, Nelson Co., 71.
Carpenter, Jesse, Nicholas Co., W. Va., 74.
Chapman, Jacob, Nicholas Co., W. Va., 81.
Crenshaw, Wm. (Creushaw), Nottoway Co., 74.
Cardwell, John, Ohio Co., W. Va., 81.
Carter, Wm., Patrick Co., 76.
Carter, Sergt. Wm., Patrick Co., 72.
Cloud, Lt. Wm., Patrick Co., 84.
Chancy, Abraham, Pittsylvania Co., 74.
Colley, Charles, Pittsylvania Co., 76.
Cullins, John, Powhatan Co., 75.
Carter, Poval, Prince Edward Co., 72.
Chievers, Joel, Prince George Co., 76.
Casey, Nicholas, Preston Co., W. Va., 80.
Colvin, Geo., Rappahannock Co., 71.
Colvin, Mason, Rappahannock Co., 74.
Croddy, John, Rockbridge Co., 79.
Custer, Richard, Rockingham Co., 77.
Collins, Jeffrey, Shenandoah Co., 78.
Council, Jesse, Southampton Co., 73.
Corbitt, Sr., Samuel, Southampton Co., 75.

Corckett, James, Southampton Co., 71.
Cason, Edward, Spottsylvania Co., 82. (Dead.)
Cason, Wm., Spottsylvania Co., 74.
Chappell, Wm., Sussex Co., 72.
Cecil, Wm., I. S., Tazewell Co., 85.
Chaffin, Christopher, Tazewell Co., 77.
Cline, Andrew, Washington Co., 85.
Cunningham, Wm., Wood Co., W. Va., 71.

Drumheller, Leonard, Albermarle Co., 72.
Davis, Wm., Alleghany Co., 77.
Davidson, Giles, Amherst Co., 72.
Davidson, Stephen, Buckingham Co., 77.
Duvall, Capt. Wm., Buckingham Co., 86.
Davis, Danl., Cabell Co., W. Va., 76.
Dinguid, Geo., Campbell Co., 72.
Dyson, Jno., Chesterfield Co., 71.
Dale, Richd., Franklin Co., 74.
Davis, Lewis, Franklin Co., 78.
Dixon, Nath., Franklin Co., 91.
Dickerson, Elijah, Floyd Co., 79.
Dunkley, Jno., Halifax Co., 75.
Dunkley, Moses, Halifax Co., 75.
Davis, Spencer Hampshire Co., W. Va., 73.
Davis, Samuel, Hampshire Co., W. Va., 73.
Davidson, Jonah, Hampshire Co., W. Va., —.
Davidson, Josiah, Hampshire Co., 70.
Davis, Wm., Lewis Co., W. Va.
Dailey, Jesse, Loudoun Co., 73.
Davis, Thos., Mathews Co., 71.
Diggs, Wm., Mathews Co., 74.
Devers, James, Monongalia Co., W. Va., 79.
Dobson, Richard, New Kent Co., 71.
Duffield, Abraham, Nicholas Co., W. Va., 71.
Dunbar, Jonathan, Nicholas Co., W. Va., 72.
Davis, Isaac, Sr., Orange Co., 81.
Devericks, John, Pendleton Co., W. Va., 79.
Dove, Sergt. Wm., Pittsylvania Co., 76.
Dickenson, Corp. Griffith, Pittsylvania Co., 77.

Dawson, Henry, Prince Edward Co., 82.
Dupuy, Lt. John, Prince Edward Co., 79. (Died Oct 1, 1832).
Davis, Wm., Prince William Co., 74.
Davis, Leonard, Rockingham Co., 72.
Drake, Ridley, Southampton Co., 72.
Dolsbury, Lyles, Tazewell Co., 74.
Dotson, Richard, I. S., Tyler Co., W. Va., 82.

Ellis, Stephen, Brunswick Co., 70.
Evers, Sergt. Sampson, Campbell Co., 81.
Edwards, Benj., Floyd Co., 77.
Emmons, Jas., Giles Co., 76.
Estes, Geo., Halifax Co., 71.
Elgin, Gustavus, Capt., Loudoun Co., 80. (Died Jan. 24, 1834.)
Elgin, Sergt. Walter, Loudoun Co., 78.
Estes, Jno., Lunenburg Co., 78.
Evans, Wm., Mathews Co., 86. (Died April 24, 1833.)
Evans, Col. John, Monongalia Co., 95.
Everley, Simon, I. S., Monongalia Co., W. Va., 71.
Ellison, James, I. S., Monroe Co., W. Va., 77.
Easter, John, Morgan Co., W. Va., 74.
East, Isham, Patrick Co., 77.
Elliott, John, Pittsylvania Co., 86.
Evans, Wm., Sussex Co., 77.
Elder, John, Wythe Co., 78.

Floyd, Mathew, Accomack Co., 71.
Fauber, Peter, Augusta Co., 77.
Fulton, Robt., Augusta Co., 74.
Fletcher, Richd., Brunswick Co., 71.
Forbes, Alex., Buckingham Co., 72.
Franklin, Thos., Campbell Co., 75.
Franklin, Thos. P., Campbell Co., 71.
Foushee, Geo., Culpeper Co., 74. (Died Aug. 13, 1833.)
Farris, Jacob, Cumberland Co., 82.
Fugate, Jeremiah, Fairfax Co., 80.
Fleshman, Moses, Fayette Co., W. Va., 74.
Foster, Jas., Frederick Co., 72.
Faudre, Thos., Goochland Co., —.

Fielder, Dennis, Grayson Co., 78.
Foggerson, Francis, Greenville Co., 72.
Ferrell, Wm., Halifax Co., 82.
Fletcher, Thos., Halifax Co., 73.
Fisher, Jacob, Hardy Co., W. Va., 77.
Flemming, Lt. Jas., Harrison Co., W. Va., 90. (Died May 14, 1833.)
Franklin, Lewis, Henry Co., 76.
Flesher, Adam, Lewis Co., W. Va., —.
Fowles, Hy., Madison Co., 78.
Fitz, Robt. W., Mecklenburg Co., 78.
Farbee, Caleb, Monongalia Co., W. Va., 82.
Fisher, Jacob, Nicholas Co., W. Va., 71.
Fitzgerald, Harvey, Patrick Co., 72.
Fowlkes, Sergt. James, Pittsylvania Co., 74. (Dead).
Fenn, John, Prince George Co., 74.
Finch, James, Prince George Co., 75.
Fainter, Martin, Rockbridge Co., 95.
Fletcher, Thos., Scott Co., 85.
Fletcher, Geo., Shenandoah Co., 90.
Feltz, Frederick, Sussex Co., 72.
Flowers, Abraham, Sussex Co., 76.
Fleenor, Michael, Washington Co., 77.

Gaines, Richd., Albemarle Co., 82.
Gentry, Geo., Albemarle Co., 68.
Grant, Robt, Amherst Co., 73.
Gillispie, Wm., Bath Co., 79.
Greene, Wm., Bath Co., 78.
Graham, Michael, Bedford Co., 76.
Groom, Jonathan, Bedford Co., 78.
Graddy, Jos., Campbell Co., 77.
Glass, Chas., Bedford Co., 75.
Gatewood, Wm., Caroline Co., 70.
Goode, Wm., Sr., Chesterfield Co., 73.
Greggory, Thos., Chesterfield Co., 83.
Griffin, Sergt. Zach., Culpeper Co., 74.
Grove, Philip, Fauquier Co., 78.
Gibson, Sergt. John, Franklin Co., 82.
Graves, David, Franklin Co., 75. (Died Aug. 20, 1833.)

Grier, Capt. Moses, Franklin Co., 90.
Grim, Jno., Frederick Co., 80.
Grinstead, Wm., Goochland Co., 72.
Gray, Jas., Goochland Co., 70.
Guill, Wm., Halifax Co., 73.
Guthrey, Jno., Halifax Co., 74.
Gilmon, Ensign Edmond, Hanover Co., 71.
Green, Sergt. Fortunatus, Hanover Co., 80.
George, Jos., Hardy Co., W. Va., 73.
Goodnight, Christo'r, Hardy Co., W. Va., 72.
Goodwin, Jno, Harrison Co., W. Va., 72.
Goff, Job., Harrison Co., W. Va., 74.
Griffith, Obadiah, Sergt., Henrico Co., 78.
Grass, Peter, Kanawha Co., W. Va., 79.
Gardner, Wm., I. S., Lewis Co., W. Va., 74.
Gibson, Nicholas, Lewis Co., W. Va., —.
Gideon, Peter, Loudoun Co., 82.
Griffith, Thos., Loudoun Co., 77.
Gibson, John, Louisa Co., 84.
Gibbs, Luman, Mason Co., W. Va., 69.
Green, Simon, Mathews Co., 75. (Dead)
Garter, Nathaniel, Monroe Co., W. Va., 74.
Gaulden, Wm., Pittsylvania Co., 81.
Giles, Geo., Pittsylvania Co., 72.
Giles, Josiah, Prince Edward Co., 78.
Gillespie, Geo., Prince Edward Co., 82.
Grubbs, Nathan, Prince Edward Co., 76.
Gill, Sergt. John, Prince William Co., 71.
Gollyhorn, Thos., Stafford Co., 91.
Gilliland, Lt. James, Washington Co., 89.

Harman, John, Accomack Co., 70.
Hickman, Jno. B., Accomack Co., 71.
Hall, Jno., Albemarle Co., 86.
Hall, Nathan, Albemarle Co., 87.
Harrison, Richd. Albemarle Co., 77.
Harris, Wm., Albemarle Co., 80.
Herring, Jas., Albemarle Co., 80.
Huckstep, Chas., Albemarle Co., 72.

Hutcherson, Jno., Amelia Co., 70.
Hamilton, Alex., Augusta Co., 75.
Hackworth, Thos., Bedford Co., 71.
Hancock, Sergt. Sam'l, Bedford Co., 74.
Haynes, Jno., Bedford Co., 81.
Holly, Jno., Bedford Co., 73.
Hudwell, Jno., Bedford Co., 70.
Henry, Wm., Botetourt Co., 79.
Hewitt, Jno., Botetourt Co., 70.
Hunter, Francis, Botetourt Co., 72.
Hall, Isam, Campbell Co., 71.
Harvey, Thos., Campbell Co., 72.
Hervard, Jas., Campbell Co., 71.
Hughes, Benj., Campbell Co., 69.
Hunter, Jno., Campbell Co., —.
Hendricks, Daniel, Charlotte Co., 73.
Hill, Wm., Chesterfield Co., 75.
Hall, Jno., Culpeper Co., 73.
Hatcher, Seth., Cumberland Co., 74.
Huff, Jno., Franklin Co., 71.
Hensell, Geo., Frederick Co., 75.
Heard, Jno., Floyd Co., 74.
Howell, Danl., Sr., Floyd Co., 75.
Hull, Hy., Giles Co., 72.
Hogg, Thomas., Gloucester Co., 70.
Hull, Geo., Greenbrier Co., W. Va., 76.
Hancock, Jas., Halifax Co., 82.
Henderson, Edward, Halifax Co., 88. (Dead)
Hamrick, Sergt. Siras, Hampshire Co., W. Va., 81.
Hawkins, Jno., Hampshire Co., W. Va., 84.
Herrin, Sergt. Wm., Hampshire Co., W. Va., 72.
Hook, Wm., Hampshire Co., W. Va., 75.
Hall, Wm., Hanover Co., 75.
Hill, Corp. Jno., Hanover Co., 84.
Hope, Jno., Hanover Co., 73.
Haddox, ———, I. S., Harrison Co., W. Va., 76.
Harbert, Edward, I. S., Harrison Co., W. Va., 72.
Harbert, Sam., Va. Line, I. S., Harrison Co., W. Va., 74.
Harrow, Jacob, Spy, Harrison Co., W. Va., 79.

Hickman, Sotha, I. S., Harrison Co., W. Va., 86.
Husstead, Moses, I. S., Harrison Co., W. Va., 86.
Hamilton, Jas., Lee Co., 77.
Hess, Hez., I. S., Lewis Co., W. Va., 78.
Holbert, Aaron, Lewis Co., W. Va., 81.
Hyde, Jacob, I. S., Lewis Co., W. Va., 77.
Harvin, Edward, Loudoun Co.
Hogeland, James, Loudoun Co., 74.
Harrison, Jno., Madison Co., 74.
Hawkins, Wm., Mason Co., W. Va., 69.
Hudgins, Anthy., Mathews Co., 75.
Hudgins, Hugh, Mathews Co., 70.
Hughes, Gabriel Mathews Co., 71.
Houston, Purnell, Mathews Co., 80.
Hull, Sergt. Wm., Mathews Co., 81.
Hurst, Richd., Mathews Co., 72.
Haught, Peter, Monongalia Co., W. Va., 78.
Hand, Christopher, Monroe Co., W. Va., 75.
Hall, Jesse, Montgomery Co., 74.
Harley, Peter, Montgomery Co., 81.
Howe, Daniel, Montgomery Co., 76.
Henry, Nicholas, Morgan Co., W. Va., 74.
Harrell, John, Nansemond Co., —.
Harrison, Henry, Nansemond Co., 76.
Howard, Miles, Nansmond Co., —.
Hale, Leonard, Nelson Co., 78.
Hargrave, Hezekiah, Nelson Co., 86.
Harper, Henry, Nelson Co., 76.
Harris, Wm., Nelson Co., 86.
Hight, Mtthew, Nelson Co., 71.
Hill, Richard, Orange Co., 79.
Hicks, Farthings, Patrick Co., 74.
Hoover, Jacob, Pendleton Co., W. Va., 83.
Hoover, Michael, Pendleton Co., W. Va., 81.
Huffman, Henry, Pendleton Co., W. Va., 77.
Harris, John, Pittsylvania Co., 81.
Hopkins, James, Pittsylvania Co., 69.
Hubbard, Jos., Pittsylvania Co., 73.
Hutchings, Moses, Pittsylvania Co., 81.

Hawk, Isaac, Pocahontas Co., W. Va., 75.
Hall, James, Powhatan Co., 73.
Hill, Wm., Prince Edward Co., 76.
Hines, Sr., Wm., Prince Edward Co., 80.
Hair, Daniel, Prince George Co., 74.
Hartzell, Jacob, Preston Co., W. Va., 83.
Hopkins, Levi., Preston Co., W. Va., 80.
Hanck, Geo. M., Rappahannock Co., 75.
Hughes, Sergt. Thomas., Rappahannock Co., 79.
Harrison, Reuben, Rockbridge Co., 76.
Hickman, Adam, Rockbridge Co., 72.
Hinkle, Henry, Rockbridge Co., 85.
Huling, Andrew, Rockingham Co., 73.
Howderskell, Law., Rockingham Co., 82.
Helsley, Jacob, Shenandoah Co., 78.
Holloway, Thos., Sussex Co., 71.
Hennigan, John, Smythe Co., 64.
Heysham, David, Tyler Co., W. Va.
Harkerider, Capt. John, Wythe Co., 84.
Helmick, John, Wythe Co., 75.

Isbel, Benj., Goochland Co., 71.
Isbel, Henry, Goochland Co., 73.
Iden, John, Loudoun Co., 82.

Johnson, Richd., Albemarle Co., 72.
Jordan, Wm., Albemarle Co., 75.
Johnson, Thos., Augusta Co., 73.
Jones, Gray, Bedford Co., 74.
Jordan, Freeman, Brunswick Co., 74.
Jameson, Lt. David, Culpeper Co., 82.
James, W. M., Gloucester Co., 76.
Jenkins Cleb., Gloucester Co., 74.
Johnson, Chas., Goochland Co., 85.
Johnson, Wm., Goochland Co., 79. (Died June 3, 1833).
Jones, Berryman, Greenbrier Co., W. Va., 77.
Jones, Jno., Halifax Co., 76.
Jenkins, Absalom, Hanover Co., 75.
Jones, Taverner, Madison Co., 79.

Jarvis, Field, Monroe Co., W. Va., 77.
Johnson, John, Morgan Co., W. Va., 100.
Jones, Elijah, Nansamond Co., —.
Jarrell, Wm., Orange Co., 81.
Jeffress, Wm., Pittsylvania Co., 75.
Jones, Elisha, Pittsylvania Co., 79.
Jones, Thos., Pittsylvania Co., 79.
Jenkins, Richard, Page Co., 84.
Jackson, Henry, Powhatan Co., 73.
Jesse, Wm., Prince Edward Co., 74.
Johnson, Andrew, Preston Co., W. Va.
Jeffries, Reuben, Rappahannock Co., 72.
Jordan, Wm., Rappahannock Co., 78.
Joyner, Joshua, Southampton Co., 77.
Jett, Lt. Wm. S., Westmoreland Co., —.

Kellam, Honsten, Accomack Co., 78.
Kincaid, Jno., Bath Co., 76.
Kemper, Ensign Chas., Fauquier Co., 78.
Kincaid, Jno., Fayette Co., W. Va.
King, Stephen, Franklin Co., 82.
Knipe, Sergt. Hy., Frederick Co., 82. (Died June 20, 1833).
King, Jno., Floyd Co.
King, Jacob, Hanover Co., 72.
Keys, Wm., Harrison Co., W. Va., 76.
Kester, Jos., Harrison Co., W. Va., 81.
Knight, Peter, Harrison Co., W. Va., 74.
King, Wm., Montgomery Co., 78.
Kidd, James, Nelson Co., 68.
Kearney, Edward, Ohio Co., W. Va., 81.
Kepps, Jacob, Shenandoah Co., 71.
Kendall, Aaron, Stafford Co., 69.
Keys, Sergt. James, Washington Co., 79.

Lohr, Peter, Augusta Co., 83.
Lambert, Capt. Geo., Bedford Co., 86.

Lowry, Jno., Bedford Co., 71.
Lemmon, Sergt. Jacob, Btoetourt Co., 72.
Lewis, Ruel., Brunswick Co., 75.
Laidley, Thos., Cabell Co., W. Va., 79.
Lindsay, Lewis, Charlotte Co., 79.
Lowry, Giles, Culpeper Co., 100.
Law, Jno., Franklin Co., 87.
Lumsden, Chas., Franklin Co., 73.
Lucas, Sergt. Basil, Frederick Co., 77.
Layne, Corp. Anthy., Goochland Co., 76.
Lowry, Thornton, Goochland Co., 74.
Littlepage, John C., Hanover Co., 85. (Private and Capt. of Virginia Troops. Died Feb. 2, 1834.)
Long, Jacob, Loudoun Co., 80.
Lee, Ludwell, Loudoun Co., 73.
Love, Robt., Mason Co., W. Va., 71.
Lucas, Capt. John, Montgomery Co., 85.
Laird, Wm., New Kent Co., 74.
Lain, Jos., Pittsylvania Co., 74.
Lifford, Anthony P., Pittsylvania Co., 79.
Lipscomb, Ambrose, Randolph Co., W. Va., 82.
Lillard, John, Rappahannock Co., 71.
Lewis, Lt. Thos., Rockingham Co., 74.
Lawson, William, Scott Co., 70.
Leneweaver, Jacob, Shenandoah Co., 71.
Love, Henry, Southampton Co., 79.
Lewis, Jacob, Tyler Co., W. Va., 78.
Leckie, Wm., Washington Co., 69.
Lloyd, John Washington Co., 71.
Leach, Thos., Wood Co., W. Va., 70.

Mears, Hilleary, Accomack Co., 75.
Maupin, Danl., Albemarle Co., 78.
Maupin, Wm., Albemarle Co., 75.
McFall, Corneli., Albemarle Co., 100.
Mayse, Chas., Albemarle Co., 71.
Miles, Thos., Albemarle Co., 74.
McFadden, Jno., Augusta Co., 74.
McCane, Sen. Samuel, Augusta Co., 79.

McCutchen, Jno., Augusta Co., 84.
McWilliams, Jno., Augusta Co., 74.
Matheny, Wm., Augusta Co., 75.
Markham, Jno., Bedford Co., 70.
Markham, Tho., Jr., Bedford Co., 77.
Meadows, Benj., Bedford Co., 70.
Mitchell, Saml., Bedford Co., 73.
Miner, Wm., Bedford Co., 81.
Moore, Sergt. Ro., Bedford Co., 83.
McComas, Jno., Cabell Co., W. Va., 77.
Mann, Jos., Campbell Co., 85.
Mathews. Saml., Campbell Co., 71.
Moore, Thos., Campbell Co., 85.
Madison, Wm., Caroline Co., 71.
McDearman, Sergt. Thomas., Charlotte Co., 76.
Mann, Peter, Chesterfield Co., 78.
Moseley, Peter, Chesterfield Co., 71.
Montague, Thos., Cumberland Co., 81.
Major, Saml., Dinwiddie Co., 74.
Munroe, Wm. H., Fairfax Co., 74.
Merry, Philip, Fauquier Co., 85.
Melton, Pearce W., Fluvanna Co., 71.
Mitchell, Henry, Franklin Co., 71.
Meadows, Jacob, Giles Co., 71.
Moore, Amos L., Goochland Co., 87.
Mortimer, Jas., Grayson Co., 78.
McMilliam, Jas., Greenbrier Co., W. Va., 71.
Martin, Zach, Halifax Co., 72. (Dead.)
Mallory, Jno., Hanover Co., 79.
Mantlo, Jno., Hanover Co., 80. (Died April 30, 1833.)
Meredith, Jas., Hanover Co., 71.
Marshall, Benj., Hardy Co., W. Va., 79.
Martin, Wm., Harrison Co., W. Va., 70.
McRee, Wm., Harrison Co., 78.
Millam, Rush, Kanawha Co., W. Va., 75.
Mardis, Jno., King George Co., 74.
Morris, Clairborne, King William Co., 80.
Martin, Jno., Lee Co., 72.
Mace, Isaac, Ind. Spy, Lewis Co., W. Va., 79.

Mitchell, Jno., Lewis Co., W. Va., 72.
Muckelwaine, Tunnis, Ind. Spy, Lewis Co., W. Va., 75.
McCann, Sergt. Patrick, Lewis Co., W. Va., 75.
McVancy, Christopher, Lewis Co., W. Va., 77.
Meade, Wm., Logan Co., W. Va., 72.
Munday, Aaron, Loudoun Co., 72.
Munroe, Spencer, Loudoun Co., 74.
Morrison, Jno., Louisa Co., 69.
Major, Humphrey, Madison Co., 76.
Morgan, Wm., Mathews Co., 71.
Morgan, John, Mecklenburg Co., 75.
Miller, Peter, Monongalia Co., W. Va., 74.
Morgan, Jackquil, Monongalia Co., W. Va., 76.
Morgan, Evans, Monongalia Co., W. Va., 81.
Morris, Amos, Monogalia Co., W. Va., 75.
Morgan, Benj., Monroe Co., W. Va., 73.
Mitchell, John, Montgomery Co., 74.
Montague, Rice D., Montgomery Co., 69.
Miller, John, Morgan Co., W. Va., 75.
Mathews, Jos., Nelson Co., 80.
Mass, Samuel, New Kent Co., 70.
Mann, Wm., Nottoway Co., 74.
McCullock, Abraham, Ohio Co., W. Va., 72.
Millingham, John, Ohio Co., W. Va., 83.
Mills, Thos., Ohio Co., W. Va., 70.
Mansfield, Robt, Orange Co., 72.
Mallows, Henry, Pendleton Co., W. Va., 75.
Morton, Edward, Pendleton Co., W. Va., 70.
Mosley, Arthur, Powhatan Co., 74.
Mosley, Hezekiah, Powhatan Co., 74.
Mathews, Phillip, Prince Edward Co., 78.
Moss, James, Prince Edward Co., 74.
Mathews, Isaac, Preston Co., W. Va., 73.
Messenger, Abner, Preston Co., W. Va., 76.
Manier, David, Randolph Co., W. Va., 79.
Miller, Wm., Rockbridge Co., 77.
Muterspaw, Phillip, Rockbridge Co., 88.
McLaughlin, Wm., Rockbridge Co., 76.
Mayer, Michael, Rockingham Co., 89.

Miller, Sergt. Christian, Shenandoah Co., 90.
Mason, Smith, Spottsylvania Co., 71.
Moore, Alexander, Spottsylvania Co., 74. (Died Feb. 4, 1834).
Marks, Edward, Sr., Surry Co., 76.
McGuire, Wm., Tazewell Co., 77.
McKay, Wm., Tyler Co., W. Va., 74.
Montgomery, Richard, Washington Co., 76.

Niceley, Saml. K., Amherst Co., 82.
Nicholas, Capt. Jno. and Col., Buckingham Co., 76.
North, Sergt. Thos., Charlotte Co., 76.
Newby, Levi, Chesterfield Co., 80.
Niles, Ro., Chesterfield Co., 75. (Died April 1, 1834.)
Nunally, Wm., Dinwiddie Co., 79.
Nutter, Christopher, Harrison Co., W. Va., 74.
Neely, Jno., Lewis Co., W. Va., 76.
Nicholas, Ind. Spy, Lewis Co., W. Va., 78.
Nicholas, Zephaniah, I. S., Lewis Co., W. Va., 78.
Norris, Sergt. Jno., Lewis Co., W. Va., 73.
Newell, Thos., Prince George Co., 78. (Died Jan. 19, 1833.)
Nance, Sergt. Wm. M., Spottsylvania Co., 74.

Osborne, Claibourne, Charlotte Co., 76.
O'Bannon, Thos., Fauquier Co., 78.
Oney, Jos., Giles Co., 81.
Oliver, Alva, Halifax Co., 70.
O'Neale, Constantis, Jackson Co., W. Va., 81.
Oldham, Isaac, Lunenburg Co., 73.
O'Rouke, Sergt. David, Shenandoah Co., 80. (Died Jan. 12, 1833.)

Persinger, Jacob, Alleghany Co., 85.
Pryor, Wm. Amherst Co., 81.
Patrick, Wm., Augusta Co., 71.
Pullen, Tho., Bedford Co., 71.
Peterson, Thos., Brooke Co., W. Va., 77.
Parrish, Jno., Brunswick Co., 84.
Payton, Henry, Cabell Co., W. Va., 75.
Prebble, Jno., Campbell Co., 75.
Patterson, Poindexter, Campbell Co., 69.
Puckitt, Nathl., Chesterfield Co., 77.

Pulliam, Thos., Culpeper Co., 72. (Died Aug. 27, 1831).
Parrish, Frederick, Dinwiddie Co., 72.
Payne, Augustine, Fauquier Co., 72.
Prater, Jonathan, Franklin Co., 76.
Pollard, Chatlen, Franklin Co., 71.
Pittman, And., Frederick Co., 74.
Perters, Ensign John, Giles Co., 79.
Pleasants, Arch., Goochland Co., 87.
Poor, Sergt. Thos., Goochland Co., 79.
Parrott, Lewis, Halifax Co., 79.
Parker, Jas., Hampshire Co., W. Va., 74.
Peters, Jno., Hampshire Co., W. Va., 80.
Powelson, Henry, Hampshire Co., W. Va., 76.
Purgett, Henry, Hampshire Co., W. Va., 81.
Price, Capt. Thos., Hanover Co., 80.
Pepper, Wm., Harrison Co., 73.
Pollard, Capt. Robt., Henrico Co., —.
Pulleam, Mosby, Henrico Co., 70.
Parsons, Joseph, Ind. Spy, Jackson Co., W. Va., 79.
Persinger, Henry, Lewis Co., W. Va., 74.
Powers, Wm., Ind Spy, Lewis Co., W. Va., 69.
Peck, Peter, Mason Co., W. Va., 79.
Pugh, Josiah, Mathews Co., 72.
Piles, Zacharah, Monongalia Co., W. Va., 77.
Parker, Elijah, Nansemond Co., 75.
Pugh, John, Nelson Co., 71.
Pledger, John, Northampton Co., 77.
Pratt, Jonathan, Orange Co., 73.
Partlow, Benj., Rappahannock Co., 70.
Parson, John, Rockbridge Co., 76.
Paxton, Samuel, Rockbridge Co., 81. (Died July 29, 1833).
Parmer, James, Rockingham Co., 70.
Pence, Sr., John, Rockingham Co., 79.
Pettis, John, Spottsylvania Co., 80. (Died July 1, 1833).
Peacock, Richard, Spottsylvania Co., 73. (Died Aug. 3, 1832).
Prewett, John, Tazewell Co., 74.
Pippin, Robt., Washington Co., 82.

Quicksnell, Adam, Alleghany Co., 79.

Read, Edmund, Accomack Co., 78.
Reynolds, Alex., Bedford Co., 71.
Runnels, Jesse, Bedford Co., 83.
Rogers, Abraham, Brooke Co., W. Va., 73.
Ragland, Jno., Buckingham Co., 73.
Roberts, Isaac, Cabell Co., W. Va., 74.
Roberts, Thos., Cabell Co., W. Va., 73.
Raynolds, Wm., Caroline Co., 73.
Rowlett, Wm., Chesterfield Co., 98.
Robertson, Mitchell, Culpeper Co.
Rossin, Reubin, Culpeper Co., 82.
Rany, Nathl., Dinwiddie Co., 70.
Rawles, Kenag, Fauquier Co., 70.
Riddle Wm., Fauquier Co., 84.
Roberts, Ambrose, Fluvanna Co., 82.
Ray, Jas., Franklin Co., 78.
Richardson, Richard, Franklin Co., 82.
Reily, Jas., Frederick Co., 76.
Rudd, Archer, Halifax Co., 71.
Rudder, Jno., Halifax Co., 77.
Randall, Ensign Jacob, Hardy Co., W. Va., 75.
Randall, Jas., Harrison Co., 73.
Rifee, Jacob, Ind. Spy, Harrison Co., 73.
Read, Jno., Harrison Co., 89.
Romine, Jno., Harrison Co., 73.
Rogers, Rhodam, Harrison Co., 77.
Reed, Jno., Henry Co., 79.
Rader, Michael, Jackson Co., W. Va., 83.
Radcliffe, Wm., Lewis Co., W. Va., 74.
Regar, Phillip, Lewis Co., W. Va., 67.
Richards, Geo., Lewis Co., W. Va., 75.
Right, Bazel, Lewis Co., W. Va. 70.
Richardson, Richd., Louisa Co., 78.
Rouch, Jonas, Mason Co., W. Va., 71.
Ripley, Richd., Mathews Co., 84.
Robinson, John, Monroe Co., W. Va., 85.
Roach, Jonathan, Monroe Co., W. Va., 73.
Rutledge, Edward, Montgomery Co., 72.

Read, Abraham, Nansemond Co., —.
Renolds, James, Nansemond Co., 77.
Ross, Jos., Nansemond Co., —.
Rossin, Jas., Nelson Co., 84.
Rexrode, Zacharah, Pendleton Co., W. Va., 73.
Rymer, Geo., Pendleton Co., W. Va., 81.
Roach, James, Pittsylvania Co., 72.
Radeer, Henry, Rockingham Co., 77.
Raynes, Lawrence, Rockingham Co., 74.
Rolstone, David, Rockingham Co., 73.
Routhon, James, Rockingham Co., 72.
Reynolds, Bernard, Russell Co., 71.
Reagan, Wm., Smythe Co., 78.
Rust, John, Washington Co., 71.

Snow, Richd., Albemarle Co., 81.
Strange, David, Albemarle Co., 70.
Smith, Sergt. Henry, Amherst Co., 73.
Shumaker, Zedekiah, Amherst Co., 81.
Sitlington, Ro., Bath Co., 86.
Stewart, Ens. Edward, Bath Co., 75.
Stewart, Jno., Bath Co., 73.
Shepherd, Jacob, Bedford Co., 73.
Stiff, Jas., Bedford Co., 77.
Swain, Geo., Bedford Co., 75.
Stevens, Jno., Berkeley Co., 76.
Simpson, Jas., Botetourt Co., 77.
Seaward, Jos., Brunswick Co., 74.
Stephenson, Jno., Cabell Co., W. Va., 71.
Story, Edwd., Campbell Co., 77.
Satterwhite, Ro., Caroline Co., 79.
Simmons, Jehu, Charlotte Co., 72.
Smith, Benoni, Charlotte Co., 75.
Smith, Isaac, Charlotte Co., 74.
Simms, Edwd., Chesterfield Co., 72. (Died June 20, 1833).
Smith, Thos., Chesterfield Co., 74.
Smith, John, Chesterfield Co., 72.
Spear, Jno., Chesterfield Co., 76.
Sims, Reuben, Culpepper Co., 79.

Sisk, Timothy, Culpepper Co., 72.
Sturdivant, Joel, Dinwiddie Co., 69.
Smith, Lewis, Dinwiddie Co., 82. (Died Aug. 20, 1833).
Seay, Sergt. Austin, Sr., Fluvanna Co., 76.
Saunders, Philemon, Franklin Co., 70.
Stewart, Wm., Franklin Co., 73.
Sperry, Jacob, Frederick Co., 80.
Shelor, Capt. Danl., Frederick Co., 84.
Stokes, Lewis, Gloucester Co., 71.
Shelton, Jos., Goochland Co., 73.
Southworth, Geo., Goochland Co., 72.
Smith, Nathl., Goochland Co., 71.
Sammons, Jno., Greenbrier Co., W. Va., 75.
Scott, Wm., Halifax Co., 71.
Seamster, Jno., Halifax Co., 81.
Snyder, Anthy., Halifax Co., 72. (Died Dec. 5, 1833).
Saunders, Jno., Hanover Co., 74.
Seay, Jas., Hanover Co., 94.
Strong, Sergt. Jno,, Hanover Co., 77.
Shinn, Isaac, Harrison Co., 74.
Smith, Danl., Harrison Co., 78.
Stout, Thos., Ind. Spy, Harrison Co., 83.
Sweger, Jno., Harrison Co., 74.
Smith, Chas., Jackson Co., W. Va., 70.
Stroud, Sr., Wm., James City Co., 82.
Staley, Peter, Jefferson Co., W. Va., 80.
Strother, Geo., King George Co., 75.
Shackelford, Alex., King and Queen Co., 75.
Spencer, Hez., King William Co., 76.
Schoolcraft, Jno., Lewis Co., W. Va., 76.
Shaver, Paul, Ind. Spy, Lewis Co., W. Va., 75.
Sims, Jno., Lewis Co., W. Va., 79.
Sleeth, David W., Lewis Co., W. Va., 72.
Smith, Geo. P., Lewis Co., W. Va., 77.
Smith, Mark, Ind. Spy, Lewis Co., W. Va., 76.
Smith, Thos., Lewis Co., W. Va., 83.
Stalmacker, Saml., I. S., Lewis Co., W. Va., 71.
Stewart, Ralph, Logan Co., W. Va., 84.
Saunders, Jas., Loudoun Co., 72.

Saunders, Wm., Louisa Co., 74.
Spicer, Jos., Louisa Co., 73.
Spaulden, Jno., Madison Co., 74.
Smith, Isaac, Mathews Co., 74.
Smith, Sherwood, Mecklenburg Co., 73.
Simpkins, Charles, Monongalia Co., W. Va., 76.
Stone, Henry, Monongalia Co., 72.
Sams, Samuel, Monroe Co., W. Va., 75.
Shank, Capt. Christian, Morgan Co., W. Va., 83.
Streater, New., Nansemond Co., 78. (Died Dec. 27, 1833).
Slater, Edward, New Kent Co., 75.
Sims, James, Nicholas Co., W. Va., 79.
Self, Thos., Northumberland Co., 74.
Sorrell, Edward, Northumberland Co., 81.
Smith, John, Orange Co., 74.
Sharp, Sr., John, Patrick Co., 81.
Simmons, John, Pendleton Co., W. Va., 80.
Seay, Capt. Mathew, Pittsylvania Co., 70.
Smith, Jos., Pittsylvania Co., 71.
Swepston, John, Pittsylvania Co., 73.
Sampson, Jos., Page Co., 72.
Scott, Wm., Prince Edward Co., 76.
Shepherdson, David, Rockbridge Co., 72.
Stepler, Geo., Rockingham Co., 75.
Self, Thos., Russell Co., 76.
Smith, James, Scott Co., 81. (Died Nov. 18, 1833).
Stewart, Wm., Scott Co., —.
Story, John, Southampton Co., 73.
Sorrell, John, Spottsylvania Co., 73.
Steers, Richard, Spottsylvania Co., 72.
Stannard, Larkin, Spottsylvania Co., 74.
Seaverge, Hartwell, Surrey Co., 78.
Smith, Jonas., Washington Co., 85.
Sorrell, Thos., Westmoreland Co., 76.
Sennett, Patrick, Wood Co., W. Va., 81.
Steffey, Peter, Wythe Co., 75.
Steffey, John, Wythe Co., 88.
Stephens, Corp. Lawrence, Wythe Co., 80.

Thompson, Lt. Robt., Bath Co., 77.
Thomasson, Jno., Bedford Co., 91.
Tracey, Wm., Bedford Co., 72.
Taylor, Paul, Berkeley Co., 86.
Trenor, Sergt. Jas., Botetourt Co., 77.
Truit, Wm., Campbell Co., 74.
Taylor, Bartholemew, Caroline Co., 72.
Thomas, Catlett, Caroline Co., 70.
Tucker, Wm., Caroline Co., 74.
Tharpe, Thos., Charlotte Co., 76.
Timmons, Geo., Dinwiddie Co., 72.
Taleaferro, Wm., Fluvanna Co., 82.
Trail, Thos., Floyd Co., 88.
Tuck., Thos., Halifax Co., 71.
Throckmorton, Rich., Halifax Co., 71.
Tinsley, Nathl., Hanover Co., 77.
Toombs, Geo., Hanover Co., 79. (Died Sept. 4, 1833).
Tichnall, David, Harrison Co., W. Va., 70.
Thomas, Evan, Harrison Co., W. Va., 81.
Tucker, Henry, Harrison Co., W. Va., 90.
Tucker, Jno., Harrison Co., W. Va., 91.
Turner, Robin., Isle of Wight Co., 74.
Thompson, Alex., Kanawha Co., W. Va., 71.
Taliaferro, Jno., King William Co., 70.
Thacker, Sackville, Louisa Co., 84.
Thomasson, Jno. (Drummer), Louisa Co., 81.
Tanner, Abraham, Madison Co., 75.
Taylor, Wm., Madison Co., 80.
Troyman, Sergt. Wm., Madison Co., 79.
Towles, Hy., Madison Co., 79.
Thomas, James, Mathews Co., 71.
Tucker, Geo., Monongalia Co., W. Va., 72.
Troy, Sergt. James, Monongalia Co., W. Va., 75.
Teaney, Daniel T., Montgomery Co., 77.
Taylor, Zacharah, Orange Co., 74.
Terry, Jos., Patrick Co., 73.
Thompson, Jennings, Pittsylvania Co., 72.
Thorpe, Thos., Page Co., 72.
Temple, Sergt. Eppes, Prince George Co., 76.

Triplett, Sergt. Daniel, Rappahannock Co., 71.
Trumble, Lt. Isaac, Rockbridge Co., 77.
Tate, Mathew, Rockingham Co., 73.
Taylor, John, Rockingham Co., 77.
Tribble, Geo., Spottsylvania Co., 78.
Twinly, Francis, Spottsylvania Co., 72.
Templeman, Lt. Samuel., Westmoreland Co., 76.

Vandall, Abraham, Fayette Co., W. Va., 76.
Vier, Jno., Franklin Co., 76. (Died March 4, 1834).
Vaughan, Wm., Grayson Co., 73.
Vanhook, Sergt. Jacob., Halifax Co., 73.
Vanmeter, Sergt. Jos., Hardy Co., W. Va., 80.
Vance, James, Washington Co., 74.

Wood, Jno, Albemarle Co., 71.
Wood, Solomon, Albemarle Co., 77.
Weaver, Jno., Augusta Co., 74. (Died Dec. 13, 1832).
Walker, Lieut. Wm. J., Bedford Co., 73.
White, Jos., Bedford Co., 83.
Wilkes, Saml., Bedford Co., 70.
Wisong, Fiat., Botetourt Co., 79.
Williams, Jno., Buckingham Co., 81.
Wilkinson, Jas., Buckingham Co., 79.
Walker, Chas., Campbell Co., 74.
Walthall, Henry, Campbell Co., 72.
Wray, Henry, Campbell Co., 71.
White, Elijah, Caroline Co., 93.
Walthall, Sr., Wm., Chesterfield Co., 76.
Whitworth, Sergt. Allen, Chesterfield Co., 76.
Williams, Jno., Chesterfield Co., 90.
Williams, Thos., Chesterfield Co., 70.
Welsh, Isaiah, Culpeper Co., 71.
Wells, Solomon R., Dinwiddie Co., 70.
Withers, Sergt. Jesse, Fauquier Co., 74.
Wright, Jno., Franklin Co., 86.
Woody, Martin, Franklin Co., 76.
White, Richd., Gloucester Co., 72.
Watkins, Jos. D., Goochland Co., 72.
Wright, Thos., Goochland Co., 75.

Wallace, Jas., Halifax Co., 73.
Willis, Jas., Halifax Co., 70.
Winn, Jno., Halifax Co., 71.
Warren, Archd., Halifax Co., 78.
Wimbish, Jas., Halifax Co., 72.
Whitecotton, Ensign Axton., Henry Co., 92.
Wallace, Jas., James City Co., 77. (Died Jan. 13, 1833).
Whitlock, Jas., King William Co., 71.
Winn, Wm., King William Co., 76.
Waggoner, Jno., Lewis Co., W. Va., 82.
Wamsley, David, I. S., Lewis Co., W. Va., —.
Wamsley, Jas., I. S., Lewis Co., W. Va., 69.
West, Alex., Lewis Co., W. Va., 74.
Wingrove, Jno., Lewis Co., W. Va., 86.
Walker, Oliver, Logan Co., W. Va., 89.
Wade, Ro., Loudoun Co., 73.
West, Jno., Loudoun Co., 80.
Wigginton, Benj., Loudoun Co., 71.
Wornell, Sergt. Jas., Loudoun Co., 70.
Walton, Joel, Louisa Co., 74.
Winston, Lt. Anthony, Louisa Co., 84.
Watson, Larner, Madison Co., 72.
Waddle, Sergt. Thos., Mason Co., W. Va., 75.
White, Sergt. Jno., Mathews Co., 78.
Wilson, Wallis, Mecklenburg Co., 78.
Wade, Geo., Monongalia Co., W. Va., 73.
Wilson, Henry, 2d, Monongalia Co., W. Va., 74.
Walker, Thos., Monroe Co., W. Va., 69.
Wilson, Robt., Monroe Co., W. Va., 74.
Wharton, Zacharah, Morgan Co., W. Va., 75.
Widmeyer, Michael, Morgan Co., W. Va., 74.
Whitfield, Solomon, Nansemond Co., 71.
Ware, Thos., Nelson Co., 71.
Williams, James, New Kent Co., 70.
Wyatt, Spivey, Norfolk Co., 75.
Walker, Thos., Orange Co., 73.
Wayt, Wm., Orange Co., 73.
White, Lt. Richard, Orange Co., 78.
Wilson, Eli B., Pendleton Co., W. Va., 79.

West, Sergt. John, Pittsylvania Co., 79.
Williams, James M., Pittsylvania Co., 71.
Woodell, Lt. Jos., Pocahontas Co., W. Va., 82.
Watkins, Edward, Powhatan Co., 87.
Worsham, Capt. Wm., Prince Edward Co., 82.
Walker, Wm. T., Prince Edward Co., 77. (Dead).
Wilshire, John, Prince Edward Co., 76.
Woodson, Jos., Prince Edward, Co., 83.
Wooldridge, James, Prince Edward Co., 74.
Whitman, Mathew, Randolph Co., W. Va., 74.
Wolford, John, Randolph Co., W. Va., 80.
Whetzell, Henry, Rockingham Co., 76.
Wilson, Abraham, Spottsylvania Co., 74.
Williams, James, Spottsylvania Co., 72.
Williams, John, Sr., Surry Co., 73. (Died Aug. 9, 1833).
Wrenn, John, Sussex Co., 72.
Welton, Ensign Thos., Tazewell Co., 82.
Wade, Hezekiah, I. S., Tyler Co., W. Va., 80.
Widener, Michael, Washington Co., 75.
Williams, Wm., Westmoreland Co., 73.

Young, Chas., Berkeley Co., W. Va., 77.
Young, Jas., Franklin Co., W. Va., 79.
Yarbrough, Elisha, Hanover Co., 77.
Young, Jno., Kanawha Co., W. Va., 74.
Youell, Wm., Madison Co., 72.
Yoho, Henry, Monongalia Co., W. Va., 82.
Young, John, Pocahontas Co., W. Va., 74.

Alphabetical List of Pensioners Residing Outside of Virginia in 1835, whose Pensions were Granted for Services as Virginia Militiamen

PART V.

This list was compiled from a report made by the Secretary of War in 1835. The ages are those given in that report, and are believed to be the ages of the pensioners in 1835. The names of the pensioners in what is now West Virginia are embraced under Part IV.

Name	Age	County	State
Abbott, Jno.	84	Green	Indiana
Adams, David		Henry	Kentucky
Adams, James,	76	Elbert	Georgia
Adams, Micajah	75	Sullivan	Tennessee
Adkins, James		Clarke	Kentucky
Alexander, James	85	Iredell	North Carolina
Allee, David	72	Cooper	Missouri
Allen, Phillip	74	Clarke	Georgia
Allen, Saml.		Pulaski	Kentucky
Allen, Vincent	78	Lincoln	North Carolina
Allen, Wm.	74	Granville	North Carolina
Alley, Isaiah	85	Warren	Kentucky
Allgood, Jno.		Breckenridge	Kentucky
Alsop, James		Mercer	Kentucky
Alverson, Jno. S.		Lincoln	Kentucky
Anderson, Alex.	73	Stewart	Tennessee
Anderson, James	69	Bedford	Tennessee
Anderson, Peter	79	Hawkins	Tennessee

Name	Age	County	State
Anderson, Jno.	77	Spencer	Kentucky
Andrews, Thos.		Fayette	Kentucky
Arbuckle, Thos.	75	Washington	Indiana
Archer, Edward		Oldham	Kentucky
Arnold, Arnold	75	Holmes	Ohio
Arthur, James	70	Butler	Alabama
Arthur, Joel	83	Jackson	Ohio
Ashbrook, Thos.	78	Owen	Indiana
Ashcraft, Amos	77	Howard	Missouri
Ashley, Danl., Sr.		Haskins	Kentucky
Ashley, Peter		Hopkins	Kentucky
Ashlock, Wm.		Nelson	Kentucky
Asherst, Wm.		Caldwell	Kentucky
Atkin, Jas.	75	Fayette	Georgia
Atkins, James	75	Fayette	Georgia
Atkinson, Ellis		Madison	Kentucky
Ayers, Henry (Died Sept. 22, 1833).	80	Robertson	Tennessee
Baber, James	72	Gwinnett	Georgia
Bailey, Noah	84	Stokes	North Carolina
Baker, Thos.		Henderson	Kentucky
Baker, Wm.		Cumberland	Kentucky
Banam, Danl.	76	Jackson	Illinois
Bandy, Thos.	86	Summer	Tennessee
Banks, Wm.	74	Putnam	Indiana
Barbee, Danl.		Mercer	Kentucky
Barber, Wm.	88	Surrey	North Carolina
Barley, Wm.	74	Spartansburg	South Carolina
Barlow, Lewis	79	Shelby	Indiana
Barnes, Benj.		Gallatin	Kentucky
Barnes, Jno.	82	Montgomery	North Carolina
Barnett, Ambrose		Nicholas	Kentucky
Barnett, Chas.	71	Granville	North Carolina
Barren, Jno.		Pulaski	Kentucky
Bartlett, Edmund	74	Randolph	Missouri
Basket, Wm. (Dead)	73	Shelby	Kentucky
Bashaw, Peter	71	Davidson	Tennessee
Bass, James	74	Bedford	Tennessee

Name	Age	County	State
Bassett, Nathl.	76	Hawkins	Tennessee
Bean, Richd.		Lewis	Kentucky
Beard, Jacob	72	Clinton	Ohio
Beasley, Leonard	67	Laurens	South Carolina
Beatty, Jno.		Montgomery	Kentucky
Beatty, Wm.	72	Scott	Kentucky
Beavers, Jno.		Barren	Kentucky
Bell, Wm.		Barren	Kentucky
Benson, Enoch	78	Gwinnett	Georgia
Bentley, Efford	74	Madison	Alabama
Berkley, Jno.	74	Scott	Kentucky
Berry, Thos.		Clarke	Kentucky
Berry, Wm.	81	Mercer	Ohio
Berry, Benj.		Mason	Kentucky
Berry, Joel		Pendleton	Kentucky
Berry Jno.		Owen	Kentucky
Bibb, Jas.		Barren	Kentucky
Bingham, Benj.	78	Blount	Tennessee
Birch, Jno.		Barren	Kentucky
Bishop, Wyatt	76	Franklin	Alabama
Black, Ro.	84	Woodford	Kentucky
Black Rudolph		Bracken	Kentucky
Blackburn, Wm.		Caldwell	Kentucky
Blackmore, Jno.	72	Shelby	Kentucky
Blackwell, David	75	Roane	Tennessee
Blackwell, Jno.	72	Shelby	Kentucky
Blankenship, Reuben	69	Shelby	Alabama
Blakely, Aquilla	94	Blount	Alabama
Blevans, Nathan	71	Ashe	North Carolina
Blevins, James	84	Lawrence	Indiana
Blomkenbaker, Nicholas	75	Shelby	Kentucky
Bond, Jno.		Owen	Kentucky
Bond, Wm. (Died June 20, 1819)		Dist. of Columbia	
Bootwright, Saml.	70	Mecklenburg	North Carolina
Borders, Christopher	71	Dark	Ohio
Boswell, Reuben	77	Mecklenburg	North Carolina
Bottom, Miles	82	Warren	Tennessee

Name	Age	County	State
Bowen, Bracy	72	Rutherford	North Carolina
Bowen, Chas.	84	Putnam	Indiana
Bowen, Jas.		Montgomery	Kentucky
Bower, Andr.	75	Montgomery	Indiana
Bowers, Brattain	71	Orange	North Carolina
Bowles, Mathew		Grayson	Kentucky
Bowling, Chas.	70	Fairfield	Ohio
Bowling, Wm.	75	Fairfield	Ohio
Bowman, Jno., Sr.		Hart	Kentucky
Bowman, Wm.	72	Washington	Indiana
Bowman, Wm.	76	Knox	Tennessee
Boy, Jacob (Died May 20, 1833)	83	Sullivan	Tennessee
Boyd, Hy.	75	Todd	Kentucky
Boydston, Wm.	81	Cocke	Tennessee
Boyers, Wm.	70	Dark	Ohio
Boyles, Hezekiah	77	Madison	Alabama
Bradley, Jno.	77	Rutherford	Tennessee
Brady, Benj.	73	Alleghany	Maryland
Bragg, Wm.	69	Cocke	Tennessee
Brandenburg, Anthony	72	Warren	Ohio
Branham, Wm.		Bourbon	Kentucky
Bramblett, James		Breckenridge	Kentucky
Brann, Jeremiah	72	Butler	Ohio
Breedlove, Jno.		Adams	Ohio

(*Fram Madison County, Va., March* 4, 1833).

Brenton, James,	70	Perry	Indiana
Bruster, James		Mercer	Kentucky
Brett, Obed.	75	Perry	Tennessee
Brewer, Barnet	71	Montgomery	Alabama
Bridges, Jno.		Mercer	Kentucky
Briggs, Benj.		Lincoln	Kentucky
Briggs, David		Logan	Kentucky
Bromigan, James		Bath	Kentucky
Brooks, Hy.	80	Orange	Indiana
Brooks, Middleton	75	Jackson	Georgia

Name	Age	County	State
Brooks, Robt.	72	Marion	Georgia
Brown, Arabia		Garrard	Kentucky
Brown, Patrick	74	Jefferson	Indiana
Brown, Stephen	78	Bledsoe	Tennessee
Brown, Thos.		Estill	Kentucky
Brown, Thos. C.		Floyd	Kentucky
Brumford, Humphrey	82	Lawrence	Ohio
Brummell, Benj.		Cumberland	Kentucky
Bryant, Benj.	82	Warren	Kentucky
Bryant, Jesse	73	Wayne	North Carolina
Bryant Jno.		Garrard	Kentucky
Burbridge, Geo.	72	Scott	Kentucky
Burch, Joseph	72	Scott	Kentucky
Burk, Geo.	75	Jefferson	Indiana
Burk, Saml.		Jessamine	Kentucky
Burke, Robt.		Owen	Kentucky
Burkett, Fredk.	83	Hawkins	Tennessee
Burns, Nathl.		Mercer	Kentucky
Burton, Robt.	70	Rockingham	North Carolina
Bush, Chas.		Henry	Kentucky
Buskirk, Jno.	69	Ripley	Indiana
Butler, James	75	Elbert	Georgia
Butler, Thos.		Madison	Kentucky
Butler, Wm.	78	Lawrence	Alabama
Cabbage, Jno.	76	Campbell	Tennessee
Caldwell, James	71	St. Francois	Missouri
Calmer, Wm.	72	Newbery Dist.	South Carolina
Campbell, Jno.	77	Hamilton	Ohio
Campbell, Lawrence		Greene	Kentucky
Campbell, Robt.		Jessamine	Kentucky
Camper, Tilman		Fayette	Kentucky
Cannon, Hy.	83	Greenville	South Carolina
Carlile, Jas. P.		Greene	Kentucky
Carney, Jno.	68	Jennings	Indiana
Carpenter, Wm.	73	Wayne	Kentucky
Carr, Geo.	87	Cooper	Missouri
Carr, James	77	Johnson	Indiana

Name	Age	County	State
Carr, Jno. F.	69	Maury	Tennessee
Carr, Moses	92	Franklin	North Carolina
Carr, Ro. (Died July 4, 1833)	75	Marion	Indiana
Carry, Wm.		Cumberland	Kentucky
Carson, James		Casey	Kentucky
Carson, Jno.	74	Rush	Indiana
Carson, Ro.	81	Warren	Tennessee
Carson, Thos. (See Jno. Perkins).			
Carter, James	78	Cleremont	Ohio
Carter, Jno.		Preble	Ohio
Carter, Joseph	74	Washington	Kentucky
Carter, Philip		Barren	Kentucky
Carter, Robt.	76	Clark	Georgia
Carter, Thomas	88	Rockingham	North Carolina
Carter, Wm.	75	Wayne	Indiana
Carter, Wm.		Ohio	Kentucky
Carver, Richd.	70	Pickens Dist.	South Carolina
Casey, James	85	Shelby	Kentucky
Cash, Jno.	77	Hall	Georgia
Cash, Wm.		Rock Castle	Kentucky
Cashin, David	75	Weakly	Tennessee
Cashone, Thos.	76	Mecklenburg	North Carolina
Catron, Peter	80	Wayne	Kentucky
Chambers, Alex.	70	Knox	Indiana
Chandler, Claiborne		Harrison	Kentucky
Chandler, Jno.		Clay	Kentucky
Chapin, Saml.	82	Crawford	Indiana
Chapman, Edmund	70	Randolph	Missouri
Chapman, Jno.		Cumberland	Kentucky
Chappell, Abner	71	Howard	Missouri
Chappel, Wm.		Bullitt	Kentucky
Charlton, Jacob	92	Hawkins	Tennessee
Charlton, Jno.	73	Davidson	Tennessee
Chethaim, Wm.		Cumberland	Kentucky
Chick, James		Knox	Kentucky
Childress, Hy.		Grant	Kentucky

Name	Age	County	State
Chinn, Peter	71	Surry	North Carolina
Chrisham, Jno.	66	Scott	Kentucky
Christian, Allen	75	Shelby	Indiana
Christian, Jno.		Fayette	Kentucky
Christie, James	85	Shelby	Kentucky
Chumbley, Jno.	74	David	Indiana
Clark, James		Mercer	Kentucky
Clark, Joseph		Montgomery	Kentucky
Clark, Patrick		Mercer	Kentucky
Clatterbuck, Reuben	79	Callaway	Missouri
Clarke, Lee	78	Guilford	North Carolina
Clarke, Lewis	71	Jackson	Alabama
Clay, Elijah		Edgar	Illinois
Claycomb, Fredk.	76	Knox	Indiana
Claywell, Shadrack		Cumberland	Kentucky
Cleaver, Wm.		Grayson	Kentucky
Clemant, Edmund	75	Spartansburg	South Carolina
Clements, Benj.	72	Stokes	North Carolina
Cleveland, Wm.		Pendleton	Kentucky
Cobb, Saml.	74	Montgomery	Missouri
Cock, Charles	72	Caswell	North Carolina
Cochran, Mathew	71	Monroe	Georgia
Cochran, Wm.		Hickman	Kentucky
Coffenberg, Geo.	73	Richland	Ohio
Coloway, Micajah	76	Washington	Indiana
Collins, Elisha	75	Greene	Alabama
Colwell, Jno.	83	Vigo	Indiana
Coleman, Thos.		Barren	Kentucky
Colville, James	76	Licking	Ohio
Colvin, Benjamin	76	Boone	Missouri
Compton, Jere H.	70	Sevier	Tennessee
Conine, Andr.		Henry	Kentucky
Conn, Saml.		Jefferson	Kentucky
Conn, Wm.		Henry	Kentucky
Connelly, Jno.	74	Bedford	Tennessee
Conner, Maxmilliam	71	Greene	Tennessee
Conner, Phileman	71	Fayette	Indiana
Conway, Richd.	72	Henry	Indiana

Name	Age	County	State
Conyers, Benj.	74	Shelby	Kentucky
Cooksly, Zach.	74	Franklin	Indiana
Copelin, Wm.	73	DeKalb	Georgia
Corbett, Jno.	79	Onsland	North Carolina
Corbin, Jno,		Holmes	Ohio
Corbin, Lewis		Bourbon	Kentucky
Corden, Benj. D.		Hart	Kentucky
Corley, Wm.	82	Wilson	Tennessee
Cornwall, Wm.	82	Jefferson	Tennessee
Corsage, Jno.	70	Shelby	Indiana
Cotterill, Thos.	84	Brown	Ohio
Cotton, James	69	Madison	Alabama
Covington, Robt.	72	Wayne	Kentucky
Cox, Andr.	77	Hamilton	Ohio
Cox, James	71	Stokes	North Carolina
Cox, Thos.	72	Gwinnett	Georgia
Cox, Wm.		Lawrence	Kentucky
Coxe, Jno.	76	Roane	Tennessee
Craig, Jno.	71	Limestone	Alabama
Craig, Wm.	76	Pike	Missouri
Craig, Wm.		Barren	Kentucky
Craig, Wm.		Rock Castle	Kentucky
Crafton, Anthony	87	Spencer	Kentucky
Crane, Wm.	85	Rutherford	North Carolina
Crawford, James		Flemming	Kentucky
Crawford, Peter	70	Rockingham	North Carolina
Creasy, Jno.		Cumberland	Kentucky
Crittenden, Richd.	72	Bartholemew	Indiana
Crockett, Ro.		Cumberland	Kentucky
Crook, Jeremiah		Grant	Kentucky
Crook, Jno.		Madison	Kentucky
Crow, Wm.	77	Jackson	Ohio
Crowder, Sterling		Jessamine	Kentucky
Crump, Joshua		Hart	Kentucky
Culton, Joseph	70	Morgan	Indiana
Cundiff, Jno.		Hardin	Kentucky
Cunningham, Ansell	74	Jackson	Georgia
Cunningham, James	78	St. Francois	Missouri

Name	Age	County	State
Cunningham, Morrell	....	Hickman	Kentucky
Curtis, Jno.	75	Bledsoe	Tennessee
Custard, Jacob	84	Perry	Ohio
Cutright, Peter	74	Sangamon	Illinois
Dabney, George	74	Wayne	Kentucky
Dabney, Jno. O.	71	Scott	Kentucky
Daird, Michael		Mason	Kentucky
Dalton, Wm.	80	Rutherford	North Carolina
Daniel, Beverly		Montgomery	North Carolina
Daniel, Buckner	74	Dupline	North Carolina
Daniel, Christopher	75	Orange	North Carolina
Danks, Jno.		Logan	Kentucky
Darnaby, Jno.		Fayette	Kentucky
Davenport, Anthony S.	76	Pickaway	Ohio
Davenport, James		Fayette	Kentucky
David, Hy.	74	Rush	Indiana
Davidson, Abraham	79	Humphreys	Tennessee
Davidson, Isaac	75	Johnson	Indiana
Davis, Thomas	72	Woodford	Kentucky
Davis, Jno.	80	Elbert	Georgia
Davis, Saml.	78	Madison	Alabama
Davis, Saml.	81	Burke	North Carolina
Davis, Saml.		Henry	Kentucky
Davis, Wm.	70	Switzerland	Indiana

(*From Kentucky, March* 4, 1834).

Name	Age	County	State
Davis, Wm., 2d.	72	Cocke	Tennessee
Day, Edwd.	73	Sangamon	Illinois
Day, Jno., Sr. (Died Dec. 4, 1833)	92	Jefferson	Tennessee
Deaver, Wm.	70	Buncomb	North Carolina
Decker, Jno.		Grayson	Kentucky
Decker, Wm.		Grayson	Kentucky
Delap, Henry, Sr.	96	Rockingam	North Carolina
Depoy, Christopher	84	Ross	Ohio
Depp, Wm.		Barren	Kentucky
Despan, Peter		Greene	Kentucky

Name	Age	County	State
Dewitt, Peter		Clarke	Kentucky
Dibrell, Chas.	77	Davidson	Tennessee
Dicken, Ephriam		Monroe	Kentucky
Dicken, Jno.		Greene	Kentucky
Dildoy, Joseph	79	Hartford	North Carolina
Dillen, Benj.	79	Dupline	North Carolina
Diller, David	79	Cuyahoga	Ohio
Dixon, Geo.	76	Warren	Indiana
Dodson, Wm.		Nelson	Kentucky
Dollins, Presley	83	Lincoln	Tennessee
Doner, Jacob	74	Tippecanoe	Indiana
Donnell, Danl.	78	**Guilford**	North Carolina
Douthat, Silas		Franklin	Kentucky
Dougherty, Wm.		Lincoln	Kentucky
Downey, Saml.		Hopkins	Kentucky
Draper, James	74	Warner	Georgia
Drum, Phillip	74	Iredell	North Carolina
Dunaway, Saml		Henry	Kentucky
Duke, Mathew		Clarke	Kentucky
Duncan, Geo.	77	Orange	Indiana
Durham, Jno.		Adair	Kentucky
Earnes, Geo.	71	Merriwether	Georgia
Earp, Josiah		Pulaski	Kentucky
Easley, Danl.	80	Montgomery	North Carolina
Elam, Godfrey		Cumberland	Kentucky
Elder, Ro.		Lincoln	Kentucky
Elgin, Saml.	75	Boone	Missouri
Elkins, James		Clarke	Kentucky
Ellington, David		Morgan	Kentucky
Elliott, Reuben	72	Ross	Ohio
Elliott, Wm.	81	Jennings	Indiana
Ellis, Jno.	98	Union	Illinois
Ellison, Jno.	72	Lawrence	Ohio
Ellison, Jno.	72	Rutherford	North Carolina
Emmerson, Reuben		Fayette	Kentucky
English, Wm.	71	Carroll	Ohio
Epperson, Francis		Fayette	Kentucky

Virginia Militia in the Revolution

Name	Age	County	State
Epperson, John,	70	Franklin	Missouri
Estes, Abraham		Lincoln	Kentucky
Estes, Jno.	82	Grainger	Tennessee
Evans, Jno.		Laurel	Kentucky
Evins, David,	77	Parke	Indiana
Ewing, John		Logan	Kentucky
Ezill, Balaam	78	Trigg	Kentucky
Faris, Elijah	72	Washington	Kentucky
Faris, Moses		Rock Castle	Kentucky
Farmer, Mathew		St. Charles	Missouri
Fast, Christian	72	Richland	Ohio
Faucett, Jno.	74	Marion	Indiana
Faudre, Vachel		Clarke	Kentucky
Ferguson, Isaac	77	Williams	Tennessee
Ferguson, Jno.	75	Franklin	Tennessee
Ferguson, Moses	72	Callaway	Missouri
Finch, Wm.	72	Oglethorpe	Georgia
Fink, David (Indian Spy)		Lewis	Kentucky
Finnell, Chas.	72	Randolph	Missouri
Fiscus, Adam	73	Washington	Indiana
Fixworthy, Jno.		Harlan	Kentucky
Fletcher, Thos.	74	Wilkes	North Carolina
Flinn, Wm.	79	Edgefield Dist.	South Carolina
Florence, Wm.	84	Hendricks	Indiana
Floyd, Geo.		Garrard	Kentucky
Floyd, Hy.	73	Union	Kentucky
Floyd, Jno.	87	Washington	Ohio
Floyd, Jno.		Garrard	Kentucky
Fons, Jno.		Fleming	Kentucky
Force, James	92		Kentucky
Force, Jesse		Oldham	Kentucky
Forqueran, Peter		Bourbon	Kentucky
Fordyce, James	72	Franklin	Indiana
Foster, Natl.		Montgomery	Kentucky
Fowler, Sherwood	74	Bedford	Tennessee
Frances, Powell	83	Elbert	Georgia
Franklin, Absolom		Christian	Kentucky

Name	Age	County	State
Franklin, Reuben		Clarke	Kentucky
Fraseur, Jno.		Fleming	Kentucky
Freeman, Jno.		Laurel	Kentucky
Freinch, Joseph	74	Fentress	Tennessee
French, Wm.	73	Shelby	Kentucky
Fretwell, Richd.	82	Newton	Georgia
Freshour, Jno.	78	Ross	Ohio
Fritter, Moses		Mason	Kentucky
Fritz, Jno.	72	Hawkins	Tennessee
Fry, Joshua		Garrard	Kentucky
Fugate, Randall F.		Scott	Kentucky
Furnish, Jas.		Harlan	Kentucky
Gabbert, Michl.		Mercer	Kentucky
Gage, Reuben	68	Hamilton	Ohio
Gaines, James, Sr.	72	Moore	North Carolina
Gaines, Robt.		Woodford	Kentucky
Gaines, Wm.	77	Elbert	Georgia
Gale, Robt. F.	68	Shelby	Kentucky
Gamble, David	82	Posey	Indiana
Gann, Saml., Sr.	83	Rockingham	North Carolina
Garth, Jno.	72	Scott	Kentucky
Garven, Isaac		Lincoln	Kentucky
Gaswell, Benjr.	73	Decatur	Indiana
Gateliff, Chas.		Whitley	Kentucky
Gates, Jno.	75	Williamson	Tennessee
Gatewood, Jno.	69	Scott	Kentucky
Gay, James, Sr.		Clarke	Kentucky
George, Jordan		Russell	Kentucky
George, Thos.		Oldham	Kentucky
Gibson, Elisha	86	Shelby	Kentucky
Gibson, Erasmus	74	Orangeburg	South Carolina
Gibson, Jno.	86	Union Dist.	South Carolina
Gibson, Jno.	73	Scott	Kentucky
Gibson, Saml.	72	Highland	Ohio
Gilliam, Jno.		Logan	Kentucky
Gist, Thos.	70	White	Tennessee

Name	Age	County	State
Glazebrook, Julius		Casey	Kentucky
Godby, (Alias Godley) Geo.	74	Rowan	North Carolina
Godsey, Wm.	70	Rockingham	North Carolina
Goggin, Richd.		Pulaski	Kentucky
Good, Wm.	80	Sullivan	Tennessee
Goodson, Wm.		Cumberland	Kentucky
Gordon, Jno.		Clarke	Kentucky
Gore, Isaac		Grayson	Kentucky
Gorin, Jno.		Barren	Kentucky
Gragg, Wm.	76	Burke	North Carolina
Graham, Amos	74	Washington	Kentucky
Graham, Thos.		Mercer	Kentucky
Graney, Wm.	76	Sampson	North Carolina
Graves, James		Jessamine	Kentucky
Graves, Jno.		Fayette	Kentucky
Graves, Thos.		Russell	Kentucky
Graves, Thos.	87	Lincoln	Missouri
Gravatt, John		Clarke	Kentucky
Gray, Joseph	80	Spencer	Kentucky
Gregory, Jno.	76	Woodford	Kentucky
Gregory, Richd.	76	Oglethorpe	Georgia
Gregg, Samuel.	77	Lawrence	Alabama
Green, Gerard		Harrison	Alabama
Green, Thos.	76	Jasper	Georgia
Greening, James		Clarke	Georgia
Greenway, Wm.	78	Washington	Tennessee
Greer, Walter	75	Overton	Tennessee
Gresham, Jno.	73	Pickens	South Carolina
Grimes, James	74	Butler	Ohio
Grimes, James	80	Ripley	Indiana
Grooms, Abraham	94	Adams	Ohio
Haggard, Hy.		Rock Castle	Kentucky
Hair, Jno.	77	Hamilton	Indiana
Haisten, Jno.	71	Fayette	Georgia
Haley, Pleasant		Monroe	Kentucky
Hall, Jno.		Davies	Kentucky

Name	Age	County	State
Hall, Joseph		Lincoln	Kentucky
Hall, Ro.	81	Laurence	Indiana
Hall, Wm.	87	Randolph	North Carolina
Halloway, Taylor	63		
(D. Sept. 24, 1832).		New Hanover	North Carolina
Hally, Benj.		Clarke	Kentucky
Ham, Drewry		Lincoln	Kentucky
Hamilton, Abner		Barren	Kentucky
Hamilton, Jno.		Caldwell	Kentucky
Hammand, Saml.	77	Edgefield	South Carolina
Hansford, Chas.		Nelson	Kentucky
Hankins, Abram	70	Knox	Tennessee
Hankins James	81	McMinnie	Tennessee
Hanks, Abram	74	Lincoln	Tennessee
Hannaman, Wm.	75	Vermillion	Indiana
Harbison, James	81	Dubois	Indiana
Harding, Ede.	77	Marion	Indiana
Harding, Hy., Jr.	70	Marion	Indiana
Hardy, Jno.	73	Rush	Indiana
Harlow, Jno.		Christian	Kentucky
Harper, Jno. W.	74	Highland	Ohio
Harison, Danl.	70	Haywood	North Carolina
Harison, John	74	Madison	Missouri
Harris, Feldman	75	Guilford	North Carolina
Harris, James		Floyd	Kentucky
Harris, Overton	73	Todd	Kentucky
Harris, Wm.		Barren	Kentucky
Harris, Wm.		Bourbon	Kentucky
Harris Wm.		Estill	Kentucky
Harris, Wm.	69	Licking	Ohio
Hartgrove, Howell	70	Stokes	North Carolina
Harvey, Chas.	73	Fayette	Indiana
Haskins, James		Henry	Kentucky
Hastin, Absolom	73	Spartansburg	South Carolina
Hastings, Zach.	83	Caswell	North Carolina
Hasty, James, Sr.	82	Richmond	North Carolina
Hatton, Reuben	72	Boone	Missouri
Hawks, Frederick	82	Madison	Georgia

Name	Age	County	State
Hawkins, Giles		Jessamine	Kentucky
Hawkins, Nathl.		Mercer	Kentucky
Hawkins, Thos. (Died Nov. 8, 1832)	73	Washington	Ohio
Hay, Thomas,	71	Simpson	Kentucky
Hayden, Benj.		Henry	Kentucky
Hays, Wm.		Pulaski	Kentucky
Hazlewood, Luke		Lincoln	Kentucky
Henderson, David	81	Callaway	Missouri
Henderson, Jno.	69	Laurence	Indiana
Hendricks, Moses		Logan	Kentucky
Hendricks, Wm.	87	Shelby	Kentucky
Henny, James	74	Tuscaloosa	Alabama
Hensel, Michl.	80	Fairfield	Ohio
Herbert, Josiah, Sr.		Campbell	Kentucky
Herring, Geo.	76	Shelby	Kentucky
Hickman, James	73	Shelby	Kentucky
Hicks, Jno.	72	Coweta	Georgia
Hicks, Jno.	73	Washington	Indiana
Higden, Joseph		Barren	Kentucky
Higgins, Thos.	73	Shelby	Kentucky
Hiles, Jno.	72	Scott	Kentucky
Hill, Clem		Barren	Kentucky
Hill, Geo.	80	Pickaway	Ohio
Hill, Ro.		Bourbon	Kentucky
Hill, Saml.	71	Rockingham	North Carolina
Hisle, Saml.		Henry	Kentucky
Hoffman, Ambrose		Barren	Kentucky
Holbrook, Jesse	69	Elbert	Georgia
Holland, James M.	78	Shelby	Kentucky
Hombeck, Saml.		Bullitt	Kentucky
Hood, Thos.	76	White	Tennessee
Hooper, Richd. B.	75	Elbert	Georgia
Hopkins, Archd.	74	Browne	Ohio
Hopwood, Wm.	70	Fairfield	Ohio
Horrell, Jos.		Pulaski	Kentucky
Horton, Joseph	75	Jackson	Kentucky
Hoskinson, Isaiah	83	Licking	Ohio

Name	Age	County	State
Houchins, Edwd.		Mercer	Kentucky
House, Geo.	71	Greene	Tennessee
Houslay, Robt.	75	Jefferson	Tennessee
Houston, James	77	Blount	Tennessee
Houston, Jno.	71	Blount	Tennessee
Howard, Adam	70	Ross	Ohio
Howard, Claiborne	70	Iredell	North Carolina
Howe, James	72	Warren	Ohio
Howell, Wm.	86	Athens	Ohio
Hubbs, Jacob		Bullitt	Kentucky
Huddleston, Ro.	75	Mecklenburg	North Carolina
Hufacre, Geo.	76	Knox	Tennessee
Huff, James	74	Perry	Alabama
Hugelay, Chas.		Henry	Kentucky
Hughes, Jonathan	81	Gallea	Ohio
Hughes, Absalom		Barren	Kentucky
Hughes, Wm.		Lincoln	Kentucky
Huling, Jonathan		Campbell	Kentucky
Hull, Jno.	83	Greene	Tennessee
Hunt, Berry	79	Caswell	North Carolina
Hunt, Littlebury	72	Franklin	Missouri
Hunt, Wilson		Fayette	Kentucky
Hunter, Henry	83	Mecklenburg	North Carolina
Hurst, Hy.		Perry	Kentucky
Hurt, Richd.		Lincoln	Kentucky
Hutchinson, Drury	72	Spartansburg	South Carolina
Hutcheson, Joseph		Breckenridge	Kentucky
Hyden, Wm.	73	Roane	Tennessee
Ice, Andr.	75	Henry	Indiana
Inghan, Thos.	72	Wilson	Tennessee
Irvine, Wm.	75	Orange	Indiana
Ivy, David	72	Williamson	Tennessee
Jack, James	77	Greene	Tennessee
Jackson, Jno. C.		Fayette	Kentucky
Jackson, Josiah		Clarke	Kentucky
Jackson, Wm.	70	Wilson	Tennessee

Name	Age	County	State
Jamison, Robert	73	Ralls	Missouri
Jeffries, Wm.		Garrard	Kentucky
Jenkins, Jno.		Harrison	Kentucky
Jenkins, Wm.	72	Surry	North Carolina
Jennings, Edmund	81	Davidson	Tennessee
Johns, Ro.	75	Knox	Tennessee
Johnson, Abraham (Died in 1834)	79	Sullivan	Indiana
Johnson, David	62	Jackson	Indiana
Johnson, David	82	Parke	Indiana
Johnson, Dalmouth		Christian	Kentucky
Johnson, Geo., Sr.	85	Wilkes	North Carolina
Johnson, Henson	70	Harrison	Indiana
Johnson, Howell	72	Spartansburg	South Carolina
Johnson, Isaac	71	Carroll	Tennessee
Johnson, James	74	Washington	Missouri
Johnson, James,		Henry	Kentucky
Johnson, Richd.	74	Greene	Alabama
Johnson, Richd.	74	Sumner	Tennessee
Johnson, Rowland	76	Spartansburg	South Carolina
Johnson, Saml.		Davies	Kentucky
Johnson, Thos.		Rock Castle	Kentucky
Johnson, Wm.	72	Anson	North Carolina
Johnson, Wm.		Estill	Kentucky
Johnson, Wm.		Graves	Kentucky
Johnson, Wm., Sr.		Harrison	Missouri
Johnson, Wm., Sr.	72	Marion	Missouri
Johnson, Wm.	80	Wilkes	North Carolina
Johnson, Zophr.	72	Greene	Tennessee
Johnston, Archd.	83	Shelby	Kentucky
Johnston, Jno.	82	Smith	Tennessee
Jones, Cadwallen	89	Wilson	Tennessee
Jones, David	69	Henry	Tennessee
Jones, David	74	Jefferson	Indiana
Jones, David	79	Robertson	Tennessee
Jones, David	72	Cooper	Missouri
Jones, Edw.	77	Sumner	Tennessee
Jones, Geo.		Henry	Kentucky

Name	Age	County	State
Jones, James	82	Robertson	Tennessee
Jones, Jno.		Calloway	Kentucky
Jones, Jno.		Garrard	Kentucky
Jones, Joshua		Grant	Kentucky
Jones, Jno.	85	Maury	Tennessee
Jones, Martin	87	Franklin	Tennessee
Jones, Richd.		Barren	Kentucky
Jones, Richd.	71	Giles	Tennessee
Jones, Thos.		Bourbon	Kentucky
Jones, Thos.	71	Stokes	North Carolina
Jones, Wm.		Hickman	Kentucky
Jordan, Geo.		Anderson	Kentucky
Keeton, David	78	Gallia	Ohio
Keeton, Jno.		Franklin	Kentucky
Kelley, Moses	84	Clarke	Indiana
Kelley, Wm.	75	Switzerland	Indiana
Keneda, Wm.	78	Lauderdale	Alabama
Kennedy, Joseph		Boone	Kentucky
Kennerly, Thos.	84	Franklin	Tennessee
Kersey, Jno.		Nicholas	Kentucky
Kesling, Peter	77	Warren	Ohio
Ketchan, Jno.	76	Anderson	Tennessee
Key, Wm. (Died Jan. 18, 1834)	73	Sumner	Tennessee
Key, Wm. B.	74	Elbert	Georgia
Keys, Matthew	74	Knox	Tennessee
Kidd, James H.	69	Jackson	Georgia
Kidd, Wm.	72	Oglethorpe	Georgia
Kilgore, Chas.	80	Davies	Indiana
Kelley, Wm.		Mercer	Kentucky
Kincaid, James	71	Lafayette	Missouri
Kinchelve, Thos.		Breckenridge	Kentucky
Kindle, Wm.	74	Sevier	Tennessee
King, Cornelius	83	Morgan	Indiana
King, Geo.		Cumberland	Kentucky
King, Wm.		Bracken	Kentucky
Kiphart, Hy.		Henry	Kentucky

Name	Age	County	State
Lewis, Thos.	70	Switzerland	Indiana
Lewis, Wm.	72	Surry	North Carolina
Light, Jno.	67	Hawkins	Tennessee
Light, Vachal	71	Sullivan	Tennessee
Ligon, Wm.	79	Smith	Tennessee
Lippard, Wm.	68	Ripley	Indiana
Lipscomb, Archd.	76	Person	North Carolina
Loch, Wm.	89		
(Alias Starr)		Jefferson	Ohio
Lockridge, Jno.		Montgomery	Kentucky
Long, Anderson	72	Marion	Missouri
Lott, Jno.	80	Jefferson	Indiana
Louts, Jacob	73	Gallia	Ohio
Love, Robt.	74	Haywood	North Carolina
Love, Thos.	79	Migs	Ohio
Loveless, Geo.	74	Trumbull	Ohio
Lowry, Thos.		Clark	Kentucky
Luck, Jno.	74	Iredell	North Carolina
Luckey, Ro.		Bourbon	Kentucky
Lumpkins, Peter	72	Burke	Georgia
Luttrell, Michael	82	Marion	Illinois
McAnnelly, Peter	78	Knox	Indiana
McCarty, Daniel		Montgomery	Kentucky
McCabe, Hugh	77		
(Died Dec. 5, 1832).		Maury	Tennessee
McCalister, David		Shelby	Kentucky
McCamish, Thos.	75	Green	Tennessee
McCauley, Thos.		Harrison	Kentucky
McClellan, Jas.	75	Columbiana	Ohio
McClelland, Joseph	69	Harrison	Indiana
McCockle, Saml.		Greene	Kentucky
McComb, Wm.	84	Clarke	Indiana
McCord, Wm.	72	Knox	Indiana
McCormick, Francis	70	Hamilton	Ohio
McCormick, Jno.	71	Fayette	Indiana
McCoy, Robt.	72	Knox	Indiana
McCreary, Jno.	82	Franklin	Tennessee

Name	Age	County	State
Kirkham, Michl.	87	Woodford	Kentucky
Kirkpatrick, Robert	70	Cooper	Missouri
Knight, Hy.	74	Rockingham	North Carolina
Lacey, Elijah	81	Owen	Indiana
Lacey, Moses	72	Dearborn	Indiana
Lackland, Jno.	79	Scott	Kentucky
Lackey, Wm.	80	Laurence	Alabama
Lain, Gisborn	81	Wilson	Tennessee
Lambert, Mathias		Madison	Kentucky
Lancaster, Wm.	87	Switzerland	Indiana
Land, Ephrain	102	Stokes	North Carolina
Lane, Drury	79	Rutherford	Tennessee
Lane, Larkin	75	Parke	Indiana
Landrum, James	72	Greene	Tennessee
Lancey, Wm.		Harrison	Kentucky
Lanter, Jacob		Harrison	Kentucky
Lanter, Thos.		Madison	Kentucky
Lashley, Howell	73	Moore	North Carolina
Latimer, Wm.		Pendleton	Kentucky
Laurence, James	74	Spartansburg	South Carolina
Laurence, Wm.		Rockcastle	Kentucky
Lawrence, Rodham		Barren	Kentucky
Law, Henry		Russell	Kentucky
Lawson, Jas.		Greenup	Kentucky
Lawson, Jacob (Died Sept. 5, 1833)	74	Hawkins	Tennessee
Layne, Ro.	76	Clarke	Ohio
Layne, Saml.	75	Laurence	Ohio
Lee, (Alias See), Jno.	73	Henry	Indiana
Lee, Jno.		Montgomery	Kentucky
Lee, Saml.		Laurence	Kentucky
Lee, Wm.		Greene	Kentucky
Leslie, Alxr.	75	Sullivan	Tennessee
Levi, Isaac	75	Switzerland	Indiana
Levisy, Geo.	70	Hawkins	Tennessee
Lewis, Jas.	78	Franklin	Tennessee
Lewis, Herbert	75	Chatham	North Carolina

VIRGINIA MILITIA IN THE REVOLUTION 281

Name	Age	County	State
McCroskey, James	74	Swift	Kentucky
McCullum, James		Hardin	Kentucky
McDade, Jno.	86	Gwinnett	Georgia
McGee, Harman	74	Stokes	North Carolina
McGee, Saml.	85	Woodford	Kentucky
McGuire, Alleghany	77	Maury	Tennessee
McGuire, Joseph		Henry	Kentucky
McKay, Robt.	81	Jefferson	Indiana
McKenzie, Isaac		Morgan	Kentucky
McKinney, Chas.	71	Limeston	Alabama
McKinney, Wm.		Adair	Kentucky
McKnight, Eli		Belmont	Ohio
McKown, James	76	Knox	Ohio
McKittrick, Jno.	75	Washington	Kentucky
McManus, Jno.	74	Pike	Indiana
McMillin, Jno.	73	Elbert	Georgia
McNeely, David	76	Madison	Alabama
McPherter, Andr.	70	Putnam	Indiana

(*Trans. from E. Tennessee, March* 4, 1833).

McPheeters, Jno.	73	Washington	Indiana
McQueen, Alex.	83	Muskingum	Ohio
McQuire, Wm.	76	Pike	Missouri
McReynolds, Joseph	70	Perry	Indiana
McSpadden, Archd.	84	Monroe	Tennessee
McVay, Hugh		Caldwell	Kentucky
Madden, Wm.	73	Harrison	Indiana
Maddox, Wilson	79	Shelby	Kentucky
Magruder, Norman B.	79	Switzerland	Indiana
Mahan, James	79	Whitely	Kentucky
Mallow, Geo.	80	Greene	Ohio
Manker, Wm.	69	Highland	Ohio
Manks, Andr.	73	————	Tennessee
Mann, Francis		Harrison	Kentucky
Mannon, Hy.	74	Laurence	Ohio
Marcum, Josiah		Laurence	Kentucky
Markham, Lewis	71	Laurence	Tennessee
Marshall, Benj.	74	Stokes	North Carolina

Name	Age	County	State
Marshall, Ezekiel	77	Sumner	Tennessee
Marshall, Francis	84	Sumner	Tennessee
Martin, Gideon	102	Warren	Kentucky
Martin, Kinchean	72	Anson	North Carolina
Martin, Wm.	72	Woodford	Kentucky
Martin, Wm.		Clarke	Kentucky
Mason, Joseph		Breckenridge	Kentucky
Massey, Edmond		Campbell	Kentucky
Massie, Jno.	69	White	Tennessee
Mathews, Benj.	70	Jackson	Alabama
Mauppin, Danl.		Madison	Kentucky
Maury, Wm.	73	Wilson	Tennessee
Mauzy, Peter		Flemming	Kentucky
Mauzy, Wm.	81	Rush	Indiana
May, Abraham	70	Greene	Indiana
Mays, Benj.	77	Iredell	North Carolina
Mayberry, Geo.	74	Perry	Alabama
Mayhew, Jno.	77	Iredell	North Carolina
Maynard, Richd.		Henry	Kentucky
Mead, Minor	71	Carroll	Georgia
Meads, Thos.	81	Pike	Indiana
Meader, Isham	73	Smith	Tennessee
Meader, Joel	75	Smith	Tennessee
Meeks, Basil		Henry	Kentucky
Middleton, Jno.	71	Highland	Ohio
Milburn, Wm.	81	Greene	Tennessee
Miller, Barney		Breckenridge	Kentucky
Miller, Edward	81	Shelby	Indiana
Miller, Edward	83	Spencer	Kentucky
Miller, Francis		Jessamine	Kentucky
Miller, Frederick	74	Preble	Ohio
Miller, Fredk.	82	Wayne	Kentucky
Miller, James	85	Claiborne	Tennessee
Miller, Jno.		Bullitt	Kentucky
Miller, Jno.	72	Ashe	North Carolina
Miller, Jno.	73	Carter	Tennessee
Miller, Jno. H.	99	Knox	Tennessee
Miller, Jno. A.	69	Floyd	Indiana

Name	Age	County	State
Milkollin, ———	70	Clarke	Ohio
Mills, Jesse		Bullitt	Kentucky
Mills, Menan		Anderson	Kentucky
Milstead, Zelus	78	Lincoln	Tennessee
Milton, Elijah	78	Woodford	Kentucky
Minton, Jno.		Henry	Kentucky
Mitchell, Chas.	75	Shelby	Kentucky
Mitchell, Geo.		Henry	Kentucky
Mitchell, Richd.		Fayette	Kentucky
Mitchell, Wm.	72	Parke	Indiana
Mitchell, Wm.	70	Franklin	Missouri
Monroe, Alex.	79	Marion	Indiana
Monroe, Jno.		Ohio	Kentucky
Montgomery, Jno.		Montgomery	Kentucky
Montgomery, Jno.	68	Parke	Indiana
Montgomery, Jno.	78	Wilkes	North Carolina
Moore, Abraham	77	Shelby	Kentucky
Moore, David	71	Cole	Missouri
Moore, George	73	Boone	Missouri
Moore, James	81	Jasper	Georgia
Moore, Thos.		Mercer	Kentucky
Moody, Thos.	72	Oglethorpe	Georgia
Moore, Saml.	73	Putnam	Indiana
Morehead, Jno.		Monroe	Kentucky
Moreland, Chas.	70	Carter	Tennessee
Moreland, Dudley	73	Wayne	Kentucky
Morgan, Benj.	72	Davidson	North Carolina
Morgan, Nathan	74	Switzerland	Indiana
Morgan, Thos.	83	Greene	Tennessee
Morrell, Adam.	69	Owen	Indiana
Morring, Jno.	70	Chatham	North Carolina
Morris, Benj.	71	Miami	Ohio
Morris, Isaac	74	Perry	Alabama
Morris, James	77	Fairfield	Ohio
Morrison, Joseph	73	Harrison	Illinois
Moses, Alex.		Shelby	Kentucky
Morton, Josiah	73	Rockingham	North Carolina
Morton, Oldin	70	Jones	Georgia

Name	Age	County	State
Morton, Saml.		Madison	Kentucky
Mosely, Thos.		Montgomery	Kentucky
Moss, Jno.		Montgomery	Kentucky
Miller, Geo.		Clarke	Kentucky
Mullins, Gabriel		Pendleton	Kentucky
Mullins, Joseph	95	Bedford	Tennessee
Mumy, Chris.	80	Morgan	Ohio
Murray, Thos.	76	Columbia	Georgia
Murphy, Joseph, Sr.	73	St. Francois	Missouri
Murphy, Wm. Sr.	75	St. Francois	Missouri
Murrell, Benj.	74	Weakly	Tennessee
Murvin, Patrick		Hardin	Kentucky
Musgrave, Saml.	69	Parke	Indiana
Neil, Lewis		Henry	Kentucky
Netherton, Jno.		Oldham	Kentucky
Nevil, Thos.	73	Rutherford	Tennessee
Nevill, James		Barren	Kentucky
Nevis, Wm.	83	Hamilton	Ohio
New, James L.	70	Jefferson	Ohio
New, Jacob		Grant	Kentucky
Newell, Saml., Sr.		Pulaski	Kentucky
Newson, Wm.	73	Maury	Tennessee
Nix, Geo.	79	Surry	North Carolina
Nichols, Wilibe	85	Carroll	Indiana
Noel, Taylor		Garrard	Kentucky
Noel, Thos.		Gallatin	Kentucky
Noland, James		Estill	Kentucky
Norshorn, Reuben		Bullitt	Kentucky
Norton, Alex.	75	Blount	Tennessee
Norton, James		Laurence	Kentucky
Oaks, Isaac	74	Perry	Alabama
Oder, James		Harrison	Kentucky
Ogglesby, Elisha	75	Sumner	Tennessee
Ogglesby, Jesse		Madison	Kentucky
O'Neal, Geo.		Jessamine	Kentucky
Orr, Joshua	73	Fayette	Tennessee

Name	Age	County	State
Osborn, Jonathan	82	Ashe	North Carolina
Osborne, Jno.	72	Laurens	South Carolina
Osman, Chas.	72	Adams	Ohio
Owen, Frk.	83	Davidson	Tennessee
Owens, Jno.	73	Smith	Tennessee
Owens, Wm.		Bracken	Kentucky
Owens, Wm.		Pulaski	Kentucky
Pace, Jno.		Madison	Kentucky
Packett, Jno.	69	White	Tennessee
Palmer, Isaac		Christian	Kentucky
Palmer, Thos.	73	Cocke	Tennessee
Pamphlin, Wm.	72	Lincoln	Tennessee
Parke, Jno.	72	Brown	Ohio
Parker, Benjamin		Hardin	Kentucky
Parker, Thos.		Jefferson	Kentucky
Parks, Wm.		Garrard	Kentucky
Parnell, Benj.	79	Todd	Kentucky
Parrot, Saml.	77	Perry	Ohio
Parsons, Thos.		Greene	Kentucky
Patrick, James		Floyd	Kentucky
Paul, Geo.		Breckenridge	Kentucky
Payne, Chas.	76	Warren	Tennessee
Payne, Thos.	71	Buncombe	North Carolina
Payton, Lewis	70	Harrison	Indiana
Peake, Jno.		Logan	Kentucky
Peake, Wm.		Henry	Kentucky
Peek, Wm.		Monroe	Kentucky
Pell, Wm.	75	Harrison	Indiana
Pemberton, Jno.	83	Lincoln	Kentucky
Pendleton, Benj.		Warren	Kentucky
Pendergrast, Edwd.	70	Ripley	Indiana
Pennington, Jas.		Jefferson	Kentucky
Peril, Jno.	75	Highland	Ohio
Perryman, Wm.		Russell	Kentucky
Petty, Rodham		Anderson	Kentucky
Phillips, Geo.		Mercer	Kentucky
Phillips, Irby	71	Rockingham	North Carolina

Name	Age	County	State
Phillips, Jno.	76	Granville	North Carolina
Pickford, Danl.		Allen	Kentucky
Pierce, James	72	Wayne	Kentucky
Piercell, Richd.		Green	Kentucky
Piles, Jeremiah	72	Preble	Ohio
Pilkington, Drura	72	Marion	South Carolina
Pilkinton, Larkin		Jefferson	Kentucky
Pool, James, Sr.	87	Laurens	South Carolina
Pollard, Edmund		Harrison	Kentucky
Pollard, Wm.		Anderson	Kentucky
Pollard, Wm.	75	Spartansburg	South Carolina
Poller, Jno.		Mercer	Kentucky
Pollock, Jno.	69	Rush	Indiana
Polly, Jno.		Russell	Kentucky
Pope, Elisha	73	Wake	North Carolina
Porter, Mitchell	75	Sevier	Tennessee
Portwood, Page	76	Anderson	Tennessee
Porter, Jno.		Bullitt	Kentucky
Potts, Thos.	73	Anson	North Carolina
Pour, Wm.		Garrard	Kentucky
Powell, Ambrose		Estill	Kentucky
Powers, Jeremiah	80	Scott	Kentucky
Pratt, Stephens	70	Wayne	Kentucky
Preddy, John	76	Fayette	Ohio
Prickard, Jno.	76	Decatur	Indiana
Prewitt, Joshua		Henry	Kentucky
Price, Sampson	72	Ross	Ohio
Pride, Burton	77	Morgan	Alabama
Priest, Jno.	83	Licking	Ohio
Proctor, Benj.	74	Cooper	Missouri
Proctor, Geo.		Rockcastle	Kentucky
Proctor, Littlepage	73	Hamilton	Illinois
Proctor, Micajah	74	Chester Dist.	South Carolina
Proctor, Nicholas	78	Hamilton	Illinois
Pullen, Ro.	78	Greene	Georgia
Pullins, Loftus		Madison	Kentucky
Purcell, Edwd.	71	Knox	Indiana
Purcell, Wm.	73	Knox	Indiana

Name	Age	County	State
Putnum, Howard	75	Knox	Indiana
Putty, Wm.	84	Wilson	Tennessee
Rains, Wm.	70	Brown	Ohio
Ralston, Jno.		Harrison	Kentucky
Ramsey, James		Montgomery	Kentucky
Ratliffe, Reuben		Morgan	Kentucky
Rhodes, Hezekiah	70	Surry	North Carolina
Ream, Jesse	76	Stewart	Tennessee
Reasor, Michael	74	Spencer	Kentucky
Reaves, Arthur	77	Greene	Ohio
Reeves, Wm.	78	Abbeville Dist.	South Carolina
Reeves, Wm.	69	Brown	Ohio
Reid, Alxr.		Garrard	Kentucky
Reid, Joab	72	Brown	Ohio
Reiley, Jno.	72	Shelby	Kentucky
Renfro, Jno.		Barren	Kentucky
Retherford, Wm. (Died Nov. 16, 1833)	85	Knox	Tennessee
Reynolds, Hy.	77	Green	Tennessee
Reynolds, Nathl.		Barren	Kentucky
Reynolds, Richd. D.		Muhlenberg	Kentucky
Rice, Jno.		Mercer	Kentucky
Rice, Phillips		Bracken	Kentucky
Rice, Saml.		Jessamine	Kentucky
Richabaugh, Adam	73	Gallia	Ohio
Richards, Joshua		Shelby	Kentucky
Richardson, Jno.	72	Highland	Ohio
Richie, Jas.	79	Smith	Tennessee
Riley, Richd.	74	Muskingum	Ohio
Ringo, Cornelius		Henry	Kentucky
Roach, James	74	Montgomery	Tennessee
Robbard, Jesse		Garrard	Kentucky
Roberts, Abner	92	Spencer	Kentucky
Roberts, John	76	Cole	Missouri
Roberts, Mourning		Rockcastle	Kentucky
Roberts, Norman		Madison	Kentucky
Roberts, Wm.	72	Caswell	North Carolina

Name	Age	County	State
Roberts, Wm.	69	Ross	Ohio
Roberson, John	74	Tuscaloosa	Alabama
Robertson, Benj.		Fayette	Kentucky
Robinson, Francis		Harrison	Kentucky
Robinson, Jeremiah	75	Madison	Missouri
Robison, Joseph	72	Clarke	Indiana
Robinson, Lewis	78	Highland	Ohio
Roebuck, Raleigh	77	Martin	North Carolina
Rogers, Geo.	70	Wayne	Kentucky
Rogers, Thos.		Bourbon	Kentucky
Rogers, Thos,	71	Rowan	North Carolina
Rogers, Wm., Sr.		Adair	Kentucky
Roper, Drury	70	Jefferson	Tennessee
Rork, Michl.	89	Hawkins	Tennessee
Rosson, Archelaus	84	Robertson	Tennessee
Roundtree, Nathl.		Hart	Kentucky
Rouse, Jacob		Boone	Kentucky
Rouse, Lewis		Henderson	Kentucky
Rouse, Saml.		Boone	Kentucky
Rousey, Edwd.	71	Fayette	Alabama
Rousk, Geo.	73	Meigs	Ohio
Rowe, Jessee	79	Fayette	Ohio
Ruble, Jno.	73	Highland	Ohio
Rucher, Wm.	89	Elbert	Georgia
Ruddell, Jasus		Boone	Kentucky
Russell, Absalom		Casey	Kentucky
Russell, Chas.	75	Gallia	Ohio
Russell, Enoc.	73		
Russell, James G.	67	Baldwin	Georgia
Russell, Robt S.		Fayette	Kentucky
Sand, Wm.	80	Stokes	North Carolina
Sanders, Jno.		Owen	Kentucky
Sanders, Reuben	71	Shelby	Kentucky
Sanders, Zachariah	75	Wayne	Kentucky
Sampson, Wm.	75	Harrison	Indiana
Sampson, Wm.		Lincoln	Kentucky
Scarborough, Saml., Sr.	74	Wake	North Carolina

Name	Age	County	State
Scogg, Hy.		Grayson	Kentucky
Sheenhan, Wm.	82	Columbiana	Ohio
Scott, Alxr.	70	Cass	Indiana
Scott, Arthur	82	Knox	Tennessss
Scott, Benj.	71	Jackson	Indiana
Scott, James		Caldwell	Kentucky
Scott, Wm.	72	Caweta	Georgia
Scruggs, Wm.		Scott	Kentucky
Seaman, Hy.	76	Greene	Ohio
Searcey, Richd.		Anderson	Kentucky
Seaton, Geo.		Breckinridge	Kentucky
Seay, Jacob	76	Washington	Kentucky
Self, Jno.		Cumberland	Kentucky
Semore, Thos.	70	Carroll	Tennessee
Serber, Jacob	90	Hamilton	Ohio
Sewell, James	76	Clay	Missouri
Shackelford, Hy.		Hardin	Kentucky
Shadly, Danl.	78	Licking	Ohio
Sharp, Jno.	71	Scott	Kentucky
Shelton, Saml.		Mercer	Kentucky
Shelton, Wilson		Henry	Kentucky
Shepherd, Thos.	79	Robertson	Tennessee
Sheverdecker, Michl. (Died March 3, 1833)	71	Preble	Ohio
Shields, David	82	Clinton	Ohio
Sharp, Archilles	79	Scott	Kentucky
Sharp, Benjamin	73	Warren	Missouri
Shoun, Jno.		Greene	Kentucky
Short, Jno.	78	Laurence	Indiana
Shropshire, Abner		Bourborn	Kentucky
Shreck, Mathew		Henry	Kentucky
Shults, Mathais		Ohio	Kentucky
Silver, Aaron	76	Hawkins	Tennessee
Simmon, Wm.		Henry	Kentucky
Simmes, James	83	Blount	Tennessee
Simmonds, Joel	76	Henry	Indiana
Sims, Rhodam	79	Ralls	Missouri
Sims, Wm., Sr.	70	Franklin	Indiana

Name	Age	County	State
Sinclair, Robt.	80	Madison	Missouri
Singer, George		Oldham	Kentucky
Sizemore, Ephriam	86	Spartansburg	South Carolina
Skaggs, Wm.		Greene	Kentucky
Skinner, Isaac		Bullitt	Kentucky
Slaughter, James		Logan	Kentucky
Slayden, Jno.		Anderson	Kentucky
Smalley, David	78	Hamilton	Ohio
Smith, Alxr.	75	Merriwether	Georgia
Smith, Hy.	80	Woodford	Kentucky
Smith, Hy.	81	McMinn	Kentucky
Smith, Jacob	85	Washington	Indiana
Smith, Jno. (Died April 4, 1833)	72	Granville	North Carolina
Smith, Jno.	92	Highland	Ohio
Smith, Nicholas		Henry	Kentucky
Smith, Obediah	71	Jefferson	Tennessee
Smith, Redmond		Flemming	Kentucky
Smith, Skiltar	72	Sumner	Tennessee
Smith, Saml. 2d		Allen	Kentucky
Smith, Thos.		Clarke	Kentucky
Smith, Wm.	80	Clark	Georgia
Smith, Wm.	73	Monroe	Ohio
Smith, Wm.		Russell	Kentucky
Smith, Zebulon	76	Sullivan	Tennessee
Smithers, Wm.		Boone	Kentucky
Smithers, Wm. (Died May 14, 1834)	93	Dearborn	Indiana
Smithey, Reuben	75	Woodford	Kentucky
Smithey, Wm.	85	Woodford	Kentucky
Smoot, Jno.		Hardin	Kentucky
Sonner, Anthony	73	Hamilton	Ohio
Spaine, Claiborne	69	Duplin	North Carolina
Sparks, Hy.		Owen	Kentucky
Sparrow, Hy.		Marion	Kentucky
Spencer, Amasa	72	Jennings	Indiana
Spencer, James	72	Clinton	Ohio
Spencer, Jesse	73	Wayne	North Carolina

Name	Age	County	State
Spencer, Wm.		Bullitt	Kentucky
Sperry, Peter	74	Ross	Ohio
Spicer, Wm.	79	Wilkes	North Carolina
Spillman, James		Clarke	Kentucky
Spillman, James		Barren	Kentucky
Springer, Benj.	75	Fayette	Georgia
Sprouse, David	74	Galia	Ohio
Staples, Isaac		Adair	Kentucky
Steed, Thos.	75	McMinn	Tennessee
Steel, Saml.	74	Marion	Tennessee
Steel, Francis, Sr.	76	Stokes	North Carolina
Stephens, Jno., Sr.		Franklin	Kentucky
Stephens, Josiah	72	Putnam	Indiana
Stepp, Geo.	77	Greene	Ohio
Stevens, Gilbert		Morgan	Kentucky
Stevens, Jacob	75	Madison	Missouri
Stevens, James (Died Sept. 3, 1832)	75	Warren	Kentucky
Stevens, Jos. L.		Barbour	Kentucky
Stewart, Wm.	71	Monroe	Georgia
Stewart, Ezekiel		Montgomery	Kentucky
Stilth, Joseph		Meade	Kentucky
Stingle, Geo.	73	Tippecanoe	Indinana
Stivers, Jno.	69	Adams	Ohio
Stone, Nimrod H.	71	Vermillion	Indiana
Stout, Elijah	91	Spencer	Kentucky
Stovell, Geo.		Allen	Kentucky
Strames, Nicholas	78	Jefferson	Alabama
Strange, Jno.	75	Highland	Ohio
Strange, Jno.		Spencer	Kentucky
Street, Anthony		Garrard	Kentucky
Stringer, Jno.		Bullitt	Kentucky
Strong, Chas.	71	Oglethorpe	Georgia
Strong, Johnson	75	Fayette	Alabama
Stubblefield, Wm. S.	70	Edgefield Dist.	South Carolina
Sublett, Abraham		Lincoln	Kentucky
Sudduth, Jared	71	Clark	Georgia
Suggett, Jno.	83	Scott	Kentucky

Name	Age	County	State
Sulcer, Wm.	79	Knox	Indiana
Summers, Jno.	76	Clark	Georgia
Summers, Jno.		Flemming	Kentucky
Sutherland, Travers		Henry	Kentucky
Swanson, Levi			Kentucky
Sweeny, Joseph	75		Kentucky
Swindle, Jno.		Boone	Kentucky
Switzer, Philip	76	Gallia	Ohio
Tait, Ro. L.	68	Madison	Georgia
Tallman, Peter	80	Belmont	Ohio
Tanner, Michael	74	Buncombe	North Carolina
Tappscott, Wm.		Greene	Kentucky
Tate, Jno.	71	Elbert	Georgia
Taylor, Hy.	82	Butler	Ohio
Taylor, Leonard		Mercer	Kentucky
Taylor, Ro.		Pendleton	Kentucky
Taylor, Wm.		Rockcastle	Kentucky
Telford, Alxr.	74	Miami	Ohio
Theobold, James		Grant	Kentucky
Thomas, Evan	78	Jennings	Indiana
Thomas, Jno.	70	Clermont	Ohio
Thomas, Jno.	80	Laurence	Indiana
Thomas, Geo.		Mercer	Kentucky
Thompson, Joseph	71	Shelby	Kentucky
Thompson, William	85	Boone	Missouri
Thornhill Wm.		Breckenridge	Kentucky
Tinder, James	72	Woodford	Kentucky
Tinsley, Wm.	71	Shelby	Kentucky
Todd, Saml.		Campbell	Kentucky
Tomlin, Saml.	79	Howard	Missouri
Tomlinson, Nathl.		Pulaski	Kentucky
Toney, Carey	71	Preble	Ohio
Torrens, Saml.	88	Hamilton	Indiana
Townsend, James	75	Athens	Ohio
Townsend, Oswold		Madison	Kentucky
Trabue, Danl.		Adair	Kentucky
Travis, James		Shelby	Kentucky

Name	Age	County	State
Tribble, James	78	Madison	Alabama
Trower, Solomon		Mercer	Kentucky
True, Jno.		Oldham	Kentucky
True, Robt.	76	Jefferson	Indiana
Truox, David	78	Preble	Ohio
Trusler, James	79	Franklin	Indiana
Trusler, Jno.	76	Franklin	Ohio
Turner, Saml.	79	Ralls	Missouri
Turley, James	72	Sangamon	Illinois
Turbyfill, Jno.	93	Lincoln	North Carolina
Turpin, Martin		Pulaski	Kentucky
Twyman, James (Died Feb. 2, 1834)		Scott	Kentucky
Twyman, Reuben	75	Woodford	Kentucky
Upshaw, Jno.	79	Elbert	Georgia
Ussery, Thos.	75	Granville	North Carolina
Urton, Peter	70	Orange	Indiana
Vallandigham, Geo.		Fayette	Kentucky
Vamssdall, Cornelius	75	Knox	Ohio
Vanbuskirk, Isaac	80	Monroe	Indiana
Vandergriff, Jacob	74	Grainger	Tennessee
Vandevander, Barnabus	73	Preble	Ohio
Vandever, Geo.	70	Pickens	South Carolina
Vanmeter, Jacob		Hardin	Kentucky
Vaughan, ——	77	Merengo	Alabama
Vaughan, Jno.	74	Spartansburg	South Carolina
Vaughan, Thos.	73	Spartansburg	South Carolina
Venard, Wm.		Harrison	Kentucky
Vest, John	83	Pulaski	Missouri
Vest, Saml.	75	Washington	Indiana
Viah, Gideon,	79	Gallia	Ohio
Vincent, Jno.	78	Franklin	Indiana
Wade, Obediah		Barren	Kentucky
Wagstaff, Wm.	82	Harrison	Ohio
Walden, Jno.		Garrard	Kentucky

Name	Age	County	State
Walden, Jno.	76	Putnam	Indiana
Wale, Thos.	71	Madison	Ohio
Wall, Wm.	75	Madison	Indiana
Waller, Jesse	75	Morgan	Ohio
Wallace, Edw.	79	Carter	Tennessee
Wallace, James.	82	Charleston Dist.	South Carolina
Walker, Jno.	69	Portage	Ohio
Walker, Joshua	75	Hawkins	Tennessee
Walker, Saml.	76	Wayne	Indiana
Walker, Wm.	75	Dark	Ohio
Wanslan, Jno.	95	Elbert	Georgia
Ward, Jno.	82	Cass	Indiana
Ward, Jno.	78	Stokes	North Carolina
Ward, Saml.	81	Oglethorpe	Georgia
Ware, Edw.	72	Madison	Georgia
Warden, Elisha		Adair	Kentucky
Warrington, Wm.	79	Hamilton	Ohio
Waters, Jno.		Estill	Kentucky
Watkins, Jno.		Harrison	Kentucky
Watson, Jno. 2d.		Anderson	Kentucky
Watson, Wm.	74	Starke	Ohio
Weaver, Wm.	74	Champaign	Ohio
Webster, Wm.	70	Washington	Kentucky
Webb, Littlebury		Henry	Kentucky
Weeks, James	85	Spencer	Kentucky
Welch, Jno.	77	Weakley	Tennessee
West, Jno. (Died Aug. 14, 1833)	75	Jefferson	Indiana
Westfall, Jacob	80	Montgomery	Indiana
Wheeler, James	74	Gibson	Indiana
Wheeler, James	75	Jackson	Georgia
White, Chas.	71	Hamilton	Ohio
White, David	79	Iredell	North Carolina
White, Joseph	74	Jones	Georgia
White, Thos.	79	Belmont	Ohio
Whitaker, Wm.		Cumberland	Kentucky
Whitecotton, James		Mercer	Kentucky
Whitman, Richd.		Hart	Kentucky

Virginia Militia in the Revolution

Name	Age	County	State
Wickliffe, Chas.		Fayette	Kentucky
Wilhite, Jno.		Owen	Kentucky
Wilder, Geo.	73	Shelby	Alabama
Wilkes, Thos., Sr.	75	Laurens	South Carolina
Wilkinson, Elisha	69	Elbert	Georgia

(*Transferred from Burke County, North Carolina, September,* 1834)

Name	Age	County	State
Wilkinson, James	71	Lincoln	North Carolina
Wilkinson, Jno.	82	Wilcox	Alabama
Wilson, Jno.	79	Greene	Georgia
Wilson, Robt.	86	Hancock	Indiana
Wilson, Saml.		Logan	Kentucky
Williams, Elijah		Garrard	Kentucky
Williams, Isaac		Grayson	Kentucky
Williams, Isaac	81	Hendricks	Indiana
Williams, James, 2d		Cumberland	Kentucky
Williams, James	78	Simpson	Kentucky
Williams, James	73	Vermillion	Indiana
Williams, Jno.	83	Currituck	North Carolina
Williams, Thos.		Cumberland	Kentucky
Williams, Thos.	80	Fontaine	Indiana
Williams, Thos.		Lewis	Kentucky
Williams, Wm.	74	Gallia	Ohio
Williams, Wm.	73	Preble	Ohio
Williams, Wm.	72	Rockingham	North Carolina
Williamson, Jno.	74	Davidson	Tennessee
Willington, Jonathan (Died Feb. 26, 1834)	97	Columbiana	Ohio
Willoughby, Alxr.		Jessamine	Kentucky
Wills, Wm.		Montgomery	Kentucky
Wingfield, Enoch		Woodford	Kentucky
Wingo, Wm.	74	Spartansburg	South Carolina
Winn, Galamer	74	Madison	Alabama
Witham, Peter	74	Owen	Indiana
Witt, Elisha		Estill	Kentucky
Wood, Ellett	82	DeKalb	Georgia
Wood, Jno.	76	Spartansburg	South Carolina
Wood, Thos.	91	Wilson	Tennessee

Name	Age	County	State
Woodall, Chas.		Rockcastle	Kentucky
Woodall, Saml.	75	Rockingham	North Carolina
Woodward, Saml.	74	Montgomery	Ohio
Woodward, Geo.		Green	Kentucky
Wooldridge, Thos.		Henry	Kentucky
Woollard, Jno.	90	Clinton	Ohio
Woods, Archd.		Madison	Kentucky
Woods, Caldwell		Lincoln	Kentucky
Wright, Bolling	75	Fairfield	South Carolina
Wright, Geo.		Hopkins	Kentucky
Wright, Geo.		Oldham	Kentucky
Wright, Wm.	72	Clark	Georgia
Wright, Wm.		Clarke	Kentucky
Wyman, Harman	68	Boone	Indiana
Wyser, Geo.	69	Claiborne	Tennessee
Yeager, Elisha		Jefferson	Kentucky
Yeargan, Thos.	71	Randolph	North Carolina
Yelton, James		Pendleton	Kentucky
Young, Jno.	77	Clarke	Indiana
Young, Mathew	69	Putnam	Indiana
Young, Ralph	74	Warren	Kentucky
Young, Wm.		Muhlenburg	Kentucky
Younger, Kanard		Henry	Kentucky
Younglove, Saml.		Christian	Kentucky
Ziglar, Leonard	72	Stokes	North Carolina
Zinn, Jno.		Grant	Kentucky

General Index

This Index is sub-divided into three parts, viz:

Index of Places.

Index of Battles and Skirmishes, which includes services against Indians and at Albemarle Barracks.

Index of Names.

The references given are to sections and not to pages.

This Index is made up from Parts II and III and does not embrace the names of pensioners set out under Parts IV and V.

Index to Places

Abb's Valley, 146.
Abingdon, 185.
Albemarle Barracks, 78, 91, 94, 103, 106, 112, 134, 172, 250.
Albemarle Court House, 81.
Alexandria, 56, 77, 216.
Amboy, 163.
Amherst Court House, 8, 106.
Amsterdam, 216.
Ashby's Gap, 243.
Augusta, Georgia, 83, 175.

Bacon's Branch, 104.
Bacon's Bridge, 172.
Baker's Hill, 82.
Ball's Ordinary, 170.
Baltimore, 46, 64.
Bannister's Bridge, 153.
Bermuda Hundred, 198.
Big Capon, 43.
Big Savannah, 97.
Bingamon Creek, 129.
Bird's Ordinary, 82, 104.
Blackmore Station, 21.

Black Swamp, 62.
Blue Bell Tavern, 64.
Bluestone, 34, 44, 145, 146.
Bluestone River, 21.
Boonesboro, Ky., 185.
Bottoms Bridge, 31, 54, 118, 130, 138, 163.
Bound Brook, N. J., 13, 46.
Bowling Green, 5.
Boyd's Ferry, 133, 196.
Brandywine, 163.
Bryants Station, 153.
Brest, 216.
Bristol, Penn., 163.
Brock's Bridge, 37.
Bruce's Cross Road, 114.
Buffalo Pond, 145.
Bullpasture River, 139.
Burnt Ordinary, 159.
Burwell's Ware House, 216.

Cabin Point, 30, 32, 50, 53, 80, 84, 116, 159, 170, 173, 196, 202, 204, 206, 217.

Calf Pasture, 86.
Calfpasture River, 139.
Camden, 21, 64, 82, 121, 173, 200.
Camp Carson, 12, 58, 71, 72.
Camp Holly, 70, 118.
Cape Capon, 119.
Cape Fear River, 107.
Cape Henry, 216.
Carter's Ferry, 195.
Cartersville, 81.
Castlewood, 185.
Catawba River, 114, 121.
Charleston, 164, 172, 175, 178.
Charleston, S. C., 64, 82, 113, 132.
Charlotte Court House, 210.
Charlotte N. C., 121, 153.
Charlottesville, 13, 25, 27, 32, 37, 38, 53, 63, 100, 116, 125, 130, 134, 148, 159, 245.
Cheraw Hills, S. C., 103, 153, 171.
Cheraw Mills, 62.
Chestnut Ridge, 142.
Chesterfield Coal Mines, 170.
Chesterfield Court House, 50, 64.
Chickamagua, 185.
Chickahominy, 31, 89.
Chilicothe, 61.
Chiswold Lead Mines, 157.
Chuckatuck Mills, 6.
Clarksburg, 57.
Clinch River, 21.
Colchester, 56, 77.
Coles Ferry, 169.
Collins Mill, 145.

COUNTIES

NOTE:—For services of Militia arranged by Counties, see Part I.

Albemarle, 9, 25, 37, 38, 42, 50, 52, 53, 61, 64, 69, 78, 81, 84, 99, 100, 113, 143, 172.
Alleghany, 106, 128.
Amelia, 24, 80, 81, 82, 104, 149, 159, 175, 181, 193.
Amherst, 6, 8, 9, 10, 17, 18, 19, 26, 31, 32, 39, 40, 41, 46, 51, 52, 56, 61, 68, 69, 77, 78, 85, 100, 106, 112, 113, 134, 189.
Augusta, 13, 20, 22, 44, 45, 46, 57, 70, 71, 72, 75, 87, 92, 95, 96, 97, 98, 100, 102, 107, 111, 114, 117, 122, 124, 130, 133, 134, 136, 139, 160, 162, 163, 168, 180, 186.
Bath, 11, 20, 33, 57, 58, 70, 71, 72, 76, 79, 97, 108.
Bedford, 47, 66, 112, 126, 153, 157, 167, 185.
Berkeley, 5, 59, 122, 148.
Botetourt, 94, 102, 103, 113, 114, 115, 118, 132, 133, 138, 141, 156.
Brunswick, 181, 214.
Buckingham, 26, 195, 197.
Campbell, 14.
Caroline, 35, 40, 85, 158, 190, 194, 200, 211, 218, 219, 223, 224.
Charles City, 234.
Charlotte, 66, 184.
Chesterfield, 2, 3, 6, 15, 31, 50, 64, 82, 170, 191, 194, 199, 200, 202, 203.
Culpepper, 85, 94, 104, 112, 117, 124, 140, 148, 149, 171, 183, 234, 249, 250.
Cumberland, 2, 6, 14, 15, 50, 54, 67, 202, 203, 207, 208.
Dinwiddie, 15, 54, 143, 144, 194, 199.
Fairfax, 56, 77, 216.
Fauquier, 59, 75, 100, 103, 188, 238, 239, 240, 241, 242, 243, 244, 245, 246.
Fluvanna, 27, 32, 51.
Frederick, 110, 129, 142, 154, 164.
Giles, 44, 146.
Gloucester, 32, 36.
Goochland, 27, 30, 42, 113, 147, 187, 189, 192.

Greenbrier, 48, 60, 61, 65, 88, 98, 102, 105, 115, 123, 125, 128, 146.
Halifax, 23, 54, 144, 173, 178, 210, 216, 217.
Hampshire, 43.
Hanover, 9, 30, 32, 35, 38, 50, 52, 93, 104, 143, 194, 200, 201, 231, 236.
Henrico, 69, 187, 194, 200, 234.
Henry, 26, 141, 152, 157.
Highland, 70, 71, 72, 180.
James City, 22.
Kanawha, 99, 115, 126, 139.
King and Queen, 36, 113, 230.
King William, 23, 35, 234.
Lancaster, 101.
Loudoun, 28, 168, 245.
Louisa, 25, 30, 38, 93, 131, 176, 177.
Lunenburg, 181.
Mecklenburg, 153, 169, 171, 172.
Monroe, 5, 12, 13, 21, 22, 34, 44, 45, 47, 49, 53, 59, 60, 62, 63, 65, 75, 88, 89, 90.
Montgomery, 21, 141, 142, 144, 145, 146, 150, 153, 155, 156, 159, 160, 161, 163, 164, 165, 166.
Nelson, 1, 46.
New Kent, 94, 111, 117, 245.
Northumberland, 246.
Nottoway, 173, 174.
Orange, 25, 32, 34, 38, 63, 112, 113, 124, 149, 272.
Pendleton, 57.
Pittsylvania, 42, 56, 62, 141, 151, 152, 171, 173, 174, 208, 209, 210, 211, 212, 213, 214, 215, 216, 217.
Pocahontas, 4, 12, 43, 48, 73, 74, 86, 87, 91.
Powhatan, 2, 15, 54, 189, 190, 191, 192, 193, 194, 195, 196, 197, 198, 199, 200, 201, 202, 203, 204, 205, 206, 247.
Prince Edward, 2, 3, 6, 7, 14, 15, 16, 23, 24, 29, 30, 31, 35, 36, 54, 55, 66, 67, 80, 81, 82, 83, 195, 197.

Prince George 15, 31.
Prince William, 21, 132, 179.
Rockbridge, 12, 20, 22, 27, 28, 44, 69, 93, 101, 105, 109, 110, 112, 113, 114, 116, 120, 121, 122, 123, 125, 130, 131, 134, 135, 137, 182.
Rockingham, 5, 20, 22, 34, 57, 62, 63, 89, 108, 119, 132, 140, 160.
Shenandoah, 49, 103, 127, 129.
Spottsylvania, 52, 93, 179, 218, 219, 220, 221, 222, 223, 224, 225, 226, 227, 228, 229, 230, 231, 232, 234, 235, 236, 237, 249, 250.
Surrey, 15, 170.
Sussex, 170.
Washington, 133.
Westmoreland, 47, 242.
Wythe, 47, 141, 146, 153.
Cowpasture River, 11, 61.
Cowpens, 103, 121, 133, 160, 171, 175, 214, 243.
Cross Creek, 42.
Crow's Ferry, 113.
Cumberland Court House, 9, 15, 50, 54.
Cumberland River, 185.

Dan River, 26, 54, 114, 141.
Deep River, 17, 19, 54, 131.
Deep Run Church, 137.
Deep Spring, 52.
Detroit, 65, 97, 185.
Dincastle Tavern, 223.
Dinwiddie Court House, 194, 199.
Dismal Swamp, 95, 105, 181, 184.

Elk River, 48, 60, 61, 80, 137, 148.
Ely's Ford, 234.

Falls of the Ohio, 36.
Falmouth, 242.
Fauquier Court House, 59.
Fayette County, Ky., 61.
Fincastle, 102.
French Broad River, 21, 141, 157.

Fluvanna, 27, 32, 51, 262.
Fort Augusta, 208.
Fort Blackburn, 184.
Fort Blackwater, 184.
Fort Buchannan, 111.
Fort Burnside, 12.
Fort Chiswell, 156.
Fort Clover Lick, 58, 70, 72, 75, 76, 88, 87, 92, 97.
Fort Cook, 12, 44.
Fort Coontie, 4.
Fort Dinwiddie, 111.
Fort Donally, 61, 102, 112, 115, 125, 133.
Fort Drennan, 48.
Fort Frederick, 49.
Fort Hatfield on New River, 209.
Fort Hinkle, 57.
Fort Hood, 31, 199.
Fort Hutton, 5.
Fort Jefferson, 61.
Fort Koontz, 140.
Fort Laverty, 34.
Fort Laurence, 5, 59.
Fort Lee, 1.
Fort Louther, 4.
Fort MacIntosh, 5, 33, 59, 88, 103, 117, 138, 139.
Fort Moultrie, 164.
Fort Muddy Creek, 115.
Fort Ninety-Six, 42.
Fort Nutter, 4.
Fort Montgomery, 1.
Fort Pickett, 271a.
Fort Pitt, 5, 43, 88.
Fort Powers, 129.
Fort Powhatan, 61.
Fort St. Lawrence, 88.
Fort Savannah, 133.
Fort Thompson, 208.
Fort Triday, 208.
Fort Vance, 58, 70, 92.
Fort Warwick, 33, 34, 58, 72, 73, 76, 79.
Fort West, 4.
Fort Westfall, 5.
Fort Wheeling, 43, 88.

Fort Wilson, 33.
Fort Woods, 44.
Four Mile Creek, 234.
Frederick, Md., 3, 28, 59, 113, 216.
Fredericksburg, 1, 3, 22, 38, 59, 64, 113, 116, 132, 136, 219, 221, 223, 225, 236.
France, Messages sent to, 216.

Garrison's Ferry, 121.
Georgia, 42.
Genito Bridge, 81.
Georgetown, 62.
Germantown, 28.
Gloucester, 36, 85, 131, 233.
Gloucester Town, 36.
Goode's Bridge, 38, 81.
Great Bridge, 82, 89, 105, 123.
Great Island, 98.
Great Miami River, 153.
Greenbrier River, 4.
Green Spring, 13.
Gregory, Camp, 182.
Gregory's Station, 6.
Guilford, 76, 192, 214.
Guilford Court House, 114, 151, 159, 204.
Gwinn's Island, 36, 66.

Hackensack, 113.
Hackets Creek, 139.
Halfway House, 25, 38, 51, 100.
Halifax Court House, 23, 54, 56.
Halifax, N. C., 82, 164.
Halifax Old Town, 2.
Hampden-Sidney College, 197.
Hampshire, 43.
Hampton, 16, 23, 24, 25, 27, 29, 55, 80, 100, 159, 174, 203, 207, 223.
Hanging Rock, 64, 137.
Hanover Court House, 93, 236.
Harrodsburg, Ky., 36
Harrods Station, 185.
Hart's Store, 84.
Hatfield Fort on New River, 209.
Haw River, 211.

Hickorynut Church, 13, 33.
Higgins Station, Ky., 36.
High Rock, N. C., 213.
High Hills of Santee, 208.
Hillsboro, 171, 194, 196, 200, 209, 215, 229, 243.
Hillsboro, N. C., 16, 35, 42, 62, 64, 121, 131, 151, 159.
Hobbs Hole, 3, 190.
Hoods Fort, 31, 199.
Hoods Landing, 192, 203.
Holston River, 66, 98, 113, 136, 141, 152, 157, 189, 209.

Indian Creek, 34.
Indian Town, 141.
Irvin's Ferry, 23.

Jackson River, 33.
James City, 22.
Jamestown, 17, 22, 23, 35, 58, 81, 89, 95, 105, 112, 113, 132, 153, 164, 181.
Jenning's Gap, 111.
Jude's Ferry, 198, 248.

Kanawha River, 61, 69.
Kemp's Landing, 82.
Kentucky, 153, 185.
Kerrs Creek, 97.
King's Ferry, 124.
King's Mountain, 119.
King and Queen, 36, 113, 230.
King William, 23, 35, 234.
Koontz Fort, 140.

Lancaster, Pa., 3, 28, 216.
Laverty's Fort, 34.
Lead Mines, 47, 65, 102, 145, 146, 153.
Leesburg, 28.
Lewisburg, 97, 133.
Lexington, 98, 109, 136.
Licking River, 153.
Lindley's Mill, 215.
Little Levels, 48, 98.
Logan Station, Ky., 21, 65, 185.

Long Bridge, 42, 148.
Long Dairy, 19.
Long Island, 113, 141, 152, 157.
Long Island on Holston, 185.
Long Ordinary, 7.
Lucas Fort, 214.
Lynchburg, 13, 47.
Lynches Tavern, 35.

McCowan's Ford, 114.
McGuire's Station, 145.
Macafee Station, 65.
Malvern Hill, 15, 25, 83, 84, 93, 94, 100, 113, 149, 193, 195, 207, 210, 216, 217.
Manchester, 93, 131.
Manakin Town Ferry, 202.
Mare's Station, 145.
Marquis Road, 25, 234.
Massey's Ferry, 151.
Mast Ferry, 35.
Mecklenburg Court House, 90.
Mecklenburg, N. C., 178.
Mecklenburg, Va., 153.
Micheaux Ferry, 198.
Midlothian Coal Pits, 207.
Moore Ordinary, 197.
Monks Corner, 113.
Monmouth, 1, 113, 124, 232, 246.
Monongahalia River, 22, 34.
Morristown, N. J., 1, 124.
Moravian Towns, 155.
Muddy Creek, 115, 128.
Mullberry Grove, Ga., 9.
Murdock Mills, 12.
Muskingum, 74, 138.

New Garden, 35, 159.
New Kent Court House, 245.
New London, 47, 66, 112.
New Market, 103, 106.
New River, 44, 141, 157, 214.
Noland's Ferry, 42, 84, 137, **212,** 213, 231, 235.
Nolachucky, 102, 157.
Norfolk, 8, 45, 82, 86, 123, 137, **143,** 148, 193, 245.

North Fork, 57.
Northumberland, 246.

Old Cumberland Court House, 166.
Old Lighthouse near Hampton, 245.
Owens Station, 185.

Pamunkey River, 22, 89, 243.
Pattonsburg, 113, 133.
Paulus Hook, 90.
Peaked Mountain, 133.
Pedee River, 35, 151.
Petersburg, 7, 16, 19, 23, 24, 29, 53, 54, 64, 66, 67, 80, 81, 82, 134, 143, 144, 162, 168, 170, 197, 199, 203, 207, 222, 248.
Peyton's Ferry, 198.
Philadelphia, 64, 148, 216.
Pipington, 15.
Pittsylvania Court House, 2, 62.
Pittsburgh, 48, 61, 97, 128.
Pogue's Mill, 234.
Point of Fork, 32, 50, 81, 82, 181, 217.
Point Pleasant, 79, 87, 97, 98, 112, 115, 117, 125, 127, 128, 130, 136, 137, 139, 141.
Port Royal, 85.
Portsmouth, 2, 3, 12, 16, 22, 29, 55, 57, 71, 72, 116, 105, 120, 123, 125, 136, 137, 143, 162, 184, 199, 217.
Powell's Valley, 185.
Powers Fort, 129.
Powhatan Fort, 61.
Prince Edward Court House, 2, 3, 16, 23, 67, 195.
Princeton, 1, 3.

Raccoon Ford, 25, 38, 202, 229, 243.
Ramsey's Mill, 54, 67, 156, 172, 173, 196, 204, 210.
Randolph Mills, 194, 200.
Rapidan River, 100, 193.
Raritan, 113, 124.
Ratcliffe's Old Field, 83.
Reading, Penn., 3, 46, 113.
Reedy Fork, 133.

Red House, 105, 123.
Rich Creek, 44.
Richmond, 1, 3, 13, 15, 22, 25, 31, 33, 35, 38, 53, 76, 78, 80, 81, 82, 93, 97, 100, 107, 109, 117, 120, 125, 130, 131, 132, 135, 137, 148, 149, 159, 169, 170, 184, 189, 193, 197, 198, 199, 202, 203, 234, 241.
Rising Sun Tavern, 28.
Roane's Creek, 157.
Rock Fish Gap, 98, 124.
Ruffin's Ferry, 23, 105, 243.
Rugley, 238.
Rugley's Mill, 75, 171.

Saint Peter's Church, 94.
Salem, 145.
Salsbury, 5, 62, 64, 75, 90, 114, 118, 121, 151, 163, 200, 218, 238.
Salt River, 65.
Sandy Point, 109.
Santee River, 21, 22, 30, 71.
Savannah, 9, 90, 113, 164, 175.
Shallow Ford, 145.
Shawnee Towns, 61.
Sherrill's Station, 157.
Simpson Creek, 129.
Simms Neck, 234.
Sinking Creek, 141.
Sleepy Creek, 48.
Smithfield, 116, 149, 204.
South Branch, 119.
Speedwell Iron Works, 45, 133.
St. Augustine, 175.
Staunton River, 50, 53, 98, 124, 219.
Stone House, 102.
Stone's Mill, 89.
Stono, 132.
Stono River, 169.
Stony Point, 232.
Stovertown, 103.
Suffolk, 6, 8, 71, 105, 192, 203, 207.
Sunbury, 164.
Sussex, 170.
Sweet Springs, 102.
Taylor's Ferry, 162, 192, 194.
Ten Mile House, 178.

Tom's Creek, 141.
Trenton, 1, 3.
Troublesome Iron Works, 92, 97.
Troublesome Creek, 173.
Tuckahoe, 199, 200.
Tygart's Valley, 22, 34, 57, 98, 111, 118, 119, 127, 139.

Valley Forge, 13, 113, 124, 163, 167, 246.
Vance's Fort, 92.
Vincennes, 61.

Warm Springs, 4, 73.
Warrenton, 243.
Ware Church, 234.
Warwick's Fort, 76, 79, 111, 117.
Watson's Old Field, 38.
Waxhauw, 168.
Wax Haw Settlement, 64.
Waynesboro, 13, 107, 111, 116, 190, 124, 136.
West Falls Fort, 119.
Westham, 1, 72, 125, 149, 198.
Westham Ferry, 200.
Westmoreland, 47.
White House, 164.
White House Ferry, 234.
White Plain, 124, 137.

Wild Goose Chase, 38.
Wilks Court House, N. C., 210.
Williamsburg, 1, 5, 7, 10, 16, 22, 24, 27, 35, 37, 39, 41, 45, 51, 58, 68, 80, 82, 85, 89, 93, 100, 102, 109, 116, 117, 118, 131, 136, 156, 157, 159, 162, 174, 179, 184, 192, 196, 197, 206, 218, 219, 221, 223, 224, 226, 227, 231, 235, 236, 240, 241, 244.
Wilton, 82.
Winchester, 12, 19, 26, 40, 49, 53, 63, 67, 75, 82, 91, 110, 114, 116, 120, 133, 134, 158, 182, 190, 195, 201, 212, 213, 219, 228, 241, 243, 244, 249.
Woodstock, 103, 119.

Yadkin, 161.
Yadkin River, 62, 114, 145.
Yellow Creek, 103.
York, Penn., 28, 53, 216.
York River, 216.
Yorktown, 27, 81, 94, 100, 102, 105, 119, 120, 132, 133, 169, 192, 193, 195, 203.
Yough-Glades, 43.

Battles and Skirmishes

Albemarle Barracks, Services at, 7, 8, 9, 17, 19, 26, 27, 31, 37, 38, 39, 40, 51, 52, 63, 78, 94, 103, 106, 112, 134, 148, 187.
Allamance, 156.
Bland's Ordinary, 15.
Brandywine, 20, 46, 122, 163, 186.
Baker's Hill, 82.
Cabin Point, 206.
Camden, 30, 35, 131, 151, 159, 191, 194, 200, 208, 229, 231.
Charleston, 113, 132.
Cowpens, 5, 62, 75, 114, 118, 121, 160, 163, 238.
Eutaw, 208, 218.
Fort Moultree, 164.
Gates' Defeat (See Camden).
Germantown, 20, 28, 148, 167, 186, 216.
Gloucester, 224.
Great Bridge, 8, 82, 105.
Guilford, 5, 10, 13, 17, 18, 19, 23, 39, 40, 45, 67, 76, 78, 92, 97, 107, 122, 137, 141, 156, 165, 167, 172, 173, 186, 191, 192, 196, 197, 198, 204, 205, 206, 208, 210, 212, 214, 215, 218, 238.
Gwynnes Island, 36, 66.
Hanging Rock (N. C.), 137.
Hickory Nut Church, 100.
Hot Water, 11, 26, 62, 79, 87, 98, 100, 104, 109, 111, 117, 119, 134, 162, 186.
Indians, Services against, 4, 5, 12, 18, 21, 22, 33, 34, 36, 43, 44, 47, 57, 58, 60, 61, 62, 65, 66, 69, 70, 72, 74, 76, 79, 86, 88, 92, 97, 98, 102, 105, 111, 113, 115, 117, 118, 119, 123, 125, 127, 129, 133, 136, 138, 139, 140, 141, 145, 146, 150, 152, 153, 157, 161, 175, 185, 189, 209, 214. (See also under head Point Pleasant.)
Jamestown, 11, 20, 22, 26, 38, 62, 72, 74, 75, 79, 87, 95, 98, 104, 118, 130, 134, 136, 160, 162, 163, 169, 210.
Long Island, 165, 179.
Monks Corner, 113.
Monmouth, 1, 13, 46, 113, 124, 232, 246.
Morgantown, 271a.
New Kent Court House, 117.
Ninety Six, 42, 208.
Osborns, 122.
Petersburg, 54, 143, 170, 197, 207.
Piscatawney, 142.
Point Pleasant, 60, 73, 74, 79, 115, 128, 136.
Point Pleasant Fort, 48, 61, 73, 74, 87, 97, 98, 112, 115, 125, 127, 130.
Portsmouth, 6, 12, 57, 72, 116.
Princeton, 1.
Quibletown, 142.
Reedy Fork, 133, 156.
Rugely, 238.
Rugely's Mill, 75.
Savannah, 157, 175.
Stono Ferry, 66.
Stono, 169, 172, 173.
Stony Point ,232.
Sudbury, 199.
Suffolk, 6.
Tories, Services against, 26, 42, 47, 62, 102, 119, 133, 141, 145, 146, 155, 156, 157, 159, 161, 210, 215, 243.
Trenton, 1.
Valley Forge, 246.
Waxhaw, 64, 168.
Witesell's Mill (N. C.), 16.
York, Siege of, 1, 5, 9, 12, 19, 22, 26, 30, 31, 32, 42, 50, 51, 59, 63, 64, 67, 68, 70, 71, 75, 78, 84, 85, 92, 93, 94, 98, 102, 105, 114, 116, 119, 120, 131, 132, 133, 134, 138, 140, 144, 147, 151, 152, 158, 160, 164, 170, 174, 179, 184, 193, 195, 196, 203, 211, 212, 213, 219, 220, 222, 224, 225, 227, 228, 234, 235, 241, 242, 243, 244.

Index of Names

Abraham, ———, 234.
Abraham, Mordecai, 234.
Abernathy, William, 263.
Adams, Francis, 269.
Adams, Geo., 280.
Adams, James, 254.
Adams, James, Jr., 262.
Adams, John, 271.
Adams, Nathan, 269.
Adams, Richard, 267.
Adams, Robert, 153, 254.
Adams, William, 268.
Ailstock, Absolom, 93.
Alexander, John, 269.
Alexander, Joseph, 276.
Alexander, Robert, 254.
Alcock, Thomas, 257.
Alcorn, John, 271.
All, Wm., 139.
Allee, David, 141.
Allen, Archer, 260.
Allen, Benj., 67, 165, 166, 260, 275.
Allen, Chas, 7, 16, 23, 24, 29, 55, 67, 275.
Allen, David, 251.
Allen, Hugh, 256.
Allen, James, 16, 23, 24, 29, 95.
Allen, John, 114.
Allen, Nathaniel, 275.
Allen, Richard, 83, 166, 211, 260, 264.
Allen, Samuel, 61, 260.
Allen, William, 253.
Allison, Charles, 280.
Alsop, Benjamin, 221, 229.
Alterberry, Thomas, 65.
Alton, James, 65.
Alton, John, 7.
Alverman, John, 94.
Ammonett, Charles, 248.
Anderson, Andrew, 95, 97, 253.
Anderson, Benjamin, 27, 262.
Anderson, Charles, 275.
Anderson, David, 2, 3, 270.
Anderson, Francis, Jr., 252.
Anderson, George, 253.
Anderson, Henry, 252.

Anderson, Jacob, 142, 211, 254.
Anderson, John, 256, 265, 280.
Anderson, Parsons, 275.
Anderson, Paulin, 193, 252.
Anderson, Richard, 270.
Anderson, Robert, 253, 260.
Anderson, Samuel, 275.
Anderson, Turner, 270.
Anderson, William, 20, 97, 253, 260.
Anson, Christopher, 140.
Anthony, Joseph, 254.
Arbogast, Adam, 4, 180.
Arbogast, David, 180.
Arbogast, John; 180.
Arbogast, Michael, 180.
Arbuckle, ———, 97, 141.
Arbuckle, Mathew, 48, 60, 61, 69, 128.
Arbuckle, William, 115.
Archer, ———, 199.
Archer, Field, 259.
Archer, Henry, 259.
Archer, John, 259.
Argabrite, Jacob, 5.
Armand, ———, 53, 184.
Armistead, ———, 1, 35, 38, 93.
Armistead, Robert, 259.
Armstrong, Andrew, 256.
Armstrong, James, 65.
Armstrong, John, 256.
Armstrong, William, 92.
Arnold, ———, 1, 53, 134.
Arnold, the Traitor, 82, 143, 181, 184, 223.
Arthur, Benjamin, 254.
Ashby, George, 269.
Ascul, William, 275.
Ash, Francis, 261.
Ashby, Lewis, 261.
Ashcraft, Amos, 271a.
Ashe, ———, 90.
Atkinson, John, 143.
Atkinson, Roger, 143.
Atwell, Francis, 261.
Austin, Henry, 37.
Avery, ———, 1.

Avery, Edward, 143.
Aylett, Thomas, 226.

Bacon, ———, 38, 258.
Bagby, ———, 270.
Bagby, William, 270.
Bagley, George, 252.
Bailey, Benjamin, 271.
Bailey, John, 99.
Bailey, Yancey, 275.
Baine, John, 260.
Baird, John, 256.
Baker, Andrew, 16, 54, 275.
Baker, Michael, 277.
Baker, Nicholas, 277.
Baldwin, John, 255.
Baldwin, Thomas, 255, 275.
Ball, Benjamin, 261.
Ball, Charles, 261.
Ball, Erasmus, 251.
Ball, Farling, 269.
Ball, George, 43, 110.
Ball, John, 261.
Ball, William, 261.
Ballard, John, 168.
Ballenger, Richard, 61.
Ballenger, ———, 106.
Ballinger, Richard, 31, 61.
Ballon, Charles, 260.
Ballon, William, 260.
Balls, Resin, 154.
Balsey, Christian, 96.
Bameslee, ———, 255.
Banks, Tunstall, 230.
Bannerd, John, 182.
Bannister, ———, 143, 197.
Bannister, John, 144.
Barbour, ———, 82, 94.
Barbour, Thomas, 272.
Barker, John, 259.
Barker, John, F., 261.
Barker, Richmond, 259.
Barksdale, John, 268.
Barksdale, Saml., 251.
Barkley, Scarlet, 269.
Barnett, ———, 256.
Barnett, Alxr., 280.

Barnett, Ambrose, 261.
Barnett, George, 263.
Barnett, James, 100, 156.
Barnett, William, 134.
Barrett, ———, 1.
Barrett, James, 102.
Barrick, Wm., 3.
Barrow, John, 263.
Barsaman, ———, 164.
Bartlett, Henry, 223.
Bartlett, Harry, 279.
Bartlett, Thomas, 226, 229, 235, 236, 279.
Barton, David, 268.
Barton, Joshua, 268.
Barton, William, 143.
Baskins, James, 253.
Bass, Archibald, 259.
Bass, Joseph, 259.
Bass, William, 252.
Bates, ———, 217.
Bates, Fleming, 42, 144.
Baxter, George, 277.
Baylor, George, 2, 3, 113.
Bayles, William, 261.
Baynham, Gregory, 257.
Beadle, John, 252.
Beard, David, 254.
Beard, Samuel, 254.
Beathe, Joseph, 70.
Beattie, David, 280.
Beaver, ———, 269.
Beazley, Jeremiah, 62, 277.
Beazley, Thomas, 257.
Beck, Jesse, 9.
Beckley, John, 210, 262.
Bedford, Thomas, 268.
Begger, Charles, 183.
Begger, Chambers, 183.
Belew, ———, 208.
Bell, ———, 164.
Bell, David, 253.
Bell, Francis, 95.
Bell, George, 263.
Bell, James, 92, 97, 134, 253.
Bell, John, 95, 97, 275.
Bell, Joseph, 98, 253.

Bell, Robert, 145.
Bell, Samuel, 95, 97, 117, 186.
Bell, Thomas, 124, 186.
Benham, John, 269.
Benham, Peter, 269.
Bennett, Jacob, 180.
Bennett, James, 264.
Bennett, John, 180.
Bennett, William, 180, 210.
Berry, ———, 164.
Berry, Francis, 263.
Berry, John, 280.
Berry, Thomas, 90.
Beverley, ———, 132.
Bias, John, 131, 270.
Bibb, James, 275.
Bibb, John, 23, 275.
Bibb, Richard, 264.
Bibb, William, 275.
Bibbing, Charles, 237.
Biddle, Lewis, 272.
Biggar, ———, 275.
Biggar, David, 270.
Biggar, William, 275.
Binns, Charles, Jr., 269.
Binns, John, 269.
Bird, ———, 67, 101.
Bird, Andrew, 277.
Bird, Mark, 90.
Bird, William, 275.
Black, Joseph, 280.
Black, Samuel, 253.
Black, William, 259.
Blackburn, William, 280.
Blackwell, James, 261.
Blackwell, John, 261, 264.
Blackwell, Samuel, 261.
Blackwell, William, 261.
Blair, Allen, 10.
Blair, John, 163.
Blair, Joseph, 253.
Bland, ———, 106.
Bland, Richard, 143.
Blizzard, Thomas, 180.
Boas, Meshack, 275.
Boas, Michael, 275.
Boatwright, John, 6.

Bobb, Peter, 263.
Bobbet, William, 271.
Bodkin, Hugh, 180.
Bogart, Cornelius, 253.
Bogg, Thomas, 277.
Boggess, Henry, 269.
Boggess, Jeremiah, 261.
Boggs, Thomas, 253.
Boggs, Vincent, 269.
Bohannon, ———, 148.
Bohannon, Ambrose, 94.
Boller, ———, 133.
Bollar, John, 256.
Bolling, Robert, 143, 252.
Bolling, Thomas, 259.
Bolling, Thomas, T., 143.
Bonner, Jeremiah, 143.
Boner, Reuben, 271a.
Bond, John, 157.
Bond, Joseph, 157.
Booker, ———, 194.
Booker, Edmund, 82, 252.
Booker, Edward, 149.
Booker, George, 252, 275.
Booker, Richard, 259, 260.
Booker, William, 275.
Booth, ———, 234.
Booth, John, 252.
Booth, Mordecai, 234.
Bott, Frederick, 144.
Botte, John, 259.
Botts, Joshua, 269.
Bough, ———, 259.
Boutwell, John, 257.
Bowen, Arthur, 280.
Bowen, Micajah, 251.
Bowen, Rees, 280.
Bowen, William, 280.
Bowling, Robert, 252.
Bowman, ———, 185.
Bowman, John, 180, 185.
Bowman, William, 10.
Bowyer, ———, 105, 162.
Bowyer, John, 116, 120.
Bowyer, William, 22, 72, 87, 117, 124, 136, 253.
Boyce, ———, 85.

Boyd, ———, 35.
Boyd, John, 22, 253.
Boyd, Patrick, 9.
Boyd, William, 251.
Boyer, ———, 13.
Boyer, John, 22.
Boyer, William, 22, 58, 72.
Bradburn, Butler, 270.
Bradford, Alexander, 261.
Bradford, John, 261.
Bradley, Daniel, 208.
Bradshaw, John, 11, 12.
Bradshaw, Robert, 264.
Bragg, William, 259.
Brame, John, 257.
Branch, Benjamin, 259.
Branch, Edward, 259.
Branch, James, 259.
Branham, ———, 231.
Branson, Amos, 263.
Bratton, James, 253.
Bratton, George, 253.
Breed, Vathan, 157.
Breeden, ———, 234.
Breeden, Caleb, 234.
Breeden, Enoch, 234.
Breeden, Moody, 234.
Brewer, James, 151, 212.
Briggs, John H., 143.
Bridgforth, Thomas, 252.
Bright, Albertus, 271.
Brightwell, John, 7.
Brinker, Henry, 263.
Briscoe, William, 251.
Britt, John, 264.
Britt, Obediah, 264.
Broaddus, Thomas, 257.
Broadnax William, 143.
Brock, ———, 223.
Brock, John, 223.
Brock, Joseph, 226, 236, 279.
Brockman, Samuel, 272.
Brookin, Vivian, 174.
Brookin, William, 174.
Brooking, Robert, 259.
Brooking, Robert E., 252.
Browlee, Alexander, 253.

Brooks, ———, 75.
Bronaugh, Samuel, 261.
Bronaugh, Thomas, 261.
Brown, ———, 60, 256.
Brown, Benjamin, 97.
Brown, Hugh, 75.
Brown, Isham, 275.
Brown, J., 157.
Brown, James, 263.
Brown, John, 20, 172, 253, 270, 276.
Brown, Joseph, 236.
Brown, Langston, 258.
Brown, Peter, 271.
Brown, Shildrake, 254.
Brown, Thomas, 252.
Brown, William, 61.
Bruce, ———, 272.
Brumagen, Jarvis, 271a.
Bryan, William, 254.
Bryant, Peter, 277.
Bryson, John, 271.
Buchanan, Andrew, 223, 224.
Buchanan, David, 253.
Buchanan, James, 116, 182, 276.
Buchanan, Patrick, 22, 86, 111, 133, 253.
Buchanan, Robert, Sen., 280.
Buchanan, William, 136, 253.
Buckhannon, Alexander, 255
Buchanon, Robert, 271.
Buchanon, William, 271.
Buck, John, 183.
Buckles, Robert, Jr., 255.
Buckner, ———, 1.
Buckner, Aylett, 261.
Buckner, Mordecia, 226.
Buckner, Phillips, 219, 257.
Buckner, Richard, 257.
Buckner, William, 272.
Buford, ———, 168.
Buford, Abraham, 64.
Bull, John, 163.
Bullock, Edward, 35.
Bullock, James, 254.
Bullock, Josias, 254.
Bullskin, ———, 269.

Bunnell, James, 185.
Bunnel, John, 185.
Burchinel, Thomas, 60.
Burfoot, Tandy, 189.
Burgoyne, ———, 94.
Burk, ———, 271.
Burk, James, 263.
Burke, Henry, 251.
Burke, John, 100, 251.
Burley, James, 27.
Burnley, ———, 31.
Burnley, Garland, 26, 91.
Burnley, Henry, 254.
Burnley, Harry, 254.
Burnley, Zachariah, J., 272.
Burner, Abraham, 180.
Burnett, Henry, 210.
Burns, ———, 145.
Burns, James, 271, 254.
Burton, John, 260.
Burton, May, 272.
Bush, Vance, 263.
Bush, William, 185.
Busher, William, 65.
Buster, Claudius, 100.
Butcher, Samuel, 269.
Butler, ———, 111, 167, 251.
Butler, Alexander, 254.
Butler, Joseph, 269.
Butterworth, Benjamin, 254.
Butts, John, 143.
Byerly, Robert, 263.
Byrnside, James, 88.
Byrk, Thomas, 275.

Cabell, Nicholas, 189.
Cabell, Samuel, 1, 27, 32.
Cackley, Jacob, 263.
Cain, Cornelius, 277.
Cain, Neil, 57.
Calbraith, William, 253.
Caldwell, David, 184.
Calhoun, William, 271.
Call, ———, 113.
Callaway, Charles, 254.
Callaway, Chesley, 254.
Callaway, Dudley, 254.

Callaway, John, 254.
Callaway, James, 254.
Callaway, William, 254.
Calloway, ———, 157, 185.
Calloway, James, 47.
Calvon, ———, 1.
Calmes, Marquis, 263.
Calvert, Samuel, 263.
Cameron, Charles, 20, 22, 75, 117, 130, 253.
Camp, John, 263.
Campbell, ———, 11, 20, 21, 23, 32, 87, 100, 117, 122, 133, 137.
Campbell, Arthur, 280.
Campbell, Charles, 116, 125, 182, 253, 271, 276, 280.
Campbell, David, 114.
Campbell, Hugh, 36.
Campbell, John, 22, 75, 134, 163, 253, 254, 280.
Campbell, Richard, 103, 138.
Campbell, Robert, 95, 253, 271a.
Campbell, Samuel, 271.
Campbell, William, 102, 271, 280.
Camper, John, 103.
Cannon, William, 157.
Canterbury, John, 21.
Caper, ———, 5.
Carey, ———, 85, 158.
Carlan, Daniel, 268.
Carlile, James, 72.
Carn, Nicholas, 277.
Carnon, William, 269.
Carpenter, Michael, 253.
Carr, Makins, 251.
Carrington, ———, 197.
Carrington, Edward, 246.
Carrington, George, Jr., 260, 275.
Carrington, Joseph, 260.
Carrothers, John, 121, 276.
Carson, Thomas, 178.
Carter, Joseph, 263.
Carter, James, 275.
Carter, ———, 184.
Carter, John, 236, 271a, 279.
Carter, Levy, 271a.
Carter, Poval, 15.

Cartmill, Henry, 133, 256.
Cartmill, John, 58, 76, 133, 253, 256.
Cartmill, Thomas, 256.
Casey, William, 275.
Casey, William, 280.
Cash, Bartlett, 18.
Cashwill, Henry, 17.
Cashwill, William, 19.
Cason, Edward, 231.
Cason, William, 232.
Cas well, ———, 42.
Catlett, ———, 1.
Catlett, Henry, 263.
Catlett, John, 263.
Cavanaugh, Charles, 271.
Cavanaugh, William, 271.
Cavander, Phillip, 44.
Cave, Belfield, 272.
Cavender, Philip, 44.
Chaffin, Christopher, 275.
Chaffin, Isham, 275.
Chaffin, Joshua, 252.
Chambers, ———, 275.
Chambers, Josiah, 275.
Chambers, Thomas, 272.
Chambers, William, 275.
Chaney, Jeremiah, 271a.
Chaney, Edmund, 271a.
Chaney, Abraham, 209.
Chaney, John, 209.
Chapman, ———, 90.
Chapman, John, 271.
Chappell, John, 252.
Charlton, Francis, 146.
Charter, Thomas, 254.
Cheatham, Henry, 259.
Cheatham, Samuel, 259.
Cheatham, Mathew, 259.
Cheetwood, Jace, 254.
Chew, Harry, 223, 225.
Chew, John, 279.
Cherokee Indians, 18.
Chilton, Charles, 261.
Chiles, John, 254.
Chiles, Micajah, 251.
Choice, Tully, 268.

Choice, William, 268.
Chrisman, George, 277.
Christian, ———, 18, 19, 61, 113, 134.
Christian, Gilbert, 280.
Christian, John, 31, 78.
Christian, Robert, Jr., 253.
Christian, Robert, 20.
Christian, William, 98, 125, 136.
Christie, ———, 141, 159.
Christy, ———, 152.
Chunn, John, L., 241.
Chunn, John Thomas, 261.
Churchill, Armistead, 244, 261.
Clairborne, Daniel P., 143.
Clark, ———, 67, 85.
Clark, Elijah, 184.
Clark, John, 157.
Clark, Mathew, 147.
Clark, Micajah, 254.
Clark, Robert, 253, 254.
Clark, Samuel, 22, 75.
Clark, William, 210, 270.
Clarke, ———, 61, 275.
Clarke, George, 255.
Clarke, George Rogers, 36, 153.
Clarke, James, 275.
Clarke, John, Jr., 275.
Clarke, Sallyson, 259.
Clarke, William, 260.
Clapham, ———, 28, 148.
Clappam, ———, 148.
Clay, David, 44.
Claypole, ———, 119.
Clayton, ———, 254.
Clayton, John, 254.
Clayton, Thomas, 279.
Clemens, Isaac, 56.
Clemmons, Casper, 253.
Clemons, William, 274.
Clement, Isaac, 151.
Clements, ———, 209.
Clendennin, George, 139, 265.
Clendenning, William, 139, 265.
Clendenum, George, 139.
Clendenum, William, 139.
Cleveland, James, 269

Cleveland, John, 210.
Cline, ———, 271.
Cline, Nicholas, 271.
Clough, ———, 2, 113.
Cloyd, ———, 271.
Cloyd, David, 276.
Cloyd, Joseph, 145, 146, 271.
Cluman, ———, 159.
Cobb, Charles, 254.
Cobb, Edward, 254.
Cobbs, John C., 252.
Cobb, Robert, 254.
Cocke, ———, 1, 23.
Cocke, Anderson, 275.
Cocke, Chastain, 252.
Cock, James, 271.
Cochran, James, 263.
Cogbill, ———, 259.
Cogbill, George, 259.
Coger, Michael, 253, 277.
Colbraith, William, 253.
Cole, Francis, 225.
Cole, James, 32.
Cole, Samuel, 270.
Cole, William, 264.
Coleman, ———, 219, 227.
Coleman, Daniel, 257.
Coleman, Francis, 228, 235, 279.
Coleman, Frank, 52, 222, 250.
Coleman, James, 269, 272.
Coleman, Julius, 257.
Coleman, Samuel, 218, 257.
Collier, William, 66.
Collin, Moses, 256.
Collins, Bartlett, 279.
Collins, John, 251.
Collins, William, 257.
Collitt, Isaac, 255.
Colston, Paul, 213.
Colston, Samuel, 213.
Colvill, Andrew, 280.
Colvill, Benjamin, 104.
Combs, Benjamin, 263.
Combs, John, 261.
Conger, Michael, 89.
Connaught, Christopher, 157.
Conner, Francis, 257.

Conner, Thomas, 245.
Conner, Wm. 257.
Connerly, Arthur, 253.
Connor, Timothy, 272.
Conoway, ———, 151.
Conrad, John, 28.
Conrad, Peter, 140.
Conrad, Stephen, 277.
Conrad, Ulrich, Jr., 180.
Conway, ———, 151.
Conway, Catlett, 272.
Conway, John, 268.
Conway, Thomas, Jr., 261.
Cook, ———, 256.
Cook, Giles, Jr., 255.
Cooper, ———, 87.
Cornstalk, 61, 112, 130.
Cornwallis, 24, 35, 62, 67, 82, 113, 171, 133.
Cornwell, Edward, 65.
Cosby, John, 270.
Coursey, ———, 91.
Courtney, Wm. 230.
Coulter, Michael, 253.
Coulter, John, 280.
Covington, Richard, 259.
Covington, Thomas, 259.
Cowden, James, 268.
Cowger, Michael, 140.
Cowherd, Francis, 218.
Cox, ———, 165, 271.
Cox, Edward, 264, 274.
Cox, Samuel, 269.
Crabtree, James, 280.
Craddock, Charles, 252.
Craddock, Henry, 252.
Craddock, Richard, 159, 252.
Craddock, William, 159, 252.
Craig, ———, 164, 226.
Craig, J., 235.
Craig, James, 63.
Craig, John, 223.
Craig, George, 97, 124.
Craig, Robert, 280.
Craig, Toliver, 272.
Crane, James, 255.
Cravens, ———, 5.

Craven, John, 261.
Craven, Robert, 34, 62, 127, 139, 140, 253, 277.
Crawford, ———, 5.
Crawford, Alexander, 92, 253.
Crawford, James, 253, 271.
Crawford, John, 95, 271.
Crawford, Nathan, 76.
Crim, Jacob, 263.
Critz, Haman, Jr., 268.
Crockett, Andrew, 271.
Crockett, Hugh, 156, 256.
Crockett, John, 271.
Crockett, Joseph, 156.
Crockett, Walter, 155, 271.
Crookshank, John, 278.
Crouch, Joseph, 253.
Croucher, ———, 222, 231.
Croucher, Thomas, 235.
Crow, Jacob, 43.
Crowder, William, 193.
Crowley, William, 252.
Crummett, Frederick, 180.
Crump, Richard, 15, 202, 207, 274.
Crutchfield, John, 270.
Cullins, John, 190.
Cummings, Alexander, 126.
Cunningham, ———, 12.
Cunningham, Ansel, 169.
Cunningham, James, 179, 276.
Cunningham, Nathaniel, 23, 195, 275.
Cunningham, Thomas, 141.
Curd, Edmund, 264.
Curd, John, Jr., 264.

Dabney, ———, 85, 100, 244.
Dabney, Charles, 30, 234.
Dabney, John, 275.
Dabney, Samuel, 270.
Dack, Joseph, 271.
Daggett, Chatton, 254.
Dance, Ezekiel, 259.
Dandridge, ———, 98.
Dandridge, Jonathan, 246.
Daniel, George, 275.
Daniel, Hugh, 263.

Daniel, James, 257.
Daniel, John, 211.
Daniel, Robert, 272.
Daniel, Vivian, 272.
Daniel, William, 77, 260.
Dark, ———, 35, 59, 110, 142.
Davis, ———, 157, 269.
Davis, Benjamin, 179.
Davis, Charles, 275.
Davis, Edward, 59.
Davis, Henry, 254.
Davis, Isaac, 251.
Davis, James, 98, 276.
Davis, Jesse, 179.
Davis, John, 179, 268, 280.
Davis, Joseph, 254.
Davis, Lewis, 157.
Davis, Nicholas, 275.
Davis, Presley, 179.
Davis, Robert, 185, 253, 271, 277. 280.
Davis, Samuel, 254.
Davis, Thomas, 179.
Davis, William, 106, 163, 265, 271.
Davidson, ———, 114.
Davidson, David, 275.
Davidson, Edward, 275.
Davidson, George, 265.
Davidson, Giles, 26.
Davidson, Josiah, 277.
Davidson, John, 105.
Davidson, Samuel, 125, 276.
Davidson, William, 275.
Dawson, Henry, 2, 23, 24.
Day, Joseph, 253.
Dean, ———, 256.
Dean, William, 271.
Debell, John, 269.
Debell, William, 269.
Dehaven, Abraham, 269.
DeJarnett, Joseph, 257.
Denicel, William, 56.
Demoss, Thomas, 254.
Dennis, John, 252.
Denny, Robert, 263.
Denny, Samuel, 246, 263.

Deering, John, 261.
Dick, ———, 56, 184.
Dickenson, Henry, 280.
Dickenson, John, 79, 87, 97, 98.
Dickerson, John, 33.
Dickey, John, 22, 75, 95, 118, 124, 163, 253.
Dickey, William, 75.
Dickinson, ———, 48, 61, 127.
Dickinson, John, 87, 97, 98, 125.
Dictum, Joseph, 127, 277.
Diggs, ———, 81.
Diggs, Edward, 261.
Dictum, John, 277.
Dillard, ———, 106.
Dillard, James, 19.
Dillard, John, 268.
Divers, John, 254.
Dix, ———, 174.
Dix, William, 212, 213.
Doak, Joseph, 271.
Doak, Samuel, 271.
Doak, William, 271.
Dobbins, Edward, 263.
Dodd, John, 269.
Doggett, Chatton, 157.
Doggett, George, 157.
Doherty, John, 271a.
Dolman, ———, 6.
Doley, Thomas, 157.
Donaldson, John, 209.
Donaldson, William, 261.
Donally, Andrew, 256, 265.
Donelson, John, 214.
Dooley, George, 254.
Dooley, John, 42, (Killed by Indians.)
Dorsey, Joshua, 263.
Doswell, Thomas, 30.
Douglass, ———, 215.
Douglass, Hugh, 269.
Douglass, William, 269.
Douthat, ———, 166.
Dove, William, 216.
Dowbman, ———, 181.
Dowell, ———, 251.
Downey, ———, 49.

Downer, John, 257.
Downing, James, 271.
Downs, John, 255.
Draggett, James, 255.
Drake, James, 274.
Drapier, ———, 271.
Drumheller, Leonard, 25, 38.
Drury, ———, 234.
Duckleman, ———, 85.
Dudley, Gwin, 157.
Dudley, Peter, 279.
Duffield, Abraham, 180.
Dugrid, William, 26.
Duke, Edward, 264.
Duncan, Benjamin, 151.
Duncan, George, 262.
Duncan, John, 185, 280.
Dundane, James, 255.
Dunmore, ———, 1, 36, 66, 74, 148.
Dunn, James, 251.
Dunn, John, 62.
Dupuy, John, 23, 275.
Durham, Joshua, 252.
Durham, Nathaniel, 275.
Durrett, Robert, 229, 279.
Durrett, Richard, 251, 257.
Durrett, William, 257.
Dusee, Lewis, 157.
Duvall, ———, 15.
Dysart, James, 280.

Early, Jacob, 254.
Early, Jacobus, 254.
Early, Jeremiah, 254.
Earn, ———, 256.
East, John, 27.
Eastham, ———, 95, 98.
Eastin, Johnston, 263.
Eavans, ———, 256.
Eberman, William, 277.
Eckard, Abraham, 180.
Eckard, Philip, 180.
Eddings, David, 256.
Edmunds, ———, 243.
Edminston, William, 280.
Edmonds, Elias, 244.
Edmunds, William, 261.

Edmondson, Richard, 153.
Edmunds, Jacob, 275.
Edmundson, ———, 120.
Edmundson, Benjamin, 232.
Edward, Robert, 252.
Edwards, ———, 271.
Edwards, Frederick, 271.
Edwards, John, 163.
Edwards, Thomas, 261.
Edwards, William, 206.
Eggleston, John, 274.
Eidson, Henry, 254.
Elam, Branch, 259.
Elam, Bartilot, 259.
Elam, Richard, 259.
Elam, Samuel, 259.
Elgin, Francis, Jr., 269.
Elgin, Gustavus, 269.
Elkins, Benjamin, 263.
Ellinipsico, 61, 112.
Elliott, ———, 1.
Elliott, James, 276, 280.
Elliott, John, 252.
Elliott, William, 269.
Ellis, Stephen, 264.
Ellis, Thomas, 257.
Ellsworth, Jacob, 180.
Ellyson, Onan, 259.
Epperson, ———, 1.
Eppes, ———, 165.
Eppes, Francis, 82.
Erwin, Benjamin, 277.
Eskridge, Charles, 269.
Estill, Wallace, 133, 256.
Estis, ———, 23.
Estis, Richard, 271.
Ethal, Anthony, 245.
Eustace, Wm. Jr., 261.
Eustis, William, 50.
Evans, ———, 122.
Evans, Andrew, 276.
Evans, Evan, 277.
Evans, Jesse, 271.
Evans, William, 263.
Ewell, ———, 132.
Ewell, James, 253.
Ewell, Samuel, 271.
Ewell, William, 254.

Eye, Christopher, 180.

Falconer, Samuel, 228.
Falkner, ———, 64, 159.
Falkner, John, 144.
Faulkner, ———, 1, 159, 194.
Faulkner, Johnson, 257.
Farley, Francis, 254.
Farmer, John, Jr., 259.
Farnsworth, Henry, 269.
Farrar, John, 259.
Feagam, Daniel, 269.
Febiger, ———, 1, 50.
Ferguson, ———, 102, 148, 152.
Ferguson, Robert, 210.
Ferguson, Samuel, 104, 271.
Ferguson, William, 141, 157.
Field, ———, 74.
Fink, Jacob, 255.
Finley, ———, 9.
Finley, James, 271.
Finley, William, 253.
Finney, John, 69, 252.
Finney, William, 252.
Fitzgerald, ———, 82.
Fitzgerald, Barclay, 113.
Fitzgerald, Francis, 252.
Fitzgerald, William, 173.
Fitzhugh, John, 257.
Fitzwater, John, 277.
Fitzwater, Thomas, 277.
Fix, Philip, 28.
Flait, William, 251.
Fleisher, Conrad, 4, 180.
Fleisher, Henry, 180, 253.
Flemming, ———, 147.
Flemming, James, 256.
Flemming, William, 274.
Fletcher, ———, 257.
Fletcher, John, 261.
Flood, ———, 24.
Flowers, Absolom, 170.
Flowers, Daniel, 261.
Flournoy, ———, 24.
Flourney, Thomas, 7, 275.
Floyd, ———, 141.
Foley, James, Jr., 261.
Fontaine, ———, 93.

Fontaine, Aaron, 270.
Fontaine, John, 268.
Fontaine, William, 8.
Ford, ———, 149.
Ford, Lewis, 193, 252.
Ford, William, 252.
Fore, Francis, 275.
Foster, George, 275.
Foster, Joshua, 275.
Foster, Thomas, 271.
Foulk, Mathew, 251.
Foulks, Gabriel, 174.
Fowler, John, 259.
Fowler, Luke, 259.
Fowlkes, Gabriel, 252.
Francis, Arnold, 163.
Fox, John, 270.
Francis, Henry, 271.
Franklin, Edmund, 254.
Franklin, James, 17, 18, 46, 68.
Franklin, Owen, 254.
Fraser, John, 275.
Fraser, Thomas, 275.
Frazier, Falzy, 251.
Frazier, George, 256.
Frazier, James, 61, 253, 277.
Frazier, John, 280.
Freeland, George, 280.
Freeze, ———, 5.
French, Daniel, 254.
French, John, 261.
Friend, ———, 258.
Frost, William, 263.
Fugue, Wm., 275.
Fulkerson, Joshua, 261.
Fulkerson, James, 280.
Fulkerson, Rodham, 261.
Fulton, Robert, 107.
Fuqua, Moses, 254.

Galispie, William, 275.
Galladay, David, 278.
Galloway, John, 128, 256.
Gaines, Richard, 184.
Gardner, Francis, 95.
Garland, ———, 1.
Garland, Edward, 251.

Gardiner, Henson, 271.
Garland, James, 9, 84, 78.
Garland, Nathaniel, 100, 251, 270.
Garratt, Alexander, 275.
Garratt, Harvey, 270.
Garrett, Henry, 270.
Garrington, John, 261.
Gartin, Nathaniel, 34.
Gaskins, ———, 50.
Gates, ———, 10, 35, 153, 159, 171, 194, 202.
Gay, John, 276.
Gentry, James, 251.
Gentry, George, 251.
George, ———, 261.
George, Frederick, 143.
George, James, Jr., 264.
George, William, 264, 269.
German, ———, 175.
Gibbs, ———, 1.
Gibbs, William, 252, 259.
Gibson, ———, 5.
Gibson, David, 107, 253.
Gibson, George, 117.
Gibson, James, 253.
Gibson, John, 88.
Gilbert, ———, 129.
Gilbert, Daniel, 254.
Gilbert, John W., 254.
Gilbert Preston, 254.
Gilbert, Samuel, 254.
Giles, ———, 252.
Giles, Isaiah, 31.
Giles, William, 81, 267.
Gilham, Peter, 263.
Gilkerson, ———, 142.
Gilkerson, Samuel, 263.
Gill, ———, 1, 181.
Gillespie, George, 29.
Gillespsie, William, 275.
Gilliam, George, 251.
Gilliam, James, 260.
Gilliam, Zachariah, 254.
Gilliland, James, 108.
Gillis, Thomas, 256.
Gilmer, ———, 61, 113.
Gilmer, George, 251.

Gilmer, James, 48, 61, 69.
Gilmer, John, 253.
Gilmer, William, 121.
Gilmore, ———, 256.
Gilmore, James, 115, 121.
Gilmore, James, Jr., 276.
Gilmore, William, 121.
Gilmore, Jno., 276.
Ginn, ———, 256.
Givens, ———, 256.
Given, David, 253.
Given, John, 87, 124, 130, 134, 253.
Glass, Samuel, 265.
Glavis, William, 271.
Glen, ———, 35, 66, 151, 211.
Glenn, Beverley, 270.
Glen, James, 260.
Gleen, Peyton, 275.
Goggins, John, 167.
Goggin, Stephen, 153.
Going, Sharod, 251.
Gooch, William, 100, 251.
Goode, ———, 15, 202, 203, 258.
Goode, Francis, 259.
Goode, Frank, 2.
Goode, Mack, 252.
Goode, Mackness, 193.
Goode, Robert, 15, 194, 199, 207, 275.
Goode, Thomas, 259.
Goodwin, Esua, 143.
Gordon, Thomas, 277.
Goodwin, Micajah, 61.
Gordon, William, 256.
Graham, ———, 265.
Graham, Christopher, 253.
Graham, Duncan, Jr., 257.
Graham, Francis, 180.
Graham, James, 253.
Graham, Robert, 257.
Graham, William, 257.
Grant, Isaac, 269.
Grant, Robert, 32.
Graves ———, 148, 171.
Gravatt, John, 257.
Graves, King, 259.
Graves, Lewis, 148.

Graves, Richard, 272.
Graves, Thomas, 148.
Graves, Thomas, N., 148.
Gray, ———, 44, 109, 113, 173.
Gray, David, 105, 123, 137, 253, 276.
Gray, John, 252.
Gray, William, 274.
Gray, William F., 257.
Grayson, ———, 13.
Grayson, William, 100, 186, 245, 251.
Green, ———, 1, 23, 39, 40, 42, 46, 54, 62, 67, 68, 121, 124, 137, 153, 156, 171, 173, 227.
Green, Abraham, 82, 252.
Green, James, 254.
Green, John, 46.
Green, Forrest, 270.
Green, Moses, 254.
Green, Samuel, 252.
Greenhill, William, 252.
Greenup, ———, 269.
Greer, James, 254.
Gregory, ———, 1, 265.
Gregory, Joseph, 129.
Grenadier, Squaw, 61.
Griffith, Benjamin, 254.
Grigg, James, 252.
Grigsby, William, 261.
Grubbs, Nathan, 30.
Guerrant, John, Jr., 264.
Gum, Isaac, 180.
Gum, Jacob, 180.
Gum, John, 4.
Gum, William, 180.
Gunn, Elisha, 173.
Guttery, Alexander, 260.
Guttery, Bernard, 260.
Guy, George, 257.
Guy, Thomas, F., 257.
Gwatkins, Chas. 254.
Gwin, David, 33. 58, 76, 92, 253.
Gwin, Joseph, 4, 12, 58, 72, 253.
Gwinn, John, 209.
Gwinn, Joseph, 253.

Habbersham, Joseph, 83.
Hackley, Samuel, 197.
Haden, Anthony, 262—(32).
Haden, John, Mozely, 262.
Haden, John M., 262.
Haden, Joseph, 262.
Haden, William, 262.
Haile, Richard, 254.
Haile, Thomas, 268.
Hairston, George, 268.
Hairston, John, 268.
Hairston, Peter, 268.
Halbert, William, 268.
Hale, Job, 141.
Hales, Peter, 275.
Hall, ———, 102.
Hall, Adam, 180.
Hall, Bowler, 252.
Hall, Bowling, 173.
Hall, James, 109, 137, 191, 256, 276.
Hall, John, 251, 257.
Hall, Nathan, 251.
Hall, Richard, 262.
Hall, William, 109.
Hamilton, Alexander, 111.
Hamilton, Andrew, 65, 159, 256.
Hamilton, Andrew, Jr., 253.
Hamilton, Charles, 253.
Hamilton, Gawen, 277.
Hamilton, James, 111.
Hamilton, John, 111, 253.
Hamilton, Patrick, 253.
Hamilton, Samuel, 265.
Hamilton, William, 256, 265.
Hammer, Balsor, 180.
Hammer, Nicholas, 38.
Hammond, Phillip, 61.
Hampkins, Uriah, 256.
Hampton, ———, 85.
Hampton, George, 237.
Hampton, Nathan, 275.
Hampton, Thomas, 263.
Hancher, William, 263.
Hancock, ———, 264.
Hancock, Benjamin, 262.
Hancock, Simon, 269.

Hand, ———, 43, 48, 61, 97, 98, 112, 130.
Hand, Christopher, 38.
Hank, Henry, 271a.
Hanly, ———, 256.
Handly, Alexander, 114.
Hansford, Benoni, 272.
Hard, ———, 1.
Hardiman, ———, 229.
Hardin, John, 279.
Harding, Thomas, 264.
Hardman, John, 277.
Hardon, George, 251.
Hardy, ———, 216, 235.
Harley, ———, 256.
Harper, Nicholas, 180, 253.
Harper, Richard, 251.
Harman, ———, 277.
Harrell, John, 263.
Harris, ———, 88, 131, 259.
Harris, Benjamin, 50, 84, 100, 251.
Harris, Francis, E., 274.
Harris, Frederick, 270.
Harris, John, 25, 38, 99, 151, 274.
Harris, John, Jr., 274.
Harris Nathaniel, 264.
Harris, Peter, 268.
Harris, Richard, 251.
Harris, Robert, 251, 253.
Harris, Samuel, 237.
Harris, Thomas, 192, 248, 261, 274.
Harris, Thornton, 248.
Harris, William, 93, 251, 270.
Harrison, Benjamin, 9, 57, 93, 239, 260, 277.
Harrison, Bevor, 261.
Harrison, James, 61, 112, 246.
Harrison, Josiah, 127, 277.
Harrison, Reuben, 253, 277.
Harrison, Richard, 42.
Harrison, Robert, 277.
Harrison, Thomas, 276.
Harrison, William, 252.
Harrod, Littlebury, 190.
Hart, Benjamin, 195.
Hart, John, 59, 255.
Hartless, William, 40.

Harvey, ———, 258.
Harvie, John, 277.
Haskins, Charles, 22.
Haskins, Crad, 6.
Haskins, Creed, 199, 211, 260.
Haskins, Edward, 274.
Haskins, John, 230.
Haskins, Robert, 259.
Haskins, Thomas, 274, 275.
Haslip, Henry, 262.
Hastie, Thomas, 275.
Hatcher, ———, 147.
Hatcher, John, 260.
Hatcher, Thomas, 264.
Hatfield, Andrew, 271.
Hathaway, James, 261.
Hathaway, John, 261.
Hatton, Reuben, 149.
Hawes, ———, 7.
Hawes, Samuel, 18, 218.
Hawes, Thomas, 257.
Hawk, Isaac, 43.
Hawkins, James, 272.
Hawkins, Reuben, 251.
Hay, James, 276.
Hayden, Anthony, 32, 262.
Hayden, Joseph, 27, 262.
Haynes, Parmenas, 254.
Haymond, Thos, 271a.
Haymond, Wm., 271a.
Haymond, Henry, 271a.
Hays, ———, 181.
Hays, John, 271.
Hays, Samuel, 280.
Hays, William, 181.
Hayth, Thomas, 254.
Hazaret, ———, 3.
Head, Benjamin, 272.
Head, James, 272.
Heale, William, 261.
Heath, ———, 132.
Heath, Andrew, 43.
Heaton, James, 263.
Heister, Daniel, 163.
Helfhingston, Philip, 263.
Helm, John, 254.
Helm, Thomas, 254, 261.

Helms, ———, 142.
Hempenstall, Abraham, 253.
Henderson, Anthony, 51.
Henderson, Bennett, 251.
Henderson, James, 256.
Henderson, John, 50, 60, 251, 265, 271.
Henderson, T., 268.
Henderson, William, 251, 253, 254.
Hendricks, ———, 1.
Hendricks, James, 226.
Henley, Hezekiah, 264.
Henry, John, 269.
Henry, Patrick, 23, 82, 148.
Henry, William, 262.
Henson, Samuel, 270.
Herndon, Edward, 187.
Herndon, John, 264, 272.
Herndon, Zachariah, 272.
Herring, James, 37.
Herring, William, 277.
Herston, Peter, 141, 152, 157.
Hevener, Jacob, 277.
Hewitt, John, 133.
Hewitt, Thomas, 253, 277.
Hicklin, Thomas, 12, 22, 70, 72, 253.
Hickman, ———, 234.
Hickman, Adam, 109, 135.
Hicks, William, 69.
Higgen, Joel, 257.
Higginbotham, Benjamin, 39, 40, 78.
Higginbotham, Caleb, 68.
Higginbotham, James, 19, 41.
Higginbotham, Samuel, 19, 61.
Hill, ———, 148.
Hill, Henry, 94.
Hill, John, 259, 263.
Hill, Richard, 199, 251.
Hill, Swinfield, 268.
Hill, Thomas, 268.
Hill, William, 35, 259.
Hines, John, 36.
Hines, William, 36.
Hinkle, Henry, 110.
Hinkle, Isaac, 277.

Hisewonger, John, 263.
Hiskill, Adam, 263.
Hiskill, Peter, 263.
Hixon, Timothy, 269.
Hockaday, ———, 1.
Hodge, James, 276.
Hodges, Robert, 143.
Hobson, Benjamin, 260.
Hobson, John, 260.
Hobson, William, 202, 260.
Hoffman, George, 180.
Hoff, James, 180.
Hogan, John, 261.
Hogg, John, 38, 69, 180.
Hogg, Thomas, 277.
Hogshead, James Jr., 253.
Holcomb, ———, 204, 205.
Holcomb, John, 7, 16, 17, 18, 19, 67, 68, 275.
Holcomb, Phillips, 80.
Holland, Richard, 7, 16, 275.
Hollady, ———, 220.
Hollady, James, 279.
Hollady, John, 229.
Hollady, Lewis, 229.
Hollman, Nathaniel, 267.
Holloway, William, 252.
Holman, Alexander, 275.
Holman, Christopher, 246.
Holman, Tandy, 264.
Holsten, ———, 133.
Holstin, ———, 256.
Holt, Thomas, 27.
Holt, William, 171.
Hondle, Hezekiah, 267.
Hood, Thomas, 227.
Hoover, Jacob, 180.
Hoover, Michael, 180.
Hopkins, ———, 1, 148.
Hopkins, James, 171.
Hopkins, John, 127, 253, 264, 277.
Hord, James, 257.
Hord, John, 257.
Hord, Thomas, 257.
Hord, William, 275.
Horseley, Richard, 263.
Hotsler, ———, 256.

House, ———, 181.
Houston, George, 108, 119.
Houston, James, 61.
Howard, ———, 64, 75, 117, 156.
Howard, Christopher, 230.
Howe, Daniel, 150, 271.
Howell, John, 143.
Howerton, James, 275.
Howson, John, 252.
Hoyd, ———, 137.
Hubbard, ———, 203, 206, 259.
Hubbard, Thomas, 274.
Hubbard, William, 66, 258.
Hubblefield, George, 272.
Huckstep, Charles, 251.
Hudgens, William, 260.
Hudnall, William, 254.
Hudson, Charles, 38.
Hudson, Irby, 143.
Hudson, John, 251.
Hudson, Robert, 252
Hudson, Tuttle, 143.
Huggard, ———, 75.
Hughart Thomas, 22, 111, 159, 253.
Hughes, Archilaus, 268.
Hughes, David, 274.
Hughes, Joshua, 270.
Hughes, Robert, 54, 196, 197, 198, 203, 204, 274.
Hughes, Thomas, 8.
Hughes, William, 270.
Hucklebery, Fred, 271a.
Hull, George, 4.
Hull, Peter, 72, 180, 253, 256.
Humphrey, ———, 269.
Humphreys, Jonathan, 253.
Hunt, ———, 174.
Hunt, David, 56, 213.
Hunt, Nathaniel, 23.
Hunt, William, 261.
Hungate, William, 161.
Hunter, David, Jr., 255.
Hunter, John, Jr., 254.
Hunton, ———, 9.
Huston, George, 277.
Huston, James, 276.

Huston, John, 277.
Hutchen, Seth, 192.
Hutcheson, James, 256.
Hutchings, Charles, 151.
Hutchings, Moses, 209.
Hutchison, James, 193.
Hutchison, William, 44, 269.
Hutton, Moses, 43.
Hylton, John, 259.

Ice, Fredk., 271a.
Ice, John, 271a.
Inglis, David, 271.
Inglis, William, 271.
Ingram, Uriah, 180.
Ingram, William, 272.
Inchminger, John, 61.
Innes, ———, 185, 223.
Innes, Harry, 254.
Irby, Charles, 173, 252.
Irey, Philip, 269.
Irvine, ———, 101.
Irvine, Andrew, 254.
Irvine, John, 254.
Irvine, Robert, 254.
Irwin, John, 115.
Ivey, Jennie, 157.

Jacobs, ———, 31.
Jackson, Henry, 194.
Jackson, William, 270.
James, ———, 29, 55.
James, Joseph, 261.
James, Thomas, 261.
James, William, 254.
Jameson, David, 257.
Jameson, James, 272.
Jameson, William, 258, 272.
Jamison, ———, 85.
Jarman, William, 25, 38.
Jarvis, Field, 47.
Jefferson, ———, 197, 207.
Jeffries, ———, 213.
Jeffries, William, 213.
Jenkins, James, 252.
Jennings, Augustine, 261.
Jennings, Baylor, 261.

Jennings, Berryman, 261.
Jennings, Isham, 275.
Jennings, James, 275.
Jennings, Joseph, 252.
Jennings, William, 261.
Jeter, Ambrose, 257.
Jeter, Henry, 254.
Jeter, Presley, 252.
Johns, Isaac, 138.
Johnson, ———, 1, 85, 115, 176, 177, 185, 272.
Johnson, Andrew, 277.
Johnson, Arthur, 252.
Johnson, Benjamin, 267, 271.
Johnson, Christopher, 270.
Johnson, George, 270.
Johnson, Henry Ashton, 270.
Johnson, James, 35, 253, 265.
Johnston, Peter, 264.
Johnston, Philip, 218, 257.
Johnston, Richard, 224, 270.
Johnson Robert, 272.
Johnson, Thomas, 254, 270.
Johnson, Walter, 264.
Johnson, William, 251, 262, 275.
Johnson, Zachariah, 136, 253.
Johnston, Benjamin, 279.
Johnston, James, 271a.
Johnston, Richard, 251.
Jones, ———, 82, 269.
Jones, Batt, 252.
Jones, Benjamin, 75.
Jones, Cadwallader, 3, 113.
Jones, Daniel, 252.
Jones, David, 152.
Jones, John, 115, 255, 257.
Jones, Joseph, 268.
Jones, Landon, 99.
Jones, Philip, 82, 252.
Jones, Richard, 252.
Jones, Thomas, 25, 38, 46, 157, 237, 251, 252, 254, 257, 268.
Jones, William, 252, 254.
Jones, Wylie, 82.
Jordan, ———, 1.
Jordan, Andrew, 180.
Jordan, Thomas, 252.

Jordan, William, 251, 254.
Jouett, Robert, 64.
Justice, Moses, 271.
Katon, Jacob, 269.
Kay, James, 257.
Kate, John, 143.
Keblinger, Adam, 251.
Keeling, George, 260.
Keister, Frederick, 277.
Keither, Alexander, 261.
Keither, Thomas, 261.
Keller, Conrad, 49.
Kelley, Alexander, 265.
Kelso, James, 116.
Kemper, Peter, Jr., 261.
Kemp, John, 263.
Kendrick, Abraham, 263.
Kendrick, Christly, 263.
Kendrick, John, 172.
Kennedy, David, 59, 263.
Kennerly, William, 117.
Kennett, Valentine, 271a.
Kenney, Robert, 253.
Kennison, Jacob, 48.
Kennon, ———, 1.
Kennon, Thomas, 269.
Kenton, Ambrose, 272.
Kenton, William, 261.
Kettering, Laurence, 271.
Kidd, James, H., 172.
Kilgrove, George, 269.
Kilpatrick, ———, 183.
Kincaid, James, 185.
Kincaid, Joseph, 185.
Kincaid, William, 34, 74, 124.
Kincannon, Andrew, 280.
Kincannon, Francis, 271.
Kincheloe, ———, 261.
King, Avra, 153.
King, Smith, 269.
King, Thomas, 269, 275.
King, William, 7, 153.
King, Zachariah, 32.
Kinkead, John, 280.
Kinkead, William, 34, 92, 253.
Kirk, Robert, 13, 97.

Kirkland, Benjamin, 143.
Kirtley, Elijah, 104.
Knight, John, 82, 174, 193, 252.
Knox, ———, 164, 184.
Kyger, Christian, 277.

Lacey, Elliott, 264.
Lacey, Mathew, 264.
LaFayette, 23, 25, 35, 38, 50, 82, 85, 87, 98, 100, 134, 148, 169, 176, 197, 199, 202, 224, 225, 229, 234.
Lambert, Jacob, 278.
Landrum, Younger, 10, 17, 18, 68, 78.
Lane, Henry, 52.
Laney, ———, 100.
Langhorne, John, 275.
Langsden, Daniel, 206.
Lanier, Thomas, 143.
Lantz, Conrad, 180.
Lantz, Joseph, 180.
Larrish, John, 263.
Laurence, James, 263.
Lawson, ———, 17, 18, 19, 67, 68, 104, 149, 152, 196, 197, 206, 210.
Lawson, McDaniel, 126.
Lawson, Robert, 29, 31, 54.
Lawton, Robert, 275.
Lawton, Thomas, 275.
Layton, Robert, 261.
Leak, Elisha, 264.
Leake, Josiah, 264.
Leake, Mark, 25, 38, 53, 99, 100, 251.
Leake, Matthew, 84.
Leath, John, 278.
Lee, ———, 133
Lee, Archibald, 275.
Lee, Benjamin, 262.
Lee, Charles, 1.
Lee, John, 275.
Lee, Young, 26.
Leftwich, Augustine, 254.
Leftwich, Uriah, 254.
Leftwich, William, 47, 157, 254.

Legg, ———, 231.
Legg, John, 279.
Leigh, Charles, 275.
Lemaster, John, 271a.
Lemon, Jacob, 118.
Leroy, ———, 171.
Lescur, Marbell, 274.
Lew, ———, 175.
Lewis, ———, 60, 61.
Lewis, Aaron, 280.
Lewis, Andrew, 74, 156, 256.
Lewis, Charles, 73, 74, 251.
Lewis, Daniel, 269.
Lewis, Griffith, 252.
Lewis, Isham, 251.
Lewis, Jesse, 50.
Lewis, John, 20, 33, 42, 60, 73, 76, 256, 269.
Lewis, John, Z., 279.
Lewis, Joseph, 264, 269.
Lewis, Micajah, 251.
Lewis, Nicholas, 251, 264.
Lewis, Robert, 264.
Lewis, Samuel, 63, 92, 105, 120, 256.
Lewis, Thomas, 119, 158, 269, 277.
Lewis, William, 251.
Ligon, ———, 24, 275.
Ligon, John, 274.
Lightfoot, Daniel, 32.
Lincoln, ———, 59, 66, 157, 169, 172, 173, 210, 214.
Lincoln, Abraham, 253, 277.
Lincoln, Jacob, 277.
Lindsay, Abraham, 263.
Lindsay, Caleb, 272.
Lindsay, Reuben, 84, 100, 251.
Lines, John, 230.
Lingul, Paul, 277.
Linton, John, 269.
Lipner, Henry, 2.
Litterell, ———, 215.
Litton, Solomon, 280.
Lively, ———, 164.
Lively, Godrell, 53.
Lock, ———, 90.
Locke, Patrick, 114, 252.

Lockett, Gideon, 274.
Lockhart, Patrick, 256.
Lockridge, Andrew, 58, 70, 72, 74, 253.
Logan, Alexander, 51.
Logan, Benjamin, 153.
Logan, Hugh, 102.
Logan, John, 61, 256.
Logan, William, 253.
Logwood, Archibald, 259.
Logwood, Edmund, 274.
Logwood, Thomas, 153, 254.
Long, William, 22, 63, 75, 85, 92, 120, 164, 257.
Long, Francis, 22, 98, 107, 133, 253.
Long, Joseph, 136, 253.
Long, John, 257.
Long, Thomas, 184.
Loony, ———, 256.
Loony, John, 280.
Loony, Joseph, 138.
Lorton, Isaac, 146.
Love, Robert, 271.
Love, William, 271.
Lovel, Markel, 271.
Lovel, William, 270.
Lovely, ———, 164.
Loving, ———, 134.
Loving, John, 10.
Lowderson, William, 253.
Lowney, John, 251, 280.
Lowry, Thomas, 257.
Lowther, William, 253.
Lucas, ———, 171.
Lucas, Edward, 255.
Lucas, John, 155, 269, 271.
Lucas, William, 255.
Lumpkin, Thomas, 254.
Lumsden, George, 270.
Lynch, Anselm, 254.
Lynch, Charles, 141, 153, 254.
Lyle, James, 276.
Lyle, John, 136, 253, 276.
Lyle, William, 105.
Lyne, Edmund, 268.
Lyne, Henry, 268.

Lyon, James, 268.
Lyon, Stephen, 268.

McArnold, William, 256.
McIlhany, ———, 100, 120.
MacIntosh, ———, 5, 33, 88, 108.
McIray, Hugh, 254.
McCalley, John, 279.
McCampbell, James, 276.
McCardle, Samuel, 251.
McCarmie, John, 75.
McCarney, John, 22, 124.
McCaul, William, 264.
McCausland, Andrew, 58.
McClain, John, 123.
McClain, Robert, 269.
McClanachan, ———, 74.
McClarry, Alexander, 195.
McClelland, Abraham, 280.
McClellan, William, 269.
McClenahan, Alexander, 136.
McClenahan, William, 138, 156, 253, 256.
McClenahan, ———, 74.
McClung, John, 105, 123, 276.
McClung, William, Jr., 276.
McCorkle, James, 150, 271.
McCorkle, John, 121.
McCormick, Francis 263.
McCormick, John, 255.
McCoy, ———, 86, 265.
McCoy, John, 4, 33, 70, 76, 253.
McCreary, John, 22, 72, 73, 253.
McCreary, Nancy, 61.
McCreery, ———, 70.
McCreery, Robert, 79, 253.
McCreery, William, 58, 253.
McCune, John, 253.
McCutcheon, Samuel, 33, 107, 124, 253.
McCutcheon, William, 124, 136.
McDaniel, Clement, 213.
McDaniel, John, 106.
McDonald, ———, 155.
McDonald, Maynus, 271.
McDowell, ———, 61.
McDowell, James, 105, 123.

McDowell, Samuel, 97, 98, 130, 276.
McFarron, Rowland, 256.
McFarran, Samuel, 256.
McGee, ———, 146.
McGee, Samuel, 271.
McGehee, William, 275.
McGeach, John, 269.
McGeorge, Thomas, 256.
McGraw, William, 210.
McGuire, ———, 44, 186.
McGuire, Neely, 157.
McKee, ———, 115.
McKee, James, 125.
McKee, John, 126.
McKee, Nancy, 125.
McKee, Robert, 276.
McKee, William, 61, 69.
McKenney, John, 107, 253, 276.
McKittrick, John, 22, 111, 118, 253.
McLaughlin, John, 57.
McLarlane, John, 271.
McLaurine, William, 207.
McMahon, John, 253.
McMaken, Alexander, 269.
McMath, William, 276.
McMicken, ———, 269.
McMullen, William, 271
McMurtry, ———, 256
McNabb, Alexander, 252.
McNeal, ———, 74.
McNeel, ———, 74.
McNeely, William, 256
McNutt, James, 61, 69.
McQuain, Alexander, 180.
McReynolds, Thomas, 254.
McRoberts, John, 256.
McWilliams, ———, 85, 228, 229, 235.
McWilliams, William, 279.
Madison, ———, 63.
Madison, Ambrose, 91.
Madison, George, 257.
Madison, James, 272.
Madison, Richard, 136, 253.
Maguhe, Samuel, 271.
Maguire, William, 271.
Mallory, ———, 100.

Mallory, Uriel, 272.
Manere, John, 252.
Mann, William, 74.
Marbury, ———, 175.
Mathews, George, 117, 136.
Marion, ———, 21.
Marks, Elisha, 269.
Marks, Hastings, 251.
Marks, John, 251.
Marks, Thomas, 269.
Markham, George, 259.
Markham, Vincent, 207, 274.
Marshall, ———, 82.
Marshall, Alexander, 252.
Marshall, Abraham, 252.
Marshall, John, 211, 252, 257.
Marshall, Samuel, 184.
Martin, ———, 93.
Martin, Azariah, 171.
Martin, Benjamin, 262.
Martin, Brice, 268.
Martin, David, 254.
Martin, Henry, 32, 262.
Martin, Hudson, 251.
Martin, John, 251, 261, 262.
Martin, Joseph, 21, 56, 185, 280.
Martin Joshua, 141.
Martin, Josiah, 134, 256.
Martin, Robert, 272.
Martin, Samuel, 275.
Martin, Thomas, 251.
Martin, Thomas Jr., 251.
Martin, William, 262.
Marx, John, 8.
Mason,———, 149.
Mason, David, 173.
Mason, George, 269.
Mason, John, 122, 279.
Massenburg, John, 170.
Massie, Nathaniel, 264.
Massie, Thomas, 1, 264.
Mastin, Thomas, 280.
Mathews,———, 35, 37, 85.
Mathews, George, 117-136.
Mathews, John, 181.
Mathews, Phillip, 7, 55, 275.

Mathews, Sampson, 11, 12, 20, 22, 57, 58, 72, 74, 79, 98, 117, 119, 124, 136, 162, 223, 253.
Mathews, Richard, 253.
Mathews, Thomas, 158.
Maupin, Cornelius, 251.
Maupin, Daniel, 251.
Maupin, William, 251.
Mauzy, John, 261.
Maxwell, Alexander, 253.
Maxwell, Audley, 276.
Maxwell, George, 280.
Maxwell, James, 271, 280.
Maxey, John, 195.
Maxey, Shadrack, 195.
May, David, 256.
May, Joseph, 274.
Mayo, Joseph, 262.
Mayo, William, 207.
Mays,———, 133.
Mays, David, 133.
Mays James, 153.
Mays, Joseph, 262.
Mays, Peter, 151.
Mays, William, 203, 274.
Mazaret, ———, 2, 3.
Meade,———, 7.
Meade, E., 16, 29.
Meade, Everett, 81.
Meals, John, 279.
Means, Thomas, 22.
Meeks, James, 34.
Megaree, Hugh, 36.
Menifee, William, 268.
Mercer, Aaron, 263.
Meredith, ———, 29, 30, 31, 55, 202.
Meredith, Elisha, 30.
Meredith, William, 6, 260.
Merriman, ———, 23, 24.
Merriott, Tapley, 274.
Meriott, Triplett, 274.
Merriweather, ———, 8, 52, 126, 170, 213, 216, 245.
Meriwether, David Wood, 270.
Meriwether, James, 229, 251.
Meriwether, Thomas, 231, 251.

Meriwether, William, 270.
Metcalf, Allen, 255.
Metcalf, John, 261.
Meteer, Thomas, 253.
Michie, James, 270.
Michie George, 270.
Michie, Robert, 270.
Milam, Rush, 126.
Milam, William, 254.
Millman, Thomas, 269.
Miles, Josias, 269.
Miller, ———,25, 37, 38.
Miller, Harmon, 217.
Miller, Hugh, 265.
Miller, John, 268.
Miller, Lewis, 272.
Miller Robert, 272.
Miller, Simon, Jr., 254.
Miller, Thomas, 264, 279.
Miller, William, 109, 121, 264.
Mills, ———, 256.
Mills, Bernard, 251.
Mills, Frederick William, 251.
Mills, Nathaniel, 272.
Mills, William, 179, 223, 255, 279.
Minnis, Robert, 277.
Minor, Garrett, 270.
Minor, John, 269.
Minor, Thomas, 229, 232, 279.
Minor, Vivian, 224.
Mitchell, Daniel, 254.
Mitchell, Evans, 252.
Mitchell, James, 97, 107, 253.
Mitchell, John, 159.
Mitchell, Thomas, 251, 252.
Mitchell, William, 174, 257.
Moffett, George, 45, 87, 97, 117, 130, 253.
Moffett, ———, 13.
Moffet, Jesse, 239.
Moffett, John, 118, 261.
Moffett, Josiah, 269.
Moffets, Robert, 271.
Monroe, George, 241.
Montgomery, ———, 9, 146.
Montgomery, Francis, 100.
Montgomery, James, 271, 280.

Montgomery, John, 185.
Montgomery, Joseph, 271.
Montgomery, Michael, 271.
Moodie, James, 259.
Moody, ———, 56, 77.
Moon, Jacob, Jr., 254.
Moore, ———, 24.
Moore, Alexander, 178- 227.
Moore, Andrew, 105, 123, 253, 276.
Moore, David, 181.
Moore, Elijah, 178.
Moore Family, 146.
Moore, Francis, Jr., 272.
Moore, George, 184.
Moor, Jacob, 254.
Moore, James, 251, 271.
Moore, Jesse, 262.
Moore, John, 7, 115.
Moore, Reuben, 272.
Moore, Robert, 181.
Moore, Thomas, 275.
Moore, William, 42, 69, 115, 120, 272.
Moorehead, Turner, 244, 261.
Moorman, James, 270.
Morby, ———, 15.
Morgan, 1, 11, 61, 62, 66, 75, 98, 104, 114, 121, 137, 164, 171, 181, 208, 238, 243.
Morgan, Benjamin, 59.
Morgan, Daniel, 167.
Morgan, David, 271a.
Morgan, Evan, 271a.
Morgan, James, 271a.
Morgan, James, Jr., 271a.
Morgan, Morgan, 271a.
Morgan, William, 54.
Morrell, John, 35.
Morris, ———, 147, 167.
Morris, Leonard, 115.
Morris, Nathaniel, 264.
Morris, Reuben, 277.
Morris, William, 115, 277.
Morrison, ———, 138.
Morrison, John, 19, 134, 136, 143.
Morrow, Charles, 255.
Morton, Jacob, 258.
Morton, James, 275.

Morton, John, 275.
Morton, Josiah, 258.
Morton, Joseph, 258.
Morton, Thomas, 275.
Morton, William, 66, 258.
Mosby, ———, 54, 270.
Mosby, Benjamin, 274.
Mosby, Hezekiah, 196.
Mosby, John, 274.
Mosby, Littlebury, 54, 197, 207, 274.
Mosby, Poindexter, 274.
Mosby, Wade, 54, 197, 274.
Moseley, Arthur, 47, 198, 254.
Moseley, Blackman, 259.
Mosley, Daniel, 251.
Mosley, Edward, 248.
Moseley, James, 56.
Moseley, John, 274.
Moseley, Thomas, 274.
Moseley, W., 229, 259.
Moss, Alexander, 262.
Moss, John, 269.
Mowby, ———, 15.
Moyer, Phillip, 277.
Muhlenburg, 49, 85, 89, 104, 105, 120, 137, 143, 163, 164, 184, 217.
Muir, Alexander, 271.
Mullemax, James, 180.
Mullemax, John, 180.
Munfort, Edward, 15, 54, 252, 274.
Munday, Jonathan, 251.
Mure, Alexander, 271.
Mure, Richard, 271.
Murphy, John, 157, 188, 268.
Murphy, William, 157.
Murray, ———, 59.
Murray, Reuben, 244.
Murray, Thomas, 254.
Myers, Jacob, 263.

Nall, ———, 5, 119.
Nall, William, 253, 277.
Namee, Cornelius, 254.
Nance, James, 173.
Nance, Reuben, 268.
Nance, Thomas, 254.

Nance, William, M., 174.
Napier, John, 262.
Napier, Richard, 32, 51, 262.
Napier, Thomas, 262.
Nash, John, 275.
Nash, William, 261.
Neale, Mathew, 261.
Neal, Stephen, 275.
Neal, William, 280.
Neely, ———, 256.
Neely, Alexander, 271.
Neely, James Jr., 256.
Neely, Robert, 256.
Neely, William, 256.
Nelson, Ambrose, 67, 275.
Nelson, ———, 37, 46 99, 174.
Nelson, Daniel, 277.
Nelson, John, 270.
Nelson, Joseph, 261.
Nelson, Thomas, 143, 236, 261.
Nevill, ———, 103.
Nevis, ———, 128.
New, Anthony, 257.
Newberry, Joseph, 259.
Newcomer, Julius, 275.
Newell, ———, 87.
Newell, James, 43, 271.
Newman, Alexander, 272.
Newman, Rice, 252.
Newsome, Nathaniel, 170.
Newsome, Thomas, 170.
Nitherson, John, 278.
Nicholas, ———, 81.
Nicholas, George, 143.
Nicholas, John, 143.
Nicholas, William, 251.
Nickle, ———, 90.
Nickle, A., 60.
Nickle, Isaac, 60.
Noble, Anthony, 255.
Noble, Joseph, 252.
Noel, John, 260.
Noland, Philip, 269.
Noland, Samuel, 269.
Nolle, William, 277.
Norment, John, 257.
Norment, Samuel, 257.

Norris, William, 261.
North, John, 143.
Null, Henry, 180.

O'Bannon, John, 240.
O'Bannon, Samuel, 261.
O'Bannon, Thomas, 238.
O'Brian, John, 263.
Ogilsby, Richard, 252.
O'Hara, James, 65.
O'Hara, John, 65.
Oliver, John, 253.
Omohundro, Richard, 262.
O'Roarke, David, 127.
O'Roarke, Philemon, 127.
Osborn, ———, 271.
Osborn, Abner, 252.
Osborn, Edward, 259.
Osborn, William, Jr., 252.
Otley, John, 254.
Ottey, John, 254.
Ousley, ———, 269.
Overstreet, ———, 24, 173.
Overstreet, James, 264.
Overstreet, John, 24, 195.
Overton, ———, 23, 24.
Overton, Thomas Perkins, 252.
Overton, Walter, 270.
Owens, ———, 275.
Owen, Christopher, 268.
Owens, James, 279.
Owens, John, 129.
Owens, Richardson, 271.
Owley, William, 269.
Orban, Zarah, 271a.

Paddy, ———, 9.
Page, Mann, 279.
Painter, Christopher, 277.
Pamplin, ———, 106.
Pannill, John, 272.
Pankey, Stephen, 191, 259.
Parker, ———, 1, 6, 123, 132.
Parker, Alexander, 179.
Parker, Charles, 260.
Parker, Glover, 275.
Parker, Joseph, 54.

Parker, Josiah, 167.
Parker, Richard, 179.
Parkhan, Nicholas, 143.
Parks, ———, 5, 59.
Parks, Ezekiel, 16.
Parks, James, 275.
Parks, Joseph, 16, 23, 24, 29, 275.
Parks, William, 271.
Parrish, Sherwood, 264.
Parrish, Tolley, 264.
Parrow, Daniel, 254.
Pate, Anthony, 254.
Pate, Mathew, 254.
Pate, Thomas, 254.
Patrick, John, F., 254.
Patters, Casper, 182.
Patterson, David, 194, 200, 259.
Patterson, John, 115.
Patterson, Joseph, 22, 95, 97, 253.
Patterson, Paul, 199.
Patterson, Samuel, 276.
Patton, ———, 101.
Patton, Benjamin, 277.
Patton, Henrv, 146, 271.
Paulet, John, 184.
Paulet, Richard, 270.
Paulin, ———, 171, 185, 256.
Paxton, John, 112, 256, 276.
Paxton, William, 256, 276.
Payne, Augustine, 240.
Payne, Francis, 261.
Payne, George, 264.
Payne, Henry, 269.
Payne, Josias Jr., 264.
Payne, Nicholas, 236, 249.
Payne, William, 242.
Peak, Aaron, 275.
Pearce, ———, 271.
Pearis, George, 271.
Pearle, Samuel, 261.
Pearson, William, 216
Peary, George, 271.
Peaseley, ———, 157.
Peck, Adam, 256.
Peebles, John, 253.
Peers, Anderson, 264.
Pemberton, ———, 35.

Pence, George, 253.
Pence, Jacob, 139.
Pence, James, 277.
Pendleton, Edmund, 148.
Pendleton, Philip, 235, 255.
Penn, Abraham, 141, 268.
Penn, Gabriel, 31.
Peper, John, 251.
Perkins, Anthony, 177.
Perkins, Francis, 264.
Perkins, John, 178, 264.
Perkins, William, 26.
Perry, Joshua, 253.
Perry, Swift, 65.
Persinger, Jacob, 128.
Persinger, John, 180.
Petalla, 112.
Petect, James, 268.
Peters, Christian, 62.
Peters, Samuel, 69, 176.
Pettis, John, 218.
Pettis, Samuel, 131, 270.
Pettus, Stephen, 275.
Pettyjoin, Amos, 271a.
Pettyjohn,, Wm., 271a.
Peyton, Henry, 261.
Phelps, John, 254.
Phillip, ———, 82, 143, 176, 177, 197.
Phillips, John, 31.
Phillips, Richard, 270.
Pickett, Martin, 261.
Pickle, Christian, 180.
Pier, ———, 147.
Pierce, John, 236.
Pierce, Thomas, 269, 275.
Pillow, Jasper, 275.
Pirkey, John, 277.
Pleasants, Samuel, 274.
Pledge, Francis, 264.
Plumley, Mathew, 278.
Plunkett, Reuben, 219.
Poage, George, 33, 70, 86, 253, 256.
Poage, James, 95, 253.
Poage, John, Jr., 253.
Poage, Robert, 276.
Poindexter, John, 270.
Poindexter, Joseph, 254.

Poland, Thomas, 259.
Pollard, Thomas, 216.
Polson, ———' 50.
Poor, William, 274.
Pope, William, 261.
Popens, Peter, 271a.
Porter, ———, 198.
Porter, Abraham, 272.
Porter, Charles Jr., 272.
Porter, Isaac, 274.
Porterfield, 255.
Proterfield, Charles, 190.
Posey, ———, 6.
Potter, ———, 142.
Potts, Samuel, 28.
Povatt, John, 274.
Powell, ———, 233.
Powell, Edward, 170.
Powell, John, 170.
Powell, Levi, 245.
Powell, Ptolemy, 233.
Powt, Robert, 15.
Powers, William, 129.
Preston, ———, 145.
Preston, John, 146.
Preston, William, 146, 155, 156, 271.
Price, ———, 159, 231.
Price, Bowen, 254.
Price, Brown, 254.
Price, Charles, 264.
Price, Evan, 278.
Price, Hezekiah, 270.
Price, John, 30, 267,
Price, Meredith, 264.
Price, Richard Moore, 272.
Price, Thomas, 154, 280.
Price, William, Jr., 275.
Prince, Hubbard, 261.
Prince, Lewis, 148.
Pringle, Samuel, 253.
Proctor, John, 272.
Prunty, Thomas, 268.
Pryor, ———, 256.
Pryor, John, 61.
Pryor, Nicholas, 61.
Pryor, William, 61, 69.
Puffenberger, George, 180.

Pulliam, George, 275.
Purvis, James, 249.
Putnam, ———, 1.
Pyles, Joshua, 263.

Quarles, ———, 50, 232.
Quarles, Harry, 234.
Quarles, James, 251.
Quarles, John, 254.
Quarles, Roger, 257.
Quirl, Thomas, 146.

Rader, Anthony, 277.
Radford, George, 274.
Ragan, Richard, 127.
Ragland, Samuel, 270.
Raine, Nathaniel, 264, 275.
Ramsey, Josiah, 280.
Ramsey, William, 216.
Randolph, ———, 7, 141, 205.
Randolph, Beverley, 16, 29, 67, 143, 197, 204, 260.
Randolph, Henry, 143.
Randolph, Peter, 81, 252.
Randolph, William, 259.
Rankin, Charles, 136.
Rankin, James, 253.
Rankin, Thomas, 136, 253.
Ransdel, Wharton, 261.
Ransdel, William, 261.
Ranson, Richard, 255.
Ratliffe, Nathan, 161.
Rawlins, Samuel, 257.
Reaburn, James, 256.
Reaburn, Joseph, 256.
Read, ———, 54, 215.
Read, Edmund, 258.
Read, John, 16.
Read, Jonathan, 258.
Reader, Adam, 253.
Reader, Anthony, 253.
Reagan, Richard, 277.
Reaner, Ulrich, 278.
Redd, John, 268.
Redford, Edward, 264.
Redford, Milner, 264.
Red Hawk, 112.

Redman, Jeremiah, 263.
Reed, Jacob, 269.
Reed, Thomas, 66.
Reeves, Frederick, 268.
Reid, John, 251.
Renfro, John, 157, 268.
Renick, William, 265.
Rennolds, James, 257..
Rentfree, Isaac, 254.
Rentfree, William, 254.
Rentfro, Isaac, 254.
Rentfro, Mark, 254.
Rentfro, Joshua, 268.
Rentfro, William, 268.
Respess, Thomas, 269.
Rexrode, George, 180.
Reynolds, George, 268.
Reynolds, M., 153.
Reynolds, Thomas M., 167.
Rhodes, ———, 178.
Rice, Benjamin, 254.
Rice, Holman, 187.
Rice, John, 34, 263, 277.
Rice, William, 275.
Richards, John, 275.
Richards, William, 36.
Richards, ———, 64, 93, 144, 159.
Richard, Elijah, 265.
Richardson, Holt, 30, 32, 35, 50, 231.
Richardson, Martin, 260.
Richardson, Samuel, 27, 31, 264, 270.
Richards, Wiliam, 36.
Richeson, ———, 215.
Richeson, James 255.
Richeson, Jonathan, 254.
Richeson, Joseph, 257.
Rigger, Richard, 89.
Riggins, Charles, 278.
Riggins, William, 278.
Rinkerbo, Casper, 263.
Rixie, Richard, 261.
Robards, Lewis, 264.
Roberts, ———, 82, 91, 159, 187.
Roberts, Alexander, 252.
Roberts, David, 139, 275.
Roberts, Jacob, 252.
Roberts James, 270.

Roberts, John, 63, 91, 249.
Roberts, Pleasant, 252.
Roberts, William, 148.
Roberts, Wilson, 64.
Robertson, Alexander, 22, 253.
Robertson, George, 259.
Robertson, James, 130, 271, 280.
Robertson, John, 259.
Robertson, William, 117, 193, 252, 253.
Robideau, ———, 101.
Robison, William, 269.
Robinson, ———, 134, 256.
Robinson, Benjamin, 219.
Robinson, Hercules, 256.
Robinson, Isaac, 256.
Robinson, James, 114.
Robinson, John, 65, 256, 272, 277.
Robinson, William, 134, 256.
Rochelle, ———, 170.
Rogers, David, 268.
Rogers, George, 261.
Rollin, Henry, 185.
Rose, Hugh, 17, 18, 68, 112.
Rosebrough, William, 280.
Ross, Daniel, 268.
Ross, John, 152, 270.
Ross, William, 199.
Rountree, William, 187.
Rowland, Thomas, 133, 256, 272.
Rowlett, John, 259.
Rowlett, William, 259.
Royall, John, 193, 252, 259.
Royall, Littlebury, 252.
Royall, William, 193, 252.
Roy, Mungo, 257.
Royston, Thomas, 264.
Rucker, ———, 62.
Rucker, Ambrose, 112.
Rucker, Anthony, 69.
Rucker, Samuel, 253.
Rudelle, George, 277.
Rudelle, John, 277.
Ruble, ———, 152.
Rubell, Owen, 268.
Ruffin, ———, 1, 38, 66.
Runley, ———, 216.

Runnels, Thomas, 157.
Rush, ———, 119.
Rush, John, 277.
Russell, ———, 98.
Russell, Francis, 269.
Russell, James, 254.
Russell, John, 269.
Russell, Robert, 269.
Rutherford, ———, 90, 157.
Rutherford, David, 264.
Rutherford, Elliot, 277.
Rutherford, Joseph, 277.
Rutledge, Dudley, 275.
Rutledge, George, 256.
Rutledge, John, 256.

Ryan, William, 268.
Sale, John, 17, 18, 68.
Sale, Samuel, 257.
Salmon, John, 268.
Samson, ———, 144.
Sampson, Stephen, 264.
Samuel, Reuben, 35, 257.
Samuel, William, 257.
Sanders, ———, 255.
Sanders, John, 270.
Sands, Samuel, 75.
Sanford, William, 216.
Saulsbery, William, 73.
Saunders, Gunnell, 269.
Saunders, James, 272.
Saunders, Jesse, 184.
Saunders, John, 269.
Saunders, Samuel Hyde, 274.
Saunders, Stephen, 47, 271.
Sawyers, Robert, 137.
Saxton, ———, 42.
Sayers, Robert, 156, 271.
Sayers, Thompson, 271.
Scaggs, Aaron, 145.
Scott, ———, 1, 56, 64, 77, 82, 223. 260.
Scott, Alexander, 18, 136, 253.
Scott, Charles, 8, 236.
Scott James, 272.
Scott, John, 66, 91, 143, 228.
Scott, John, Jr., 272.

Virginia Militia in the Revolution 331

Scott, Walter, 259.
Scott, William, 66, 143, 256.
Scurry, Eli, 271.
Seamond, Ephriam, 251.
Seaton, William, 261.
Seay, John, 270.
Sehorn, John, 278.
Semley, Alexander, 256.
Sepner, Henry, 2, 3.
Settle, William, 261.
Sevier, John, 157.
Sevier, Robert, 157.
Seybert, Nicholas, 180, 253.
Shackelford, Edmund, 272.
Shackelford, Zachary, 272.
Shaffer, ———, 269.
Shanklin, Andrew, 277.
Sharp, Robert, 64.
Sharp, Linn, 244.
Sharp, Moses, 275.
Sharpe, Robert, 64.
Sharpe, Sinsfield, 261.
Sharpe, Thomas, 279.
Sharpe, William, 74.
Shaw, James, 280.
Shaw, Joseph, 271.
Shaw, Robert, 253.
Shearman, Caddy, 61.
Sheets, George, 180.
Shein, Samuel, 163.
Shelby, ———, 141, 152.
Shelby, Evan, 185, 280.
Shelby, Isaac, 61.
Shelby, James, 280.
Shelby, John, Sr., 280.
Shelton, ———, 112, 165.
Shelton, Francis, 26.
Shelton, Peter, 270.
Shelton, Samuel, 270.
Shelton, Thomas, 131, 270.
Sheperdson, David, 131.
Sherman, Paddy, 61.
Sherwin, Samuel, 252.
Shirley, David, 255.
Shirley, Valentine, 253.
Shore, Richard, 269.
Shore, William, 143.

Shores, Thomas, 269.
Short, Archibald, 200.
Short, Edward, 268.
Short, Samuel, 200.
Short, Thomas, 252.
Shrieve, John, 269.
Shumaker, Zedekiah, 61, 69.
Shumate, Daniel, 261.
Simerall, James, 263.
Simmons, ———, 67.
Simmons, George, 180.
Simmons, John, 67, 180.
Simmons, Leonard, 180.
Simmons, Mark, 180.
Simmons, Michael, 180.
Simmons, Peter, 180.
Simpson, Alexander, 253.
Simson, Jeremiah, 271a.
Sinclair, John, 269.
Singleton, Manoar, 272.
Sinkfield, ———, 175.
Sisson, Caleb, 272.
Sitlington, Robert, 76.
Skelton, Thomas, 265.
Skelton, James, 268.
Skillern, ———, 48, 61, 102, 127.
Skillern, George, 98, 256.
Skippish, Henry, 166.
Skipwith, ———, 165.
Skipwith, Henry, 83, 260.
Skidmore, John, 253, 277.
Slater, ———, 269.
Slaughter, ———, 94.
Slaughter, John, 254.
Sledd, John, 201.
Sleth, John, 3.
Small, Matthew, 268.
Smallwood, ———, 121, 238.
Smith, ———, 45, 63, 124, 142.
Smith, Augustine, 261, 275, 277.
Smith, Boswell, 42, 277.
Smith, Daniel, 253, 277, 280.
Smith, Edward, 264.
Smith, Francis, 200.
Smith, Gideon, 268, 272, 274.
Smith, Henry, 256.
Smith, James, 102, 207, 217, 256, 271.

Smith, John, 13, 143, 212, 253, 263, 275.
Smith, Jonathan, 254.
Smith, Joseph, 217, 261, 277.
Smith, Luke B., 197.
Smith, Mark, 180.
Smith, Nathan, 269.
Smith, Obadiah, 264.
Smith, Philip, 68, 230.
Smith, Rolly, 261, 274, 275, 277, 279.
Smith, Sebastian, 180, 263.
Smith, Thomas, 22, 95, 97, 98, 130, 133, 253, 261, 268.
Smith, William, 57, 261, 270, 272, 274, 277.
Smithers, ———, 130.
Smizer, Michael, 37.
Snapp, Philip, 278.
Snide, Christian, 271.
Snider, Jacob, 255.
Snider, Jacob, Jr., 255.
Snider, John, 180.
Snider, Nathaniel, 255.
Snoddy, John, 280.
Snow, Richard, 251.
Sorrell, John, 219.
Southerland, Philmon, 275.
Southerland, William, 275.
Southerlin, Kenneth, 251.
Spaulding, John, 275.
Speake, Francis, 216.
Spencer, ———, 131, 200.
Spencer, James, 268.
Spencer, John, 229.
Spencer, Joseph, 229.
Spencer, Sharpe, 275.
Spinner, Richard, 251.
Spradling, John, 251.
Springer, W., 88.
Spurr, ———, 269.
Stagg, Charles, 275.
Stanard, Larkin, 226.
Standifor, Luke, 268.
Standifor, William, 268.
Stanhope, William, 269.
Starke, John, 143,

Stears, John, 221.
Stears, Richard, 220.
Steel, Alexander, 254.
Steele, David, 124.
Steel, James, 92, 253.
Steel, Samuel, 276.
Steel, Thomas, 276.
Stegar, Hans, 274.
Stegar, Thomas, 274.
Stephens, ———, 45, 137, 271.
Stephen, Adam, 20.
Stephens, John, 169.
Stephens, Robert, 255.
Stephenson, John, 253.
Sterling, Lord, 142.
Sterling, William, 36.
Steuben, Baron, 6, 19, 23, 29, 35, 50, 100, 136, 143, 234.
Steuart, Edward, 70.
Steuart, John, 72.
Stevens, ———, 35, 62, 45, 85, 89, 131, 151, 159, 171, 194, 234.
Stevens, Edward, 10.
Stewart, Alexander, 253.
Stewart, John, 19, 249, 256.
Stewart, Francis, 143.
Stewart, Ralph, 253.
Stith, Joseph, 254.
Stokes, ———, 1.
Stone, Joshua, 213.
Stone, Sebastian, 180.
Stout, George, 180.
Stovall, ———, 202.
Stovall, George, 274.
Stovall, Littlebury, 202.
Stover, ———, 269.
Strachan, Thomas, 251.
Strange, David, 251.
Stratton, John, 274.
Stratton, Seraiah, 277.
Straughton, James, 148.
Street, Joseph, 270.
Sterns, Peyton, 257.
Streshly, William, 257.
Stribbling, William, 263.
Strother, Joseph, 250.
Stuart, ———, 106.

Stuart, Alexander, 276.
Stuart, John, 249.
Stubblefield, ———, 3, 140, 151, 279.
Stubblefield, George, 52, 229, 235, 272.
Stubblefield, Harry, 235.
Sturgis, William, 255.
Sullivan, ———, 5.
Summerfield, Thomas, 180.
Summers, George, 269.
Summers, Paul, 180.
Sutherfer, Richard, 261.
Sutton, Coleman, 158.
Sutton, James, 257.
Swann, John, 274.
Swearingen, Josiah, 138, 255.
Swearingen, Van, 255.
Swift, Flour, 271.
Syler, William, 278.

Tabb, Edward, 252.
Tabb, John, 252.
Tacey, Mace, 145.
Talbott, Haile, 254.
Talbott, Henry, 157.
Taliaferro, ———, 1, 85.
Taliaferro, Francis, 223, 235.
Taliaferro, George, 272.
Taliaferro, Wm., 224.
Tankard, ———, 219.
Tankersley, ———, 220, 222.
Tankersley, John, 279.
Tankersley, Richard, 61.
Tarflinger, Henry, 269.
Tarlton, 32, 50, 64, 72, 104, 112, 113, 116, 120, 125, 130, 134, 159, 163, 171, 243.
Tatum, Edward, 157, 254.
Tate, James, 75, 107, 118, 133, 163, 253.
Tate, Jesse, 254.
Tate, John, 133.
Tate, Nathaniel, 153.
Tate, William, 253.
Taylor, ———, 1, 9, 32, 51, 63, 85, 112, 106, 134, 271.

Taylor, Coleman, 158.
Taylor, Edmund, 35.
Taylor, Francis, 91, 187, 249.
Taylor, George, 268, 269, 275.
Taylor, Isaac, 146.
Taylor, James, 77, 229, 279.
Taylor, John, 251, 269.
Taylor, Joseph, 259, 261.
Taylor, Richard, 263.
Taylor, Skelton, 254, 260.
Taylor, William, 263, 268, 276.
Teaney, Daniel, 163, 245.
Tedford, John, 276.
Tee, Widow, 45.
Temple, Samuel, 223, 257.
Terrill, George, 257.
Terrill, Harry, 167, 254.
Terrill, Peter, 254.
Terrill, Thomas, 207.
Terry, Jasper, 157.
Terry, Joseph, 210.
Terry, William, 141, 157, 254.
Teter, Paul, 253.
Thacker, Nathaniel, 251.
Thatcher, John, 269.
Thilman, John, 257.
Thomas, Absolom, 251.
Thomas, Austin, 268.
Thomas, Enoch, 269.
Thomas, James, 253.
Thomas, John, 28, 35, 251.
Thomas, Joseph, 251.
Thomas, Moses, 269.
Thomas, Ralph, 99, 251.
Thomas, Robert, 272.
Thomas, Rowland, 272.
Thomas, Thomas, 269.
Thompson, ———, 124, 265, 270.
Thompson, Alexander, 253.
Thompson, Andrew, 277.
Thompson, Barlett, 260.
Thompson, Christopher, 234.
Thompson, George, 27, 251, 262.
Thompson, Henry, 271.
Thompson, James, 61, 69.
Thompson, John, 30, 35, 257, 275.
Thompson, Joseph, 270.

Thompson, Josiah, 274.
Thompson, Leonard, 251, 262.
Thompson, Levi, 32.
Thompson, Nelson, 84, 251.
Thompson, Robert, 11, 79, 253.
Thompson, Roger, 251, 262.
Thompson, Smith, 46, 162, 270.
Thorn, John, 148.
Thornbery, Thomas, 255.
Thornhill, William, 254.
Thornton, Anthony, 158.
Thornton, Anthony, Jr., 257.
Thornton, Francis, 258.
Thornton, George, 223, 257, 279.
Thurmond, Philip, 19, 40.
Thurman, Thomas, 27, 262.
Thurston, Charles, 142.
Tilford, ———, 137.
Timberlake, Benjamin, 201.
Timberlake, Epapproditus, 261.
Timberlake, Lewis, 257.
Timberlake, John, 270.
Tilman, Daniel, 262.
Tinsdale, Thomas; 262.
Tinsley, ———, 106.
Toley, James, 261.
Tompkins, Francis, 257.
Tompkins, Robert, 257.
Tompson, James, 61.
Tommis, John, 129.
Toney, John, 203.
Topp, Roger, 280.
Torbert, John, 47.
Tosh, ———, 138.
Tosh, James, 256.
Towles, ———, 100, 195.
Towles, Oliver, 1, 221.
Towles, Stockley, 264.
Towles, Thomas, 223, 225, 279.
Townes, John, Jr., 252.
Townes, William, 260.
Trent, John, 189.
Trible, George, 224.
Trigg, Abraham, 145, 161, 271.
Trigg, Daniel, 146, 254, 271.
Trigg, William, 254.
Trimble, James, 22, 74, 98, 111, 253.

Triplett, Frank, 75, 243, 261.
Triplett, Simon, 245, 269.
Triplett, William, 153.
Trout, ———, 34.
Trowton, ———, 215.
Truman, Obadiah, 270.
Tucker, ———, 67, 100, 106, 205.
Tucker, Daniel, 252.
Tucker, James, 274.
Tucker, St. George, 217.
Tucker, Thomas, 204.
Tuggle, Benjamin, 275.
Tuggle, Thomas, 275.
Tunstall, William, 268.
Turnbull, George, 254.
Turner, Daniel, 257.
Turner, George, 257.
Turner, James, 42, 178.
Turner, John, 257, 268.
Turner, Richard, 42.
Turner, William, 78.
Turnley, Francis, 222.
Turpin, Horatio, 54, 197.
Turpin, John, 267.
Turpin, Sugly, 267.
Turpin, William, 260.
Tutt, James, 279.
Twiner, Daniel, 257.
Tyler, ———, 85.
Tyler, George, 257.
Tyler, John, 257.
Tyler, Richard, 257.

Upshur, James, 257.
Upshur, Jeremiah, 257.

Vance, ———, 159.
Vance, Samuel, 12, 33, 58, 70, 76, 253.
Vance, Thomas, 137.
Vance, William, 263.
Vancel, Edmund, 271.
Vandevender, Isaac, 269.
Vanover, ———, 269.
Vardaman, Peter, 268.
Vardiman, William, 254.
Vass, Phillip V., 225.

Vaughan, Edmund, 274.
Vaughan, James, 252.
Vaughan, Reuben, 169, 172.
Vaughan, Robert, 252.
Veal, David, 255.
Venable, Charles, 275.
Venable, Robert, 275.
Venable, Samuel, 197, 275.
Vimands, Elijah, 256.
Vincell, Adam, 269.
Vines, Thomas, 134.
Vineyard, George, 135.

Wackub, John, 92.
Wade, Dabney, 264.
Waddell, Joseph, 253.
Waddy, Samuel, 270.
Wade, West, 43.
Wagoner, Adam, 180.
Walden, Lewis, 270.
Walden, Richard, 254.
Walker, ———, 152, 252.
Walker, Alexander, 276.
Walker, David, 143, 275.
Walker, E., 80.
Walker, Edmund, 80, 81.
Walker, Edward, 80.
Walker, George, 67, 275.
Walker, John, 113.
Walker, Robert, 143.
Walker, Samuel, 128, 216.
Walker, Thomas, 89, 143, 251, 275.
Walker, William, 275.
Walker, William T., 80.
Wallace, Adam, 1, 6, 8, 271.
Wallace, Andrew, 61, 69, 128, 184.
Wallace, David, 276.
Wallace, John, 276.
Wallace, Samuel, 120, 276.
Waller, George, 268.
Walt, Charles, 217.
Walter, John, 269.
Walter, William, 276.
Walthall, Archd., 194, 200, 259.
Walthall, John, 252.
Walthall, William, 259.
Walton, Robert, 275.

Wamsley, James, 180.
Wamsley, John, 180.
Wamsley, William, 180.
Wandless, Ralph, 86.
Ward, Alexander, 271.
Ward, Benjamin, 80, 81, 252, 259.
Ward, David, 280.
Ward, John, 149, 252, 254, 271.
Ward, John, Jr., 254.
Ward, Rowland, 159.
Ward, Rowland, Jr., 252.
Ward, William, 265, 271.
Ware, Jacob, 43.
Ware, James, 264.
Ware, John, 264.
Ware, Robert, 219.
Warren, William, 261.
Warwick, Jacob, 57, 73, 253.
Washington, Gen., 1, 75, 77, 93, 113, 133.
Washington Charles, 279.
Washington, Samuel, 255.
Wasley, Robert, 270.
Watkins, Abner, 83, 275.
Watkins, Charles, 153.
Watkins, Edward, 205, 206.
Watkins, George, 67.
Watkins, Joel, 258.
Watkins, John 143.
Watkins, Robert, 167, 254.
Watkins, Samuel, 252.
Watkins, Silas, 26.
Watkins, Thomas, 275.
Watman, Henry, 276.
Watshall, Archer, 82.
Watson, ———, 80, 81.
Watson, Douglass, 66.
Watson, Drury, 275.
Watson, James, 131, 270.
Watson, Jessee, 275.
Watson, Luke, 252.
Watson, Robert, 83.
Watson, William, 252, 258.
Watterson, Henry, 276.
Watts, John, 157.
Watts, Thomas, 254.
Waugh, George, 272.

Wauchub, John, 253.
Wayne, ———, 9, 11, 22, 25, 38, 62, 94, 100, 104, 149, 176, 177, 198, 243.
Weaver, Tilman, 261.
Webb, ———, 171.
Webb, Charles, 153.
Webb, Isaac, 153.
Webb, John, 261.
Webber, Philip, 264.
Webb, Richard C., 272.
Webster, John, 275.
Weedon, ———, 131, 234.
Weir, George, 276.
Weizer, Henry, 164.
Welch, Sylvester, Sr., 246.
Wells, Isham, 259.
Wells, John, 268.
Wells, Joseph, 259.
Wells, Matthew, 268.
Wells, Thomas T., 252.
Wells, William, 252.
Welsh, ———, 148.
West, ———, 28.
West, George, 269.
Westfall, Jacob, Jr., 253.
Whatley, James, Jr., 269.
Wharton, John, 99.
Wheatley, ———, 215.
Wheatley, Joseph, 261.
Wheeler, Micajah, 251.
White, ———, 101, 173, 177, 208. 269, 279.
White, Ambrose, 257.
White, Chilion, 257.
White, Daniel, 100, 251.
White, Elisha, 190.
White, James, 271.
White, Jeremiah, 272.
White, Joel, 269.
White, John, 220, 253, 270.
White, Richard, 272.
White, Robert, 263.
White, William, 270.
Whiteman, Henry, 180.
Whitlock, Josiah, 275.
Whitten, Richard, 169.

Whitten, Thomas, 280.
Wickliffe, William, 261.
Wier, Bezaliel, 210.
Wier, Samuel, 253.
Wiglesworth, James, 279.
Wiglesworth, John, 223.
Wilbern, Thomas, 275.
Wildman, Joseph, 269.
Wiley, Alexander, 276.
Wiley, Andrew, 137.
Wilfong, Jacob, 180.
Wilkerson, John, 157.
William, ———, 210.
William, Charles, 174.
William, Joseph, 209.
Williams, ———, 156.
Williams, Charles, 212, 261.
Williams, John, 48, 269.
Williams, Otho H., 16.
Williams, Phillip, 252.
Williams, Samuel, 260, 265.
Williams, Solomon, 264.
Williams, Thomas, 151, 269.
Williamson, ———, 175.
Williamson, George, 192, 203, 205, 206, 274.
Williamson, John, 262.
Willis, ———, 15, 22, 105, 111.
Willis, John, 62, 104.
Willis, Moses, 272.
Willis, Robert Carter, 255.
Willis, Young, 62.
Willson, Thomas Branch, 252.
Wimer, Philip, 180.
Wilson, ———, 22, 159, 252, 260, 270, 276.
Wilson, Abraham, 250.
Wilson, Benjamin, 253.
Wilson, Charles, 252.
Wilson, Daniel, 217.
Wilson, David, 253.
Wilson, John, 22, 33, 70, 97, 253, 280.
Wilson, Joshua, 161.
Wilson, Hugh, 263.
Wilson, Mathew, 133, 253.
Wilson, Richard, 85.

Wilson, Samuel, 136.
Wilson, William, 136.
Wiltshire, John, 83.
Winckleback, Henry, 88.
Windle, Philip, 278.
Winfrey, Henry, 259.
Wingfield, Charles, 251.
Winn, Benjamin, 257.
Winn, James, 188, 238, 244.
Winn, John, 210.
Winn, Minor, 261.
Winn, Richard, 252.
Winslow, ———, 223, 226.
Winslow, Beverly, 223, 279.
Winston, ———, 93.
Winston, Anthony, 131, 270.
Winston, James, 270.
Winston, John, 30.
Witcher, ———, 210.
Witcher, William, 214.
Withers, James, 261.
Withers, Spencer, 243.
Withers, William, 261.
Witherson, John, 278.
Wolfe, Henry, 263.
Wolfe, John, 263.
Woodel, James, 87.
Wood, ———, 128, 271.
Wood, Archibald, 44, 265.
Wood, Edward, 275.
Wood, Isaac, 251.
Wood James, 99, 251, 263, 276.
Wood John, 251.
Wood, Peter, 254.
Wood, Samuel, 61, 69.
Wood, Solomon, 84.
Wood, Thomas, 157.
Wood, William, 193, 257.
Wood, William, Jr., 252.
Woods, ———, 44.
Woody, William, 262.
Woodfin, Nicholas, 44.
Woodford, ———, 8, 38, 87.
Woodliff, Peter, 143.
Woodruff, David, 19.
Woodson, Anderson, 275.
Woodson, Hughes, 196, 203.
Woodson, Isham, 264.

Woodson, Jacob, 275.
Woodson, John, 67, 275.
Woodson, John Stephen, 264.
Woodson, Joseph, 81.
Woodson, Josiah, 264.
Woodson, Miller, 260.
Woodson, Obadiah, 275.
Woodson, Tarleton, 100, 251.
Woodson, William, 251.
Wooldridge, Edmund, 206.
Wooldridge, Robert, 259.
Wooldridge, Thomas, 259.
Woolfork, ———, 85.
Woolfork, Charles, 257.
Woolfork, John, 257.
Wooten, Hinman, 254.
Wooten, William, 275.
Worsham, ———, 1.
Worshum, William, 82, 252.
Worthington, Ephraim, 255.
Wray, David, 214.
Wrinker, Jacob, 103.
Wright, ———, 265.
Wright, Andrew, 58.
Wright, Archibald, 275.
Wright, David, 254.
Wright, James, 275, 276.
Wright, Thomas, 12, 28, 65, 72.
Wright, William, 272, 275, 279.
Wyatt, Richard, 257.
Wycoff, ———, 269.
Wylie, Alexr., 280.
Wylie, John, 137.
Wynne, Thomas, 262.
Wysong, Fiatt, 138.
Wysor, Henry, 164.

Yates, Robert, 279.
Yancey, St. Charles, 270.
Yeager, John, 180.
Yores, Thomas, 134.
Young, Charles, 157.
Young, Henry, 275.
Young, James, 253.
Young, John, 91, 107, 139, 253.
Young, Patrick, 253.
Young, Richard, 226.
Young, William, 272.

END